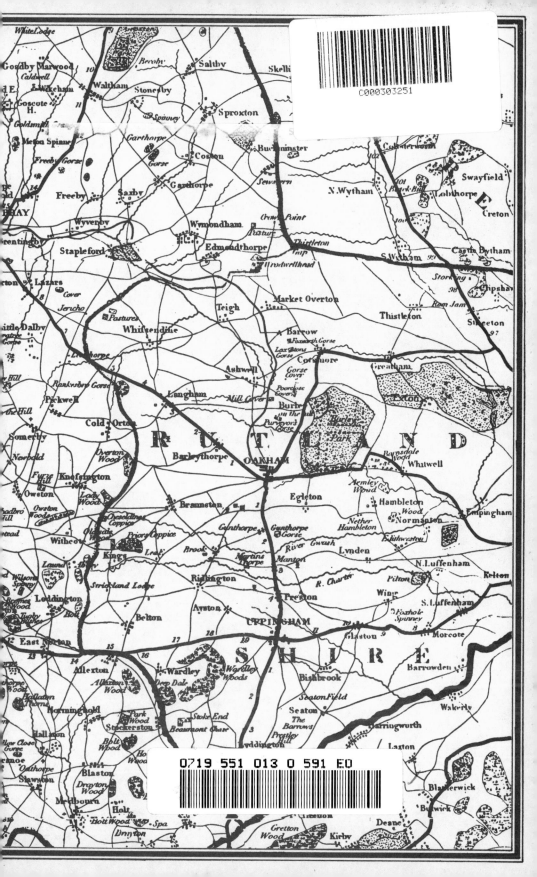

Foxhunting in
Paradise

Foxhunting in Paradise

MICHAEL CLAYTON

Line drawings by John King

JOHN MURRAY

Text © Michael Clayton 1993
Line drawings © John King 1993

First published in 1993
by John Murray (Publishers) Ltd,
50 Albemarle Street, London W1X 4BD

A catalogue record for this book can be obtained from the British Library

ISBN 0-7195-5101 3

Typeset in 11/12½ pt Plantin by Colset Pte Ltd, Singapore
Printed and bound in Great Britain by Cambridge University Press

The endpapers show part of 'Combe's Map of Leicestershire and the Surrounding Country', 1835. All the country around Melton Mowbray was, and still is, among the choicest riding terrain for the Leicestershire packs. There is additionally some excellent country south of this map, near Market Harborough, in the modern Fernie country.

Contents

Illustrations

The Author and publishers would like to thank Jim Meades for permission to reproduce the following photographs: 6, 9, 11, 12, 14, 16, 17, 20, 21, 27, 29, 30, 34, 35, 39, 43, 44, 45, 47, 50, 52.

Foreword

Captain Brian Fanshawe

Over the last twenty-five years foxhunting has been extraordinarily lucky to find among its friends, Michael Clayton. As an ex-Leicestershire MFH who has frequently benefited from his wisdom and advice, it is a great privilege to be asked to write the foreword to his latest book.

Michael has always hunted for fun, deriving his pleasure from all the various aspects of hunting: the hooroosh of the chase, the venery of a fit pack of hounds ably conducted, the access to the countryside, and the social whirl of the local hunting community.

Foxhunting in Paradise is a précis of the histories of the four Leicestershire Shires packs; the Belvoir, Quorn, Cottesmore and Fernie. In particular, it records the hunting of the post-war years and the Masters and huntsmen involved.

Much of the recent hunting has been experienced by Michael himself, with many of the personalties of the hunting field mentioned in this book his friends or acquaintances.

The book portrays many of the problems that beset modern hunting, such as increased urbanization, changes, in farming policies, hordes of motor cars following the Leicestershire packs, the political threat and direct action from other people, ranging from the genuine vegan to the arch social anarchist.

No individual has done more to address these problems either locally or through the columns of *Horse and Hound*. Hunting has benefited from his flair for good public relations (to see him conducting a press conference is an education), his oratory and his scribing talents, and his dedication and energy in promoting hunting with hounds towards the end of this century.

Michael has truly made his mark in Leicestershire, occasionally on the land, painfully and unintentionally! His efforts on behalf of the sport should ensure future generations of foxhunters will be able to enjoy their foxhunting in paradise.

Preface

I have defined the scope of this book by selecting the Leicestershire Hunts traditionally regarded as 'Shire packs'. The Badminton Hunting book asserts that 'The Shires' are limited to three counties; Leicestershire, Rutland and Northamptonshire.

'But a geographical definition will not serve,' says Badminton. . . . 'The distinction is really one of fashion, not of geography.' Badminton firmly defines the Shire packs as the Belvoir, the Cottesmore, the Quorn (which then included what is now the Fernie) and the Pytchley.

'So some unwritten law, dating from what era we know not, has ordained,' says Badminton.

The Pytchley is certainly a great Shires pack, with one of the most glorious histories in foxhunting. It is, essentially, a Northamptonshire pack, and therefore not within the scope of this book. The golden past of the Pytchley is splendidly related by the late Guy Paget in his excellent writings on that Hunt.

Similarly, the Atherstone is not within the scope of this book. It hunts a substantial part of south-west Leicestershire, but also a large area of Warwickshire, yet is outside the Shires definition – although it has a splendid history and has long attracted foxhunters who have found every virtue of the Chase within its boundaries.

The Quorn, Fernie, Belvoir and Cottesmore each deserve individual, full-length histories and therefore I have had to be exceedingly selective in combining them in one book. Much has been written about these Hunts up to 1939, but this is the first attempt to treat fully their history up to the present day. I have, of course, used literary sources detailed in the bibliography, but I am especially grateful to Ulrica Murray Smith for allowing me to quote from her book, *Magic of the Quorn*, and from her fascinating articles in *Horse and Hound*, together with many an enlightening conversation. Sir Henry Tate, President and former Joint Master and huntsman of the Cottesmore kindly gave me a marvellous interview.

In attempting to refer to individual foxhunters I am thoroughly conscious that many are omitted who should be in such a book if the weight of their contribution is to be adequately measured.

I have long been contemplating this work, but was especially prompted to undertake it by the spate of misinformed, inaccurate nonsense which appeared in the press and other media during the 1991–2 season, when those who would like to see hunting abolished sought to use the Quorn video case as justification. The reverberations from that affair have materially affected foxhunting throughout the United Kingdom, since the Masters of Foxhounds Association has made major rule changes, and I have attempted to deal with these in some detail.

It may be argued by some that this book pays but little attention to Charles James, the fox – subject of the Chase. I would reply that foxes abound in the hunting countries I describe largely because of the habitat, the careful culling and the close seasons maintained by the Hunts for well over two centuries. The Leicestershire hunting countries are conservationist marvels due to the enlightened self-interest of generations of foxhunters.

If this work throws a little more light on this aspect of hunting alone, I shall have succeeded. Hopefully, it will encourage those who love foxhunting everywhere to take a greater interest in the fountain of the sport we know today: the country where Hugo Meynell evolved the science of hunting the fox in the open with a pack of hounds, according to a code of conduct, made possible only by the goodwill of Leicestershire's farmers and landowners.

An immigrant from the deep south of Beckford's Dorset hunting grounds, I owe so much to all those who have made me welcome in the Shires, and I am proud and pleased to be a resident of Rutland. As *Horse and Hound's* Editor and Hunting Correspondent 'Foxford' since 1973, I have had the fortune to hunt with nearly two hundred packs of hounds. This has at least enabled me to view Leicestershire in the context of foxhunting elsewhere. It is no slight on anywhere else that if I were to be given one last day's foxhunting it would be with one of the Shire packs.

I am especially in the debt of those who have looked after my horses, especially Geoff Brooks of Widmerpool, and nowadays Mick Smith of Withcote.

It has been a privilege to enjoy the friendship of Masters and their staffs, and so many others I have met at the covert-sides. Most of all I owe, 'the best of my fun' to our hosts, the aforementioned farmers and landowners.

To them I dedicate this story of 'foxhunting in paradise'.

My best thanks are due to the following who read sections of the manuscript and gave me their thoughts: Jonathan Inglesant, Joanna Spencer and Tim Hall-Wilson. I am particularly indebted to Joe Cowen, Senior Joint Master of the Fernie.

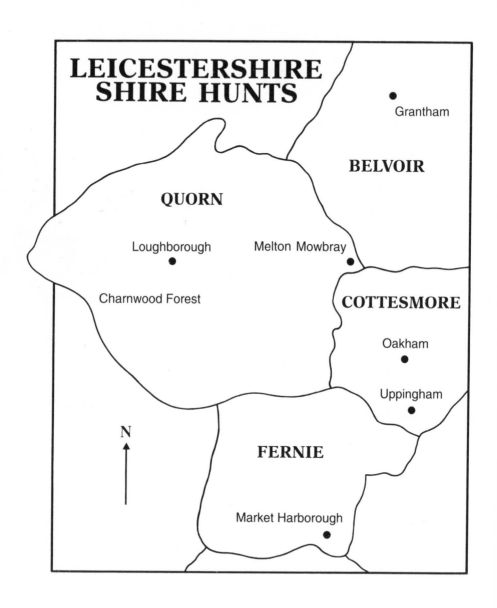

LEICESTERSHIRE
SHIRE HUNTS

Grantham

BELVOIR

QUORN

Loughborough   Melton Mowbray

Charnwood Forest   COTTESMORE

                                    Oakham

                                    Uppingham

N

FERNIE

Market Harborough

1

The Hunting Landscape

In the absence of all perfection, it is as a
hunting country as nearly approaching to its
nature and art can make it, and its fame may
be said to have reached the remotest corners
of the civilised world

Thus Nimrod, Charles James Apperley, the greatest hunting correspondent, summed up Leicestershire in the early nineteenth century. Apperley (1777–1843) adored the countries around Melton Mowbray with a passionate loyalty which entertained many, but affronted some.

There has always been amongst some foxhunters a certain provincial resistance to Leicestershire. Perhaps this is because at times it has seemed to epitomize the merely fashionable rather than the truly sporting. In this they are profoundly mistaken. The foxhunting world does not divide as neatly as some would have us believe, into those who merely hunt to ride, and those who ride to hunt.

A love of foxhunting inevitably involves a delight in the countryside you are privileged to cross. Leicestershire may seem to the non-resident, non-hunting person a fairly unremarkable East Midlands county; not an especially attractive terrain from the car window on the M 1, nor from the train window on the line north to Nottinghamshire and beyond. The truth is that Leicestershire's subtle beauty, with its wonderful miniature uplands, charming valleys, uncluttered hinterlands, unspoilt woodlands, copses and hedgerows, and its miles of undulating old turf, is best appreciated from the back of a horse.

Streams, hardly known to most residents of the Midlands, follow their secret and circuitous courses toward the river Trent in the north, the Welland to the south, or to the Tame and Warwickshire Avon to the west. The foxhunter knows the streams well; foxes often dwell on their banks and are found by hounds. Foxhunting history is full of brave leaps over the streams and brooks of Leicestershire. In a classic account of one such run, Nimrod describes the field encountering the Whissendine brook, in the Cottesmore country, north of Oakham. This meant a leap of twenty feet for a horse.

'Who is that under his horse in the brook?' asks one member of the field.

'He will be drowned,' says another rider.

'I shouldn't wonder,' says another.

Nimrod adds; 'But the pace is too good to enquire.' With this, Nimrod continues his account of the run.

As you ride up each new incline, the vista spread before you is, in the best of the hunting country, a patchwork of pastures divided by thorn hedges patched with rails, the pointed spires of village churches in the distance. The first steeplechase is reputed to have been in Ireland, but the term point-to-point refers to the practice of Meltonians larking across the country, riding in fierce competition towards the point of a village spire.

The ancient green lanes, gated roads, and wide grass verges beside even the busiest of highways, are superb routes for the horseman. From the saddle he sees so much more of this beguiling landscape than the motorist whose windscreen is often below the level of the hedge tops. When the view, framed by a horse's ears, includes a first-class pack of hounds streaming away across the landscape; the prospect ahead is irresistible for the 'true foxhunter', he who adores horse and hound.

Thus, since the late eighteenth century Leicestershire has appealed to those who have the nerve and skill to ride good horses across superb grass and obstacles, which include timber and, best of all, fly fences – the name given to hedges which may be taken in a flying leap, a bold horse easily clearing a ditch on take-off or landing side. Many visitors have had their few Leicestershire seasons and have since returned to their home countries, with golden memories of hunting the Shires. More than a few have been visitors from all over the world, especially the United States of America, the Commonwealth countries and Europe.

Comparatively few foxhunters settle permanently in Leicestershire, although as we shall see, there are communities entirely created by the love of the Chase. Many others continue for much of their adult lives to make annual pilgrimages to the county, either staying for the winter, or more often travelling long distances in their cars once or twice a week in order to hunt. They keep their horses in the hunting countries throughout the winter at livery stables, thereby investing heavily in the local rural economy.

Historically, during times of agricultural recession, Leicestershire has benefited economically from its foxhunting magnet which has attracted considerable expenditure from outside the county. The hunting lodges of Melton Mowbray, Oakham, Market Harborough and many villages were notable examples of investment created by the sport. Foxhunting has also enriched the rural and town communities with jobs and businesses, largely stimulated by the host of horses kept at livery, producing a ready market for locally grown forage, and the many ancillary services necessary to keep horses and their riders fit and happy through the long season from September to the end of March, or early April in bygone years when there was less arable farming.

Even today when horse transport from outside Leicestershire is much easier, hunting stimulates major expenditure within the county. Compare this with a non-hunting, heavily intensive arable district where farm labour has been cut to a handful of highly qualified men capable of using modern machinery, and where the horse population has dropped, thereby reducing a source of intensive labour. In such areas we see villages denuded of young people and a landscape of monotonous plough, with all too many of its hedgerows gone forever.

Leicestershire is still a delight for the foxhunter and is still worthy of its description as 'this little paradise' in the Badminton Library volume on Hunting published in 1889; although it must be admitted that the author's description of Melton Mowbray as being 'isled in a sea of grass' is far from accurate nowadays. Arable farming has increased hugely in the post-war years.

The Shire hunting countries of Leicestershire may be thought of as lying on the spokes of a wheel, with Melton Mowbray as the hub. The Fernie country, in the south of the county, is the exception but this was originally part of the Quorn. To the north-east of Melton lies the Belvoir; the Quorn is north-west, south and west of Melton; the Cottesmore is south-east, with Oakham as its largest town; the Fernie, at the southerly end of the Quorn country, borders on Market Harborough.

Geologically, Leicestershire is extremely varied: carboniferous limestone in West Leicestershire, in Charnwood Forest ancient volcanic rocks, and from Belvoir Castle down to the Laughton Hills near Market Harborough, a hard band of iron-bearing limestone, a marlstone rock bed. The honey-coloured marlstone rock can be seen in the buildings of East Leicestershire and Rutland, where the churches, barns, and cottages all benefit from this warm stone. Further east still there is Lincolnshire limestone, providing the well-known building stone found at Clipsham and Ketton. The vales are clay and tend to ride heavier in the Cottesmore country. The upland wolds provide thinner soil and therefore lighter going for a horse, but it needs to be really wet to provide a good scent for foxhunting. The East Midlands are among the drier areas of Britain and there are all too many blue, hazy, bad scenting days in the autumn. This usually disappears early in the New Year when scent improves greatly, and the lighter going allows horses a far better passage across country than they get in, for example, the south-west of England where the clay vales produce mud baths for horse and rider in January and February.

I have included Rutland as part of Leicestershire not merely because the politicians ensured that it was absorbed within the latter's boundaries and administration from 1974. No area of the East Midlands retains its individual identity more strikingly than Rutland; it is still a superb foxhunting country, all within the Cottesmore boundaries. Designated a Rural District, Rutland still yearns for its previous status of smallest county of Britian, although with a population of only 35,000 people it could scarcely cope with financing the full administrative apparatus of a modern county. As a Rutland resident, I write with no shred of impartiality in averring that the character of the undulating country surrounding Oakham and Uppingham still has a distinctive charm which sets it apart from much else in Leicestershire; it is not necessarily better but it is noticeably different. The villages have the honey-coloured, stone-walled cottages; there are still ancient thatched roofs nestling against steep hillsides; there are surprisingly steep valleys, vistas of old turf, criss-crossed with neat hedgerows in a landscape which swells contentedly against a large, spare skyline whose sunrises and sunsets are often breathtaking. The imposition of Rutland Water, the huge reservoir east of Oakham, has been absorbed as an area of beauty.

The spirit of friendliness, of equality in the Shires hunting fields compares well with any other Hunt. I affirm this as one who has hunted with nearly two hundred packs of foxhounds throughout the United Kingdom and abroad. Those who have hunted for many seasons with the Leicestershire packs know that their sport depends on the same basic precepts, the same emphasis on goodwill with the landowners and farmers, as the smallest, humblest Hunt in the land.

The true secret of the success of the Leicestershire packs was, and still is, based on successful venery in the most congenial environment imaginable for this demanding sport. Tracing the fascinating history of the Leicestershire Hunts it is clear that their peaks were achieved by brilliant individual exponents of the exceedingly difficult art of hunting the fox in open countryside with consistent success. Hound breeding, horsemanship and preservation of the countryside are all vital in Leicestershire to achieve so much hunting for so many followers. Those of us who have been merely spectators on horseback, the mounted field, can best justify our allegiance by declaring that the most important element present in abundance in that delectable country at the heart of the Shires is sheer enjoyment. A foxhunting country is more than its fabric. It exists in the hearts and minds of those who love it, who relish its virtues, and who will do anything possible to conserve them.

It is to the everlasting credit of a significant number of Leicestershire landowners and farmers that they continue to nurture the qualities of the landscape as a hunting country, no matter what horrors are inflicted by urban development and agricultural change caused by commercial pressures.

Paradise is not lost, but it has changed.

2

Enduring Changes

Hounds making a tremondous cry, were
quite invisible and the few remaining riders
appeared like legless Centaurs; one hoped
the fences would be big enough to appear
above the cloud – it was like a weird dream,
and terribly exciting

It is all to easy to bemoan the huge changes wrought in Leicestershire's
hunting countries, whilst forgetting the inestimable prize which remains –
the co-operation and hospitality of the vast majority of landowners and
farmers.

Improved fertilizers have enabled farmers to grow corn crops con-
tinuously, and modern technology has led to machinery capable of
improved drainage of often heavy land. Hedgerows have all too easily be
rooted out allowing the machinery to operate effectively over vast acreages
of plough. Riding over stubble has rapidly became an almost forgotten
autumn luxury, and ploughing commences in a trice after harvesting. The
popularity of winter wheat, and the use of rotary ploughs right up to the
edge of fields has made them virtually unrideable.

In the eighteenth and nineteenth centuries, Leicestershire had a fine
reputation as a sea of grass. At the first Agricultural Census, in 1866,
it was estimated that sixty per cent of the county was under permanent

grass. Grass cover increased further in this century, and those who hunted between the wars undoubtedly had the best of it. An official survey in the 1920s and '30s showed that eighty-five per cent of Leicestershire was then down to permanent grass. In fact much of the so-called arable land east of the A 1 road was extremely lightly farmed at that time, I have been told. It had returned to rough heathland, easy to cross on a horse, and containing many natural fox coverts.

The Second World War began a trend towards plough in the county, reducing the pasture to forty-one per cent by 1943. This trend was encouraged by government subsidies and the guaranteed market for cereals. By the 1970s only a little more than one-third of rural Leicestershire and Rutland were under permanent grass, and there have been further reductions since.

The policy of set-aside land initiated by the government in the 1990s may appear to be economic lunacy – paying farmers not to grow food – but it was beginning to be noticeable in reducing the areas under intensive plough cultivation. In wet weather, however, set-aside land rides abominably, probably worse than plough. It tends to become a sea of mud after heavy rain, and horses stumble and wallow about while endeavouring to cross it.

Leicestershire's changing face is simply part of a British rural revolution in which forty-four per cent of ancient woodlands, ninety-five per cent of herb-rich meadows and half the country's fenlands have vanished. In the eight years previous to 1992 it has been estimated that 24,000 miles of hedgerow have been destroyed throughout Britain, and pesticides have continued to deprive many birds of the insect diet they need to survive. Apart from the major changes in the areas still designated as rural, it has been estimated that since 1945 one and three-quarter million acres of Britain have been 'urbanized'; an area equivalent to all of Greater London, Berkshire, Oxfordshire and Hertfordshire. At night the broad horizons of Leicestershire are lit with an eerie glow – the street lights of the sprawling urban conurbations at Leicester and Nottingham penetrating the darkness. The urbanization of much of Leicestershire began during the Second World War when the county was used extensively for new military aerodromes: at Cottesmore and Luffenham in Rutland; at Castle Donington, Ratcliffe, Rearsby, Bitteswell and at Stoughton, Bruntingthorpe and Lubenham in the Fernie country. Only two aerodromes have survived to become major post-war developments – Cottesmore is a large NATO airbase and Castle Donington has become the East Midlands civil airport, serving Derby, Nottingham and Leicester.

Leicestershire's main roads have seen major developments such as the dual carriageway on the A 6, which bisects the Quorn Monday country from above Thrussington to Willoughby; and dual carriageways on the A 50 and A 6. The first major road disaster for foxhunting was the construction of the M 1 scything through Charnwood Forest in the north-west of the county; followed by the M 69, connecting the M 1 and M 6 that scarred the Atherstone country, and then most recently, the development of the M 42 from Staffordshire up to the Kegworth inter-change on the M 1, which has cramped the already hard-pressed area hunted by the Quorn on Saturdays to the west of the M 1.

Rutland lost 3,000 acres in the River Gwash valley above Empingham when the area was drowned by a huge reservoir now known as Rutland Water. Completed in 1976, a lake the size of Windermere now sits in the valley. Three per cent of Rutland is under water as a result. The Eye reservoir, south of Uppingham, contributes to this. Rutland Water is Britain's largest man-made lake and has become a trout fishery, winter wildfowl reserve and sailing centre. Foxes abound on its shores, and the Hunt performs useful culling work here. The fox population unchecked could wreak havoc among the other wildlife in the area. Alas, Rutland Water was afflicted with a plague of blue algae in the late 1980s which can be poisonous to drink. Significantly, this was discovered when several hounds of the Cottesmore Hunt died after drinking from the water during hunting. Some local dogs and sheep were also afflicted.

Rutland was absorbed by Leicestershire in 1974 under the Government's misguided boundary changes, but retains much of its character and certainly its tenacious spirit of independence. There had been a whole series of independence battles before 1974; notably that of 1963 when Sir Kenneth Ruddle of the Rutland brewery firm led a victorious struggle against a take-over by Leicestershire. There were high hopes early in the 1990s that Rutland could regain its independent status when discussions of further boundary changes were taking place. The concept that 'little is good' was perhaps beginning to filter through to bureaucratic thinking in a recession-hit world.

As if intensive farming, disappearing hedgerows, new roads and reservoirs are not enough; major seams of coal were discovered more than 1,300 feet below the surface of the Vale of Belvoir in the 1970s. Luckily, the mining threat was largely averted; the change of policy towards reducing coal production and closing down mines in the 1990s has probably saved the heart of the Belvoir Vale. However, just north of Melton Mowbray, Asfordby Mine has been developed at enormous cost, swallowing up the famous Welby Osiers covert and some of the Monday Quorn country. In the light of subsequent pit closures and a contracting coal market, the Asfordby development seems to be an expensive error.

Paradise lost? Despite the related tale of woe in terms of conservation, Leicestershire has amazingly remained a heaven for foxhunting during the post-war years, even if it is somewhat eroded. The Hunts have made enormous efforts to ensure that the cream of their country has been bought by hunting enthusiasts whenever possible, and are engaged in a constant campaign to keep their countries rideable. Hunt staffs build bridges, put in small hunting gates, cut back overhanging trees on rides, and generally create the sort of environment most enlightened Britons wish to see in their countryside. We hunt for today; it is no good allowing our sport to be spoilt by constant reflection that the country was so much better in the days of our forebears. It is still possible to taste the 'quick thing' on grass, to jump Leicestershire fly fences fifty or so abreast, and to tackle open brooks and ditches. Our horses must be more versatile than ever before, and the best of them combine the skills of keeping their feet on modern slippery roads with a talent for jumping timber and hedges at speed.

The county has largely been saved from the worst forms of growth and sprawl in its villages. Leicester and Nottingham have grown but their hinterland does not form the sort of ex-urbia achieved by London in the Home Counties, whereby 'real countryside' cannot be found; it is simply suburbia spread more thinly, with plenty of golf courses, sewage farms and innumerable other developments associated with twentieth century man's insatiable appetite for new diversions. Try to foxhunt successfully in the neighbourhood of a modern theme park, garden centre, or novelty zoo! The Pytchley, Whaddon Chase (now amalgamated with the Bicester), Grafton and to some extent the Heythrop, have all seen changes. In most of these hunting countries, the impact has been even worse than in Leicestershire.

The real value of the Hunts in Leicestershire is now starkly apparent for those who care to examine the rural fabric of the county in detail. Why were the coverts carefully planted and maintained? Many coverts were originally patches of gorse, pronounced 'goss' in Leicestershire, and were a great harbour for foxes. They give the landscape much of its character. The Hunts have invested hundreds of thousands of pounds over the past two and a half centuries in the upkeep of an environment which modern conservationists agree is an ideal habitat for birds, insects and mammals. Foxes need 'bottom' in coverts; growth at ground level where sanctuary can be sought. Thus, the good fox covert has a wealth of thorns and bushes, as well as trees. The Hunts can be proud of their record right up to the 1990s in encouraging tree and shrub planting in the coverts, and especially in fostering the preservation of that great feature of the Leicestershire landscape – the fly fence, a thorn hedge, often guarded by a ditch and patched with timber rails.

True, the foxhunter promotes hedges because he likes to jump them, but enlightened self-interest is surely the best way to achieve results in conservation? The Hunts hold annual hedge-cutting contests throughout the county, as do many elsewhere in Britain, but nowhere is the fly fence seen to better advantage than in the foxhunting Shires.

'The history of the hedge is something like this,' wrote Otho Paget. 'The quick, as the young thorn is called, was planted, and was protected by post and rails on each side with a ditch to carry off the water. Whilst the rails were new, this was a formidable obstacle to encounter, but time and weather speedily perish all wood except oak.

'In seven or eight years the thorn fence was cut and laid, and then, if properly done, a hedge grew up that would stop the wildest bullock from straying, and turn over any horse that tried to go through it.

'Cutting and laying a fence is an art confined to the skilled labourer. The thorn is cut half-way through as close to the ground as possible, and is then bent down between stakes, the latter being bound together by twisted briars or some other pliant wood. The thorn that is cut still lives and grows, whilst a wealth of young shoots are thrown out from the bottom.

'In ten or fifteen years the old layers would have commenced to die out, and the young shoots would have developed into a tall bullfinch. Every year after that the hedge would gradually be showing more daylight at the bottom, and the fly-stricken bullock or the impetuous fox-hunter would have no difficulty in forcing a passage.

'The good farmer would then proceed to cut and lay again, so that the youth and vigour of the fence might be revived. In this way the hedge, in a period of twenty years, varies from the new-cut stake and bound to the high, straggling bullfinch. It is not the custom to lay all the fences on the farm in one year, but to do a length every winter, so that the foxhunter finds the thorny obstacles in every stage of growth, giving him that pleasing diversity of jumps which is one of the greatest charms of riding across Leicestershire.'

Since Otho Paget's day, farmers increasingly use mechanical hedge cutters and may dig out ditches with farm excavators. These often make for an extremely formidable combination. The hard-packed, bushy nature of the fence can be deadly if your horse gets a knee on it and the unforgiving, steep-cut mechanical ditch is all the more likely to bring your horse down on landing.

Jumping timber is fine; we can do it as well as our ancestors, but nowadays all too often the timber has barbed wire attached to it, or wrapped around it, and a broken rail spells disaster because the wire will probably bring your horse down.

However, one great contemporary advantage over the early nineteenth century, when horsemen were endeavouring to set new records in jumping and galloping, is that land drainage has improved tremendously. Formerly the land must have been extremely holding in winter. Nowadays, the best old turf in Leicestershire is superb for galloping and jumping; it has a spring in it, quite unlike the grassland in most other areas of Britain. High Leicestershire, where the best of the old turf still exists in the Quorn and Fernie countries, has the most marvellous examples of this natural going for the horse.

Leicestershire foxhunters are well acquainted with another local feature; the ridge and furrow, which is found on old, permanent pasture, usually near to existing or abandoned villages. It is a relict of the method of farming clay land before subsoil drainage was developed. On flat land, grass and corn could perish during a wet winter. The only chance of a crop of either was to throw the soil up into ridges with the plough. Nothing much grew in the furrows, but even in an exceptionally wet season there were hopes of a crop on the top and sides of the ridges. Prices for wheat were good at that time, but subsided later, when the greater value of the land for stock rearing became more profitable.

Fortunately, the horseman in Leicestershire is still bestowed with a marvellous network of bridle paths, green lanes, and roadside verges, usually more generous in width than those to be found anywhere else in the Midlands, and often opening out into common-land meadows near crossroads.

Enclosure in Leicestershire did not occur abruptly; it is likely that land was enclosed over the centuries between the later Middle Ages and the early years of Queen Victoria's reign. The mid-nineteenth century saw an acceleration in the establishment of Enclosure Acts in the county to end the old open field systems whereby the land was farmed on a communal basis in strips of arable cultivation. Instead of planting hedges and enclosing; boundaries between the increasing areas of pasture were formed by leaving strips under grass leys for longer periods.

It is the drovers' tracks, busy in the eighteenth century with cattle herded on the hoof from Scotland and Wales, which form the verges and green lanes of today. Without them foxhunting would be desperately impoverished, since they allow horsemen to bypass the huge arable fields where hounds may be running, and to reach the next pocket of pasture land.

It is all too easy to assume that the current agricultural pattern is immutable. In the twenty-first century it would not be impossible for far less of Leicestershire to be under intensive cereal production, with the remainder down to grass or perhaps permanent set-aside which would be markedly more rideable than the present temporary set-aside arrangements.

What is certain is that the preservation of the coverts is vital, and who better to achieve this than hunting folk? Geoff Brooks of Widmerpool, who has voluntarily carried out much of the work on coverts with his own farm staff and helpers says; 'The Quorn owns some twenty coverts in its country. We do a tremendous amount to maintain them, and many others privately owned, where all the landowners welcome us. We have planted 30,000 trees, paid for by the Hunt, in the last five years. The work is never ending and, of course, it makes a large contribution to the conservation of the British countryside.'

The British Buttterfly Society contacted the Quorn in 1991 to arrange for certain species, such as buddleia, to be planted in coverts to encourage butterflies to use them as habitats. The Hunt was happy to co-operate in such work.

Let us explore the hunting countries of the Shires packs from north to south. I will not give detailed lists and maps of coverts; in modern England they need protecting from vandals, some of whom would seek to trespass in the totally misguided aim of spoiling foxhunting – whereas they are simply spoiling habitats for wildlife – whilst others will venture in search of mindless destruction.

I have not dwelt on the identity of most landowners and farmers in the best hunting country. It would be invidious to do so; the Hunts have the invaluable prize of co-operation with landowners large and small; they are all depended upon and all appreciated to the full by the Hunts. To select some for special mention would be to disregard many others who are equally important.

Belvoir

To achieve a vision of the attractiveness of Leicestershire to the foxhunter, stop at the top of Broughton Hill on the A 606 road from Melton Mowbray to Nottingham. The huge sweep of the Vale of Belvoir lies below. Looking north, the Quorn country is mainly to your left; the Belvoir to your right. The boundary, in fact, lies to the right of the road; it is the river Smite, a famous name in Shires foxhunting since so many foxes are found on its bank, and many hunts have taken place along it, and there have been more than a few adventures in crossing it. The range of hills eastward from Broughton Hill is broken in your vision by woodland coverts which are vital to foxhunting in the Belvoir country. Holwell Mouth is a dense, sprawling covert clothing the hillside; the Smite runs down from it into the Vale. Foxes abound in this covert, and it needs persistent work by hounds to get a fox away for a good hunt in the open, but it can be done.

Further east along the hillside is Clawson Thorns, overlooking the village of Long Clawson, the village that is true to its name, stretching one and a quarter miles from one end to the other, with fourteen right-angled bends! Stilton cheese is made in Long Clawson from milk supplied by the small dairy farms which cover the floor of the Vale, keeping it mainly down to grass even in the late twentieth century. The old corn mill, now without its sails, stands above the village but below the covert. Long Clawson is the fixture for the first Saturday of the season, and hunting usually takes place in the Vale northwards. The Vale villagers have been brought up with foxhunting as part of their lives; they love it, and many are among the most knowledgeable of the Belvoir hounds' regular observers. A good hunt from Clawson Thorns above the village, is one of the greatest treats in the Belvoir country, hopefully soaring past the village to right or left, involving the clearance of some daunting drop fences, and then going down to the pastures below, each one well fenced and equipped with drainage ditches which must be cleared before or behind nearly every thorn hedge or timber fence.

Further east still, there is Brock Hill, and the range of Harby Hills, overlooking the village of Harby, the largest in the Vale, and another centre of Stilton cheese production. Foxes live in the coverts all along the hillside, and are hunted down to the Vale, which is all Saturday country, or above it to the south, which is Wednesday country. The exception is Old Hills, the covert south of the village of Holwell, on the hill country above the Vale, Scalford Ashes, and Melton Spinney, near Scalford. This is a delightful upland area, which rides well in the main. Old Hills is in a small basin, with beautiful pastoral country all around, much of it mined for ironstone in the last century, and then returned to grassland. The Melton brook can be an interesting obstacle in a hunt in this area – I have seen some exciting swimming displays when horses have flopped into it. Melton Spinney can easily afford runs north and west into the Wednesday country. There are great blocks of arable land to the west, but to the north it is a varied country which is indeed pleasant to ride.

In the Vale, to the south-west of Long Clawson is the fine covert, Sherbrooke's, start of so many excellent hunts with the Belvoir hounds, which may take you anywhere; sometimes westwards across the Smite and into some of the best of Quorn Monday country; where the pastures of Muxlow Hill rise above Upper Broughton, and at other times, to the north of the long hill known as The Standard, which guards the village of Hickling. From Long Clawson north to Colston Bassett, the narrow Canal Lane travels through some of the choicest Vale country. It crosses the Grantham Canal which meanders in a loop, running west to east from the Trent at Nottingham, to Grantham. Just on the south side of the canal by

Canal Lane is Hose Thorns, the marvellous covert affording hunts throughout the Vale, best of all, perhaps, is a run southwards, which then either
runs up to Harby Hills, or sweeps below Long Clawson village westwards.
It is a ride which tests the bravest horse if you cross it at speed and mean
to be near hounds.

Leicestershire gives way to Nottinghamshire in these parts; the county
boundary runs along Canal Lane. Further north the great covert of Kaye
Wood is in Nottinghamshire and is on the left before the village of
Colston Bassett. Still in Leicestershire, travelling east from Canal Lane
are the villages of Hose, Harby, Stathern, Barkestone-le-Vale and Redmile,
with the Grantham canal marching just to the north. Stathern and Plungar,
with huge woodlands above them, are excellent foxhunting areas. The
arable land now encroaches and the country becomes a flat vale with ditches
or even dykes, large bushy thorn hedges, and a plenitude of tracks and
paths to take you past most of the plough with comparative ease. There
are plenty of long, grass verges. Yet your horse needs to be able to manage
plough as well as he can grass. In a wet season he must be fit indeed to
tackle this country. Some of the fences are as daunting as those you will
meet anywhere in Leicestershire, especially in the Plungar and Stathern
districts.

Hounds can work well in these areas, and you will see some pretty hunting, even if the riding lacks the grass and fences of the Vale further west.
Langar, with its abandoned airfield, Barnstone, Granby and Barkestone-le-
Vale lie further north-east. North of Grantham canal lies a further stretch
of vale country around Bottesford where there is regular Saturday hunting;
with meets at Normanton, Kilvington, Allington and Elton. The Belvoir
farmers in this area are among the most sporting, and I have had tremendous fun in these flat, arable lands, mainly with a view of Belvoir Castle
on its knoll above the Vale. On Wednesdays the hunting is mainly to the
south of the Saturday country, much of it lying above the range of hills
behind Clawson and Harby. The area lying between the arms of the A 606
road from Melton and the A 607 towards Grantham forms much of the
Wednesday country. Waltham-on-the-Wolds, Chadwell, Wycomb, Scalford,
Goadby and Eastwell are among the meets.

The dismantled railways are useful coverts here, and you will often hack
along high embankments whilst hounds draw either side. Sometimes I
wonder whether helicopter travel will in the late twenty-first century make
Britain's motorways similarly redundant, and hounds will draw the motor-
way verges as they do the abandoned railways, pride of the nineteenth
century.

The opening meet of the Belvoir is held on a Wednesday at Croxton

Park, on the Duke of Rutland's estate, where the Manners family enjoyed relaxation at their poolside lodge. The wooded, hilly areas around the Castle are nowadays well-run shooting country, but foxes are well preserved and the Hunt draws the Castle coverts after the shooting season. Branston, Woolsthorpe and Knipton are in wooded, hilly country where there are plenty of foxes, and the fences can give the Wednesday country some stiff challenges at times. To the south, Mr Joey Newton ensures that his farmland around Saltby is well fenced for hunting. Swallow Hole and Joey's coverts usually hold well, and there are a wealth of good coverts further south stretching to Garthorpe: among them Stonesby Spinney, Sproxton Thorns, Coston Covert and Freeby Wood.

I have elected to concentrate on Leicestershire, but it should be stressed that the Belvoir's Lincolnshire country is equally important in foxhunting terms. The Belvoir doghounds, hunting the Lincolnshire country, much of it east of Grantham, on Tuesdays and Fridays; have a loyal and enthusiastic following in the mounted field and in foot and car followers. For sheer foxhunting, Lincolnshire country is a splendid area in which to watch and follow hounds. The meets include Hough on the Hill, Old

Somerby, Welby, Swarby, Cranwell – where hounds meet at the RAF College – Horbling, Honington, Walcot, Osbournby, Westby, Barrowby, Burton Pedwardine, Threekingham, Oasby, Aswarby, Carlton Scroop, Pickworth, Burton Coggles and Ropsley. Saturday meets include Long Clawson, Kilvington, Langar, Normanton, Landyke Lane (above Long Clawson), Plungar, Wartnaby, Ab Kettelby, Elton, Granby, Allington and Ponton. Wednesdays include Croxton Park, Goadby, Waltham-on-the-Wolds, Branston, Thorpe Arnold, Hose, Stonesby, Freeby, Sproxton and Buckminster Park.

Quorn

The Quorn Monday country starts in the northernmost districts of Nottinghamshire. The sprawl of urbanization has curtailed hunting to some extent, but it is still only a short drive from the city southwards before you arrive in some of the best Quorn country. Drive down the A 606 past Keyworth and soon on your right is the village of Widmerpool, within easy reach of some of the most favoured coverts and best riding country. Flint Hill and Green Hill lie south of Widmerpool; further south is the village of Willoughby-on-the-Wolds with its delectable coverts to the west of Willoughby Gorse and a cluster of others, and to the south, above the Wymeswold Road, Ella's, which is a beautifully sited covert, with an exciting line of hedges and rails in all directions. To the west lies Wymeswold in the centre of yet more good riding country. Alas, running east from Ella's is desperately difficult nowadays, unless the fox chooses to cross the bridge over the four-lane highway which is now called The Fosse. The A 46 follows the route known as The Fosse Way made by the Romans running from Exeter in Devon up to Lincoln. Continuing south, parallel to the Fosse, you will come to the important coverts just west of Six Hills. No one knows why it is called 'Hills' as there are none, but there may have been ancient tumuli. The 'Six' used to be written as 'Segs' or 'Segg' named after the owner of the Wold in about twelve hundred. The coverts are Cradock's Ashes, named after J.D. Cradock, the Quorn's distinguished Hunt Honorary Secretary (Chapter Four) and Walton Thorns. A modern day descendant, Mrs Pat Weldon, hunted for years with the Quorn and still lives in Wymeswold. If hounds run out of the Thorns and down the brook towards Burton-on-the-Wolds, you need a good horse to keep you near the front as the hedges are well guarded, with especially daunting ditches.

East of the A 46 lies a great swathe of excellent Quorn Monday country, much of it still down to grass; from Kinoulton, right down to Asfordby, just west of Melton Mowbray.

Immediately south of the old Grantham canal, is Hickling, below the long hill called Hickling Standard. On its northern slope is Parson's Thorns, which was on Hickling Glebe, hence its name. This can provide superb hunts over the Standard, swooping over the shallow valley beyond and over the grass and fences so carefully preserved on the land of late Dr Tom Connors (Chapter Eight) at Muxlow Hill. If hounds run east, they are soon in the Belvoir country, and I have enjoyed glorious incursions with both Hunts across the border here. One of the newest coverts in the Quorn country is called 'Miss Hepplewhite's,' named after the late Miss Alice Hepplewhite who followed the Quorn Hunt for a great many years by car with her sister Dora. The covert is on the land at Muxlow.

On the west side of the A 606 is Curate's Gorse. The name refers to Parson's Thorns in the saying that 'If the Parson cannot perform the service, the Curate will.' This is invariably true today when it comes to finding foxes which will run in the open. If hounds run due south there is a marvellous swoop over Mr Bob Chaplin's grass and fences to Upper Broughton and Nether Broughton, leaving Old Dalby on the right. If you are lucky, hounds would run on up Green Hill, just to the west of Broughton Hill, and I have enjoyed hunts in which they then ran back down the Hill, crossed the Melton road and swooped over the grass behind Nether Broughton, either going on to Slyborough Hill in the Belvoir country, or turning north again and landing us back on the grass below Muxlow Hill.

Above Green Hill is the Wartnaby estate, now largely arable but always with well stocked coverts and a warm welcome. Continuing south there is Saxelby Pastures, and the Asfordby country, but the new coal mine there has largely curtailed hunting in this district, and has, as mentioned previously, swamped Welby Osiers, planted by the 2nd Earl of Wilton in the 1870s.

Just to the north-west, by the Melton to Wymeswold road is the famous Shoby Scholes covert, a hillside covert at the source of a stream which theoretically gives access down to the Hoby Vale, one of the best loved Quorn hunting heavens, but which in the latter twentieth century has largely been put to plough. Old Dalby Wood, Grimston Gorse and Bridget's are famous coverts around Old Dalby, still providing excellent hunts.

The Monday country has small enclosures, fairly neat hedges and timber, and is a marvellous place for the 'quick things'. It has become increasingly difficult as an environment for the longer hunt, simply because of the multiplicity of roads and lanes and their business with modern traffic.

Foxes are all too easily headed, and the huntsman needs the patience of a saint. In Michael Farrin such saintliness seems abundant, but I wonder just how many members of his mounted field realize what huge difficulties he has to contend with in this area nowadays.

Monday meets include Wymeswold, Saxelby Park, Hickling, Six Hills, Wysall, Widmerpool, Old Dalby, Grimston and Roehoe.

The Quorn's Friday country lies due south of Melton Mowbray, running down to the A 47 road between Leicester and Peterborough, the modern boundary with the Fernie country (Chapter Ten).

My own interpretation of Quorn history is that the Friday country is in many ways the heartland of the old Quorn, and that the far northern end of the Monday country was considered far too wild and woolly by the nineteenth century Meltonians. Muxlow, for example, was then undrained and considered to be a huge bog.

The lovely hunting estates of Lowesby, Baggrave and Quenby dominate the mid to southern end of the Friday country, and thank heavens still continue to do so. For historical reasons I will mention some of the owners. Lowesby Hall, of Ketton stone, dates from the seventeenth century, with early eighteenth century development. It is a beautiful setting for the Chase, set amid sweeping vistas of pasture dotted with long-cherished Quorn coverts; a masterpiece of landscape that must never be erased. It was formerly the seat of the Fowkes family. In the 1830s it was rented by the Marquis of Waterford, who in 1838 performed the jolly feat of jumping his horse, Don Juan, over a gate in the dining room; not so jolly for the horse, I suspect. This feat was quite common in roistering parties among sportsmen; remember, they had no fast cars nor power boats in those days. The gate was preserved in the stables. Waterford is said to have shot out the eyes of some of the Fowkes family portraits because he said they were staring at him! W. Bromley-Davenport celebrated the virtues of the estate in his sporting prose essay *Lowesby Hall*.

In the twentieth century it was the home of Sir Keith and Lady Nuttall who had lived in Cheshire previously. Mr David Wilson, the master builder, who bought Lowesby in recent years is a marvellous supporter of the Hunt, having enjoyed many seasons in the mounted field. He keeps this superb estate down to grass, and the fences and coverts are in top-class order.

Baggrave, the estate just to the west, was the pre-war home of Major Algy Burnaby, the Quorn's Joint Master, then Sir George and Lady Earle, and after the war, Mr and Mrs Stuart Blyth. Stuart, a devoted foxhunter, who had been Joint Master of the South Notts, maintained the estate ideally for foxhunting, with plenty of fly fences and timber to jump. The Household Cavalry Ride used to take place there with Stuart and Jenny Blyth as hosts.

The next owner was Asil Nadir, the Cypriot financier, who spent a fortune in developing the estate for intensive cattle production which made it necessary to put in a great many Hunt jumps. Now the owners are Mr and Mrs Tom Scott who are most co-operative with the Hunt.

The third great estate surrounds Quenby Hall, the notable early seventeenth century house, home of Sir Harold Nutting, the former Quorn Joint Master (Chapter Five) and his family before and after the war. Then, fortunately, it became the home of Squire de Lisle and his family, devoted foxhunters, who have always maintained the estate with foxhunting in mind. Among the famous coverts in this area are Carr's Brigg, near the footpath from Twyford to Hungarton, as it crosses the Queniborough Brook, possibly named after a Mr Carr who was vicar of Lowesby in the late eighteenth century; Prince of Wales's covert, just west of Baggrave Hall, made in 1871 in honour of the Prince of Wales, later Edward VII and the Diamond Spinney which is one of the many excellent coverts on Lowesby.

The eastern side of the Friday country is bounded by the range of hills, running north to south, where the Cottesmore country begins. It is a complex of little hills and valleys, dotted with coverts, and provides excellent foxhunting, although your horse must be fit to pull up the hills. Great Dalby village nestles below Gartree Hill to the east, and is usually the first covert after the Quorn's traditional opening meet of the season at Kirby Gate. Hounds have a long hack from the Melton to Leicester road, through Great Dalby to Gartree where the covert stands on a hilltop, giving superb views over the Quorn Friday country and the Cottesmore country to the east. I suspect Gartree had a sinister usage, since one of the fields was known as Gallowtree Hill in the early seventeenth century. Hilltops were quite popular hanging sites so that all should see what fate befell lawbreakers. A ride around Gartree, and a run from there in most descriptions is still one of the special treats of the Quorn, and the Cotttesmore are known to run into Gartree from their draw over their border at the Lakes Spinney, near Little Dalby.

Advancing further south, to the west lie Cream Gorse, so well maintained by Mrs Joan Crosfield; Ashby Pastures, one of the oldest and best coverts, and coming east again, above Thorpe Satchville is Adam's Gorse, re-enclosed and re-sown by Otho Paget for Lord Manners in 1184–6. Burrough Hill stands highest in this range of hills, at about seven hundred feet, and between this hill and Gartree lies Sir Francis Burdett's covert, named after the radical politician (1770–1844).

The Friday country pushes out westwards towards the A 607, and just beyond, but the urban sprawls around East Goscote, Queniborough and Syston, curtail the huntable country. On the eastern side there is far less development, and the hunting is good, although more steep inclines confront the foxhunters as they approach Tilton-on-the-Hill and Cold Newton just westwards. John O'Gaunt, presumably named after the Earl of Leicester, who bore that name, was already well established in the early nineteenth century and lies close to the B 6047 Melton to Harborough road, just below Tilton.

To the north of Billesdon, now the Quorn's boundary with the Fernie, lie three famous coverts: Lord Morton's, made in this century by that Earl who hunted from Cold Newton as Lord Aberdour; Billesdon Coplow, a dark triangular landmark, and next to it, Botany Bay, a name signifying 'a long way from anywhere', dating from the 1790s when convicts were exiled to Botany Bay in Australia; it was a long hack to the covert from the Quorn kennels.

The area around Barkby and Beeby is still hunted regularly; although perilously close to the boundaries of Leicester it is remarkably rural. Barkby Holt covert goes back to old Hugo Meynell's Mastership in the late eighteenth century. There is an old Quorn joke about a foxhunter who bragged about his acquaintances and when asked if he knew Barkby Holt, said: 'Yes, of course, I dined with him last week.' The antiquity of the coverts in the Friday country is among the most striking evidence that fox-hunting has indeed influenced the landscape in which it takes place. Fridays include Beeby, Great Dalby, Cold Newton, Queniborough, Eye Kettleby, Lowesby, Walton-le-Wolds, Ashby Folville, Thorpe Satchville and Quenby.

The Quorn's Saturday and Tuesday countries lie to the west of the Monday country. Many who have hunted with the Quorn for years have never hunted on that side; it is a varied area, among the hardest hit by urbanization in the form of the M 1 and M 42 motorways, and an increase in the size of towns and villages.

Charnwood Forest, an ancient hunting ground dating back to pre-Norman times, known jokingly to former Meltonians as the home of the 'beasts of the forest', offers a totally different environment, with small pastures set among heathland and stone walls. With small fields, and the doghounds hunting persistently, many a Leicestershire-born foxhunter has learned to enjoy the Chase in this area, and then graduated to the Melton side. Bardon Hill, on the west flank of Charnwood Forest, is the highest point in Leicestershire, at nine hundred and twelve feet, and offers a marvellous panorama of Midland landscape.

Much of the Quorn's basic strength as a Leicestershire pack is due to the loyalty and enthusiasm of the people who hunt regularly on Tuesdays and Saturdays. As I have remarked, the Donington country, west of the M 1, has been hard hit by road developments, and in 1992 the Saturday country was, in effect, being pushed eastwards, which then posed problems through the possibility of encroaching on the Monday country.

Tuesday meets include Woodhouse Eaves, Swithland, Greenhills, Quorn, Ulverscroft, Whitwick and Gracedieu. On Saturdays hounds may be found at Diseworth, Hoton, Owthorpe, Kinoulton, Burton-on-the-Wolds, Thrussington and Osgathorpe.

The Quorn met for many years on Boxing Days in the centre of Loughborough, and we received a warm welcome from thousands of residents and visitors, followed by a drink with the District Council, and a long hack to the first draw. I recall hunting on one such Boxing Day and much enjoying a hunt on a fox found in a clump of rhododendron bushes behind a public lavatory in the woodland near Nanpanton. Surrounded by scores of youthful foxhunters on ponies, my mare Josephine cantered about among the trees, filed along narrow paths behind garden walls, and clambered about among rocks, until hounds marked to ground.

For the first time in 1992 the Quorn met elsewhere on Boxing Day, at Ingarsby, and plenty of people turned up to welcome the hounds. There is a strong anti-hunting faction within Charnwood Borough Council; they did not forbid the Hunt to meet in Loughborough, but they certainly made it unwelcome. Have they improved life for Loughborough citizens, and the keen youngsters who ride ponies in the area? Have these young riders not been robbed of their birthright, having been born in the most famous hunting country in England?

Cottesmore

As I explain in more detail in the Cottesmore section (Chapters Thirteen and Fourteen) this hunting country has suffered somewhat more than its neighbours in terms of grass country. The Quorn has enough grass for most Mondays and Fridays to take place on pasture; the Belvoir has virtually an all-grass Saturday once a fortnight, and a part-grass and arable Wednesday; once a fortnight the Cottesmore has an all-grass Tuesday, although it may sometimes run into a little arable that day, and a part-grass, part-arable Tuesday alternately. Its Saturdays, Mondays and Thursdays see plenty of arable as well as some grass.

From a foxhunting viewpoint, however, the Cottesmore is inestimably blessed in its fine, wild country, and its splendid coverts. No motorways march through it; the A 1 and the A 47 are busy, but cause few problems. There are huge blocks of land in the Cottesmore, with no village sprawl, and far less urbanization than many other hunting countries in the Midlands.

You may see a wild Cottesmore fox go away from a large covert in fine style, and it can run a long distance, not too likely to be headed by traffic on roads. Rutland is an especially beautiful area and much of the country is beguiling to the eye when seen from horseback.

Let us explore first the cream of the Tuesday riding country – from the western side of Oakham it is only three miles to the village of Knossington, with its thirteenth century church of St Peter, which has a square tower instead of a spire. On either side of the route to Knossington is some of the best country, especially that to the south above Braunston which retains its character as a stone-built Rutland village. It is replete with stables, now largely unused, which serve as a reminder that it was a highly popular centre for Cottesmore foxhunters over many years.

Great hunting forests surrounded the villages in medieval times, and the undulating, rideable nature of the country must have been much appreciated by huntsmen whose quarry was then the stag. The forest clearance has left rounded uplands above Braunston where you may clearly see hounds working in front of you, as you skim across the superb old turf, your horse leaping neat thorn hedges and timber. It looks somewhat easier to cross than it is. Visitors are sometimes caught out by the scoops, instead of ditches in front of hedges. A horse can easily get into the scoop instead of standing off to jump, and this can bring him down if he fails to get his knees up high in take-off; alternatively he may be brought down by jumping short and landing in a scoop. Boldness tends to pay; kick on, and your horse should jump scoop and hedge off a long stride.

Wilson's, a covert owned by the Honourable Mrs Ursula ('Urky') Newton, is a great place to find a fox and start a hunt in this paradise of grass; it lies just west of Oakham. Above it to the north is Orton Park, a corruption for Cold Overton Park Wood, a large covert where innumerable great Cottesmore hunts have started, or ended. Below, by the Knossington lane, is one of the finest coverts in Leicestershire, Lady Wood, where foxes can take you on hunts over grass and fences in all directions. It is just a short ride, but a good one, across country south to Preston Lodge, home of Sir Henry Tate who is host for the opening meet at his home, Preston Lodge. His famous woodlands behind the house, Owston Little Wood, and the Big Wood on the far side to the west, are superb coverts, always holding foxes, and are an invaluable asset in severe weather when hounds can hunt there happily for hours. I have remarked elsewhere on the perils of deep going in these coverts for horsemen.

Arable dominates much of the country around this heavenly centre of the Tuesday country, but there are excellent stretches of grass too. To the south above Braunston is the famous Priors Coppice covert, standing on a hilltop, with the valley of the River Chater beyond it, the land rising again to the hilltop village of Ridlington. Taking the Braunston road towards Tilton, on your left lies the beautiful valley of grass centred on Launde Abbey, originally a priory for Augustinian canons, founded in the early twelfth century, but since destroyed and rebuilt several times, being much modernized in the nineteenth century. It is among the most beautiful sites in Leicestershire, the grass parkland guarded on hillsides around it by the huge coverts; Launde Park Wood and Big Wood. Due west in another complex of small hills and valleys, some quite steep, are a range of good coverts, Tilton and Skeffington Woods, Priest Hill, Tugby Woods and Loddington Reddish. The Eye brook runs south from this area, via the Eyebrook reservoir, eventually to join the River Welland near Caldecott. Much of the land is ploughed, but there are grass tracks in all directions, and I have enjoyed some superb hunting in this area, especially during the Mastership of Brian Fanshawe. Out of season the hacking in this area is a pure delight.

The remainder of the Tuesday country runs mainly to the west; it includes Leesthorpe, home of the Joint Master, Mr Tony Ruddle, on the Oakham-Melton road, Little Dalby just to the west, Somerby, Burrough-on-the-Hill, Marefield, and Owston, plus the Tilton country on the Cottesmore side. This is arable and grass mixed and includes the escarpment of hills on the Quorn boundary. There are coverts clothing the hills between Burrough and Little Dalby, and thick woodlands above the village, which hold foxes well. Abandoned railway lines near Owston, running into the Quorn country, provide self-sown coverts.

The Saturday country nowadays includes that above Oakham, and near, or below Uppingham to the south. Wardley Wood is a famous covert near Uppingham, and in the country east of Uppingham and north up to Stamford, there are plenty of coverts, giving runs over this huge terrain of large arable fields and wide horizons. The villages just west and south of Rutland Water – Egleton, Gunthorpe, Manton, Morcott, Glaston and the Luffenhams, provide mixed country, with plenty of havens for foxes. Manton Gorse is a very old and famous Cottesmore covert. The River Chater runs through this area to join the Welland at Stamford. Just to the north the River Gwash runs into Rutland Water.

Above Oakham, the Cottesmore hunt the country above and around Burley-on-the-Hill, the great mansion standing above Oakham to the north, built by the first Duke of Buckingham in the early seventeenth century, destroyed in the Civil War and rebuilt; then much added to, and restored in the eighteenth and nineteenth centuries. Burley Woods, clothing the hills below the house, are marvellous for foxhunting at all times of the season. The house and estate are owned by Mr Joss Hanbury, former Cottesmore Master (Chapter Seven). East of Burley is Exton, seat of the Gainsborough family, founders of the Cottesmore Hunt, and this major estate remains another invaluable Cottesmore hunting ground. West of Burley lies the Catmose Vale where the old abandoned Oakham to Melton canal winds below Cottesmore, Market Overton and past Edmondthorpe. Just to the north is Stapleford Park, nowadays a country house hotel run by enterprising Americans, Bob and Wendy Payton, who hunt with the Cottesmore and perform great services in helping to defend foxhunting.

Laxton's covert lies just south of Stapleford, producing runs in the Whissenthorpe country, now heavily under the plough, and once the delight of Meltonians, with the challenge of jumping the Whissendine brook adding extra spice to a hunt.

On the west side of the Melton road, near Langham, stands the famous covert of Ranksborough Gorse, where a hunt could involve swooping down eastwards, over the Melton road to tackle the vale country between Langham, Ashwell, Teigh and up to Wymondham. The Burton Flats, an extension of this vale, lie north-west under Burton Lazaars, just south of Melton Mowbray. This is now arable land, but is still hunted, and if hounds run northwards they are soon in the Belvoir country around Freeby and Garthorpe. Ulrica Murray Smith recalls in the 1930s: 'The Burton Flats was ideal for these not so brave, as hounds always seemed to run fast there, and the fences were tiny, although some of them had big ditches which could come as a shock to the unwary.

'I shall never forget one evening hunt across the Flats with the Cottesmore, when the moon was up and there was a ground mist, covering everything like a cloud. Hounds, making a tremendous cry, were quite invisible, and the few remaining riders appeared like legless Centaurs; one hoped the fences would be big enough to appear above the cloud – it was like a weird dream, and terribly exciting.'

On Thursdays the Cottesmore hunt the country mainly to the east and north of Rutland Water, again much of it arable, and with some big shooting estates, but a huge terrain of largely open country. Hambleton, now a peninsular in Rutland water, is still a fixture, and so is Empingham and surrounding country at the eastern end of the reservoir.

The Monday country, in Lincolnshire on the east side of the A 1, has been far more intensively farmed in the post-war years than before, but it has a great record of producing plenty of good hunting, abounding in coverts, some of them very extensive woodlands, such as the woodlands at Greetham, Pickworth, Clipsham, Stretton and East Morkery. Brian Fanshawe took the Cottesmore hounds early in the season as far east as possible to the Lincolnshire fenlands, hunting the multitude of foxes in and around the fens as a valuable education for the young hounds.

Saturday meets include Seaton, East Norton, Belton, Glaston, Burley, Beaumont Chase, Egleton, Bisbrooke, Wing, Preston and Caldecott. Monday meets include Witham on the Hill, Edenham, Holywell, Dunsby, Twyford and Toft. Tuesdays include Preston Lodge, Withcote, Knossington,

Braunston, Brooke, Tilton, Loddington, Cold Overton, Owston, Somerby, Burnough, Pickwell, Leesthorpe and Little Dalby.

Fernie

Drive from Billesdon down the Melton Mowbray road to Market Harborough, and you pass through some of the most attractive landscape in the East Midlands; it certainly catches the eye of a foxhunter, and so it should, since so much of it is drenched in hunting history. The Fernie country is bounded in the north by the A 47 Leicester to Peterborough road, and on the west by the A 426 from Leicester to Lutterworth. Its eastern boundary runs from Market Harborough up to Great Bowden and Welham to the Eye Brook near Caldecott, going by Stockerston back to the A 47 near Allexton. To the south it follows the line of the River Welland from Market Harborough through Lubenham and up to Ashby Magna. Joe Cowen, the Fernie's senior Joint Master, tells me that Stoughton and Bruntingthorpe airfields, built during the war, substantially affected the hunting country. Between the wars perhaps the finest area to hunt over had been the far Thursday country, relying on Thurnby covert, Norton Gorse and Tamborough as the principal coverts to be drawn.

Stoughton airfield substantially damaged a significant portion of the country between Thurnby covert and Glen Gorse, although this was mitigated by the fact that the area could still be hunted due to the very light use made of the airfield in the post-war years, allowing hounds to continue to draw the rough places on its perimeter and to hunt over the runways. However, the days of large grass pastures and big hedges in this area had gone forever.

Yet this part of the country only ceased to be hunted after the Co-op Society ban on its Stoughton estate. The Fernie has since that ban hunted two days a week, Saturdays and Wednesdays, and manages to organize itself so that those who hunt on either day enjoy a fair proportion of grass as well as arable.

Bruntingthorpe airfield caused the immediate loss of Gilmorton covert. In the early days of the century when Arthur Thatcher was huntsman, he and others always considered that the country between Jane Ball, Walton Holt and Gilmorton covert was the best of all, known to many foxhunters as 'the Elysian Fields'. Bruntingthorpe increased in size after the war when it was developed as a USAF bomber base, eventually ceasing this role in the early 1960s. The Americans were generally very hospitable and welcomed hounds to meets there sometimes, Joe Cowen recalls. The old airfield then became an intensively used semi-industrial site.

Lubenham was used for more than a decade after the war as a storage dump for old Army vehicles, preventing entry by hounds. Then it became the site of Gartree prison, now permanently established, with the remainder of the area restored to arable farming.

Bosworth covert was part of a bomb testing range during the war and thereafter could not be entered by the Hunt because of the danger of unexploded shells. Sadly, Mowsley covert was also removed, but this was due to farming interests.

Charles Simpson in his excellent *Harborough Country* says the Fernie changed in the eighteenth and nineteenth centuries, 'from a gorse-grown common, or series of commons divided by boundary fences and broken by lands under the plough, to a strongly fenced grazing country, almost every field of which has helped to make hunting history.'

The Fernie consists mostly of a rolling upland, intersected by deep broad valleys in the eastern part, falling gently down to the Soar valley in the west. The country west of the A 6 in the Harborough district, just north-west of Market Harborough, is still among the finest to be found anywhere. There is some glorious turf, well made fences of thorn and timber and the Hunt has worked hard to ensure that it is crossable by building Hunt fences where necessary, constructed on as broad a front as possible, greatly reducing the need to queue. No wonder old Meynell relished Gumley, and no wonder at all that subsequent Meltonians rued the day the Quorn ever lost this country to an independent Fernie Hunt. Gumley Wood is north-east of the village, and Gumley covert lies on the southern slope. To the south lies the Laughton Hills where there is a range of spinnies, Bunker's Hill at one end and Saunt's Close at the other; all offering the opportunity of grand hunts down into the Lubenham Vale, or along the Laughton Hills. Smeeton Gorse, Holloway Spinney and the coverts at Saddington Reservoir above Gumley, all hold well, and just to the east is Furnivals. Further east still on either side of the A 50 road, near Shearsby, are the great glories of the Fernie country, the wonderful coverts, John and Jane Ball. John Ball was a covert made by Mr Oldacre, a skilled man in creating thorn coverts, the work being carried out for Squire Osbaldeston when he was Master of the Quorn (1817–21). Oldacre also made Jane Ball on the other side of the Welford road. It is thought that the name John refers to a child of Mr Oldacre's, christened at the time, and Ball may refer to a Leicestershire term meaning to cake or gather in lumps, like snow on a horse's feet, which may be appropriate on account of the rounded summit of the hill on which the covert stands.

Knaptoft, just to the south, is the site of a ruined church, supposedly burnt down after the Battle of Naseby by the Roundheads because Knaptoft

Hall was owned by a staunch Royalist. Over this hill Prince Rupert's beaten Dragoons passed after the Battle of Naseby (1645). It is a magic area for foxhunting, and I shall always treasure the special hunt I enjoyed there in 1977 after the meet at Foxton. The annual Harborough cross-country ride is held at the end of each season over the marvellous old turf around Saddington, and that is a gallop I shall always recall with much pleasure. Colonel Tony Murray Smith used to give the heavyweights, of whom I was one, a field start over the lightweights, affording us special pleasure until the latter on their Thoroughbreds came pounding past us.

Coming south from Billesdon you pass two famous coverts on the right, Tamborough Hill, planted in Mr Fernie's time and Shangton Holt, referred to in hunting reports in the late eighteenth century, and still a wonderful covert. The Billesdon country is nowadays mixed grass and arable, but affords excellent hunting; to the east are Noseley Wood, Glooston Wood, and beyond that the Hallaton country; fine upland Leicestershire, with marvellous views, but with heavy incursions of plough in the post-war years. The steep, wooded hills, Park Wood and Bolt Wood, lie below Stockerston, further to the east.

The Fernie is an especially cherished country; the Hunt is exemplary in investing in fencing and covert maintenance. The Hunt Trustees have pursued a policy of buying important coverts when they become available and have acquired Slawston covert, Holt Wood, Gwens Gorse, Reggies, the Colonel's Spinney (named in memory of Tony Murray Smith), and Allexton Wood, partly in conjunction with the Cottesmore.

Among the meets are Hallaton, Woodside Green, Medbourne, King's Norton, Blaston, Mile End Green, Smeeton Westerby, Great Easton, Tugby, Fleckney, Kibworth, Stonton Wyville, Drayton, Goadby, Gaulby, Alexton, Foxton, Peatling Magna, Thorpe Lubenham, Thorpe Langton, Peatling, Stockerston, Illston, Laughton, Aythorpe, Willoughby Waterleys, Saddington, Ilston on the Hill and Mowsley.

3

Meynell: Father of Foxhunting

He complained of having to find fault with
the Universities of Oxford and Cambridge,
for disgorging annually such a parcel of
fools to torment him

The Quorn, indeed foxhunting as we know it, owes its existence to Hugo
Meynell. Like so many great institutions, the Hunt, and a new way of
hunting the fox in the open, were born because Meynell was the first to
recognize a blindingly obvious fact which had escaped his brother sportsmen. He was only in his twenties when he formed the view that the swathe
of rolling grass country from Nottingham down to Market Harborough
could form the most perfect hunting country imaginable. Further, he
evolved new techniques, 'the Meynellian science', which revolutionized the
hunting of the fox with hounds. His achievements were rightly to earn him
a title, 'The Father of Foxhunting'. The Hunt he founded was to retain
the reputation as Britain's premier pack – but this was due to its environment, and to those who inherited and cherished the great traditions founded
by old Hugo.

Meynell was a good horseman, but his interest was in venery; in hunting
the fox effectively with a pack. He did not come to Leicestershire to jump
the fences; when he founded the Quorn, there was little to leap compared

with the country when he completed his Mastership at the end of the eighteenth century. Meynell was a Derbyshire squire, born in 1727. He was the early inheritor of a considerable fortune and estates centred at Bradley, near Ashbourne. His father, Lyttelton Poyntz Meynell died in 1751, disinherited his eldest son and left all his estates in Derbyshire and Staffordshire to his younger son, Hugo. It was perfectly normal for someone born in such circumstances to include hunting in winter-time recreation. Although foxhunting was still primitive in execution, suffering from the aftermath of deer hunting, the traditional sport of kings.

The clearance, or reduction, of many of the great forests throughout Britain during the seventeenth century made the hunting of wild deer difficult. Deer hunting was beloved by the Normans who brought harsh law and order to English venery with the Conquest. The deer and the hare were Britain's premier 'beasts of the Chase'. As the preservation of the red deer and fallow deer herds became far more difficult the hunting squirearchy began to turn to the hitherto despised fox as a quarry likely to provide sport, even if he could not be eaten. Early foxhunting was far different in character and technique from the sport which Meynell was to evolve in Leicestershire. Slow, lop-eared hounds, bred to have excellent scenting abilities and loud voices, were used to follow the scent, or drag, of a fox soon after dawn. The fox would be returning to its earth after nocturnal hunting expeditions. Giving tongue joyously, hounds would patiently follow the line and would mark enthusiastically when they finally arrived at the earth. Often such a hunt would be abortive because the hunted fox was still above ground and could usually escape such a pack in a run in the open. Long, slow hunts of many hours were not uncommon. In such hunting during the Stuarts' reign, horses would scramble through or over obstacles, but the technique of galloping at a fence to take it in one bound, was hardly known, and certainly not widely practised. 'Craning' was common; the horse stopping for both mount and man to inspect the intended obstacle. If there was a jump it would be from a standstill. Considering the lack of surgical and medicinal skills available to treat injury, the cautious approach to jumping was eminently sensible. Ordinary life without risk taking was still all too short, and exceedingly uncomfortable in varying degrees, for the squire and the serf.

Meynell's triumph was to breed faster hounds capable of running up with the fox, and to perfect the technique of drawing coverts to find the quarry afoot, instead of hitting the line by chance in the open.

There had been some continuity of hunting in what was to become the Quorn country. Thomas Boothby, the Squire of Tooley Park, eight miles south-west of Leicester, hunted parts of Leicestershire, Derbyshire and

Staffordshire, where he owned scattered estates. Tooley Park is in the country which became the Atherstone, but undoubtedly parts of the Quorn country north of Leicester were in his foxhunting domain. He was, therefore, the ancestor if not the founder of the Quorn Hunt. It is almost certain that young Hugo Meynell first discovered the joys of delectable terrain up to Melton Mowbray and beyond, through hunting with Squire Boothby's hounds. Boothby is credited with hunting his widespread country for fifty-five seasons, from 1698 to 1753. He achieved a certain fame in the Midlands among hunting folk, and undoubtedly entertained sportsmen over a wide area. Unfortunately, there are no reliable records of the standard of sport achieved, nor the methods employed, or the type of hounds bred by Mr Boothby.

Since the environment has a huge influence on these matters, and Leicestershire was naturally a hunting paradise, one can only assume that there was plenty of fun to be had with the Squire, although far removed from the foxhunting evolved by his successor.

'Fielding, the novelist, was closely connected with the Boothbys, and it was always supposed that more than one character in *Tom Jones* was drawn from the Tooley Park district, while Mrs Boothby is said to have been the original of Sophia Western,' wrote William Blew in his *The Quorn Hunt and its Masters* (1899). Squire Boothby had more than a slight reputation as a man with a taste for amorous diversions.

Hugo Meynell was a gentleman of sophistication, considerable intelligence, and possessing great tact and diplomacy. As any foxhunter knows, all are qualities as much to be desired in an MFH in the 1990s as they were in the mid-eighteenth century. An instinctive understanding of public relations is essential in an MFH if he is to make a real success of his role. It is doubtful that Meynell could have gained the allegiance of Leicestershire's landowners, great and small, if his skills stopped short at breeding an exceptional pack of hounds.

He took the rent of Quorn on Lady Day, 1753; Thomas Boothby having died in August the previous year, aged seventy-five. Ten years later he also rented Langton Hall, now in the Fernie country, then well to the south of the new Quorn territory. Meynell was adopting the ancient practice of moving house to hunt different parts of his country more intensively. Quorn Hall was built in 1680 as a two storey H-plan house, after a fire had destroyed the original manor house of the de Farnham family on that site. In 1793 Meynell was to add another half-storey, a dining room between the wings on the north front, and major kennels and stables. The position of Quorndon on the Leicester to Derby road was no doubt convenient for Meynell. He retained strong links with his native county; he was High Sheriff for Derbyshire in 1758 and represented Lichfield in Parliament for seven years up to 1778. What a pity that modern MPs cannot combine their duties with those of MFH!

The proximity of Charnwood Forest to Quorn was another advantage. Meynell found it ideal as a place to enter his young hounds, since it was a better refuge for foxes than the rolling, grass country he was hunting at the height of the season.

Hugo Meynell's second marriage helped to establish the invaluable element of continuity in a hunting country. His first wife, Ann Gell, having died in 1758 leaving one son, Meynell married Ann Boothby Skrymshire the following year, a grand-daughter of the old Squire Boothby. Soon Meynell bought Quorn Hall and the surrounding estate. His brother-in-law, 'Prince' Boothby was a considerable ally and another partner was Lord Richard Cavendish, a son of the Duke of Devonshire. Meynell needed allies and powerful connections because he set out to acquire the hunting 'rights' to a huge swath of England where local jealousies could all too easily be aroused. He proved adept at taking over the 'right' to draw coverts on many an estate, almost before the local squires had realized that this was to be the established order of things. Meynell clearly had charm to accompany a firm resolve, some would say ruthlessness. He would doubtless have made a great success as a City tycoon organizing take-overs with suave decision if he had been born into the twentieth century.

To the east the Dukes of Rutland at Belvoir Castle needed no such manoeuvrings. They ruled by might, hunting their own vast acreages, and their importance ensured the co-operation of lesser landowners who were their neighbours. Similarly, the Cottesmore was founded largely by those who owned the land.

Part of Meynell's triumph was that he owned not an acre of Leicestershire when he took Quorn Hall, and his closest allies were, in effect, his first Hunt subscribers. They backed his new Hunt with cash as well as practical support. Meynell was to found the most successful subscription pack in Britain on the basis of excellent relations, carefully maintained, not only with the landowners but with the yeoman farmers. At first he had only two subscribers, Lord Richard Cavendish, and Mr 'Prince' Boothby. Meynell paid the graziers who hunted with him 'the compliment of giving them half an hour's law (at the meet) when he knew that there was a fair in the neighbourhood,' says one contemporary observer. But this was just one example of his concern for the maintenance of good relations with the rural community where his hounds hunted.

These are the very conditions which ensure the continuance of hunting in the late twentieth century. Truly, the Father of Foxhunting set an example to be followed with confidence by us all at every level.

What of the sport that Meynell produced? Why did an increasing number of foxhunting pilgrims journey to the Quorn country? There does not appear to be a record of his first huntsman, although some hunting writers assert that Meynell never hunted hounds himself. This is highly doubtful, since his role was far more fluid in the hunting field than a modern MFH not hunting the hounds. Meynell clearly instructed a huntsman and whippers-in and participated in the hunting of the hounds when he felt it to be necessary. It is likely that he actually hunted hounds, with professionals acting purely as whippers-in when he was a young man. How else would he have developed the new style of hunting the fox in the open? He certainly directed the hunting of his hounds with a firm hand, his professional huntsman adopting the style and practice which Meynell evolved in ensuring that hunting the fox in the open was never to be the same again.

Although there is no record of who the first huntsman was, we note that John, often known as Jack, Raven filled this exacting role, probably from 1775 when the Quorn advertised in the *Leicester Journal* for a huntsman. Raven hunted hounds for the remainder of Meynell's Mastership and must have been most effective. He had to meet the standards of a Master who seldom missed a day's hunting and kept the closest eye on the handling of hounds, usually riding up with the huntsman. He has been described as tall, wiry and possessing a melodious voice. His horsemanship and hound control were exceptional. On one occasion a famous hound called Guzman was hunting a hare, and when the whipper-in galloped on to stop the hound, Raven called: 'Let him alone; he will stop of his own accord when he sees that he is running.' Sure enough, Guzman did just that.

Raven went on to hunt hounds for Meynell's successor, Lord Sefton. According to the Quorn historian William Blew, Raven died in an accident while returning home after 'a pipe and a glass'. He slipped into the river Soar, not far from the Hunt kennels, and was drowned. Meynell's whipper-in, Thomas Jones, was a great character, known as 'Cork Leg' Jones because of an amputation which did not prevent him from riding to hounds. He was inclined to leave his leg in odd places all over the countryside during a celebratory night out, and great searches for it took place next day. Jones wrote a diary, published in 1816, which provides a complete record of Meynell's fixtures and runs from 1791–1800, but it throws little light on any but the bare statistics of the sport.

Let us defer to the view of the greatest hunting correspondent of all time – yes, greater than Surtees whose genius lay in fiction. I refer of course to Nimrod, the pseudonym of Charles James Apperley, who admitted that he only saw Meynell in the last year of his great Mastership, but had the ability to discern the qualities of the Meynellian style. Nimrod wrote:

I well remember the lessons he gave to all would-be huntsmen. I remember the steadiness and docility of his hounds, and the superior manner in which they hunted through hares, cattle, or sheep; the quiet way in which they waited for them to recover the scent when lost, and his division of his pack when they made their casts, instead of having them driven after his huntsman like a flock of sheep. I also fancy I hear his chiding voice and his cheering holloa.

The one was efficient without unnecessary noise; the other musical, distinct, and thrilling through the heart and nerve of every one who was near enough to hear it. His scream, in a view, naturally acute, was remarkable and susceptible: he had a wonderfully quick eye to the faults committed by his hounds, which he could the better discern from the reliance he placed on their own powers in chase.

He allowed them to spread, and to use those powers at a very gentle pace, which, from his command over his field, it was fortunately in his power to do. Of blood, he was more indifferent than most owners of fox-hounds are wont to be.

The wildest packs of hounds, he has been heard to say, 'are known to kill the most foxes in cover, but very seldom show good runs over a country.'

Mr Meynell made no display of his riding in the field, but when with his hounds in chase nothing that he considered feasible would stop his being in his place. As a companion he was the delight of every society in which he appeared.

The key to his success in the field was his ability to breed hounds which were faster, whilst retaining their scenting abilities. He did this by selective and very close breeding, sometimes mating brother and sister, but never parents and offspring.

The strands of breeding which led to the modern foxhound compromised the Talbot – hounds brought to this country by the Normans, and later called the Northern hound; and the old Southern hound, used prior to the eighteenth century mainly to hunt the hare. There were original Celtic breeds of hounds which became the Welsh hound, and various importations from France, often brought in by monks. At a time when selective breeding was increasingly used to improve farm cattle and sheep, Meynell was using this system to evolve hounds suitable to his country. Leicestershire's rolling landscape, but light going, means that fox and hounds can accelerate remarkably.

Meynell made his breeding decisions based largely on very close observation of the hunting prowess of individual hounds in his pack. Whether he evolved detailed pedigrees is not clear, since none survived, but it is highly likely that he did keep such records and relied upon them increasingly during his Mastership of half a century in which the brilliance of his pack clearly grew enormously. He took into the hunting field far more hounds than most other huntsmen did then and were to do later in the sport's history. Thirty or forty couple were not uncommon in his pack in his earlier years of Mastership, but later he cut the size of the hunting pack to no more than twenty couple. His policy of careful selective breeding had doubtless evolved hounds he could trust to work together effectively in smaller groups.

One curious eccentricity was his habit of entering his young hounds to hunt hare, and later switching them to foxhunting. Since all foxhounds have ancestors bred primarily to hunt hare or deer there is no doubt that left to their own devices they will hunt these quarry naturally, but have to be 'entered' to hunt the fox which is itself a predator. Meynell probably resorted to some hare hunting when entering his young hounds because he was short of coverts in the open country on the Melton Mowbray side.

He was known to make a cast by dividing his pack into two or three groups; he would take one; the huntsman another and sometimes the whipper-in a third. The effect, of course, was to draw very widely, which was no doubt effective in the wide open rough pastures of eighteenth century Leicestershire. Some reports indicate as many as one hundred couple on certain occasions, and have described hounds' combined voices as the 'sound of an angry sea' when in full cry. I suspect these reports were exaggerated, but certainly Meynell was reported by most observers as taking out far more hounds than today, when huntsmen manage with well under twenty couples. No wonder that hound control was such an essential part of Meynell's hunting practice.

Those who oppose hunting say that a foxhound's natural tendency to hunt deer and hares is a major argument against foxhunting, since they claim the fox is not a 'natural' beast of the Chase. This is nonsense, for it is clear that hounds were in fact used to hunt fox and wolf back into pre-recorded history. But deer and hare were preferred as the quarry for the royal packs as long as the environment was more suitable for these forms of hunting.

'The quick thing' – the famous twenty or twenty-five minute's dash, ending with a kill above ground – was born during Meynell's Mastership. It was certainly never the most frequent form of hunting run achieved; many were just as painstaking, and involved numerous checks as those experienced in provincial hunting countries. The twenty minute hunt is a hallmark of Shires hunting which was emulated although never bettered elsewhere, simply because no other country had a more suitable terrain for the Chase at its fastest and most thrilling.

Unfortunately, Meynell did not write his own detailed treatise on his breeding methods and pedigrees. The greatest book on foxhunting in his time was produced far away in Dorset by Peter Beckford; his *Thoughts on Hunting* was published in 1781. Beckford certainly knew of Meynell's success, and wrote in his famous book: 'You say you wish to see your pack as complete as Mr Meynell's. Believe me, my good friend, unless you breed as many hounds, it is totally impossible. Those who breed the most hounds have the right to expect the best pack; at least it must be their own fault if they have it not.'

The success of the Quorn hounds meant that Leicestershire's appeal to the hard-riding follower was soaring. The potential of the Shires was becoming more widely recognized. Already visitors came regularly from London, and Meynell turned Quorn Hall into a sort of hunting hotel, accommodating many friends and acquaintances for the season. Others rented houses nearby. It was the start of a huge investment in the county by foxhunters, which was to add enrichment to its farming community and country towns during good and bad times in agriculture. Foxhunting became a Leicestershire rural industry.

The *Sporting Magazine* declared: 'Meynell's hunt is a species of sport at present so truly refined to a degree of perfection, by the speed of the hound, the excellence of the horses, and the emulative and determined resolution of the riders, that the scene has certainly never before been equalled in the Kingdom.'

Granted that such journalism in the eighteenth century was flowery and effusive, there is no doubt that Meynell, the first gentleman to exploit Leicestershire's natural advantages as a foxhunting country, had earned a reputation which was as well-known in fashionable London as it was in the great country houses throughout sporting England. Meynell's relationship with his mounted field was more like that of a squire with his friends than a Master appointed to produce sport for a committee and a long list of subscribers.

The growth of hard riding meant that foxhunters were keeping large studs of top-class hunters standing in yards close to Quorn. There were two good days a week on grass in the country to the east, but there were far less popular days in Charnwood Forest, or near to Leicester, which were not to the taste of the hard riders.

Meynell's cubhunting took place mainly on Charnwood Forest, and in country which is now part of the Cottesmore: in the neighbourhood of Stockerston and Allexton, south of the Leicester to Peterborough road.

During the full season Meynell hunted considerably in the country north of Loughborough, two or three times a month to the Melton side, which became the Monday country, occasionally to the country south of Melton

Mowbray, which was to be the Friday country much later, with occasional excursions to such places as Whetstone, Newbold Verdon, Braunstone (now part of Leicester), Market Bosworth and Oakley Wood. His visits were a treat for the local gentry and farmers. Sometimes he would stay with them, bringing a few distinguished visitors.

It can be seen, however, that he was hunting the delectable country south of Melton Mowbray far less than it deserved. The young men who were coming to Leicestershire to stay for the season, bringing their studs of hunters, were not getting enough days per week to suit them in the Quorn's open, pastoral country, and hence they were inclined to drift eastwards to Melton Mowbray, the ideal centre for hunting on the best days of the Quorn, the Belvoir and the country that was to become the Cottesmore.

Meynell had that extraordinary stamina, no doubt nurtured by many days in the saddle in all weathers, which the great foxhunters have always needed if they are to pursue their sport for a lifetime. To maintain a Mastership for forty-seven years in the eighteenth century when medical knowledge and standards of care were rudimentary was indeed a tribute to his fortitude. He ate a significant portion of veal for breakfast before hunting, and instead of hard spirits, he carried during the day a small flask containing tincture of rhubarb, of which he was very fond. Meynell's new style of hunting, producing the 'heroosh' of the Chase, seemed to encourage hard riding which was not to his taste when it involved members of the field interfering with his hounds. According to Colonel John Cook in his excellent *Observations on Hunting*, published in 1826, Meynell was himself a 'wild huntsman' as a young man in Staffordshire, but 'that wildness he soon restrained to proper eagerness, keeping in bounds the finest spirits and energy that perhaps man ever possessed. His voice and articulation were delightfully harmonious and energetic – his view-hallo thrilled everyone near him – and his language was too pertinent to be misunderstood.'

There was no misunderstanding Meynell when he chided the thrusters who began to harass him in the hunting field. Cook reported the observations of an old Leicestershire hunting man who said that Meynell's 'indignation in the field was sometimes excessive'.

> Frequently expressed by looks, sometimes by deputies, but when by words, he seldom or ever degenerated into rudeness.
>
> After rebuking a man once or twice, he would tell him he was incorrigible, and it was of no use to admonish him. He complained of having to find fault with the Universities of Oxford and Cambridge, for disgorging annually such a parcel of fools to torment him; to whom, if they attempted a vindication of their riding, or being troublesome, he would courteously reply, 'You may be perfectly right gentlemen, and I may be wrong, but there is gross ignorance on one side or the other.'

Many generations of Masters of Foxhounds have since expressed similar sentiments in widely varying degrees of sarcasm or more crudely expressed abuse. Colonel Cook relates an anecdote illustrating the high level of hound control in Meynell's reign; '. . . the circumstance of Mr Meynell's hounds waiting in the same field, while a few couples selected from the pack were running hard in an adjoining gorse, nor did they attempt to break from the whipper-in until cheered to the cry by Jack Raven.' This technique was used to avoid the full pack from chopping the fox in covert, which was very likely to happen with the huge packs of hounds that Meynell took into the hunting field.

Meynell, hunting three days a week, was likely to kill about thirty-six brace of foxes a season, according to Cecil in his *Records of the Chase*. Many packs hunting much smaller areas would kill more foxes today, indicating the increase in coverts in the nineteenth and twentieth centuries, even though the area of rural Britain is now shrinking.

Mellowing as he grew older, Meynell retained his good health but he did not make the mistake of continuing to administer the Hunt when his vigour was fading. He handed over the management of his kennels and stables to his son Hugo a few years before the end of his Mastership in 1800, and Mr Loraine Smith acted as his deputy in the field. Although Meynell was not then in control, there occurred in 1800 on Monday 24 February, one of the greatest of Leicestershire hunts: the Billesdon Coplow run. Hounds found in the covert which still dominates the southern end of the Quorn Friday country, just south of the road from Tilton to the A 47 Leicester road. The twenty-eight miles run was recorded in verse by the Reverend Robert Lowth, from Hampshire, who was visiting a friend near Melton and was offered a mount on a young Thoroughbred horse which had probably never seen hounds. Lowth experienced the great hunt, and recorded it in naive rhyming couplets in a poem which has become a minor classic in hunting literature, although it smacks of McGonagle in style. It conveys the scope of hunting at the end of Meynell's Mastership. There were some two hundred riders at the covert side. Hounds found their fox very quickly, ran up to Tilton, headed for Skeffington, Norton, Great Stretton and on to Wigston and Ayleston. The much depleted field now faced the formidable task of crossing the river Soar, fox and hounds swimming it ahead. A Mr Germain was first in the river, riding a horse called Melon which had belonged to the great initiator of desperate riding, William Childe. Several riders sank in the river, but struggled through, and the few remaining galloped on after hounds who were now running hard to Enderby Gorse. The huntsman, Jack Raven, arrived on a borrowed horse just in time to stop the pack. The Billesdon Coplow fox escaped with his brush because it got among other foxes.

The rest of the poem dwells on the individual fortunes, or misfortunes of mounted followers who either fell or had to pull-up their exhausted mounts. A horse named Carlo Khan, ridden by a Mr Price, died after a fall, and judging by the grim reference by Lowth, the horse was a grey.

> In a fatal blind ditch, Carlo Khan's powers failed,
> Where nor lancet, nor laudanum either availed . . .
> At the death of poor Khan, Melton feels such remorse,
> That they've christened that ditch the Vale of White Horse.

Lowth ends with a triumphant tribute to Shires hunting. He was obviously an instant convert:

> Thus ended a chase which for distance and speed,
> Its fellow never have heard of or read,
> Every species of ground, every horse does not suit,
> What's a good country hunter may here prove a brute,
> And unless for all sorts of strange fences prepared,
> A man and his horse are sure to be scared.

> This variety gives constant life to the Chase,
> But as Forester says: 'Sir, what kills is the pace.'
> In most other countries they boast of their breed,
> For carrying, at times, such a beautiful head;
> But these hounds to carry a head cannot fail,
> And constantly too, for by George, there's no tail.

> Talk of horses and hounds and the system of kennel –
> Give me Leicestershire nags and the hounds of old Meynell.

Hunting too often imposes a heavy price on those who devote their lives to its best interests. Meynell tragically lost his son Hugo who died from the effects of a fall in the hunting field in 1800, thus denying his father the prospect of a family succession in the hunting field.

Old Hugo moved into a little house near Quorn Hall which had formerly been the huntsman's, and he continued to ride to hounds occasionally until his death aged eighty-one in 1808. He was buried in the family vault at Bradley in Derbyshire.

No Master of the Quorn has since held office for any period approaching the half century achieved by its founder. This is not only a tribute to Hugo's own vitality, but it reflects the increasing pace and pressures of the sport he virtually invented.

The size of the task he handed on to his successors was illustrated by the almost bewildering rapidity with which Quorn Masterships changed at some periods of its history. This nearly wrecked the Hunt on several occasions, but it endured and thrived because the superlative qualities of the country continued to attract fresh generations of sportsmen from outside – and because the Meynellian tradition of co-operating with landowners and farmers bred generations of native Leicestershire foxhunters, or friends of foxhunting, who have to this today ensured that old Hugo's legacy is still a golden thread running through the history of the Shires.

4

The Quorn in the Nineteenth Century

But spurs must go in, knees must press and
horses must be driven hard

Inevitably Hunt histories are shaped by Masterships. So far we have placed
great emphasis on the Quorn's first great Master – and with good reason – he
greatly influenced the sport throughout the United Kingdom and beyond.

The nineteenth and twentieth century history of the Quorn illustrates that
the instrumental figures in producing great hunts are great huntsmen.
Assheton Smith, Osbaldeston and Captain Forester were great amateurs, and
three professionals stand out in the Quorn's history: Tom Firr (1872–
99), George Barker (1929–59) and Michael Farrin who took the horn in 1967
and thankfully is still hunting hounds after a quarter of a century. Not only
the quality of their skills as huntsmen counted for much, but their endurance in holding down this especially exacting role was a key factor in maintaining continuity of standards: a consistency of sport which continued to
attract visitors who would pay handsomely to keep foxhunting alive at top
level in the Quorn country, no matter how often the Masterships changed.

And change they did. T.F. Dale, the historian of the neighbouring
Belvoir hunt reports somewhat acidly that Quorn Masterships altered 'with
bewildering rapidity' compared with the ordered series of successions of

the Dukes of Rutland who reigned at Belvoir. Since Meynell's time, only one Master has achieved a Mastership anywhere near approaching his half century: Mrs Ulrica Murray Smith who was Joint Master for twenty-five years, until 1985. Few have reached a decade of Mastership, and the current senior Joint Master, Captain Fred Barker, has set a remarkable precedent in serving for thirteen years in his first term, and then taking over for a second term when the Hunt was in the dire crisis of the 1991–2 season.

When Meynell handed over in 1800 the problems of holding together and administering his huge hunting country soon became apparent. There were periods during the nineteenth century when the Hunt's future was in considerable doubt, largely due to weak and ineffectual Masterships. Some would-be Masters arrive in a country with great reputations already made as consummate experts in venery. Many simply proffer a seemingly limitless cheque book; while others combine wealth with a flair for management and politics which enables them to organize a hunting country with great success; cleverly delegating the science of venery to a well selected huntsman and staff.

The stresses and strains on professional huntsmen throughout Britain have long been underestimated by all too many of those who ride to hound, and alas, by some Masters. Hunting hounds is a lonely task, and requires the utmost in tactful support and consideration from the Masters, with discipline exerted from a position of deep knowledge and understanding of the huntsman's task.

It is notable that the truly great huntsmen have ascended beyond the role of 'Hunt Servant'; they have been spoken of in terms of admiration, even reverence, by those who have enjoyed the brilliant sport they produced so consistently. Yet when a mere mortal is the huntsman, he is subject to all the gossip and speculation accorded to any sports star when his fortunes wax and wane. A series of bad scenting seasons is recognized by the true hunting man as a huge, natural obstacle to good sport, but many less knowledgeable followers will begin to blame the huntsman. The professional huntsman has no opportunity either to explain to his mounted field that the current Mastership is meanly providing him with exceptionally bad horses, that the Hunt Committee is doing a bad job in maintaining coverts, consequently holding far less foxes than before, or that the Field Masters are dunderheads who keep riding over the hounds, with an uncontrolled mounted field in tow. The more experienced observers will deduce these problems; the majority are blithely unaware of such desperate difficulties with which a professional huntsman is expected to cope. The contrast between a professional huntsman, constrained to hold his tongue during a day's sport, and the abrasive, sometimes ranting and raving, out-pourings of some well-known amateur huntsmen in the hunting field illustrates the frustrations which the former cannot express, while the latter inclines, if anything, to be far too unbuttoned in exposing his ire.

In a hunting country the Hunt kennels is in a veritable spotlight of attention. Thus the stresses and strains of his professional life are fully shared by the huntsman's wife and family. Indeed, the importance of a huntsman's wife is well recognized when appointments are made. Having 'a bad wife' can lose a professional an appointment; the poor lady is of irreproachable reputation morally, but may be known to get somewhat tetchy when the umpteenth futile telephone enquiry has to be answered. The huntsman, of course, has the doubtful benefit of living on the job.

Top-class professional huntsmen, and indeed some of those with lesser reputations, have been well looked after. But considering the wealth of many of those who enjoy hunting in the major packs, professional huntsmen have never been remotely in the same financial bracket as professional golfers, tennis players, footballers and indeed many other sportsmen – although the professional huntsman will entertain many thousands of people throughout a long and arduous career, with a major physical risk factor, and the quality of the sport he achieves can provide a huge range of ancillary jobs and incomes, even influencing the prices which country houses will fetch in his area.

I have outlined the special demands of character and self control for the huntsman because successful foxhunting in the Shires has always depended on these professional gentlemen of the Chase. Even the comparatively few great amateur huntsmen who have found fame in Leicestershire would be the first to praise the quality of the professional staffs supporting them.

Hugo Meynell's first successor, Lord Sefton, brought great wealth and enthusiasm to the Quorn. He also brought great personal weight: he was some twenty stone in the saddle, and was certainly one of the first foxhunters to introduce the second horse system; indeed Sefton was inclined to ride three horses a day. He employed in the Quorn country his own huntsman, Stephen Goodall, from Oxfordshire, who hunted the unfashionable forest side of the country to the west, while Meynell's huntsman, Jack Raven, continued to hunt the grasslands on the Melton side. The enclosure of land speeded up during this Mastership, with greater opportunities to leap fences occurring during a run. The influx of wealthy young bloods increased as Sefton spent freely to run the Hunt in great style.

Five years of all this was enough for Lord Sefton, probably finding the physical strain the major problem. He was succeeded by Lord Foley, but only for one season, and hounds deteriorated during his Mastership.

The Quorn's reputation was suffering badly in comparison with its great neighbours, the Belvoir, Cottesmore and Pytchley – and far better sport was being provided in Warwickshire and Gloucestershire.

Fortunately, a great decade of sport erupted with the arrival of one of the greatest amateur huntsman of any age; Thomas Assheton Smith. He combined tremendous drive as a huntsman with an extraordinary capacity for crossing the most formidable of country on any horse. His Mastership was instrumental in establishing the Quorn country to be visited if you wanted to enjoy the ride to the ultimate. He exploited the huge natural advantages of the Leicestershire turf and fences to the full.

There is no quicker way to earn the admiration and loyalty of a mounted field than to consistently give them an inspiring lead across country. Nowhere is this more true than Leicestershire. Accounts of Assheton Smith's feats have become part of hunting history. No one was more eloquent in his praise than Nimrod:

> From the first day to the last, he was always the same man, the same desperate fellow over a country, and unquestionably possessing on every occasion, and at every hour of the day, the most bulldog-like nerve ever exhibited in the saddle. His motto was: 'I'll be with my hounds' and all those who have seen him in the field must acknowledge that he made no vain boast of his prowess.

Nimrod affirms that this do or die policy assisted Assheton Smith as a huntsman because it enabled him to cast hounds widely over the most demanding of terrain without keeping hounds waiting. Assheton Smith would ride for a fall if it was the only way to get past an obstacle. 'Over, under, or through he would go', is a famous hunting saying, born out of Assheton Smith's exploits. His drawbacks were that he had a rough tongue at times, and could be harshly sarcastic in the hunting field. He was also inclined to be somewhat jealous as a rider, and did not relish anyone rivalling his own abilities during a run. These characteristics were tolerated, but he was held in esteem rather than warm affection by those who followed him.

Smith was inclined to 'ride to the gallery' but he should not be blamed for this. Foxhunting is an entertainment, and he was certainly a great entertainer. I have no doubt the field enjoyed his crashing falls as much as his successes.

'So you won't have it gentlemen?' he would ask the field before essaying some enormous leap over a seemingly impossible obstacle. He was far more than a rough rider. He had mastered the technique of the bounce jump which we see nowadays at Badminton Horse Trials. Smith could leap a huge gate into narrow lanes, and collect his horse to leap a facing gate out of the lane in the next stride. His hands and seat were impeccable.

'What's the use of opening gates for a flying 'ossman?' asked a bewildered countryman when about to open the second gate for the huntsman. Undoubtedly the factual history of Assheton Smith's prowess grew into unlikely legend, but there is no doubt that no one has crossed the Quorn country better.

After eleven seasons, Assheton Smith retired from the Quorn. He hunted the Burton country to the east, and then took hounds to hunt his family estates at Tedworth. He collected a pack from fifteen different kennels and hunted that unpromising country in Hampshire and Wiltshire with tremendous success from 1826 until his death in 1858. Some foxhunter!

Another remarkable sporting figure, of even greater eccentricity and renown, succeeded Assheton Smith at the Quorn: Squire George Osbaldeston brought his hounds from the Atherstone country to Quorn in 1817. He was an extraordinary all rounder: a hero of the turf, the road and the Chase. His greatest fame was as Master of Hounds; on the racecourses he lost a prodigous fortune. He was an amazing shot: on one day he killed one hundred pheasants with one hundred shots, and he once bagged ninety-seven grouse with the same number of shots. A tremendous cross-country rider, he raced over fences and on the Flat. At an age of sixty-eight he rode his own horse in the March Stakes at Goodwood. He performed tremendous feats of endurance as a driver of four-in-hand teams; he was a tireless athlete, a top-class cricketer, oarsman, tennis player, loved coursing – and indoors excelled at billiards and whist.

How did he do it? How did he fit it all in? Osbaldeston's autobiography still leaves the reader wondering at the vitality of the man. However brilliant he was, I cannot believe that such an all rounder could have been more successful in each sphere than a genuine specialist. If a time machine gave me the choice of a day with either, I would choose a day's hunting with Assheton Smith rather than Osbaldeston. I am not at all sure that Osbaldeston much liked the Quorn. It was as if he were simply adding another sporting challenge to his extraordinary tally. In his autobiography he is exceedingly tetchy about the cares of Mastership at Quorn:

> It is not at all an enviable distinction to hunt that country, because it is almost impossible to give universal satisfaction to the Meltonians, who are only birds of passage.
> They were like a handsome spoiled young lady, who doesn't know her own mind for a week together and changes it as often. I believe they expected that I ought to make a good scent every day and show a run. . . . They are never satisfied at Melton.

Other records indicate that sport with the great Osbaldeston sometimes fell short of expectations in the Quorn country. There was exasperation on both sides, and Osbaldeston is expressing the huntsman's side of the age-old tension between the man who carries the horn, and those whose only intent is to follow his hounds.

Fitting two Quorn Masterships into such a life was clearly no exceptional effort for such a phenomenon as Osbaldeston. Yet he had to overcome the sort of penalty which the Goddess of the Chase can extract even from any rider, even an all round sporting genius.

Osbaldeston was Master from 1817, but had to give up for two seasons from 1821 because he smashed his leg appallingly in a hunting fall – in a visit to the Atherstone country. He was riding a Thoroughbred called Cervantes, and was in the lead in a run from Bosworth towards Charnwood Forest, when he took a drop fence. Sir James Musgrave was close behind, and crashed into Cervantes when Osbaldeston took a pull to balance his horse before jumping. Cervantes was knocked over, Osbaldeston parted company and as he lay on the ground Sir James's horse jumped on him, breaking two bones, probably tibia and fibula, in his leg.

'Oh Musgrave! You have broken my leg. The bones feel as if they were pounded,' shouted Osbaldeston.

'Sir James rode on with the hounds the instant he and his horse were free!' Osbaldeston recalled in his autobiography.

It was a very bad compound fracture and took a long time to mend. Osbaldeston's remarks on over-riding could be echoed by generations of Shires hunting men ever since: 'I always disliked having anyone ride close behind me after this mishap, and often wished I could act as a friend did to rid myself of a follower, which, of course, I was unable to do as I always hunted my hounds.'

Osbaldeston then recounts that his friend was greatly annoyed by someone constantly using him as a pilot, so he led him far astray. Eventually the follower remarked that he could not see hounds, and the pilot replied: 'Of course you don't. I'm on my way home across country.'

One can only admire Osbaldeston's fortitude. Whatever his complaints about the Meltonians, expressed in his autobiography when he was a very old man, he was keen enough to rejoin the Quorn after two seasons off to allow his leg to mend. When he took over the Mastership he resumed his arduous programme of hunting hounds six days a week for much of the season – and they were long days involving huge hacks to and from meets.

During his two seasons off (1821–3) he handed the country to his friend Sir Bellingham Graham. Like Osbaldeston he liked 'hopping about' from one country to another, but he was a fine horseman and a good huntsman – and showed excellent sport in his brief Mastership. He certainly had the foxhunter's essential quality of durability. On Boxing Day in 1822 he suffered a tremendous fall jumping a gate, was unconscious for twenty-four hours, and confined to bed for a week. Next day he went out in a carriage to see hounds hunting, but called for a horse and began to hunt hounds. He used to lead the field often on a famous horse called Cock Robin, the sort of horse which would win Badminton or Burghley Horse Trials today. Cock Robin escaped from the mounted field entirely one occasion by slipping away from covert, and performing a consummate bounce jump in and out of two huge sets of rails.

Let it not be thought that Osbaldeston was merely resting in his two years absence from the Quorn. He simply exchanged countries with Bellingham Graham, taking the less challenging Hambledon in Hampshire and it is believed also hunting the Holderness in Yorkshire.

Osbaldeston tells of a violent element in the Quorn country which rings a bell with modern foxhunters forced to face the attacks of Hunt saboteurs. The stocking makers and weavers from Leicester and surrounding villages would gather in crowds at the covert sides and would prevent the fox from going away. This was probably not their intention, but an unruly crowd round the covert is anything but helpful at this vital stage of a hunt. Osbaldeston said persuasion and kind words failed, and so did force.

'At last we had recourse to bribery; we used to give every village two sovereigns a year for drink, and this plan had a far better effect, though on occasions the people were still unruly.'

The early nineteenth century Leicestershire villagers liked their own hunting with terriers and cur dogs and would draw the Quorn's prized fox coverts on Sundays. Hunting with dogs on Sundays was an offence punishable by fines or prison at that time. Clearly foxhunters were well represented in the judiciary. There were tough elements prepared to risk the consequences. The bad feeling resulted in a fight at Sileby where two men came out of a public house and began kicking and striking the Quorn hounds on their way home from hunting. Osbaldeston was pulled off his horse, but beat off an attacker when on his feet. In the fracas an attacker knocked one of the horses' eyes from its socket. Osbaldeston and his two whippers-in barely escaped with their lives when a crowd of about fifty stocking makers joined in the affray.

Osbaldeston also describes a later incident in the Harborough end of the Quorn country when he and his whips wished to take possession of a badger the terriers had found in a drain. The stocking makers had already bolted the badger and put it into a sack. Osbaldeston wished to take it back to the Hunt kennels as 'we had some young terriers at home and wanted the badger to try them with'. The stocking makers refused, so Osbaldeston and his two whippers-in charged them in line, and Osbaldeston wielded his whip end to beat the man carrying the sack, forcing him to drop it. Neither the reason for requiring the badger, nor the fight, make good reading in the late twentieth century when badger baiting is abhored by hunting folk as much as anyone else, and when Masters prevail on their followers to exercise total restraint when provoked by the saboteurs. Yet the incidents recounted by Osbaldeston indicate that many of the working classes were by no means subservient at that time, and that their reason for dispute with the Hunt was largely based on counter claims of their own on what they considered to be their sporting rights. In the early nineteenth century, Britain's newcomers to the ranks of industrial workers had by no means lost their rural links and regarded sport with long dogs and terriers as part of their rightful inheritance as Englishmen.

It has been argued that much of the antipathy between town and country over so-called blood sports originally arose because British landowners were too inclined to protect game from so-called poaching by harsh laws, ruthlessly enforced – a practice introduced as long ago as the rule of William the Conqueror. A poacher of deer in royal forests could be punished with death, maiming or blinding after 1066. The battle between poachers and game-keepers has remained part of country life to the present day.

Unlike venison or game, the fox is not an edible commodity. Foxhunting was to unite most of the rural community through offering a sport which all could enjoy, whether mounted or following on foot. Its success in over-ruling the anarchy of freelance hunting with terriers has been in the best interests of foxes who can suffer far more from a cruelly conducted dig and fight with the terriers than during the Chase in the open.

But we are here describing times long before the advent of the Masters of Foxhounds Association and a nationally applied set of rules and standards for registered Hunts.

Osbaldeston managed to hunt eight packs of foxhounds as Master, and after his second Quorn term (1823-7) he went on to take the Pytchley (1827-34) where his fame was further broadcast by Nimrod. As well as hunting hounds, Osbaldeston was one of those who helped to found National Hunt racing through the practice of match-making contests in rides across natural hunting country. The cash prizes were vast by contemporary standards. One of the most famous in the Quorn country occurred on 31 March 1826, when Mr Francis Holyoake's horse Clinker was ridden by Captain Ross in a match against Assheton Smith's horse Radical, ridden by a Mr Douglas. Osbaldeston was contemptuous of the ability of both riders, and the race was something of a farce. Starting from Barkby Holt in the Quorn Friday country, both horses became jammed in a gap trying to jump out of the first field, giving Mr Douglas a fall over his horse's head. The bridles of the two horses became hopelessly entangled. Amazingly, each was allowed a pilot to guide them across country. Ross on Clinker went well ahead, and Douglas suffered another fall, this time remaining embedded in a deep ditch while his rival crossed the winning post under Billesdon Coplow.

Osbaldeston remarked that 'two greater tailors never exhibited in a steeplechase'.

So much for the good old days? Riding standards were clearly as uneven in the hunting field as they are today. Osbaldeston recounts that he rode in six steeplechase matches – and naturally won them all! He raced five miles against the same Captain Ross at even weights, across the Quorn country for five hundred guineas on 5 December 1829. They started between Skeffington and Rolleston, finishing at Carlton Clump in the Quorn's Harborough country which was to become the Fernie's. They were together until about one mile from the winning post when Captain Ross's horse, Polecat, fell into a ditch on the landing side of a fence, the mount being 'very distressed'. By the time he emerged, Osbaldeston had won.

After Osbaldeston the Quorn experienced, sometimes suffered, a series of changes. Osbaldeston generously gave forty couples of hounds to his successor, Lord Southampton, then aged only twenty-four, who had much enthusiasm, but apparently little real knowledge of foxhunting. He moved the kennels from Quorn to Leicester and took a house there, possibly at Humberstone Gate. The kennels were somewhat unfortunately built next to a Methodist chapel!

It proved to be a stop-gap Mastership. Lord Southampton departed after four seasons, but had been an absentee in the last one. Sport was apparently above average in his third season. Later he became a successful Master of the Grafton.

Sir Harry Goodricke's Mastership (1831–3) promised much, but was cut short by his fatal illness. He moved the kennels to new buildings at Thrussington on an unsuitable site on the bank of the river. Sir Harry spent money prodigously, and rode across country well; two activities which earned him much early popularity with the Meltonians.

There were some notable hunts during his Mastership. Here is a run which modern Quornites would relish. Hounds found at the Curate's covert, running to Willoughby village, and Walton Thorns, then on to Thrussington Wolds, Ragdale, Schoby Scholes and Lord Aylesford's. The fox ran on to Old Dalby and Nether Broughton, and was eventually caught near Stapleford after a run of some two hours.

Alas, at the end of the 1832–3 season, Sir Harry caught a bad cold while visiting Ireland for the otter hunting, and died within forty-eight hours.

The Quorn Mastership was taken by Sir Harry's friend and heir, Mr Francis Holyoake, owner of Clinker mentioned previously. He hunted the country for one season, and half of it for another. Holyoake then retired from the country and became very religious. In his second season he had handed over the Donington area of the Quorn country, on its west side, nowadays bordering the Meynell, to the Second Marquis of Hastings whose estate was nearby. The Donington country was to be re-joined with the Quorn in 1851 under Sir Richard Sutton.

Mr Holyoake was succeeded in 1835 by Mr Rowland Errington from Cheshire. He was likeable and enjoyed a convivial time with the other young men hunting with the Quorn. He introduced Charles Payne as huntsman, later earning his greatest reputation with the Pytchley. Errington probably went as far as his finances reasonably allowed – two seasons – and handed over to Lord Suffield, whose Mastership proved to be the most disastrous the Quorn had experienced. He had already lost a fortune in racing, but he went ahead to spend lavishly on yet another new kennels establishment, this time at Billesdon. Suffield took Lowesby Hall, but he was desperately short of money. He brought a poor pack of hounds in Northumberland, and provided inadequate horses in the Hunt stable. Yet in his one and only season the Goddess of Hunting smiled on him in providing one of the best hunts experienced by many: hounds found at Cream Gorse, ran to Burrough Hill, down to John O'Gaunt, and away from Tilton down to Lowesby, hounds running about fourteen miles over delectable country at a hot pace.

For the next two seasons (1839–41) Mr Thomas Hodgson from Yorkshire took the Mastership with little success. He appears to have spent far too little money to please the Meltonians, endeavouring to run the Quorn as economically as possible. This would not have mattered so much in most departments, but it was alleged that he was guilty of that cardinal foxhunting sin: mounting the huntsman badly. It is true of all hunting countries, but especially in the Shires, that the mounted field hate to see the huntsman unable to cross the country well behind hounds because he is riding a bad horse. Nimrod and others claimed that Mr Hodgson's huntsman, Webb, was slow across Leicestershire, however effectively he may have crossed the Holderness country previously. After one season with the Quorn he was replaced by Tom Day who had hunted the Warwickshire with success, and had previously whipped-in to Assheton Smith and Osbaldeston. He was described as a fine horseman with beautiful hands, and a thoroughly competent huntsman; he was built like a jockey. Although his Mastership lasted only one more season, Tom Day was to remain huntsman of the Quorn for eighteen seasons.

Despite his lack of popularity, Mr Hodgson had provided consistently good sport for two seasons and was certainly a knowledgeable foxhunter. He hunted his own hounds on the Charnwood Forest side with success.

The appointment of a local man as the next Master, and one with no previous experience of Mastership, was gloomily predicted to be a short-term disaster. Fortunately, Mr Henry Greene, of Rolleston, proved to be one of the most successful Masters during the nineteenth century, and the Hunt's fortunes revived remarkably. A bachelor devoted to the Chase, Mr Greene had been riding in the front rank of the Quorn field for some twenty years before he took the Mastership. A lightweight, nicknamed 'the fly', he went well, was popular, and knew the country and its people intimately. These are enormous advantages at the start of any Mastership. He used the Billesdon kennels which were close to his home, Rolleston Hall, and also the old kennels at Quorn. He appears to have been nearer to the modern concept of an acting Master, since he was heavily dependent on the committee for cash to run the Hunt.

According to *The Sporting Magazine* Mr Greene paid a subscription of £100 per season, whereas others paid subscriptions ranging from £25 to £300.

'When he is out of pocket, it is only to call a meeting of the habitues of the Hunt to secure the necessary supplies', reported the magazine. Greene in fact mounted himself and the Hunt servants, and paid their wages, calling on the *ad hoc* committee for expenses above these. This is much nearer the arrangement on which many Hunts were to run in the twentieth century.

The Quorn, of course, had no rules nor constitution, preferring to wait for about another one hundred and fifty years for such fripperies.

Greene reduced the pack to about fifty couples of working hounds, and he and Day produced an effective combination. Sport was often excellent, and there is no doubt the field were given a fine lead by the Master and his huntsman, superbly mounted. The Hunt stables had a stud of some twenty-seven horses, not considered inordinate at that time, but they were of top-class quality.

A run recorded in Mr Greene's Mastership, on 9 December 1841, is interesting because it covers country still huntable, indeed country hunted regularly today by the Quorn and its southern neighbour, the Fernie. They found at Thorpe Trussells, ran by Great Dalby, up towards Burrough, having passed Marefield. They ran on to John O' Gaunt, bore left for Halstead, on to Skeffington and Tugby Spinney where the fox was headed. Tom Day recovered the line and hounds and they hunted on towards Rolleston where the pack caught their fox by a small brook. This was a hunt of one hour and twenty minutes, across lovely country, with hounds for the first fifty-two minutes up to the check.

Mr Greene ruled successfully by general consent, although there were grumbles expressed in the sporting press that he was too inclined to hunt the grass country around Melton Mowbray, and neglected to hold enough meets in less favourable riding parts of the country, especially on the western side. Other reports indicated that a wide section of the community thoroughly enjoyed the Quorn's sport. A frame-work knitter at Woodhouse Eaves, Benjamin Fouldes, became famous as a regular footfollower, wearing a scarlet coat. He was by no means a lone figure. Whole villages of workers would turn out to follow hounds when they were in the district; 'the stockingers leaving their dusty frames for the purer air of Charnwood Forest and its heights', according to William Blew.

The consequence of Mr Greene's success in establishing consistent sport on a high level for six seasons was that on his retirement in 1847, the Mastership was sought by Sir Richard Sutton, one of the great aristocratic figures in the hunting world. He hunted the Burton country for eighteen years from 1824, and the Cottesmore for five, before taking the Quorn. For years the Quorn hounds had been scratch packs, assembled by purchase, and then various drafts, as each new Mastership had all too swiftly succeeded the last. Sir Richard, one of the wealthiest men in the Kingdom, brought with him a beautiful pack of hounds which he had bred and hunted from his first season with the Burton. He transferred his establishment from the Cottesmore, and set about hunting the entire Quorn country with extraordinary energy and huge expense. His income included £40,000 a year from the rents in one parish in Westminster – he had deep pockets. He took Quorn Hall, bringing his three daughters and some of his seven sons, to live there. After one season he dispensed with subscriptions, which must have added to his popularity enormously. At the same time he actually increased the sport available by re-taking the Donington country to the west, and hunted six days a week for two seasons.

Then, in effect, he hunted eight days a week by having two packs out on the same day twice a week. He hunted the Harborough country separately, and this led to the eventual separation of this area, and the formation of the Fernie. It was a highly convenient separation for foxhunters living at the Harborough end of the Quorn. Local loyalties to the separated pack grew among farmers and landowners, and still thrive today, as we shall see.

The 1850s and '60s saw Leicesteshire drawn into the railway network. It was not until 1858 that Leicester had a direct line to London; it was a matter of changing at Rugby before that. The railways were assisting trade; they were also aiding sport, since many a foxhunter could venture to Melton with far more speed and comfort. There were plenty of takers for the large number of hunting days provided so generously by Sir Richard Sutton. The Quorn now had a genuine houndman as Master. Although he revelled in Leicestershire as a setting for the Chase, he did not care for the over-riding of his precious pack by the Meltonian thrusters. One story is that he sent home two of his favourite hounds in a carriage on learning that one notorious hard rider was at the meet. Another legend is that he instructed one follower not on any account to ride over a particular hound which he valued above all. The gentleman courteously replied: 'I will do anything I can to oblige you, Sir Richard, but I have a wretched memory for hounds, and I am afraid that he will have to take his chance with the rest.' Sir Richard's reply is not recorded! I know more than a few contemporary Leicestershire Masters who would simply have retorted: 'Go home!'

During this Mastership the Quorn fixture's were advertised as 'Sir Richard Sutton's hounds', emphasizing the Master's priorities in the hunting field. Good houndmen may have to discipline the mounted field, but inevitably they please the riders through the prolific amount of good sport provided by a top-class pack. For a man in his late fifties, the sheer weight of the sporting load which Sir Richard was bearing, in terms of organization and leadership, as well as continual expense, was enormous. It was not surprising that in his eighth season, which happened to be a bad scenting winter, with all too many disappointing days, that the Baronet let it be known that he was contemplating relinquishing the Quorn at the end of the following season. Great was the consternation which this news evoked throughout the country. Yet he had not negotiated his departure when the next season arrived, and Sir Richard's zeal and enthusiasm seemed to be re-charged. Alas, on 14 November 1855, the Master died suddenly at his London home, aged fifty-seven. His contribution at Quorn had become so all embracing that his passing during the season produced nothing less than a crisis for the Hunt. Two of his sons, Richard and Frank Sutton, managed affairs for the rest of the season, but they sold most of the horses and hounds after the last fixture.

Meetings of leading followers failed to find another Master for some months, but eventually an emissary was sent to ask, even plead, with Lord Stamford to give up the Albrighton pack in order to take the Quorn. The connecting link was a large estate which Lord Stamford owned near Quorn, but without any residence. Quorn Hall was purchased by Mr Edward Warner of Loughborough, who put the stables and kennels at the disposal of Lord Stamford, the Earl taking up residence at Bradgate House, near Groby. Aged thirty when he took the Mastership in 1856, Lord Stamford was a man of many interests and Meltonians soon perceived that foxhunting was his pleasure, but not his passion. They became used to his frequent absences from the hunting field to engage in other interests, of which shooting was certainly one.

Tom Day, nearly sixty, went down to the Harborough end of the country, taken over by Mr Tailby, the first move towards the eventual break away of this country which was to become the Fernie. Old Tom had a good season, but Lord Stamford's huntsman, Ben Boothroyd, who had come from the Donington country, was considered too slow for the Melton's old turf, fences and small coverts. Boothroyd probably had major problems in sorting out some eighty couples of hounds, collected from all too wide a variety of sources, including the entire Bedale pack from Yorkshire.

Lord Stamford, a mild mannered man who was easy to like, was tough enough to take firm action, replacing Boothroyd next season with a new appointment: John Treadwell who was the son of the James Treadwell, huntsman to the famous J.J. Farquharson, the 'Meynell of the West', who hunted most of Dorset. As so often, choosing the right huntsman is the major service a Master can render a country. If he makes an error in that appointment all the organization and expenditure he cares to make will be in vain. John Treadwell had wide experience, having been in service with packs as far apart as Scotland and Hampshire where he was with the Hambledon and the Vine. He knew Leicestershire, having served in the Cottesmore country. He was a top-class horseman and houndman; sport rapidly accelerated in every way, much to the delight of the Meltonians. On 18 December 1858, he achieved a remarkable hunt of four hours and ten minutes in the western side of the country. They found near the meet at Bardon Hill, and caught their fox after a long circular hunt, taking in Gisborne's Gorse, Chartley Knoll and Chartley Wood. Records for the 1958-9 season showed that hounds hunted one hundred and thirty-six days, none of them blank, had killed fifteen brace during cubhunting, twenty-three and a half brace during the season proper, and ran thirty-seven brace to ground. It is often said that foxes were far less plentiful in the nineteenth century, and this appeared to be true at times, but the aforementioned figures compare well with today's tally: a total of nearly forty brace is comparable with a good season for foxhunting in Leicestershire. It is not clear whether any of the thirty-seven brace run to ground were then despatched in the earth.

Despite his affable nature, Lord Stamford had differences of opinion within the country, and twice threatened to resign unless a promised covert-fund was forthcoming. After Sir Richard Sutton's subscription-free reign, the re-introduction of subscriptions was lackadaisical. Lord Stamford gave up the Quorn in 1863, partly due to his displeasure over shortfalls in the covert-fund. It was described as a 'hopeless muddle' by the Hunt historian Blew. Lack of control over 'unruly fields' was another problem which persuaded Lord Stamford to end his Mastership.

Clearly a firm hand was needed, but the Hunt was to have three short Masterships, despite the need for continuity and a tough leadership.

Mr Samuel William Clowes took the Mastership for three seasons (1863–6). He was a son-in-law of Sir Richard Sutton and a man of substance and worth, but he found the Quorn too much financially, and a burden to organize properly. In his retirement speech he nobly denied that he had been at all 'misused'. He had asked for a guarantee of £1,600 a year from the country, and had received about £2,000 in his first season, although it had fallen short thereafter.

'The bother of the country and the coverts was too much for any one man to cope with,' said Mr Clowes. His summing up should have been handed down to future generations of Quorn foxhunters inclined to criticize their Masters.

Mr Clowes sold his hounds, being auctioned by Tattersalls at the Hunt kennels, and fetching a total of £1,401 guineas – a considerable sum in 1866. One of the results of the rule ending commercial sales of foxhounds, made by the Masters of Foxhounds Association in the twentieth century, is the better establishment of a continuous breeding line in Hunt kennels, because the pack is handed from one Mastership to the next.

Every time the Quorn Mastership changed in the last century scratch packs had to be set up, unless the new Mastership could import a long established pack wholesale. None of this was good for sport.

The Quorn lurched into disaster with the next Mastership: Harry, 4th Marquis of Hastings, was an extravagant madcap incapable of running his own life, let alone a major Hunt. He was to die aged twenty-six in the November following his resignation, having lost much of his fortune on the turf. It was common for him to arrive late at the meet, keeping hounds and the field waiting, and then to leave the hunting field early, eager to dash off to some fresh misadventure.

'Blow your horn, Harry!' said Lord Wilton on one occasion when the fox had gone away with only one couple of hounds after it.

'Impossible,' said Hastings. 'Do you want to see me sick in front of the whole field?'

There were dire forecasts that the Quorn would not survive much longer. Tom Day, the former huntsman had now seen seven dispersal sales of the hounds in recent years.

Although he only reigned for two seasons, Mr John Chaworth Musters deserves much credit for rescuing the Quorn from dismemberment and possible oblivion. He was a true foxhunter through and through, and a Midlands Master who knew how to hunt hounds in a Leicestershire environment, although he was not born in the county. As a grandson of Jack Musters, he was irrevocably linked with the neighbouring country of South Nottinghamshire, where he had already formed an excellent pack of hounds. He brought the entire pack with him to Quorn, and took on the country without a guaranteed subscription. Yet again it was not the allure of hard riding, nor the thrill of hunting among the swells, which had saved the Quorn. It was the challenge of an extraordinarily appropriate setting for the Chase which attracted a genuine foxhunter.

Chaworth Musters had another inestimable asset – he was good with people. He could achieve reasonable discipline with harmony; his staff and his mounted field co-operated readily with his cheerful lead.

The last thirty years of the nineteenth century was to be another golden period for foxhunting. Those who had made their money in the industrial revolution included many who wanted to hunt; they wanted the best and were prepared to pay for it. The Quorn was soon able to prove again that it was the best. It was a paradise for the horseman. The main roads of today were then country lanes winding through a sea of grass; barbed wire was unknown; the fences were maintained by hand, and were nearly all practicable for a good man mounted on a top-class horse.

Frank Gillard hunted hounds for Chaworth Musters on the Melton side, and was later to become one of the greatest of huntsmen for the Belvoir. The Master himself hunted hounds on the Donington side, producing excellent sport in this rougher country. Masters need to be lucky, and Chaworth Musters was blessed with good scenting conditions in his first season. Foxhunters flocked to the Quorn country. During the season of 1869–70, the Quorn hunted one hundred and five days, killing forty-three brace of foxes, and running eighteen and a half brace to ground.

Alas, when all else was right, there were problems with the Master's health. At over seventeen stone it is likely that the physical stress of riding hard over the Quorn country hastened his retirement. After only two seasons he was compelled to give up, much to everyone's regret. He did not leave the Hunt in the lurch, but formed a partnership with a wealthy ship broker, Mr J. Coupland, who had made his money in Liverpool, and lived in Cheshire. The partnership was quickly dissolved, but Mr Coupland was to remain sole Master for fourteen seasons. In his third season he made the inspired decision to appoint Tom Firr as huntsman. The fame of the Quorn was sealed, benefiting from two further Masterships, those of Captain Warner and Lord Lonsdale.

Tom Firr is to foxhunting what Fred Archer or Lester Piggott are to racing, or W.G. Grace to cricket. Was Firr the greatest ever huntsman? There is no way of telling because unlike cricket and other games, hunting has failed to keep reliable, detailed statistics against which performance can be measured. Such statistics would help in comparing reputations, but they would not be conclusive because the environment varies so radically in different countries throughout our small island. In measuring modern huntsmen against the great Firr, one should always bear in mind that he hunted the Quorn country when it was at its best. Wire was coming in and there was some trouble occasionally with hounds on railway lines, but urbanization of rural England as we know it was far away. Doubtless Firr would have coped with today's main roads, diesel fumes, arable land, and barbed wire, but he could hardly perform the hunting miracles with which his fervent admirers credited him during his twenty-seven years hunting the Quorn hounds (1872–99).

Frank Gillard stayed for Mr Coupland's first season. He was succeeded by James MacBride, son-in-law of Tom Day, but MacBride's excellence as a first whipper-in was not evident as a huntsman; a not uncommon problem. It is often said that excellent whippers-in seldom make good huntsmen – although that could not be said of Michael Farrin.

Firr was fortunate in having a businesslike Master, who loved foxhunting all his life, having kept his own pack in India as a young man, and had hunted with the sporting packs in Cheshire, as well as keeping a stud of twenty-five horses in the Quorn country. Mr Coupland's wealth enabled him to provide a stable Mastership, providing top-class backing for his huntsman. The Quorn establishment was now to be run under consistently able management at last. Coupland's Mastership is the third longest in the history of the Quorn, behind Meynell's half a century and Mrs Ulrica Murray Smith's marvellous twenty-six years.

Firr was thirty-one when he arrived at Quorn with his wife and young family. According to his excellent biographer Roy Heron (*Tom Firr of the Quorn*, published in 1984):

> His frame had not an ounce of spare flesh. He weighed around nine stones and stood about five feet eight inches, wiry and strong and with a quick eye, a musical voice, a good brain and iron nerve. His face was generally solemn – indeed he had been likened to an archbishop – but his twinkling eyes betrayed his sense of humour. Like all great sportsmen, he was fastidious about his dress and equipment: his stock always looked as if it had been carved from marble, his coat was spotless and his boots shone like mirrors.

He was further described by Lady Augusta Fane who saw him in the hunting field for many years:

> In appearence, Firr closely resembled a fox. He had a sharp, thin face, and clear, keen eyes, and nothing escaped his notice. His hounds loved and trusted him implicitly, obeyed the slightest wave of his hand and flew back to work at the sound of his inspiring voice that set the blood coursing through one's veins and made the most timid rider ready and anxious to jump the biggest fence.

Whatever else, Firr was indisputably the right man in the right place, at the right time. The Quorn was ready for a huntsman of genius who could exhibit the full value of a remarkable environment for the Chase, which had been first fully recognized by Hugo Meynell. Firr was born on 12 April 1841 at the Essex Kennels, the son of the kennelman. He had started work as a boy in the South Oxfordshire kennels, was second whipper-in successively to Mr Hobson's Harriers in Hertfordshire, the Cambridgeshire, the Craven, the Tedworth, the Quorn in 1863 for one season, the Eglinton and the Pytchley. In 1869 he became huntsman of the North Warwickshire and swiftly showed natural gifts for this role.

John Coupland went to the North Warwickshire with John Chaworth Musters to see Firr in action before they sought to engage him for the Quorn. He fulfilled the prophecy of *Baily's Magazine* that he was the 'coming huntsman; before many years he will be quite the head of his profession.'

It is clear that Firr had the strength of character to enable his great sporting gifts to endure. As I have already remarked, huntsmen are sporting entertainers whose reputations are at the mercy of the most ignorant and jealous of observers. He had gifts as a speaker, could sing well, and was held in high repute locally at Quorn, quite apart from his skills as a huntsman. What was it that distinguished him in the hunting field? We do not lack for enthusiastic reportage, since much of Firr's sport was recorded by the great correspondent of *The Field*, Captain Edward Pennell-Elmhirst, who used the nom de plume, Brooksby. He based himself at Brooksby Hall, which was rented by his brother-in-law Mr Ernest Chaplin. Firr receives indirect praise in Brooksby's accounts, but the latter fails to paint an adequate pen portrait of the great huntsman, and he is shy of describing hunting technique in detail; the ride is all.

A much quoted snapshot of Firr in his second season, by Brooksby, puts us at the covert-side.

> Go place yourself where you have just seen a fox stealing across the main ride of Walton Thorns and get two yards to leeward of Tom firr as he cheers them to the cry.
>
> If it doesn't make a boy of you, it will make you an old woman on the spot. You must either stiffen in your saddle with concentrated excitement, or you must turn round and cry over your dotage. 'Huic! huic! huic!Yoo-oi! at him there, old bitches! Yo-oi!'

His successor at *The Field*, the excellent J. Otho Paget, gives confirmatory impressions of the great huntsman. He recalls a day, when there had been no run, 'and the shadow of despair was gradually settling upon us. . . . Nearly the whole covert has been drawn and we relapse into sorrow, when all of a sudden there is a shrill tally-ho! from Firr that fills our souls with joy.'

There followed thirty minutes at racing pace from Walton Thorns to Burton Spinneys, by Seagrave village, and back to the Thorns. Paget asserted that Firr rode just as well after twenty years, ready to face the stiffest obstacle; 'but never jumping for the sake of jumping.' He describes an occasion when hounds had been holloaed away from Botany Bay covert. Firr was still in the covert and had to make haste to follow them.

'Arriving at the gate out, which had always previously only wanted a push of the whip to open, he found it chained up,' Paget recalls.

'Most of us in a similar position would have been disconcerted, and lost time in fumbling at the hinges, but Firr never hesitated a moment, and turning his horse round, popped quickly over the gate as if it had been a gap.

'The performance was a masterly exhibition of nerve, quickness and horsemanship, a collection, I may remark, that is not often found in men who have reached the ripe age of fifty-eight.'

One of the many Firr legends concerns two gentlemen who were jealous of each other in the hunting field. One day during a run Firr found himself confronted by a particularly formidable piece of timber virtually guaranteeing a fall. He turned his horse half round and exclaimed, as if to himself: 'Ah! I wish Captain A was here; he would soon show us the way over.' The remark had the desired effect in galvanizing Captain A's deadly rival, Mr B, into dashing gallantly at the timber, levelling it to the ground, and taking a heavy fall. The huntsmen then rode on after his hounds.

Firr's superb handling of his hounds was, of course, the key to his success. He gave them freedom to hunt their fox, but disciplined them to obey his voice and horn at crucial moments during the Chase. His speciality was the galloping cast. After the pack had made its own cast unavailingly he would summon with a call or a whistle, and move forward at an increasing pace, casting them widely until they had hit the line of the fox. Hitting the line at speed requires hounds with good noses, but this was achieved on Quorn old turf, which carries a great scent. At best this tactic achieved a tremendous zip, because hounds picked up the line and surged ahead, giving the mounted followers every opportunity to gallop and jump as soon as the line was recovered.

It must have required good judgement to ensure that hounds had their heads down when being cast widely at speed, unless we are to assume that

Firr merely lifted them and galloped them on in the hope of hitting the line of any old fox, let alone the hunted one. This is what happened when a huntsman was merely playing tricks to provide sport. Contemporary, knowledgeable opinion was that Firr was capable of providing enormous fun for the field whilst hunting the fox he had originally found within the proper limits of venery.

I have no doubt, however, that he was a natural entertainer, and thoroughly understood the need to provide maximum fun for the mounted followers. This led to jealous jibes that the Quorn field was invariably riding after Tom Firr rather than a pack of hounds hunting a fox. There was also the charge that he was too inclined to change foxes during a run in order to keep up the tempo, rather than painstakingly hunting the fox originally found in covert.

One incident is recorded in which the Quorn hounds found a well-known bob-tailed fox at Holwell Mouth, and achieved an excellent hunt to Ab Kettelby, back to Old Hills, Scalford Spinney, Freeby Wood, past Chadwell and down the Belvoir Vale past Clawson Thorns, to catch their fox in the open after a hunt of two hours and fifteen minutes. In answer to the 'know-alls' who claimed that hounds had changed foxes, their huntsman simply held up the bob-tail fox's short stump.

Guy Paget, that great authority on Leicestershire, vouched for Firr's integrity thus: 'Much as Firr liked blood, he was scrupulously fair. No mobbing, or nicking, and above all no bagmen!' (Crowding round a fox with mounted and footfollowers to make it easier for hounds to catch it; nicking a fox's pad so that the blood droplets made it easier to hunt; keeping a fox captive and then releasing it from a bag before hounds were to hunt.) These are all practices totally forbidden according to the rules of the Masters of Foxhounds Association since its formation in 1881 which crystallized and enforced the abhorrence of such practices by reputable foxhunters.

Paget averred that Tom Firr hated digging for foxes. 'His hounds were never short of blood, so it was only necessary when a notorious outlaw slipped into the nearest drain.'

Connoisseurs of Shires hunting compared Firr's casting technique with that of the great Frank Freeman of Pytchley fame. Both were capable of spreading their hounds in front of them like a fan when casting.

I like the legend I was told one sunny morning at Shoby Scholes, the hilltop covert near Six Hills. A veteran Quornite said his father told him that Tom Firr would canter towards the small covert, cracking his whip as he approached. A fox would go away on the far side, and Tom would lift hounds round the covert to hit the line at speed, then gallop down hill to the delights of the Hoby Vale, then a delectable vista of grass and fences; nowadays mainly under plough. I doubt that even the great Tom Firr could achieve this every time, and I hope he did not indulge in such showy manoeuvres too often. Yet it is an example of hound control, for not every huntsman could ensure that his hounds are biddable enough to execute the trick neatly, nor could he hit the line right the other side.

Miss Evelyn Firr, daughter of the great huntsman is quoted by Roy Heron as saying: 'Father would sit for hours, just looking at them (his hounds) without a word. For years he never took a holiday and hated to be even one night without his darlings.'

She said her father 'had a tremendously strong will – I think this accounted, partly, for the great control which he had over animals.'

Mr Coupland's fourteen years of Mastership gave the Quorn the opportunity to build up a pack with proper continuity. He bought the nucleus of his pack from the Craven in Berkshire, and there were drafts from the Belvoir. Benefiting by the stability provided by the Dukes of Rutland, the Belvoir kennel was much prized as a source of consistently bred hunting hounds, long before the Masters of Foxhounds Association was to start the official Foxhound Kennel Stud Book in 1886.

Tom Firr's hounds were certainly bred for work, and they must have been reasonably light framed, and speedy to achieve the bursts over the grass so ecstatically described by Brooksby and others.

The Quorn exhibited its hounds in shows sometimes, although Firr was not particularly keen on the show ring. One of his favourite doghounds, Quorn Alfred, by Mr Garth's Painter, out of Craven Affable, won the Stallion Hound class and the championship cup at York Hound Show, and won his class at Alexandra Palace Show, in 1875.

Alfred had been despatched to the Quorn kennels as a small whelp in a basket. According to Daphne Moore*: Alfred (1872) became a firm favourite with Tom Firr, who regarded him as, 'a perfect model of a twenty-four inch doghound and well fitted to fly over the green pastures of Leicestershire.' Alfred's pedigree contained such a variety of blood that he was looked askance by some Masters, wrote Miss Moore. His ancestors included Lord Henry Bentinck's Contest, Brocklesby Rallywood and Osbaldeston's Furrier. He was obviously a top-class working hound, and among his admirers was Lord Willoughby de Broke who bred four litters by Alfred in 1878 and '79 which founded a celebrated dynasty in the Warwickshire kennel.

Tom Firr's own diaries are quoted at length in Roy Heron's biography of the huntsman. They are fascinating to those who know the Quorn country well, since they indicate many remarkable similarities between the route of foxes taken nowadays and over a century ago.

---

* *The Book of the Foxhound*, first published in 1964 by J.A. Allen, London.

They are the laconic, terse records of a professional, and seldom contain any descriptive passages. The season 1883–4 was celebrated by Brooksby as, 'The Best Season on Record', also the title of his book of the collected reports for that season.

Here is Firr's account in his diary of Monday 7 January 1884, when hounds met at Old Dalby:

> Another splendid day's sport. Found in Grimston Gorse and ran at a tremendous pace through Saxelby Wood by Wartnaby, to the left of Cant's Thorns and Welby and on by Old Hills and Wycomb to Goadby Gorse, to ground in the main earths not a hundred yards in front of hounds. A finer forty-five minutes could not be seen. Found in Welby fishponds and ran fast for twenty minutes, then a good hunting pace by Melton Spinney, towards Freeby Wood; back to the left by Wycomb and stopped hounds at dark at Melton Spinney. Fine day's sport. Last run an hour and twenty minutes.

Any modern Quorn or Belvoir foxhunter knows that these two runs would today take the Quorn hounds across the Hunt boundary well into Belvoir Saturday and Wednesday country. In the nineteenth century, judging by hunting reports, the Quorn and Belvoir hunted the area north of Melton Mowbray from east to west, more or less at will. They certainly cross the same boundary today, but seldom press quite as far into each other's country, as recounted here.

Now compare Brooksby's view of the same run recorded by Tom Firr. After leaving Saxelby, hounds accelerated, and Brooksby exclaims:

> Ye gods, how they fly! The mottled pack, now running in a broad mass, is skimming up the second grass field in front; we are crowding through a gateway, into a rough meadow that is built for anything but rapid galloping.
>
> But spurs must go in, knees must press and horses must be driven hard. . . . The Duke of Portland is the only man within close hail of the pack; and is making the best of such a chance on his good bay mare (the plum of Mr Younger's recent sale).
>
> The fences are just what they should be when good turf leads up to their feet – broad, strong, fair and clean. They come easy now, with the last hound flicking through each, as we skim the one before, with never a moment for the veriest coward to funk or crane. How long this may last we know not. Suffice it that we conjure nothing better for the seventh – seventeenth heaven. There are some awkward ravines and gullies in this happy district, we know only too well – and the Wartnaby Bottom has been a terror and a hindrance to generations.

Here it is, by all that's disappointing and terrifying – with its black fence frowning and its brookbanks yawning.

But again do fox and hounds of themselves help us in dire extremity. We know of no bridge or opening for a mile – and here, as in blank despair we follow men and hounds into the lowest corner, an old hidden gate is flung open by the foremost horseman, and we are free to hurry forward at our best.

On the big pasture opposite Wartnaby Hall, a flock of sheep dash across the front of hounds; a man stands in his gig in the open road above, pointing onwards towards Cant's Thorns. The fox no doubt had eyes as ready and keen as those of the passing traveller; but the swing of the pack in their own forward cast takes in the turn without a second's loss of time: and with undiminished pace they are onwards over succession of tight little meadows at the back of Kettelby.

Captain Smith and Mr A. Brockleshurst land together into the road by the village – Firr joining them at the same instant as if from the clouds; certainly no other man could have made up the ground with fifteen minutes of extricating himself from the gorse covert, fully fifty people being then between him and hounds.

The little brown is almost burst by the effort; but, very shortly afterwards, Mr Coupland snatches an opportunity to change horses – setting his huntsman on the grey – while a moment's breathing time easily enables the blown one to bring the Master to the end of the run.

Another unjumpable bottom is to be crossed where bullocks have put fence and brook on the same level, and where only a hurdle answers all purposes of winter gap-mending. How thankful we are – but many yards we lose when such an outlet has to be carefully forded or a gate has to be unlatched!

And on a day like this we can almost measure by ear the distance of the flying pack – so clear and sharp and regular is its rapidly fleeting music. Now we are in the Nottingham and Melton road. Where are the hounds that we hear so plainly?

Yonder they flit by the railway side (the Holwell ironstone track). We have ridden the exact reverse of the line already this year with the Belvoir – and to this perhaps we owe the gallop of today. But what is really curious lies in the fact that we shall ride these very fences, creep these very holes, open these very gates, in a second run today. Let that remain I promise myself and you to inflict no minute repetition. 'Tis all I can do to separate two runs so oddly entangled.

The next I remember in this hurried chase is half a dozen hot-faced men huddled in a corner – looking one to the other for assistance, and each looking less capable than the other of giving it.

A new white oxer in front, a drop beyond – two refusals against the side fence – and 'bellows-to-mend' all round. But the good sorrel warhorse, that has become almost as famed and familiar as his master, is equal to this or any other similar occasion. The white rails are shown to be no impossibility – and the next comer, bringing still further evidence, and weight to bear, removes their self-assertion altogether.

The pack runs the waggonway for half a mile; most of us run it a mile, and join the bridleroad throng from Wartnaby, Kettleby, and Holwell. But Mr Cochrane carries the principle of seniores priores by boring a way through the overhanging bullfinch alongside – and carries out also the huntsman and a grateful following from the trammels of the waggonway – though he bears an honourable scar on his cheek for the rest of the day, perhaps for the rest of the week.

The covert-lined glen of Old Hills is at this time just to the right; and we top the hill to double two more roads, to leave Clawson Thorns wide on the left – and to gallop up to another ironstone railway. (It has been my fate to write of hunting for some fifteen years – and I aver, in sorrow, and in truth, that the word railway is at the end of my pen at least fifteen times oftener now than when I was first entered to ink.)

An old man fumbles willingly at the padlocked gates by his farmside; Firr rides lucklessly down to another pair of white gates some fifty yards away, where there are not even a pair of clumsy willing hands with a key – while in anguish of soul he marks bold and bedraggled Reynard toiling up the next field, hounds a hundred yards behind him, and a flock of sheep scuttling between. Who shall say that a huntsman's career is without its agony? To make matters worse, two quarrymen stoutly aver that they have stood for quite a quarter of an hour in the very gateway through which the fox has actually passed!

Such is information from the passing clod, whose eyes, startled from accustomed vacancy or the ground, have risen to the coming fray. But for the quarrymen, but for the sheep, but for the locked railway gates, that fox might have been handled within half an hour.

As it is, he is able to stay above ground for forty-five minutes, and to bring his brush safely to the main earths in Goadby Gorse – his point and goal throughout. This little check is the only one of a straight and superb gallop.

Recognising familiar ground as we go, we find ourselves opening two of the bridle gates by which we canter from Melton to a meet at Piper Hole. Now we are bearing down upon the Spinney of Scalford Bog (the fences happily diminishing in size as jumping power fades); and now Captain Ashton views the beaten fox once more just before hounds.

At the little hamlet of Wykeham, midway between Scalford and

Goadby Marwood, foot people are running, shouting, and pointing on both sides. One fox has passed between the houses; but the hounds never leave their game, race him up the road, and dash into Goadby Gorse – only to worry and tear at the tiles of the artificial earth instead of wetting their teeth on his savoury sides. So a gallant fox lives – after as true and honest a gallop as ever did credit to the Quorn, or helped to make a season famous.

They do not write hunting reports like that nowadays! So much for *Foxford's Hunting Diary*! Oh for the space which *The Field* accorded their correspondent for such reports back in the 1880s. Brooksby sometimes writes in the present tense, and hots up the pace, the emotions, and the risks. Yet he reveals clearly here that hunting the Quorn hounds was by no means a case of sailing onwards over an easy sea of undulating country. The rural scene was far more populated in those days and it was highly possible that farmhands, quarry men and other workers would be in the wrong place at the wrong time, however much they may have wished to assist the Hunt. The ironstone railways, and the quarrying were clearly considerable handicaps to hunting in parts of the Quorn and Belvoir countries during this period. As he says, Brooksby finds it necessary to mention both hazards far more frequently than he would wish.

Virtually all the country referred to above is crossable today and the ironstone railway is more accessible, since it is long since abandoned, and there are no locked gates. The Hunts regularly use the disused track as a bridleway, and foxes often inhabit the cuttings and embankments as natural coverts; a welcome sanctuary from intensively farmed arable fields.

For Tom Firr and the Quorn, the 'best season on record', 1883–4, ended on a sour note: suddenly Mr Coupland announced that he was resigning as Master. His shipping business in Liverpool was suffering from a slump in freights. Mr Coupland held a sale of his hunters at the end of every season, but far more serious, he was intent on selling the Quorn hounds on resigning; he asked some £3,300, a high price at that time.

This would have been an enormous blow, since the pack had been carefully bred and produced by Firr to the highest pitch. Starting yet again with a scratch pack of drafted, imported hounds, was asking too much of such a huntsman, at the height of his career. The Quornites were, in the main, more interested in the quality of the ride than the pedigree of the hounds, but they well understood the risks to the standard of their sport if hounds were to be sold. Three of the most devoted, and wealthiest, Quorn subscribers came to the rescue: the Duke of Portland, Lord Wilton, and Mr Julius Behrens of Leeds. They took equal shares in the ownership of the hounds, and the Duke of Portland paid Tom Firr £50 a year – the difference between his present income and that which had been offered from an illustrious quarter, the Royal Buckhounds, who hunted carted deer in Berkshire. This post provided a house in Windsor Great Park and a pension on the civil list. One cannot imagine such a great huntsman of foxhounds being satisfied, nor fulfilled, hunting carted deer. So it could not have been an especially difficult decision for Firr to continue at the Quorn under these terms. Although he had to consider his income and his future security, since he had a young family to bring up.

Mr Coupland's retirement was a blow in many ways. His business-like approach to Mastership was ahead of his time, and he recognized the worth of his huntsman, allowing him to carry out his task without interference, but with real support when needed. In return, Tom Firr never fell into the trap of becoming vain and spoilt, despite the plaudits heaped upon him.

The new Master was Lord 'Hoppy' Manners who lived at Quenby Hall in the Friday country. At the age of twenty-eight, he was already a famed and popular sporting character, having ridden his own horse Seaman to victory in the 1882 Grand National which was run in a heavy rainstorm. Another member of the Quorn mounted field, Count Kinsky won the National the following year on Zoedene. Lord Manners agreed to take the Mastership on a short-term basis, and continued for two seasons – alas not blessed with good scenting conditions. His Mastership was marked by the enclosure and planting of the famous covert, Adam's Gorse, and by the happy appointment of Fred Earp who was to prove the best of Tom Firr's many whippers-in, filling that role excellently for eighteen years.

In 1886, the appointment of Captain William P. Warner as Master heralded one of the happiest periods of Tom Firr's time at the Quorn. The Warners lived at Langton, in what was to be the Fernie country, and they knew Leicestershire and its people extremely well. William Warner was exceptionally amiable, which ensured his popularity, and he was well supported financially, since Mr William B. Paget of Loughborough was a partner in the management and expenses, becoming Joint Master four years later. It is probable that Mr Paget had much to do with achieving an important change in the effective Quorn borders: at the end of the 1886-7 season the Donington country was reclaimed from Earl Ferrers, not without some protest apparently. This was important, since it was clear that the feud at the southern end of the country, the Harborough area, was not going to be won by the Quorn. Mr Fernie was appointed as Master of the Harborough country in 1888 effectively sealing off that area as a separate Hunt forever.

It cannot be claimed that the Donington country was anywhere near as attractive as the Billesdon–Market Harborough district which became the Fernie, but it was a sensible decision to regain the Donington area.

Although no one could have foreseen the huge erosion of hunting countries which was to take place in the latter half of the next century, making every acre of huntable country so precious. The retention of the Quorn's pack, so carefully nurtured by Tom Firr, produced brilliant sport during Captain Warner's Mastership.

'I look back upon this Mastership as being the period I enjoyed most, although I have had many happy days before and since', opined Otho Paget. He summed up Captain Warner's Mastership:

> There were many good runs during his time in office, but what I think more to the point is that hounds nearly always provided some sport whenever they were able to hunt.
>
> Captain Warner was very methodical and did things thoroughly, so that the business of the Hunt was carried on without a hitch. One of the things on which he insisted, and which I consider most important, was that the country should be drawn and hunted fairly.
>
> It is a matter that not only affects sport, but is essential in keeping on good terms with covert owners and occupiers of land.

The resignation of Captain Warner and Mr Paget in 1893 brought major change. It could hardly have been otherwise, since the new Master was one of the most notable personalities of late Victorian England, Lord Lonsdale, called the 'Yellow Earl' because it was his favourite colour and he used it in his staff liveries and the exterior of his carriages. Hugh, 5th Earl of Lonsdale, was thirty-six when he took the Quorn, having succeeded to the title and the great wealth of the Lonsdale's Cumberland estates, including rich coal mines; after the death of his father and brother, the 3rd and 4th Earls, within ten years. Although he was an Etonian he had not been brought up with the expectation of becoming the Earl, and lived a wild youth in which horses and hunting had played a great part. He was a natural horseman and claimed to have been 'brought up in the stables'. His firmest Leicestershire connection was his family's Mastership, and his own, in the Cottesmore, and we will refer to his character in more detail when dealing with that country. His extraordinary personality was to have a major impact even on the Quorn where wealthy extroverts were hardly unknown in the mounted field.

Like so many outwardly bombastic people, Hugh Lonsdale's imposing, even intimidating front, concealed a far less secure and shy personality. This made his dealings with people sometimes less than successful, but he had great powers of leadership, drive and organization. He believed in change and did not shirk plenty of shaking and stirring in getting his way. He was a great spender, and believed in magnificently high standards of turnout as well as performance. Unfortunately, he felt that everyone else should spend just as generously, and this caused some unpopularity. His first innovation at the Quorn was a new uniform for the Hunt servants: white leather breeches and dark-red coats with Lowther buttons. Tom Firr, remarking on the change from buckskin to leather said he had 'never known what it was to ride in comfort before.'

Brooksby recorded his astonishment on re-visiting the Quorn to find Tom Firr 'an old picture hung in a new frame . . . leathered as to the legs, hung with swan-necked spur, crossed with a stirrup strap, and mounted (superbly mounted) on a hog-maned steeplechaser with a long tail.'

Brooksby described the total effect as 'Tom Firr en aspic', but the correspondent admitted that the great huntsman was working as effectively as ever in the field.

The Earl even produced a Hunt livery for Harry Houghton, the runner; he was also equipped with a patent Lonsdale combined pick and spade, and other devices to bolt foxes from drains.

Second horsemen were sent out with well equipped first-aid boxes, and a yellow ambulance van was in attendance, sometimes ungratefully referred to by the field as 'the fever van'.

Many Quornites were more critical still of the new Hunt button introduced by the Earl; it had a large coronet above, and a small Quorn below. One or two refused to sew on the new ones, fastening their coats with safety pins and declaring that they were 'not his Lordship's lackeys'. Such independent spirits were soon to be defeated in the hunting field when Hugh Lonsdale delivered his famous 'tick-offs'.

Unfortunately for misbehavers, the Earl was a true countryman, and despite all the pomp and show, knew a vast amount about foxes, hounds and horses.

'You shouldn't hunt, sir. Paper-chasing is in your line. You'd make a damned good hare,' he would roar at a particularly irritating thruster who had dared to ride too close to hounds.

Hugh ordered Firr to take hounds home after one noble peer had twice disobeyed his orders to 'Hold hard'.

'You can do what you like; I'm going home myself,' replied the angry Lord.

'In that case the rest of us can continue,' said Lonsdale with a satisfied smile.

According to a correspondent in *The Field*: 'Men and women obey Lord Lonsdale as well as trained wolves obey their instructor, going on only at the word of command.'

One can only hope this was a journalistic exaggeration, but certainly the Yellow Earl made his presence felt. Aggrieved Quorn members must have been mollified, however, by the huge amounts of cash he spent from his own purse on the Hunt above the £3,000 in subscriptions guaranteed to him by the Committee, a lavish sum at that time. His Mastership may have been a mixed blessing, but it was never dull. He was intensely keen that his hounds should catch their fox. The meets were showpieces, with ladies and gentlemen stepping out of elegant carriages to mount top-class blood horses, all superbly turned out to the highest standards. In the hunting field the standards of venery were in no way sacrificed to show or fashion. He insisted on hounds hunting the fox accurately across country until they had caught it, preferably above ground.

Hence his ire if anyone should interfere with the work of hounds.

Colin Ellis in his history declares that if the Quorn had not appointed Hugh Lonsdale:

> It would have been the poorer for a colourful episode. I am bound to say, however, that in the opinion of many people the times in Lord Lonsdale's Mastership which were the happiest for all concerned were the frequent occasions when he was absent and his brother, Lancelot Lowther, acted as his deputy in the field. Tom Firr was then allowed to kill his foxes in his own way and it never seemed to be necessary to send hounds home because of the behaviour of the field.

Hugh Lonsdale's preoccupations included the Road and the Turf as well as the Chase; he had a complicated social and business life. His energies were prodigious. It was inevitable that his Mastership was to be meteoric and memorable, but not one of the longest. The Committee grew restive as the Master's expenses soared. J.D. Cradock resigned the secretaryship in 1897 and his successor, Tempest Wade, had to increase subscriptions immediately. Lonsdale's Mastership put extra strains on Tom Firr, although he was certainly intelligent enough to appreciate the benefits as well as the debits. Firr was said to have offered his resignation to Lord Lonsdale after the Earl changed the traditional practice of drawing Gartree Hill covert after their opening meet at Kirby Gate on the first Monday in November. The Earl had mistakenly taken this decision for the best of motives: as a mark of respect to the landowners, the Hartopps, whose mother had died during the summer. Had he consulted the family he would have discovered that he had upset them more by not drawing the covert. Next morning Hugh disarmed his huntsman with a frank apology and the resignation was withdrawn. There were differences with the huntsman over hound breeding policy, but one suspects that despite his brashness, Hugh Lonsdale's deep knowledge and sympathy for foxhunting enabled him to maintain a working relationship with one of the greatest huntsman in the history of the sport.

Alas, on the last day of 1897 Firr suffered a terrible fall. Going away from Walton Thorns after killing one fox, hounds ran past Six Hills and on to Wymeswold. Then disaster struck: 'I unfortunately jumped a fence into a pit and was completely knocked out, my skull being fractured,' Tom Firr recorded in his diary.

'I was taken home in a carriage and, some weeks afterwards, went to Brighton for a month, which did me good. But I did not recover sufficiently to hunt again that season, except for one day.'

Tom's health was seriously impaired by this fall. He returned to the saddle at the start of the 1898–9 season, but he suffered another serious fall during cubhunting on the Forest side. He fell over a wall by a gate at the edge of Barrow Wood, by Charley Hall. He seemed dazed, but remounted and soon jumped through a bullfinch; when the next man landed he saw Tom lying motionless. He regained consciousness, but now his health was shattered, and he aged fast. Unable to return to the saddle, with the greatest reluctance he had to accept retirement in February 1899 after twenty-seven years as Quorn huntsman. The Hunt raised over £3,000 in a testimonial – a very substantial sum at that time.

Tom Firr died of a cancer of the throat on 16 December 1902, and was buried in the graveyard at Quorn. He was only sixty-one; it could truly be said that he gave his life for foxhunting with the Quorn.

Lord Lonsdale's Mastership ended abruptly, through financial pressure of course. In the summer of 1898 he had to inform the Committee he could not continue the season ahead. He sold his eighty-four hunters for 18,228 guineas. Despite his bombast, he had achieved a notable Mastership, emphasizing the Quorn's position in most eyes as England's premier Hunt. One of the great runs occurred during his Mastership: on 14 December 1894, hounds found at Barkby Holt in the Friday country, and ran twenty-seven miles before marking their fox to ground in Stockerston Bolt Wood, south of Uppingham in the Cottesmore country.

The furthest point was sixteen and a half miles, and the distance from the find to the finish was thirteen miles. Hugh Lonsdale and all the Hunt staff, Tom Firr, with whippers-in Fred Earp and Walter Keyte, were there at the finish, plus Lady Gerard and 'hardly anyone else', according to a report in *Baily's Magazine*.

5

The Quorn in the Twentieth Century

Look out! Look out! Here comes a loose
horse with a lady on it!

The Yellow Earl's successor, Captain Tommy Burns-Hartopp, a member of an old Leicestershire family, had far less money, but a great heart, a warm personality and enormous fortitude. These qualities carried him through a Mastership (1890–1950) which was among the most popular in the Hunt's history. He was dedicated to proving that hunting was for fun – a formula which is compatible with the highest standards of venery. He first put on the second whipper-in, Walter Keyte as Tom Firr's successor, but although a bold horseman Keyte was not able to produce the sport achieved by Firr. It is probable that Firr's hounds and their forebears had learnt to hunt in a certain manner which worked splendidly with the great huntsman but could not be reproduced by an average huntsman.

Galloping casts are not recommended to most huntsman on taking over a new pack of hounds. Much better to let hounds work things out for themselves at first, rather than try the degrees of wizardry achieved by Firr through his genius for hound control.

In 1902 the Quorn brought in Tom Bishopp from the Grafton. A calm, competent huntsman, Bishopp worked hard to improve the pack's performance after Keyte's attempts to 'do' a Tom Firr. There were criticisms that the Quorn pack was 'not what it was'. This in no way deterred huge mounted fields from continuing to support the Hunt during the Edwardian era, and there is no doubt that they had tremendous fun, even if too much of the sport apparently consisted of short bursts over the delectable grass and fences, with the longer hunts becoming rare. Although the Boer War undoubtedly made an impact on British society, there is no evidence that it had any noticeable effect on the numbers of people who enjoyed hunting, shooting and fishing. People were blissfully unaware of the horrors of a world war ahead, and the Indian Summer of 1900–14 saw confident middle and upper classes continuing to relish country sports in much the same way they had in the nineteenth century, even if costs were already rising – although labour remained remarkably cheap.

It was as well that the Quorn Committee decided during this period to build new kennels on another site. The old ones at Quorn could no longer be refurbished without huge expense, and the landlord, Mr E.H. Warner, eldest brother of the previous Master of that name, asked the Hunt to make a move. He was fully supportive and gave a new site at Pawdy Crossroads, near Sileby, as a gift.

For some £14,000 the Committee built excellent kennels, cottages and stables, which served the Hunt splendidly from 1905–91. As we shall see, it was the environment not the buildings which caused the next move. Despite his financial problems, Hugh Lonsdale generously proffered a £5,000 interest-free loan, and others donated readily to the new buildings which formed certainly one of the best kennels and Hunt stables in Britain; far better than the Victorian 'workhouse' design all too often seen in some other Hunt establishments. Former Quorn Hunt Secretary Jonathan Singlesant tells me that Hugh Lonsdale never came forward with his proferred loan. The last of the debentures raised to build the kennels was paid off with the money from a foot and mouth disease insurance claim in the 1925–6 season.

The much regretted resignation of Captain Burns-Hartopp was followed by the appointment of one of few amateur huntsmen to succeed in Leicestershire, apart from a latter day tradition of amateurs in the Cottesmore country. At first, however, it was insisted by the Committee that Captain Frank Forester (Master, 1905–18) should not hunt hounds, but must employ a professional. There was considerable prejudice against amateur huntsmen in the Quorn Committee. Even today some Hunts are still nervous of the prospect of ejecting an amateur huntsman should he prove ineffectual, whereas not re-engaging a professional's contract at the end of a season is a less embarrassing option.

Frank Forester proved to be a truly formidable figure in the hunting field, as Field Master and later as huntsman. He rode the country with a total absence of fear, taking all obstacles, including the most challenging, at a great pace. Woe betide anyone who impeded him or interfered in any way with hounds. He seems to have had quite a lot in common with the Cottesmore's great amateur huntsman, Captain Brian Fanshawe, who retired in 1992, but the latter is a more polished horseman who correctly varies his pace in taking fences.

Captain Forester gave up the Forest side of the Quorn country after one season, devoting himself to the Melton side on Mondays and Fridays. The vacuum was filled by inviting the Earl of Harrington to bring his hounds over from Derbyshire twice a week. Known as 'Whiskers' because of his flowing white beard, the 8th Earl was a totally dedicated foxhunter whose heirs have continued this tradition in England, and latterly in the County Limerick Hunt in Ireland.

The outbreak of the 1914–18 War brought undreamt of social change to Britain, and the rest of the western world. Foxhunting's resilience, and its hold on the rural way of life was demonstrated by its ability to survive, and to flourish again after such a profound change in so many aspects of the nation's life-style. Foxhunting did not cease during the First World War, but the huge numbers of men, women and horses eventually drafted into military service reduced Hunt establishments to skeleton staffs, and much smaller mounted fields became the norm. The green Elysian fields of Leicestershire remained virtually a sea of grass and jumpable fences, and much solace they gave to the few who managed to escape briefly on leave from the hell of trench warfare on the continent.

Captain Forester, as part of war economies, was now able to take over as huntsman, and quickly proved himself first class in the role. His persistence, thoroughness and drive ensured that hounds caught a high percentage of foxes above ground. The coverts were scrupulously cubhunted, and foxes knew well the importance of flying into the open when hounds arrived during the season proper.

Despite dire forecasts that the War would mean the end of hunting through its decimation of the flower of Britain's youth, and the dwindling of family fortunes; foxhunting in Leicestershire soon entered another heyday after the War, partly for the wrong reasons. The manic gaiety of the 1920s, and the despair in the 1930s when Europe was on the march to another war, produced a pleasure-seeking set of young, and not so young people for whom hunting in the Shires was part of a giddy round of hectic pastimes. As referred to in more detail in Chapter Eight, the hunting lodges around Melton Mowbray at times reflected the desperate appetite for diversion, fuelled by the possibility of sharing them with such glamorous personalities as Edward, Prince of Wales and his set.

There is little cause for censure; compared with the sexual licence of the 1960s, the mid-war years were decorous for most people. The rigours of riding Leicestershire still indicated an early night as the best medicine for many spending the winter in the Shires. Such gaiety as took place is sadly missed nowadays when all too many outside foxhunters do not stay one night in the Quorn country, but dash to and fro on day visits to the Hunt fixtures.

Those who benefited from Leicestershire's last spell of predominant pastoral farming in the twentieth century were of the generation whose early years had been clouded by family bereavements in the First World War, and were all too soon to be called upon to make more sacrifices after 1939. The other 'wrong reason' for hunting's golden patch between the wars was the increasingly parlous state of farming economics. Much land was farmed lightly, if at all, and foxhunting inevitably always benefits from wilder country where there is ample sanctuary for foxes, and less chance of upsetting farming operations during a hunt. The state of agriculture was not of course the fault of foxhunting; indeed, hunting helped to alleviate the low incomes from traditional farming.

The Quorn had been fortunate in its secretaryship as well as in its professional huntsman. When the great J.D. Cradock resigned in 1897 during Lord Lonsdale's turbulent reign, the new secretary appointed was Mr Tempest Wade who proved excellent in this role until his death in 1919. He ran the sales at Leicester Horse Repository, and his skills as a horseman and businessman, and his integrity and tact, earned the greatest respect from Quorn subscribers, and local landowners and farmers.

When Captain Forester resigned in 1918, the Committee carried on hunting the country for one season, and had the good fortune to appoint one of the best huntsmen in Quorn history, Walter Wilson, who came from that grand grass country, the Cheshire. He served the Quorn for ten years, proving himself a top-flight hound man and cross-country rider. Colin Ellis tells a revealing story of Wilson's hounds running perilously on the railway line at Thorpe Trussels at a time when it was operative. Wilson jumped a set of rails, and slid his horse all the way down the steep cutting bank. At the bottom he 'stood by the railway and quietly waved his hounds off the line. By the time the foot people got down to help him he had the situation completely under control. He was a marvellous horseman and very quiet with his hounds.' Nowadays the cutting back is thickly clothed with bushes and trees, and the track is bare of rails, making a useful bridleway across the country. The cutting bank is a fine sanctuary for foxes and other wildlife.

In 1919 the appointment as Joint Masters of Major Algy Burnaby to take charge of the Melton side of the country, and Mr Edward Paget the Forest side was another stroke of good fortune. They were highly respected foxhunters, the Major making a huge success of the arduous role of Field Master on the hectic Monday and Friday fixtures. His relationship with the mounted field, especially those who transgressed, involved the use of shafts of wit, or sarcasm, which have become part of hunting legend. They are not as funny in the re-telling as they were at the time. The fact is that at moments of stress on a pulling horse in front of more than two hundred other people on pulling horses, anything other than 'Hold hard!' could be regarded as witty.

'Look out! Look out! Here comes a loose horse with a lady on it!' was one of his remarks.

He was also known to exclaim: 'The pretty ladies can go ahead, the ugly ones must stay behind me!'

Despite such jokes against the ladies, Algy Burnaby was by reputation anything but a misogynist.

Mr Paget was an excellent organizer and played a great part in ensuring a well-run Hunt establishment, while keeping the Forest side well hunted since its restoration to the Quorn from Lord Harrington. After Mr Paget retired in 1928, Major Burnaby continued as sole Master for two seasons, to be joined in 1930 by Sir Harold Nutting, who owned Quenby, the lovely house and estate in the Friday country, now in the possession of those great supporters of hunting, the De Lisle family.

Sir Harold, whose fortune derived in part from bottling Guiness, certainly poured his resources generously into the Quorn. One estimate was that he was spending £15,000 a year on the Hunt in the 1930s. He was a stickler for the highest standards in horses, turnout and the 'correct' use of hunting parlance. Ulrica Murray Smith, who was a friend and protégé of Sir Harold and Lady Nutting, recalls in her entertaining reminiscences *Magic of the Quorn*: 'If anyone spoke of "cubbing" or the "whip" instead of whipper-in, he would nearly have a stroke. There were many pitfalls in speech about hunting into which I may say even the most educated and eminent used to fall, much to Harold's disdain.'

Sir Harold could be extremely irascible, but foxhunting has always been a trial for any Master with a tendency to perfectionism. In contrast to today, when 'second horses' is printed on the meet card, Sir Harold kept as a close secret where hounds would draw, where horses would be changed, or the likely place of end of day. If anyone dared to telephone him to ask where to leave a car, he would reply firmly: 'In your garage I hope' and ring off.

Second horsemen were still used to bring the horses for the latter part of the day; horse boxes were rarely used, although the train was still relied upon in many hunting countries to transport horses to distant meets. The Quorn used trains to take horses to meets on the far western side of the Saturday country. The second horsemen would assemble at the meet, to be put under the instructions of the huntsman's second horseman. They trotted for miles along the roads until the Master ordained a change of horses. No second horseman was allowed to go off on his own, and if the mounted field crossed a Hunt boundary into a neighbouring Hunt country during a run, the second horsemen had to wait in the Quorn country, being forbidden to cross a boundary. All this meant that hunters were remarkably fit, and when a second horse was mounted for the afternoon's hunting it was already reasonably exercised and 'had its back down'.

Shortage of labour and the proliferation of horse boxes, has made the Leicestershire 'second horses' arrangement virtually a second meet in post-war hunting. Many livery owners and grooms whisk the first horses back to their stables, and return at the end of the day to pick up the riders at another pre-ordained spot. The modern arrangement certainly produces a fresh horse, too fresh at times, and it may be required to undertake exertion all too soon after being unboxed. It has to be admitted that arriving by car to collect your first horse, and having your car moved to end of day is the most luxurious arrangement I have ever enjoyed, and it is most welcome for someone who leads a busy life earning a living on days when he is not hunting.

Yet some of my happiest hunting memories are of more traditional arrangements: hacking a tired hunter miles back to the stable in the dusk, chatting with friends about the sport one has enjoyed, and then a farmhouse Hunt tea, a meal to be appreciated more than any other because you are genuinely tired and hungry.

The inevitable abandonment of the second horsemen's role after the war robbed hunting of some of its best professional recruits. More than a few excellent Hunt staff started their careers as second horsemen. Through trotting the roads and lanes for much of the day they became knowledgeable about the sport, which they had to observe closely in order to keep in touch. Young grooms learnt to ride reasonably well, and they had an excellent view of the huntsman at work.

In 1929 Walter Wilson left the Quorn, and his young first whipper-in, George Barker, was appointed in his place – a somewhat daring decision. George was born and bred in the Quorn country, the first huntsman with this background since Mr Meynell's John Raven. An agreeable personality and a natural flair for public relations is a major asset in a huntsman, and George Barker had these qualities in abundance. He had served successively as second and first whipper-in, with Wilson setting an excellent example in kennels and the hunting field, exercising discipline with a firm hand. Despite this, Wilson had one weakness according to eyewitnesses, he liked a drink rather more than was wise in a huntsman and was alleged to have arrived or departed from a meet somewhat too well liquored. This was a symptom of depression in his bereavement after the death of his wife.

Discipline in Hunt kennels still maintained long held traditions of strictness. One ex-Hunt servant who worked under Wilson said the huntsman was, 'a man of very few words; he only had to look at you, and that was enough.'

George had been a brilliant whipper-in, and knew exactly what needed to be done and the huge challenge that lay ahead as huntsman. He met the challenge with considerable success, and provided stability and continuity for the next thirty years. Success was not achieved without organization and discipline which he had learned from Wilson. Ted Hill, who was to be a distinguished huntsman of the Barlow, was second whipper-in to George Barker just after the war. He recalled that George was charming to him – until he put on his scarlet coat.

'Then,' Ted said, 'I don't think that I ever met a sergeant-major as strict!'

He described Barker as a very hard taskmaster of whom Ted was 'frightened to death', but he said his season at Quorn did him as much good as anywhere he worked in a lifetime.

Ulrica Murray Smith says she can still hear Sir Harold Nutting's incredulous 'No! Where?' on hearing that a ploughed field had been seen in the Friday country. She recalls Sir Harold as 'a marvellous organizer, but he had a very little voice (he was kicked in the throat by a horse when he was in the Army) which made him sound rather cross. He was nearly decapitated once out hunting when he rode into a clothes line which probably did nothing to improve his voice, or his temper, but he was a very good and conscientious Master.'

Apart from the second horsemen, people watched from the road only if they had travelled on foot or bicycle. The huge attendant body of car followers was a post-war phenomenon. Sir Harold reputedly encountered one driver of a small car at a meet and asked him what he intended to do.

'Follow the hunt of course,' replied the driver. Sir Harold's response was brief; 'Go home!'

Undoubtedly the pastoral nature of the country and the lack of road traffic greatly increased the prospect of longer runs in the 1930s. Sir Harold's secrecy about the day's arrangements, and the strict discipline of the second horsemen were designed to limit the possibility of foxes being headed or disturbed before hounds had found them.

Jack Littleworth, who whipped-in to George Barker, and was to succeed him, recalled a day in 1936 when the Quorn hounds found in Carrington Spinney, just south-west of Ashby Pastures, and ran in a big circle before their fox made his point just to the west of Oakham in the Cottesmore country – a point of thirteen miles, twenty-eight as hounds ran. Only a handful of mounted followers finished from some four hundred who started.

From Windmill Hill in their Saturday country, the Quorn hounds ran east across the Monday country to Welby Osiers, a ten mile point and almost straight, without a check.

Jack Littleworth recalled that George Barker finished the hunt by running on foot across the last three fields, while Jack had to retire five fields away because his horse was absolutely done.

Whether Barker was a 'great' huntsman as a purist is not claimed by those I have met who hunted with him, but he was certainly highly effective, and of course most of those who recall him can only do so in the latter years of his long career at Quorn. His qualities of character enabled the Hunt to maintain its high levels of popularity with most resident landowners and farmers whilst continuing its extraordinary record of attracting huge fields of subscribers from outside the country who were not merely tolerated but welcomed in Leicestershire. Colin Ellis remarked that, 'George Barker could convince anybody of anything. To convince the Quorn farmers that he came as a benefactor had been his role for years.' His success in keeping the Quorn kennels in operation during the Second World War alone deserves the highest praise. He worked exceedingly hard to keep hounds at top-class working level, growing vegetables behind the kennels to augment their diet. After the war, he made a notable contribution in reviving Quorn hunting according to the old standards. He died on 5 October 1975, aged seventy-eight, one week after his golden wedding anniversary when he made one of his amusing speeches, having enjoyed a happy retirement in the Quorn country, latterly at Twyford in the Friday country.

The former distinguished Hunt secretary, Denis Aldridge wrote in *Horse and Hound* in paying tribute to George Barker; 'To show sport in the Shires at any time requires exceptional ability and to hunt hounds with a hard riding field thundering on one's heels calls for nerve and patience.'

Sir Harold Nutting had pulled the Quorn through the difficult finances of the 1930s when even some of the wealthiest subscribers were hit by the economic slump. The total subscription income dropped from £11,426 in 1929–30 to £7,882 three years later. When he retired in 1939 there were reserve funds in hand. He continued to support the Hunt wholeheartedly as Chairman, and despite his occasional testiness he earned the appreciation of everyone who cared about foxhunting in Leicestershire.

The sport continued throughout most of Britain from 1939–45. The Ministry of Agriculture accepted the packs' role in fox control and allowed limited rations for the hounds and for a few Hunt horses. The 'dig for victory' campaign of home food production brought new jobs for British agriculture. In Leicestershire old turf went back under the plough for the first time in more than two centuries.

Apart from George Barker and a scratch staff, the Quorn owed its wartime survival to a devoted foxhunting eccentric, Major Philip Cantrell-Hubbersty of Ragdale Hall, near Six Hills in the Monday country, nowadays a health establishment. He was a foxhunter of the deepest dye; it was his passion; it entirely dominated his way of life. He was fearless across country, knew the Quorn country intimately and could take his own line. 'That bloody man . . .!' Harold Nutting would yell as Cantrell-Hubbersty chose his own direction across country, taking a lot of others with him. This is reported by his nephew Simon Blow in the splendid pen portrait of Cantrell-Hubbersty in Blow's excellent Leicestershire record *Fields Elysian*. The Major rose to the challenge when war broke out, and took on the role of acting Master for the Committee and Hon. Secretary throughout the war years. According to Simon Blow, Cantrell-Hubbersty had no small-talk outside hunting. He did not bother to address a woman unless she hunted, and he did not care for a constant flow of visitors. Sometimes at meals he would say to his wife, Phyllis, in front of guests: 'When are they going Puppy?' (his term of endearment for her). The degree of his preoccupation with hunting is best summed up by Ulrica Murray Smith's story of Teddy Bouskell-Wade making his first appearence with the Quorn hounds after the war.

'Philip Cantrell-Hubbersty rode up and asked him where he had been and why he had not been out hunting. Teddy replied that he had been abroad fighting the war.

'All Philip said was, "Well, you will find subscriptions have gone up" and rode away.'

Continuity is so important that a gap of five or six years could make the resurrection of a viable Hunt almost impossible. Englishmen hunted throughout the Napoleonic wars and all the subsequent international struggles, keeping alive the great field sport for those able to return and claim it as one of the fruits of victory.

Philip Cantrell-Hubbersty's contribution was therefore of major importance. The strain on a man of advancing years was illustrated in March 1947 when he was out with the hounds at the Beacon: he suddenly fell from his horse and died.

'His death was exactly as he would have wished,' opined Simon Blow.

The Quorn Committee marked its debt, and made a sound decision, in appointing Philip's widow, the redoubtable Phyllis, as the first lady Joint Master in the Hunt's history – with Mr Fred Mee, of the Grange Farm, Shepshed, as her Joint Master. He was the first Quorn farmer to assume that office, and had played a great part in helping to keep the pack going during the war.

6

The Quorn after the War

Those who made the hack to Walton Thorns
for the last draw were well rewarded. The
air was still; the evening sun a golden ball;
and the trees and hedges were black against
the pale green turf. A time to tighten your
girths and perhaps to shorten your leathers

Phyllis Cantrell-Hubbersty had given up riding for some years when she
became Joint Master, but she made a valuable contribution at the helm
while civilian life revived.

Clothes and petrol rationing were still in force, but foxhunting quietly
recruited new subscribers, and new Masters, making remarkable progress
in a post-war Socialist Britain where a whole generation of young people
who had emerged from the restrictions of war wanted to enjoy their
heritage: country sports.

The huge impact of the war seemed likely to some to produce an English
countryside where foxhunting was no longer required, no longer relevant.
How wrong they were: the spread of incomes in the post-war years, the
greater mobility of people with surplus incomes, and the surge of enthusiasm for horse riding, all combined to ensure that foxhunting was to
achieve fresh heights of popularity in the second half of the century. There
would be waiting lists to become subscribers up to the 1990s.

Foxhunting had to make new adjustments to a changing environment, new methods of organizing itself. Some of these were to be painful. The new world of instant communication was to be used against foxhunting by the late twentieth century phenomenon of extremist Animal Rights fanatics. The Quorn was to experience the harsh realities of this opposition as well as basking in the popularity of new generations who would thrill to its challenge, even if the undiluted sea of grass was now but a memory.

Mrs Cantrell-Hubbersty and Mr Mee were joined in the Mastership in 1948 by Major the Honourable R.G. (Ronnie) Strutt, heir to the 3rd Baron Belper, a member of a Derbyshire family whose fortunes derived from the development of mechanical cloth making through an association with Richard Arkwright. The family seat is at Kingston on the Derbyshire borders of the Quorn where he lives in retirement.

Born in 1912, Major Strutt was a fine horseman who scored considerable success as an amateur rider over fences in the 1930s. He was injured during distinguished war service with the Coldstream Guards, and after the war was to make a considerable contribution to foxhunting in Leicestershire, being Joint Master of the Quorn from 1948-54, and then serving in the Belvoir Mastership from 1955-64. He returned as Acting Joint Master with the charming and hard working Mrs Ann Reid-Scott in the 1972-3 season when there was a need for a new arrangement at short notice. I much admired the lead he gave across country, and he exhibited a certain dry sense of humour. At a Belvoir meet in 1972 I was introduced to him when he was Field Master. On being told I had come from Dorset, he barked with a suspicion of a smile: 'Well, I should go back there! Hunting up here is just a racket! Just a racket!'

He soon proved during a rumbustious day with the Belvoir that the racket of leading a large mounted field over a grass country was one to which he was well accustomed, and still much enjoyed. He wore a top hat as Field Master at that time, and when asked why, he replied: 'Because I am now an acting Master.'

When he resigned from the Quorn Mastership in 1954, Sir Harold Nutting, as Chairman, immediately invited Lieutenant Colonel Tony Murray Smith to take over as sole Master. It was fortunate that he felt able to do so, as at the time he had duties as High Sheriff of Leicestershire and Colonel of the Leicestershire Yeomanry. Tony was essentially a Shires hunting man, born and bred to it, but he had much wider experiences of life and sport; he fitted that hackneyed description, one of nature's gentlemen, and had a natural charm and modesty. He spoke with just a very slight stutter at times, which in itself was disarming. It was always a pleasure to be in his company, and I relish the Hunt teas I spent with him after visiting the Fernie during his Mastership. Tony was by any reckoning a great Master of Foxhounds. He was essentially a Fernie man, and was to provide that Hunt with influential leadership for a significant part of the post-war period. At the Quorn he was invaluable in many ways, not least because he truly understood and appreciated hounds as well as horses. It is perfectly possible for Masterships to succeed without hound men, but it cannot but benefit a Hunt if there is at least a leavening of those who are genuinely knowledgeable and appreciative of hounds and their breeding, perhaps becoming knowledgeable judges, and certainly involving themselves effectively in the breeding of their own packs. Tony certainly made his own decisions about hound breeding. Born in 1913, he was the inheritor of the Gumley estate near Market Harborough in the Fernie country, but he lost his father in the First World War and was brought up in County Meath, Ireland, where he learned to ride and hunt in that wonderful country of grass and formidable open ditches. He had seen hounds work from close quarters throughout his formative years. Taking a commission in the Royal Horse Guards (the Blues) he kept his horses at Gumley as a young man and hunted with all the Shires packs. He was a consummate horseman and was often in the frame in point-to-points and military steeplechases. In Leicestershire he met Ulrica Thynne, who was to emerge as one of the most remarkable personalities in twentieth century foxhunting. She came to the Quorn country from her native Sussex for a month's hunting holiday early in the 1930s – and virtually never went home, setting up a hunting box with her friend Diana Fellowes in the Quorn country, and latterly staying with the Nutting family at Quenby. She is slim, elegant and has a delicious, dry sense of humour, and is a natural horsewoman, with beautiful hands and seat, and an unshakeable nerve. These qualities enabled her to ride across Leicestershire with style and verve until her very late seventies. One of my best strokes of fortune at *Horse and Hound* was Ulrica's acceptance of my invitation to write occasional articles on her reminiscences and observations on the Chase. These were distilled eventually into her warmly recommended book *Magic of the Quorn.* Tony and Ulrica married in 1936, and their shared passion for foxhunting was to benefit Leicestershire immensely. Ulrica followed her husband to the Middle East during his war service, and engaged in an adventurous wartime of her own, working for SOE in India.

After the war, the couple returned to Leicestershire and resumed their hunting. In the hunting field Tony gave a great lead across country, achieving authority over the mounted field with courtesy and affability. No bluster is needed by a Field Master who is truly respected by the followers. Constant journeys from Gumley were wearing, and Tony bought a house at Gaddesby, where Ulrica has lived ever since. In 1959, Ulrica joined her husband in the Quorn Mastership, but only one year later the marriage broke up. Tony returned to Gumley, and one year later he married Sally

Hanbury, former wife of the Master of the Belvoir, James Hanbury. She suffered a devastating accident, riding in a point-to-point, and Tony supported her with great care and solicitude until her sad death in 1976. It is good to record that he and Ulrica remained the best of friends up to his death in 1991.

In 1960 it would have been difficult to forecast that Ulrica would remain in the Quorn Mastership to achieve the second longest term to that of the great Meynell. Ulrica has proved, as much as any successful MFH I have ever met, that successful Mastership is a triumph of personality. Crashing falls, disappointments and misunderstandings, must all be endured stoically if the Master is to remain a respected and much liked personality in the local community. The late Dorian Williams, the great Master of the Whaddon Chase, remarked that fortitude is more important than courage, although both are necessary, and courtesy and respect for other people are absolutely essential.

Ulrica was an excellent Field Master in the Quorn Saturday and Tuesday countries; she particularly likes the the latter country, with its walls, woodlands and well foxed coverts. There are sometimes formidable obstacles to be jumped in both countries. Madam, as Ulrica was always addressed in the hunting field, was a hard act to follow in every way. Her former skills as a showjumping rider were apparent when she would deftly wheel her horse off a lane, and with beautiful balance, present her mount on the right stride to a particularly awkward obstacle, leaving some members of the field struggling repeatedly to get their horses over the same fence.

She set the fashion for lady Masters wearing gold buttons with black coats. 'I had no wish to wear a scarlet coat, as I had a terrible feeling that might look like the "Tally Ho Band" ' she remarked. Madam put in two days a week on Tuesdays and Saturdays as Field Master, and rode at or near the front of the Monday and Friday fields for most of her long Mastership. She liked large horses because it lessened the chance of other horses knocking them over, and she rode many of them in large gag bits on one rein in latter years.

I seldom saw her take a fall in the hunting field, although I saw her bucked off once at a meet at Old Dalby. It was clearly a very painful fall, but she bore it with the stoicism of one who can recall lightly that she has broken 'quite a few' bones in the hunting field 'and came to know the pay-bed wing at Nottingham General Hospital rather too well, at one time.'

Ulrica instructed me that when lying stricken in the hunting field one should croak: 'Take me to the Nottingham pay-beds.'

When I shattered my leg on a cubhunting morning with the Belvoir, I duly beseeched to be taken to Nottingham only to find that the pay-beds were no more, but I cannot speak highly enough of the devoted care I received in the Queen's Medical Hospital, Nottingham, under the NHS.

Ulrica speaks warmly of some of the changes since the pre-war years:

'There is no doubt at all that Masters were far fiercer before the war than they are the present time; subscribers held them in great awe, which I do not find to be the case now!

'Hunting was far more regimented and I think there is a happier, more relaxed atmosphere today. Pre-war everyone had to be at the meet on time, properly turned out.'

She agrees that for those who only hunt to ride and to jump fences, the hunting field was undoubtedly better pre-1939 when it was all grass, and not a strand of wire.

'If you love to watch hounds,' says Ulrica, 'they hunt just the same today as in our grandfather's time (I suspect better) and they certainly have more difficulties with which to contend. I would not decry the famous names of the past, but both huntsmen and Field Masters have a far trickier job to perform today, and I would say that it is much more of a challenge to cross country.'

George Barker was succeeded as huntsman in 1959 by his first whipper-in since the war, Jack Littleworth. He was a superb whipper-in, one of the best the Quorn has seen, and although adequate as huntsman he appeared to prove the adage that exceptional whippers-in do not always achieve the heights as huntsmen; there are plenty of exceptions to this. He was a top-class horseman, and good with hounds, but his health was poor; he suffered from an ulcer and sadly had to retire in 1967 with a tumour on the brain. He was born at the Warwickshire kennels where his father Alfred was first whipper-in. Before coming to the Quorn as second whipper-in in 1935, Jack was with the Grove and Rufford for four seasons. After war service in the Leicestershire Yeomanry, he returned to the Quorn in 1947.

Ulrica Murray Smith was joined in the Mastership in 1960 by Colonel Tim Llewellyn-Palmer; he was popular with the farmers and remained in office for two seasons until he married and returned to Wiltshire. The third Joint Master was the late Eric Crosfield who lived at Ashby Pastures with his wife Joan, one of the most ardent supporters of the Quorn, and easily one of the most popular hunting people resident in the country. Joan Crosfield only gave up riding to hounds recently, but follows regularly by car and welcomes hounds to her splendid Cream Gorse covert on her farm near Gaddesby where the grass and fences are always a treat. Her daughter Susan, has made a great success of her Mastership of the Meynell and South Staffs.

In 1962 Brigadier 'Dolly' Tilney replaced Tim Llewellyn-Palmer in the Mastership. The toll which riding across Leicestershire can exact was emphasized in February 1965 when the Brigadier suffered a horrendous fall, receiving severe head injuries from which he never properly recovered. His daughter, the delightful Lady 'Annie' Elton hunted with the Quorn for many years.

Ulrica Murray Smith was then joined by another new Master, Captain David Keith, a devoted hunting man and a landowner in Norfolk. He was a complete foxhunter, taking interest in hounds as well as horses, and judged at many puppy shows and at Peterborough Royal Hound Show. He was an excellent Field Master, courteous but firm, and I was one of many who enjoyed happy days following his lead across the country which was still far more pastoral than today. He told me in 1967:

There has been some increase of plough in the Quorn country in recent years, but it is still mainly grass. We have been more fortunate than some neighbouring Hunts so far, but there is no doubt that a further substantial increase in plough would change the character of Leicestershire hunting considerably.

At present the country is largely unchanged with most of the famous coverts still in existence. Perhaps the biggest problem is road traffic. We get a large number of cars following a hunt which is bound to increase the possibility of a fox being headed, and also causes many hold-ups to through traffic on the roads, for the which the Hunt may be blamed.

However, I would be the last person to discourage car followers. Their numbers reflect the great interest in foxhunting still evident throughout Leicestershire. For example, when we met in Loughborough a crowd of about 15,000 attended the meet.

It is important to note that all Masters and the huntsman and his staff after about 1970 have had to contend with just the changes which Captain Keith envisaged would change the country substantially. The task of keeping the country rideable, and capable of producing consistent sport in Shires style, when vast new acreages of plough have appeared, roads have become busier, and villages more built up, has been of increasing severity in the past twenty years. It is easy for mere subscribers to overlook these problems which appear gradually season by season. We owe an enormous amount to the Masterships, Hunt staffs, and all other officials and helpers who have made foxhunting possible within the huge changes wrought in farming and building development.

Key figures in any Hunt, who have had insufficient place in this outline history of the Quorn, are Hunt Chairmen and Secretaries. Jonathan Inglesant was a great success as Hunt Secretary for eighteen years until his retirement in 1976. Always courteous, meticulous in knowing the country and all who lived and hunted there, Jonathan was the ideal Secretary. He is a true foxhunter, and since he gave up Hunt officialdom he has continued to follow the Quorn, and the Cottesmore on foot in which country he resides. Jonathan sees far more of the day's sport than most of us on horseback and thoroughly enjoys and understands hound work. Latterly he has been working hard for the establishment of a national hunting museum at Melton Mowbray, acting as secretary to the trustees and management committee.

When Jack Littleworth's health broke down, Ulrica and David had to make a swift decision in appointing a new huntsman.

'There was never any doubt in our minds,' Ulrica recalls.

'If we looked for a new huntsman we should try to find someone exactly like Michael Farrin – he crossed the country with consummate ease, was a very fine horseman, and certainly had a flair for hunting the fox. His only possible disadvantage was his youth; he was just twenty-five, but time would undoubtedly alter this!'

The appointment has proved to be one of the most successful in the history of the Quorn. A farmer's son from the Atherstone country, Michael was a Pony Club member and hunted whenever the opportunity arose. He has always been a natural horseman, but after leaving school a brief experience in a racing yard was not to his liking. In November 1958 he became second horseman to Captain Brian Parry, Master of the Atherstone. Here he worked in the stables and kennels for one season, but the next season Brian Parry was out of the Mastership and was laid up for much of the time. Michael, aged sixteen, hunted three top-class hunters, with the Fernie, the Cottesmore and the Belvoir. He came to the conclusion that hunting was the greatest fun!

Next season Brian Parry took the North Cotswold Mastership and put Michael on as whipper-in. He hunted three days a week, and worked in kennel with the kennel huntsman, Jim Roberts, who did not ride. It was an intensive education for a future huntsman.

When Steve Andrews was appointed to replace Jim Roberts at the North Cotswold, Michael feared he would be demoted to second whipper-in because Steve was certainly a riding kennel huntsman. He expressed the wish to go elsewhere as first whipper-in to a professional, and his first thought was a move to the Warwickshire, but that vacancy was already filled. The Quorn had a vacancy, and after an interview on a Thursday, it was confirmed next day that he had the job. He was appointed first whipper-in to Jack Littleworth in 1963. Michael had to hunt hounds for a short spell in the first season, and carried the horn in the 1967 season because Jack was ill and did not hunt after just one cubhunting fixture. However, the 1967–8 season was cut short because of the national foot and mouth disease epidemic in cattle which involved stoppages on animal movements, Hunts voluntarily halting their fixtures in the interests of farming.

Fortunately, Michael's potential as a huntsman had been adequately demonstrated. Sixteen months after his appointment as huntsman he married, and has two sons Stephen and Andrew; his second marriage to Di has been eminently successful.

The 1992–3 season was Michael's twenty-fifth as huntsman of the Quorn; his fiftieth birthday was in February 1993. During that quarter of a century many photographs of the Quorn huntsman in action, by Jim Meads and others, have appeared on my desk. In every picture Michael is sitting his horse beautifully, his mount superbly balanced, and he is seen to be hunting hounds with decision and style.

The 1991–2 season, when the video furore erupted, was his worst test (Chapter Seven) but he emerged from this appalling experience with dignity, and his reputation intact in the hunting world as one of the most brilliant professional huntsmen ever to hunt hounds in Leicestershire. I have enjoyed so many superb days with Michael Farrin hunting the Quorn hounds that it is impossible to select the best. In the 1981–2 season fierce frosts and heavy snowfalls assailed Leicestershire in the first week in December, and this weather prevailed until the end of January. But what wonderful sport we all enjoyed thereafter: the snow and frosts had cleaned the land and left remarkably good scenting conditions for hounds, plus excellent going for the horses. There were many good days in the best February I can recall. Michael Farrin and the Quorn hounds were supremely successful in making the very best of the thaw. Here is an extract from my Foxford's Diary in *Horse and Hound*, published on 26 February 1982:

On Monday, 8 February, when we met at Old Dalby, hounds benefited from the serving scent which had persisted since the thaw arrived in January.

Riding Leicestershire is, of course, always a tremendous pleasure, but just watching Michael Farrin hunt hounds is a special joy in itself.

The combination of the two on a good scenting day, in a historic piece of hunting country where the farmers and landowners are so splendidly co-operative, is something to savour and appreciate ever afterwards.

After a convivial meet at Old Dalby Hall, hounds were soon speaking enthusiastically in Old Dalby Wood. This is an ancient woodland which used to cover a very large area of the Quorn country over two hundred years ago; it is much reduced, but has an excellent bottom to it, which is so essential if foxes are to dwell in any covert.

A good strong fox went away, and then the field was soon enjoying a flier over the grass towards Green Hill, then left-handed down the hill towards Nether Broughton, running over Mr Robin Lovett's land. There was special amusement in jumping the steep-sided brook below the village.

Hounds ran on to the back of Upper Broughton, then came back down the hill, and one suspects that foiled ground eventually ended this hunt.

It was a longish hack back to Grimston Top, hounds drawing Bridget's Gorse without success on this occasion. This cover used to be known locally as Dalby Rough Field, but was made into a proper covert by Mr J.C. Phillips, who christened it after his niece, Miss Bridget Drake.

There was a great crash of hound music soon after the pack began to draw Grimston Gose; a fox went away down the line of the Saxelby Brook where there is an enticing stretch of grass and fences.

They ran on just short of Asfordby, made a couple of loops down the valley and back to the covert, before hunting their fox across the Six Hills road where he braved a line of cars.

Hounds hunted nicely across superb old turf, finally catching their fox in the open by that famous covert, Shoby Scholes, and almost at the feet of the Chairman of the MFHA, Captain Ronnie Wallace, who had binoculars trained on hounds all day.

It was a delightful ride across the hilltop at Shoby Scholes, which affords such wonderful views of High Leicestershire.

Those who made the hack to Walton Thorns for the last draw were well rewarded. The air was still; the evening sun a golden ball; and the trees and hedges were black against the pale green of the turf. A time to tighten your girth and perhaps shorten your leathers.

At twenty minutes past four hounds spoke enthusiastically and Tony Wright lifted our hearts with a stirring holloa from the bottom end of the Thorns.

Joint Master Mr James Teacher, Field Master on this day, led us over the superb grass and fences on Mr Evan's farm. There was a short check when the old customer took temporary refuge under a hen house, but ran on very strongly to the farms of the Knight family to whom we are indeed indebted for a wonderful ride over their challenging fences and broad ditches. On one downward swoop over a drop fence I swear that there was time to check my watch carefully before landing!

Hounds came back left-handed, and then ran right-handed and up over the Barrow-on-Soar road, going on towards Seagrave. In fast gathering dusk, hounds were hunting on Mrs Gibson's farm, short of Seagrave village, when it was wisely decided to blow for home.

Tired horses and happy riders hacked back after a memorable run of more than fifty minutes over some of the best country you could wish to ride.

There is a special magic about really good evening hunts, with a reduced field and the shadows lengthening. I hope I never forget this one.

David Keith was succeeded as Joint Master in 1973 by Captain Fred Barker from the VWH country in Wiltshire. His first Mastership, lasting thirteen years, provided a firm hand guiding the Hunt during the changes which his predecessor had feared were on the way, notably more arable development and even busier roads. His second Mastership was undertaken as an immediate and selfless response to the greatest crisis in the Hunt's long history. I will describe this in more detail but I can state that at the time of writing, at the start of the 1992–3 season, the Quorn's debt to Fred Barker is immense for shouldering onerous responsibilities in the most difficult of circumstances, and seeing them through. Cometh the hour; cometh the man. Having hunted with the Quorn throughout Fred Barker's first Mastership I can testify that his tendency to occasional volatility is so much froth on the surface of a personality given to firm commitment and consistency.

'Go home' is an injunction he has used, but very sparingly indeed during such a period of riding in front of the Quorn field. He looks like a Master of foxhounds; he sounds like a Master of foxhounds; he *is* manifestly the holder of that office. These attributes have certainly ensured his credibility at times of stress not only with Hunt followers, but with farmers, landowners and the general public. It was to stand him in good stead when the television cameras attended Quorn meets as if they were political press conferences.

A considerable landower in Wiltshire, Fred was born into a way of life where foxhunting was a natural part of the order of things. His late father, Major E.P. 'Gar' Barker, a considerable disciplinarian at times, and his mother, were both Joint Masters of the VWH in the early post-war years. Fred's aunt, Miss Effie Barker, is a widely popular figure in the hunting and equestrian world, and was a most successful Master of the Garth and South Berks. When he took the Quorn Mastership, Fred was married to the former Venetia Quarry, step-daughter of Lord Mancroft. Venetia, in impeccable habit, rode side-saddle at the head of the Quorn field, a figure of considerable elegance and popular with everyone in the country.

'I must say I find it extremely difficult to ride the country as straight as one should', she confessed to me one day.

I replied that I admired any attempt at all to ride the country anywhere near straight. The most profound changes in the form of arable land, increases in barbed wire and electric fencing, and busier roads came in during Fred's Mastership. Any measurement of sport during the past twenty years must take account of these major deteriorations in the riding country, compared with the comparative heaven before that. The most important factor was to retain the confidence and co-operation of the vast majority of farmers and landowners, and Fred and his Joint Masters achieved this.

Fred's second wife, the beautiful former Penny Oppenheimer, is a polished horsewoman, and dedicated to foxhunting. She has made a particularly effective contribution in assisting Fred's second Mastership.

Fred's Mastership with Ulrica Murray Smith was assisted in 1975 when James Teacher joined, as Master in charge of the Friday country. He is one of the most amusing and congenial personalities you would wish to meet in any sporting sphere – but with an underlying seriousness of purpose. His qualities include exceptional powers of public speaking, especially after dinner, and this made him a special asset at the Hunt functions which make up the calendar during and outside the hunting season. The farmers in each area of the Quorn have separate Hunt dinners, and there are dinners and dances for the supporters, Hunt cricket club and other groups. The Quorn has a lively and popular Farmers' Dinner Dance in addition, but it does not have a grand Hunt Ball, which may surprise the Fleet Street scribes who like to stress the Hunt's mythical exclusivity.

James's affability was a great help in the hunting field; no one was in any doubt that he hunted for fun. There were just a few occasions when his enthusiasm led him to gallop the Friday field between the huntsman and some of the hounds, but he established a particularly happy partnership with Michael Farrin and there was excellent sport on Fridays, with James giving a good lead. Hunting with him was always tremendous fun. He was helped in every way by his wife, Chloe, daughter of that remarkable politician, bullion broker and keen foxhunter, the late Sir Henry D'Avigdor-Goldsmid. James and Chloe bought Carlton Lodge, at Gaddesby, to alleviate driving regularly from their home in Kent. Everyone admires Chloe's courage and resolution in fighting back to full health and vigour after receiving a serious head injury in a fall while following the Quorn on a visit after James's Mastership had ceased in 1983.

The retirement in 1985 of Ulrica and Fred marked a considerable change in the Hunt's management. Still operating without a written constitution and rules there were some signs of strain in the appointment of the new Joint Masters, due mainly to some confusion as to whether individuals should apply or wait to be invited. The latter course prevailed, and a trio of Joint Masters were appointed who worked well, establishing a particularly happy atmosphere for the next six years: Jim Bealby in charge of the Monday country; Joss Hanbury in the Friday country; and Barry Hercock in the Saturday and Tuesday countries. They brought a variety of traditional landowning, farming and business backgrounds to the Mastership which served it well in coping with the challenges of the 1980s.

Born of yeoman farming stock in Lincolnshire, Jim Bealby farms successfully in the Belvoir country near Grantham. He is blessed with a supportive sporting family, in which two sons, Chris and Ashley, are well-known as amateur race riders over fences. Jim had the major advantage of experience as Joint Master of the South Notts with the genial Bill Strawson who is also a well-known member of the Quorn field. With unremitting support from his wife, Sue, Jim Bealby has earned a high reputation with the mounted fields in the Quorn Monday country, over five enjoyable seasons. He worked hard in keeping the family open and maintaining excellent relations with the farmers. He has a natural gift for working with other people.

Joss Hanbury broke a record by becoming simultaneously Joint Master of both the neighbouring Cottesmore and the Quorn, having taken the Cottesmore Mastership since 1981 when Brian Fanshawe took over as Joint Master and amateur huntsman. His family is steeped in the history of the Shires, in foxhunting and equestrianism. A tall, slim figure, he is a fine, natural horseman; one of those comparatively rare riders who can make green, unmade horses go well for him with deceptive ease. He likes horses for their own sake, not merely as conveyances, and takes the greatest interest in breeding, buying and making youngsters for cross-country work, latterly looking as far afield as Poland for new recruits to his stable. Joss inherited Burley-on-the-Hill, the remarkable seventeenth century hilltop manor house, above Oakham, with its fine colonnaded court yard, large enough to accommodate the main ring of the annual Rutland Show. He sold the house to the Cypriot financier Asil Nadir, and then bought it back at considerable profit when Nadir's empire crashed.

It was during the same year, 1991, that the Quorn video row erupted, resulting in the expulsion from the Masters of Foxhounds Association of Joss and his Joint Masters, and their resignation from the Mastership. His father, the late James Hanbury, was a highly popular Joint Master of the Belvoir (Chapter Twelve), and his mother was a gifted horsewoman who secondly married Tony Murray Smith when he was Master of the Fernie. Possessing a quiet self-deprecating sense of humour, and exhibiting great dash in the hunting field under a calm exterior, Joss had already achieved much popularity among the Cottesmore mounted field, especially in their best Tuesday country. Those of us fortunate to have followed his lead across country, and enjoyed his company in the hunting field, owe him a special debt. His grace under pressure later in his hunting career is a quality I particularly admire. His laid back attitude to the ups and downs of life was well illustrated when he was asked for a comment on his highly successful deal in buying back Burley-on-the-Hill for a reported two million pounds, having sold it to Nadir originally for seven million pounds.

Joss's comment was simply; 'Well, I'm glad something has gone right this year.'

Barry Hercock, a successful Leicestershire businessman in the solid fuels industry, brought considerable enthusiasm and experience in organization to the Mastership. He likes all aspects of foxhunting, not merely the ride, and is inclined to go down to Exmoor at the end of the Quorn season to see Captain Ronnie Wallace's hounds performing great feats of venery in their moorland country where jumping is not the name of the game. Barry's wife, Barbara, has been a stalwart Quorn supporter, contributing much as District Commissioner of the Pony Club.

The 1990–1 season's end was a turning point in Quorn history. There had been notable retirements, those of Jim Bealby and in the preceding season, the late Major Charles Humfrey, who gave up after fifteen years as Hunt Secretary. Charlie, he of the Desert Rat moustache, and his wife Ginny, contributed much. Alas he died after a short illness in April 1993. In Leicestershire the Secretary's role is full time, and as life becomes more complicated it has involved spending increasing time in liaising with farmers and landowners, plus the essential task of collecting subscriptions and caps and ensuring that subscribers are happy. A lifelong horseman, Charlie's passion other than foxhunting was polo, and he performed great services at Rutland Polo Club. He was a descendant of Parson Dove, the nineteenth century hunting parson referred to at length in Whyte-Melville's *Market Harborough*. After his retirement as Hunt Secretary, Charlie continued to hunt regularly in the Quorn mounted field with his wife Ginny. Early in the 1991–2 season, they each suffered a nasty fall in the Friday country while tackling the same fence at different places during a snow storm. They battled their way to full recovery and were out again on horseback later in the season. A special end of season bye-day was held in March 1991, with caps going to a testimonial presentation for Charlie's retirement. The meet was at Barry and Barbara Hercock's new home in the Friday country, and the new Hunt Secretary, Michael Hemphrey, sported a flowing false moustache in tribute to his predecessor.

Although the sun beamed relentlessly, the old turf in the Friday country was riding superbly. One of the benisons of Leicestershire, exceptionally well-drained pasture land, enabled us to enjoy the sort of sport impossible in many grass countries elsewhere at that time of the year when horses' hoofmarks are not always so welcome, especially in grazing vales.

We had most of the Friday country available, and hunted it from north to south, starting at Botany Bay, crossing the beautiful Quenby and

Lowesby estates, taking in the Thorpe Satchville pastures, with Michael blowing for home at Thorpe Trussels at about half-past five on a sunny springtime evening.

Joss Hanbury was relinquishing his Cottesmore Mastership after ten years, and was to devote himself solely to the Quorn. He had purchased a strategically vital grass farm at Thorpe Satchville and generously vastly improved the fencing for the benefit of the Hunt. Following the much regretted retirement of Jim Bealby, he and Barry Hercock were to be joined in the Mastership in the following season by two keen foxhunters born into a background of the Chase and the Turf; Diana Turner and Alastair Macdonald-Buchanan. Di Turner's parents, the late Victor and Bunny McCalmont, established one of the finest centres for foxhunting in the world at their home at Mount Juliet in Kilkenny. Major Victor McCalmont who died suddenly in March 1933, aged seventy-three, was Master of the Kilkenny since 1949; he hunted hounds for forty years with immense success, not only being a remarkable horseman, but a gifted breeder and handler of hounds. His beautiful Kilkenny hounds carry off championships regularly at Ireland's major annual hound show, and they have won honours at Peterborough when brought over to show in England. Victor succeeded the long Mastership of his father, Dermot, in the Kilkenny. For a decade up to 1975 Victor was also Master and huntsman of the Wexford, giving a great lead over those daunting narrow stone-faced banks. Those of us who have stayed at Mount Juliet as guests of Victor and Bunny, and who have enjoyed superb sport with their hounds, would include it among the greatest fun in our foxhunting experience.

Alastair Macdonald-Buchanan's family are staunch Pytchley foxhunters, and have an extensive estate in that country, at Cottesbrook which Alastair manages; his grandfather was a famous Joint Master; Alastair himself was brought up in the Heythrop country and learned his foxhunting during Ronnie Wallace's great Mastership.

There seemed much to celebrate in the Quorn country that summer. Best of all was the successful completion of the new Hunt kennels, worth at least one million pounds, and demonstrably the most modern and lavish new layout of kennels and stables in the United Kingdom.

The real strength of the Quorn's support from successful business folk as well as traditional landowning and farming was apparent in the success with which the Hunt negotiated a marvellous deal in moving its headquarters. Buildings at the kennels at Pawdy Crossroads were still in excellent order, having been built only in 1905 – as recorded earlier – but the road past the site was becoming alarmingly dangerous for the exercise of horses and hounds. Heavy lorries were constantly passing the kennels. The Hunt negotiated with a property developer and builder to hand over the site and buildings in exchange for a new development in a less developed area. The Committee chose a green field site at Kirby Bellars, south-west of Melton Mowbray.

The planning authority, to its credit, gave permission, and a magnificent new kennels complex was completed on the site, well back from the road. It comprises spacious, well designed buildings for hounds and horses, with plenty of modern labour saving features. The kennels have four lodges, with yards designed for twenty couples in each; the stables are in a modern barn, with twenty-one boxes and plenty of support facilities. Excellent, separate houses for the huntsman and the stud groom, and a row of adjoining houses for other staff. The development is set in sixty acres; it should last the Hunt for another century at least, and it is a handsome group of buildings, blending into its pleasant, grassy setting. Cedric Ford gave planning advice; Ian Phillips, the Hunt Treasurer, organized the financing; David Wilson gave technical help and advice; and the architect was Messrs William Saunders. The special booklet produced to herald the opening of the new kennels pays special tribute to Geoff Brooks, of Manor Farm, Widmerpool: 'Without his foresight and perseverence these kennels would probably not have been started or finished. With a project such as this, many people had a view, often a lengthy one, on how, why and when it would be done, but everyone will agree that when the going got tough and the job really needed sorting out, it was Geoff who was telephoned day and night and through his total dedication, enthusiasm and hard work – the kennels were built.'

Celebrations for the opening included a summer Ball in a huge marquee in the new kennel grounds, followed by a charity luncheon next day, largely organized by Mrs Jim Bealby.

It had been a good summer. The new Mastership was full of confidence. Even the hot, dry conditions for cubhunting did not dampen enthusiasm. The Quorn had every reason to look forward to a great future.

No one suspected that the increasing presence at the covertsides of a slim, fair haired man, bespectacled, and apparently self-effacing was to produce a grievous blow against the Quorn – and against foxhunting throughout the United Kingdom.

There was really only distinguishing feature about the newcomer among the regular footfollowers; he always carried a video camera.

7

Trust Betrayed

I just tagged along

The video scandal which rocked the Quorn and foxhunting everywhere during the 1991–2 season was part of an orchestrated propaganda campaign designed to achieve the abolition of the sport. In this it failed, but it did succeed in dragging hunting on to the political agenda for a short time.

The new Labour government in 1945 had not been obsessed with divisive issues such as a ban of foxhunting; it had many more priorities in endeavouring to cope with national rebuilding, and a host of international crises. However, there were individuals determined to exert the force of their prejudices against hunting in the new Socialist post-war climate.

Yet one of the best defences of hunting was to be expressed in the House of Commons by the then Labour Minister of Agriculture, Mr Tom Williams, when a Private Member's Bill to abolish hunting was soundly defeated in the Commons in 1949. Labour as a party did not espouse the anti-hunting cause until 1983 when Michael Foot included it in his manifesto for a General Election in which his party was heavily defeated. Neil Kinnock was to continue tilting at the windmill of anti-hunting in both General Elections he lost. The Liberal Democrats became the second party openly opposed to hunting when they voted to make abolition party policy at their annual conference in 1992.

Hunting was not, of course, an influential issue in any General Election, but Labour party involvement in an issue previously considered to be one of private conscience was another strand of evidence in the accusation that politicians of the left wished to create a 'nanny state' in which people would be compelled to follow paths of 'political correctness' deemed suitable by their enlightened rulers. This is extremely unpalatable to the British electorate and produced one more element in Mr Kinnock's humiliating defeats at the ballot box. This clearly escaped the Liberal Democrat conference; the party may yet repent. The Conservative party has continued to adhere to the view that hunting is a matter for private conscience and not government intervention.

The majority of the British have consistently indicated that they want a pluralist, tolerant society. Foxhunting can exist and flourish in such a society, and if it is ever abolished by government decree it will be one more significant indication of the destruction of personal freedoms in the United Kingdom; it will certainly not be a step forward for wild animal welfare. This depends on the preservation of habitats, the management of a species according to the resources available, and such management should be carried out with a humane method of culling, observing a close season during the animal's breeding cycle. Foxhunting with hounds, according to the code of conduct of the Masters of Foxhounds Association, falls within all these criteria.

The Quorn and the other Leicestershire Hunts can justifiably claim to have invested more in habitats for wildlife in the county in the post-war years than any other single body, and these have been invaluable at a time of severe erosion in the fabric of the rural area.

In 1992 the anti-hunting lobby had secured the co-operation of a prominent Labour MP, Kevin McNamara, the shadow Northern Ireland Minister. Having drawn well in the ballot for Private Members' Bills he had agreed to frame a Bill which would effectively ban all forms of hunting with hounds in Britain. The chances of such a Bill becoming law were virtually nil whatever its fortunes on the floor of the House of Commons at second reading. A General Election was in the offing soon after, and Parliament would not have time to see such a Bill progress to the statute book. Yet the Labour Party was likely to repeat its commitment to include anti-hunting action in its General Election manifesto. A concerted campaign throughout the winter of 1991–2 followed by a Labour victory at the polls could be followed by government action to halt the hound sports at last.

That appeared to be the calculation of the hard core of anti-hunting activists. It is impossible to state which individuals led the anti-hunting campaign, but certainly the League Against Cruel Sports took most of the initiatives, backed at varying times by the more militant part of the RSPCA executive, and a wealthy body which, at that time, had a low profile in Britain; the International Fund for Animal Welfare which was to spend huge sums on an anti-hunting poster and cinema commercial campaign.

The anti-hunting scenario that winter was first to gain seats for hunting abolitionists on the Council of the National Trust, increasing the risk of the Trust forbidding the use of land for hunting; the targeting of the Quorn for a video 'exposé' of allegedly cruel practice; a subsequent barrage of press and television propaganda and advertising; the McNamara Bill's second reading on 14 February; followed by the injection of anti-hunting propaganda into the General Election campaign, up to polling day in April. Just to stiffen the battle, there were to be new attempts by Labour groups in some County Councils to attempt to ban foxhunting on Council owned land. Altogether, it amounted to the most serious assault ever on country sports, and the rural way of life enjoyed throughout Britain, headed by urban-based animal rights zealots.

The Quorn was clearly chosen as a target because of its high prominence and long held reputation as the most famous and prestigious of Hunts. Whenever referred to in the popular press the Hunt was described as 'Prince Charles's favourite Hunt'.

The anti-hunting lobby lost the battle in all spheres. Lessons were learned the hard way by the hunting world, and action was taken to remedy the problems with a speed and thoroughness which was extraordinary from a somewhat loosely knit, voluntarily supported group of sporting enthusiasts.

Yet much damage was done in the public relations field. Significant doubts were raised about the rules and disciplinary procedures of the Masters of Foxhounds Association, and the ability of that body and the British Field Sports Society to produce an adequate response in a major public relations crisis. Hunting emerged stronger from the battle, and better able to face new challenges. Foxhunting found that it had a remarkable gallery of eloquent friends; the articles in serious newspapers in favour of the sport were well written, hard hitting statements of faith from an extraordinarily wide range of journalists, politicians and other leading figures, ranging from Michael Heseltine, the Conservative cabinet member, to Bernard Levin, the highly independent writer in *The Times*, and John Mortimer, the Socialist-leaning playwright and barrister.

On 27 October, the *Mail on Sunday* published an 'exclusive' story that a spy or 'mole' representing the League Against Cruel Sports had been taking video pictures of recent cubhunting operations by the Quorn, who were, in one instance, allegedly breaking Masters of Foxhounds Association rules. The cameraman, it transpired, had been posing as a Hunt supporter and had earned the tacit trust of other supporters and some members of the Hunt staff. Copies of the video had simultaneously been widely circulated to television companies, newspapers, and were soon to be received by many MPs. Clips from the video were shown on the Sunday and many times on succeeding days on national and regional television. Reporters wanted instant answers and reactions from all concerned. A trial by television was under way.

The video film appeared to show one fox being shot in a hole while being held by the terrierman, and another being pulled from a hole and thrown into a hedge, then apparently running headlong into the pack of hounds which immediately killed it. The latter manoeuvre was described as a case of 'throwing the fox to the hounds', although anyone with long experience of foxhunting could see that this was not the intention; it appeared to be a botched attempt at bolting the fox. A voice-over commentary included what was alleged to be a recording of a telephone conversation between the 'mole' and Quorn huntsman Michael Farrin. It appeared that the huntsman believed the films were being taken for the benefit of the Hunt supporters' club by the enthusiastic new footfollower wielding the video camera.

Digging a fox and shooting it in the ground will never be a pretty operation; recorded in close-up, and shown on the nation's television sets it was unattractive enough, but especially when accompanied by an anti-hunting commentary which only put the case against the sport. Every time the subject was mentioned the television news and current affairs programmes showed just a brief clip of the dig as a reminder to the viewer. It was the most successful anti-hunting propaganda on a mass scale ever achieved.

Hunting needed loud and clear to put over the message that the fox does need to be controlled in the British countryside; that the alternative methods of shooting above ground, snaring, trapping, gassing and poisoning all involve far more chance of real and prolonged suffering by the fox. When a fox is caught by hounds in the open it is immediately killed; when it is dug and shot in the earth it is similarly destroyed immediately; if it is bolted from an earth by terriers it should be given plenty of law to escape into the country before hounds are put on the line again. The nub of the matter is that when a fox is hunted by a pack of hounds under MFHA rules it is either killed cleanly, or it escapes completely unscathed; the lingering agony of gunshot wounds which cannot always be successful when the fox is shot in the open, the desperate agony of a fox in a snare, and the inconclusive effects of poisoning and gassing are manifest to anyone with real experience of the fox's life and death in the British countryside.

Cubhunting is the time of the year when Hunts cull the fox population more heavily. It is unfortunate that traditional hunting terminology conjures up a picture of baby cubs being slaughtered. Born very early in the year, foxes are adult in size and capacity in the autumn, and it would take an expert to tell the difference between foxes born in the current year, and much older animals. The number killed by Hunts during cubhunting varies enormously according to the density of the local fox population, and the wishes of the landowners and farmers.

Ironically, the tradition in High Leicestershire has been for little or no terrier work. If a fox is marked to ground it is invariably left, and hounds are taken on to draw another covert quickly on Mondays and Fridays. The Quorn employs only a part-time terrierman, although this is a full-time job in many other Hunts. Changes in farming practice were providing sanctuaries in the new stacks of huge straw bales. Farmers were often keen to see foxes bolted from these bales by the Hunt, and some extra terrier work was involved. A spate of dry winters also meant that more foxes took refuge in drains where bolting was required. The video incident occurred in the Forest side of the country where the terrain is far less open, and foxes are more likely to be marked to ground in the many existing earths.

A major public relations problem immediately presented itself after the widespread broadcasting of the video. The Masters of Foxhounds Association swiftly announced that it would investigate the matter, and take disciplinary action if justified. Under its rules there had to be a period of at least fourteen days before the Committee sat in its disciplinary role; this was hardly an unreasonable wait before a disciplinary inquiry could be arranged, and compares very well with any other self-regulatory body, let alone official legal processes which can take months. However, the gap before the inquiry meant that the MFHA could not fulfil a role as spokesman for the sport in general at a time when it was vitally needed because the Quorn incident was now subjudice. This caused more than a little confusion because Masters of Foxhounds normally think of the MFHA as guide and friend when difficulties occur, but in this instance the Association now had to act as judge and jury.

What was badly needed in the Quorn country was the closest possible guidance and liaison with the ruling body if further public relations disasters were not to occur. Alas, the wait for MFHA disciplinary procedures meant the Hunt was virtually going it alone while the pressure from the media mounted. Spokesmen for the British Field Sports Society, the umbrella defence organization, were fielding some queries from press and television, but it was a response rather than an initiative. Peter Atkinson, head of public affairs at the BFSS, did his best in very difficult circumstances. No doubt the Society was constrained by its need to co-operate closely with the ruling body of foxhunting, which meant not appearing to prejudice or pre-judge an official inquiry. Some members of the sporting press, including this author, contributed numerous broadcasting interviews to put the case for foxhunting, but we could not speak as officials running the sport.

The MFHA Committee, chaired for twenty years by Captain Ronnie Wallace viewed the nine minute video film issued by the League. Afterwards the Committee announced that it took 'a very serious view of the contents' and required the Quorn Masters and Hunt staff concerned to attend an inquiry.

Meanwhile media coverage was fuelled by the Quorn's own independent actions immediately after the first showing of the video. These were made with the best of intentions, and undoubtedly they succeeded in confirming locally that the Hunt took the matter very seriously and meant business. However, each step taken by the Hunt provided a continuing thread of interest for the national media, keeping the story well to the fore, and increasing the public relations damage to the sport in general.

The MFHA had for at least two years been requesting Hunts throughout Britain to ensure that each one had a written set of rules and a constitution on lines modelled and approved by the ruling body. There was a body of opinion in the Quorn Committee that this was not a desirable step. The Hunt had run very successfully for over two hundred years with a Committee who simply invited new members when it felt appropriate, and with an annual meeting which rubber-stamped the decisions of the Committee rather than holding any meaningful form of inquiry into, let alone censure of, such decisions. New Masters were similarly 'invited' by the Committee, and such appointments were endorsed by the Hunt as a matter of course. Defining the 'Hunt' was somewhat difficult; was a subscriber a member? Was a landowner or farmer over whose land the Hunt operated a member? Certainly the Committee represented all such factions within the country, and in recent years the hard financial decisions were ably taken by an inner finance committee which exercised real power in ensuring that the Hunt was viable. This was essential for a sporting body which, in subscriptions alone, was bound to have a turnover measured in hundreds of thousands of pounds.

Was this well tried, benign system to be handed over to over-lordship by the MFHA? Operating according to MFHA rules of conduct was fine, but some in the Quorn Committee doubted the wisdom of all the new fangled ways which an MFHA constitution would involve: regular elections of Committee members when set terms of office were completed; a specific definition of Hunt membership; and general meetings which actually inspected the accounts in full, and had to give official endorsement to appointments and financial decisions. Without written rules, without a rigidly defined constitution, the Quorn set about dealing with the worst crisis in its history, and one which posed challenges of public relations which would have tested a thoroughly experienced London public relations expert.

Hounds met on Monday, 28 October to fulfil their fixture at Old Dalby. Reporters and cameras were in attendance. The country was buzzing with concerned telephone calls. It was a test of stoicism for the Huntsman and his staff in providing a day's sport as usual. The following evening the Quorn Hunt Committee held an emergency meeting, lasting over four hours. Lord Crawshaw, Chairman for over twenty years, and the four Joint Masters offered their resignation if the Committee felt it would help matters. Next morning Mr Rad Thomas, a devoted hunting farmer from the Forest side with wide experience in National Farmers' Union matters, issued a statement which made it plain that the Hunt was going it alone in taking full responsibility.

'The Committee examined the evidence and admits a degree of culpability to the allegations made,' declared the statement. It was promised that the Hunt would enact 'its own strict code of practice, the primary function of which will be the elimination of unnecessary suffering associated with any limited use of terriers digging.'

'This code of practice will be wide ranging, comprehensive and rigidly enforced. All employees of the Quorn Hunt will receive full instructions as to their future conduct.'

Although the statement declared that it did not wish to prejudice an MFHA enquiry, after the admission of some 'culpability', the result of the forthcoming MFHA procedures could hardly be in much doubt. The Quorn Committee then delivered a bombshell by announcing the suspension of the two senior Joint Masters, Joss Hanbury and Barry Hercock, and stated that it would consider the offer of resignation by the Chairman. On Friday, 1 November, the Committee met again, and thereafter announced that it had accepted the resignation of all four Joint Masters and the Hunt Chairman. This was a 'ministerial' resignation.

It had invited Captain Fred Barker to take over as sole Master forthwith, resuming his Mastership which he had filled for thirteen years up to 1985. He remained a member of the MFHA, having been in office as Master of his home pack, the VWH, in the interim. Mr David Samworth had been elected as the new Hunt Chairman, and was similarly of excellent standing with the MFHA, as a former Master (1976–85) and afterwards Chairman of the Cottesmore, and a much respected Quorn landowner. He is a highly successful businessman in the food industry, and is well experienced in re-modelling and increasing efficiency in any enterprise.

There had been huge disquiet expressed by some farmers and landowners after they had seen the video clips on television, but the Committee's drastic decisions were not universally welcomed and inevitably placed huge stresses on the intricate system of checks and balances, friendships and co-operations which make foxhunting possible on a major terrain of privately owned parcels of land varying widely size in and shape.

It is a testimony to the binding nature of the alliances built up in the Quorn country over two hundred and thirty-eight years that it stood the shocks and strains of the 1991–2 season. In the end loyalty to the Quorn hounds was the prevailing factor which carried the Hunt through its season of crisis. At the end of day it is a spirit of neighbourliness, of caring for one's friends best interests, which still shine through rural life – and should not be derided, nor eroded by modern 'values' based on quick judgements made by the mass media, and largely influenced by strident pressure groups such as the animal rights movement.

The actions of the Masters and Chairman in accepting the doctrine of accountability to the letter was noble, and well meant. Inevitably, however, it was interpreted widely, although mistakenly, as a total admission of 'guilt'.

The Daily Telegraph, whose Editor Max Hastings is a keen supporter of field sports, commented: 'The Quorn resignations are welcome, as a sign of responsibilities acknowledged. This sad episode will not have been wholly in vain if it teaches other foxhunters, shooters and fishers that in an age when they face intense public scrutiny, they must conduct their affairs properly – or face being unable to continue their sports at all.'

What, in fact, was the Quorn 'guilt' in breaching MFHA rules? The MFHA's crucial rule number one simply states: 'Foxhunting as a sport is the hunting of the fox in his wild and natural state with a pack of hounds. No pack of which the Master or representative is a member of this Association will be allowed to hunt a fox in any way that is inconsistent with this precept.' A rule also stated that, 'when a fox is run to ground, the Master must decide what is to be done. If the decision is that the fox be killed, it must be humanely destroyed before being given to the hounds.'

The outcome would depend on the MFHA Committee's interpretation of these rules which were anything but specific.

The effects of the video broadcasts were evident on all sides. The National Trust banned the Quorn from hunting on two hundred acres of land at Calke Abbey, Derbyshire, and on eighty acres at Ulverscroft, Charnwood Forest.

In the House of Commons the anti-hunting element flexed its muscles by tabling a motion calling for legislation to ban hunting with hounds, welcoming what it called the 'exposé of the widespread and flagrant abuses by members of the Quorn Fox Hounds of the Masters of Fox Hounds Association rules.'

On the plus side, the appearence of Fred Barker as sole Master had a positive reaction from the media. He appeared at a Monday meet at Roehoe, and gave effective television interviews in which he promised to ensure there would be no problems over fox digging or any other aspect of hunting in the Quorn country. He was perceived to be firmly in charge, and totally at home in a role to which he was well accustomed. It looked effortless; in fact, taking on such a Mastership suddenly is an immense undertaking. The former Masters backed him discreetly but effectively; all the horses they had purchased for the Hunt staff continued to be fully available, and they worked hard to ensure that the vital task of liaison with landowners and farmers was continued in all four areas of the country.

The annual meeting of the National Trust occurred in the teeth of the Quorn controversy, on 1 November. Baroness Mallalieu, the Labour peer, spoke eloquently on behalf of hunting, and after a lively debate, none of the seven anti-hunting activists seeking election to the Council was elected. The anti-hunting lobby suffered a further reverse when their motion to end proxy-voting by the Chairman was defeated.

On 14 November the MFHA held a Committee of inquiry, and heard evidence from the former Quorn Masters, the Chairman, and huntsman Michael Farrin. The verdict and penalties were the stiffest ever handed out by the Association in its one hundred and eight years. The Committee decided that the Masters had breached rules one and five. 'The Committee found that a fox had been handled in such a way that it should have been destroyed and not hunted further,' said the MFHA statement.

Rule one is that already quoted above. Rule five contained a provision that members of the MFHA had to bind themselves to abide by its rules and instructions. The two senior Joint Masters, Joss Hanbury and Barry Hercock, were expelled from the MFHA for four years before they could re-apply for membership; the two junior members, who had only been in office since 1 May that year, were expelled until the start of the next season, 1 May 1992.

Captain Wallace stated after the inquiry: 'The rules must be obeyed in letter and spirit. The Association has dealt firmly in the past with anyone who has breached the rules and will take action again if anyone breaks them.' In Leicestershire we were, and are, saddened by the severe ban on Joss Hanbury and Barry Hercock as Masters of Foxhounds. However, the areas of country where the incident took place were specifically in the charge of Barry, although he was not present on at least one of the days filmed, and Joss's Mastership responsibilities included specific authority over the Hunt staff and kennels. The MFHA has no direct sanctions against Hunt staff; their actions are deemed to be totally the responsibility of the Masters. Informing Hunt staffs fully of MFHA rules, and ensuring their adherence, is among the most important of Mastership responsibilities. The buck stops firmly at Mastership level.

The League Against Cruel Sports denied allegations that the video had been in any way edited to reduce the time between the pulling of the fox from the earth, and the moment when it was caught above ground by hounds. However, League spokesmen said at a press conference held in the House of Commons that they agreed that much of what was shown in the video was not against the specific rules of the MFHA. Their wish was to ban the entire practice of killing foxes in the course of sport, regardless of the rules imposed by the sport.

Hunting's answer to this argument is that the alternative to registered, authorized hunting under rules would be anarchy, and the fox would certainly suffer far more because unregulated control would continue.

Self-regulation by the ruling body has to work; has to be seen to work. The MFHA's exceptionally tough action was therefore predictable in these circumstances. History had repeated itself in one respect: the boundary row between the Quorn and the Fernie in the nineteenth century had a major impact on foxhunting's ruling body, the Committee of Boodles Club, proving to be one of the catalysts which produced the MFHA. This time, the Quorn affair resulted in the most profound changes in MFHA rules. With legal advice from Mr Timothy Preston QC, in 1992 the Committee made radical alterations to its rules, which were announced in September when Captain Wallace, retiring after a record twenty-one years as Chairman, had been succeeded by Mr Edmund Vestey, Joint Master of the Thurlow. Significantly, the new rule is far more specific on the subject of digging: '. . . when a hunted fox is run to ground in a natural earth, there shall be no digging other than for the purpose of humanely destroying the fox.' The rule further states that 'a fox which has been handled must be humanely destroyed immediately and under no circumstances hunted.' The rules also grasp the nettle in dealing with the subject of bolting. Hunts continue to be allowed to bolt a fresh fox, and may bolt a hunted fox which has taken refuge in any man-made structure, such as drains, stickheaps, straw bales and the like, and also in rocks and places in which digging is impossible. It is now stated that, 'the practice of bolting should only be undertaken when hounds have been taken away such a distance that they are out of sight of the place of refuge and are unable to hear any operations at the place of bolting'; a fox when bolted 'must be given a fair and sporting chance of escape before hounds are laid on.' The distinction between 'natural' and 'man-made' structures in bolting is necessary because digging is clearly impossible in the latter case, and the same applies to the exception of rocks in the case of natural earths.

The Association expanded its disciplinary rules: 'if the Committee has reason to believe that a member has acted or permitted the Hunt staff to act contrary to the rules on the conduct of the sport, or in any way prejudicial to the interest or good name of foxhunting, he may be suspended from membership forthwith for twenty-eight days, must provide a written explanation, or appear before the Committee, or both.'

This clearly prevents another Quorn case in which the Mastership's decision to resign pre-empts anything the MFHA Committee may wish to do. Under the new rules, suspension for up to three years, or expulsion, are the prescribed penalties for proven cases, and the name of the Hunt may be erased from the list of recognized packs. At the same time the MFHA issued a new 'Code of Good Hunting Practice' which was widely circulated to Hunts and hunting people throughout Britain. Among the most significant sections is that dealing with cubhunting in which Masters are urged to limit the involvement of volunteer footfollowers and members of the public in terrier work.

Who was the 'mole' who so easily gained the trust and friendship of the Quorn Hunt staff to take video pictures? He revealed himself in Court in August 1992, when the League Against Cruel Sports gained still more publicity from the affair by engaging in a private prosecution against the Quorn's part-time terrier man Alan Betts, and kennelman Christopher Doherty. Giving evidence against them was Michael Huskisson, who stated that he was the video cameraman who had operated on behalf of the League. Explaining how he had been accepted by the Hunt, he said merely: 'I just tagged along.' A totally dedicated anti-hunting activist, he admitted that in the past he had served prison sentences for his part in desecrating the grave of the great Lakeland huntsman Tom Peel, and for taking part in a raid on an animal laboratory in the Home Counties. Yet again Huskisson's video footage proved useful to the League. The court saw a ten minute film which showed Betts being handed a loaded pistol by Doherty, and Betts then shooting a fox in an earth. The court was told that Doherty had a licence for the gun, but Betts did not. Loughborough magistrates convicted them both for offences against the firearms regulations and fined them a total of two hundred and fifty pounds. They had pleaded not guilty, and Doherty claimed it had been their job to kill the fox as quickly and humanely as possible once it had gone to ground. The court heard that the Crown Prosecution Service had decided not to prosecute in this case, but the League had gone ahead with its own prosecution.

As the Masters of Foxhounds Association spokesman, Brian Toon, said to the press after the case: 'No stick is too small for the League to beat foxhunting.'

In March 1993 Leicester Crown Court allowed Christopher Doherty's appeal against conviction for breaching the Firearms Act by not keeping a pistol and ammunition secure, because he was summoned two months longer than the legal limit.

As I have indicated, the sudden departure of four Joint Masters and the immediate appointment of Fred Barker caused inevitable tensions within the Quorn country. Alas, these erupted into the press during January 1992 in a manner which caused considerable anxiety to those endeavouring to ensure that hunting's case would be well fought and won in the forthcoming McNamara abolitionist Bill debate, due on 14 February – the first time the issue had been the subject of a vote in the House of Commons for over forty years.

Despite the previous autumn's public relations disasters, there appeared to be some in Leicestershire who still did not understand that such a high profile Hunt as the Quorn could not hope to have any form of dispute in private. And there was clearly a dispute as to the composition of the Mastership in the next season, 1992–3. Hunts organize their affairs so that a new Mastership takes over on 1 May and therefore arrangements are made as early as possible in the previous season. Mysteriously, there was a major failure of communication or understanding, in that some members of the Committee clearly thought that Captain Barker had returned for one season only, and that was the end of it. After that they could go ahead and form a completely new Mastership. The Captain's expectations were entirely different, and he certainly deserved consideration after stepping into the breach at the Committee's invitation. As a member of the mounted field that season I can testify that Fred Barker, immediately on his appointment, imposed a much tougher rule as Field Master than had been imposed for some seasons. There was to be little galloping and jumping unless hounds were running; no one was to gallop past the Field Master, except in the most exceptional circumstances during a run; there was iron control when necessary to ensure that fences, crops and stock were given full respect during the Hunt's somewhat stately progress across country. And of course, terrier work was abandoned forthwith; there was to be no bolting from round bales, or any other underground sanctuary. Rightly, Captain Barker was taking no chances of the Quorn becoming involved in any more damaging 'incidents' in the hunting field. Safety first was an eminently sensible policy, but inevitably it sat uneasily with the heroosh of the Chase.

None of this would have mattered a scrap in a wet, cold season with plentiful scent. But the 1991–2 season was one of the worst on record in the Quorn country. Arid, dry days were afflicted with that desperate enemy of foxhunting, thick fog which makes hunting virtually impossible in the open when a large mounted field is to be entertained. On other days there was often an irritating blue haze which is usually accompanied by very poor scent. The drought rendered the ground bone hard and dusty for much of the first half of the season, and there was not enough moisture even in the new year to produce a serving scent. The high wolds of the

Quorn Monday and Friday country suffer particularly in such conditions. In contrast the Cottesmore was having a great season to the east, but its country undoubtedly rides heavier and carries more moisture, and its large coverts are a great boon in a dry season. We should also state that both the huntsman, Captain Brian Fanshawe, in his last season before retirement, and the hounds he had so carefully bred and nurtured for a decade in this kennel, were bang on top form. The Belvoir were suffering from the poor scenting conditions, but the deeper vale country undoubtedly carried better scent during a drought than did the higher ground in Leicestershire.

The Quorn huntsman and his staff had the additional burden of the demoralizing effect of the Hunt operating in a major media spotlight throughout the season. Much that was written and said was unfair, inaccurate, and intentionally hurtful. There were abusive telephone calls and letters, and threats of sabotage; all sparked by the video film television showings. It could hardly produce a congenial atmosphere, and a pack of hounds quickly responds to atmosphere. Captain Barker was to sum up the season at the next annual meeting as 'a stinker'. As a lifelong hunting man he knew the problems; he also knew there were no easy answers, no quick solutions. He soldiered on; without his presence, let alone his time and commitment, it would have been virtually impossible to maintain a full season, since the Master had to be a member of the MFHA.

Alas, behind the scenes the Hunt was drifting into a new crisis. A new package of Joint Masters was being prepared for the next season – and it did not include Fred Barker. The proposal was that the two junior Joint Masters, who would become eligible for re-entry to the MFHA on 1 May, be reappointed. Completing a quartet would be Mr John Blakeway, who had just achieved much success as Joint Master of the Belvoir (1983–91) and Mr Charles Geary, a Leicester businessman who was new to Mastership, but full of enthusiasm, and volunteered to look after the Forest side of the country. The Quorn Committee duly voted by an unannounced majority for this new package of Masters. There immediately erupted a major Hunt row which threatened to split the country, and which spilled into the national press in a deluge of publicity. This was desperately unwanted by the leaders of the newly formed national Campaign for Hunting, striving to present hunting's case in the House of Commons and in the media.

It has to be said that, as in all public muddles, every individual concerned believed he or she was acting for the best. Fred Barker was swiftly besieged by the press, and he spoke out. Those who criticized him for this, should bear in mind that he had borne the brunt of intense media interest throughout his Mastership of the Quorn, and he had established a public mood of confidence that the Quorn had sorted out its problems, and now no more would be heard. It would have been asking too much for him to remain silent at this time, and with hindsight it would not have been the best course, since tensions and dissatisfactions would have continued to rumble below the surface among those who backed him steadfastly in the country. He declared that he had 'clearly lost the confidence of the Hunt Chairman and the Committee' and complained that he was 'very distressed and disappointed.' He was contemplating immediate resignation. His critics muttered that he was behaving petulantly, having lost a democratic vote. The other side said this missed the point entirely. All the public relations gains made by appointing Fred Barker to take over would be lost. He was perceived by the public as the man who came in to 'clean up' the Hunt, whether in fact the situation in reality was as stark as that.

David Samworth in the hot seat as the new Hunt Chairman emphasized that he had tried hard to find a compromise satisfactory to all members of the Committee, but in the end he felt he had to resort to a vote. In effect the situation was finally resolved in the Quorn's true environment: the hunting field. At what could have been his last meet as Field Master, Captain Barker was warmly cheered by a mounted field of about one hundred and forty and over two hundred and fifty footfollowers; it was all recorded on television. At the meet at Kinoulton, Mr Geoff Brooks, of Widmerpool used a megaphone to propose a vote of thanks to Captain Barker. The Master was naturally somewhat overwhelmed by the spontaneous roar of support, and perhaps it was a good omen for the Quorn that when Michael Farrin took hounds to their first draw they went away with a great cry, and the field enjoyed a day of sport well above average for that season.

The Friday meet on 17 January was a disaster in sporting terms – thick fog caused the mounted field to wait for over an hour at Twyford before the fixture was abandoned – but it saw the end of the Great Hunt Row. There had been a great deal of behind the scenes peace making. Two people in particular had to resolve their differences: Captain Barker and Mrs Di Turner who was seen to be the prime mover in organizing the alternative Mastership package. They met in the horse box lines after hunting was abandoned and had a serious talk. That afternoon Mr David Wilson made available his manor house, Lowesby, and all parties concerned attended a meeting which finally resolved the future of the Mastership. John Blakeway, as one would always expect from him, adopted the most helpful attitude, immediately offering to stand down if it would help matters. He explained that he had only come into the Mastership to assist the Quorn, and was perfectly happy to withdraw.

The new Mastership announced was the compromise which the Hunt so badly needed to see everyone working together in the best interests of foxhunting: Captain Barker, Mrs Di Turner, Mr Alastair Macdonald-Buchanan, Mr Charles Geary and Mr Rad Thomas. Mr Thomas had played a great part in struggling to achieve solutions to the Quorn's troubles and in handling much of the pressure from the press and television.

One of the many lessons learned so painfully by the Quorn and by foxhunting in general, was that in the 1990s it is exceedingly difficult to have a dispute in private, behind closed doors, if you are running any sort of high-profile operation. The communications explosion at all levels, with the growth of local radio and television, and the ease of transmission of news, has made dramatic differences to the way a great many organizations conduct their affairs. For example, in the summer of 1992 the British public was amazed by the volume of publicity in all media directed at what would previously have been regarded as the private lives of members of the royal family.

The hunting world in general had been aghast at the publicity attending the Quorn row. Although the peace that had broken out was a spontaneous compromise, which has worked exceedingly well, the situation had spurred the Masters of Foxhounds to attempt to take another hand in resolving matters. Some thought that such a step should have been made much earlier.

It was claimed that signals from the MFHA had been less than clear previously, with the new Mastership package claiming to have received total approval from the ruling body in presenting their proposals to the Quorn Committee. However, on 16 January, the day before compromise was achieved, the MFHA issued a statement declaring that the Chairman of the Quorn Hunt had been informed that the Hunt must adopt an acceptable constitution by 1 May. Until this was achieved, the MFHA warned that it would not consider any proposals from the Hunt Committee for new Mastership proposals for the 1992-3 season. Captain Wallace declared: 'There is no question of any of the proposed new Joint Masters assuming office during the current season which ends on 30 April. If Captain Fred Barker, the present sole Acting Master, resigns before 30 April, he will have to be replaced by another acting Joint Master or Master acceptable to the Association. Rumours that any or all of the proposed four new Joint Masters might take office before 1 May are unfounded.'

The reference to 'acting' Master indicated that the MFHA was well aware that ultimate power in the Quorn country lay with the Committee, and especially its inner finance Committee, headed by the Honorary Treasurer Mr Ian Phillips, an astute businessman and life-long hunting man, who was known to have reservations about accepting the MFHA style constitution.

In Hunts throughout Britain full Masters are given a guaranteed sum by the Hunt Committee, and spend it as they will, but topping it up with their own contribution – although calls for extra cash are seldom open-ended nowadays; the Committee will agree to limits on such extra expenditure by the MFH. In the case of acting Masters the Committee retains full financial control throughout the season. Although being an acting Master can still be a highly expensive undertaking, especially if – as in the case of the Quorn – this requires the purchase of horses by the acting Masters. Their own hunting expenses inevitably escalate well above those of ordinary subscribers, and the Master's workload is enormous.

David Samworth agreed with the MFHA view. He asserted that one of the conditions under which he undertook the chairmanship was the Hunt would carry out the reform of producing a constitution. This he proceeded to do, and he deserves immense credit for much hard work behind the scenes in ensuring that this was achieved with considerable success. It enabled the MFHA to approve the new Mastership of five, and the 1992 Annual General Meeting of the Quorn was one of the best attended, and certainly more meaningful than such meetings had been for a long time. There was total endorsement for the new rules and constitution. It was clear that the new Mastership was already taking effect. The Quorn started the 1992–3 season in good heart. There was an excellent atmosphere at all levels, and hounds were working well. Huge efforts were being made to produce harmony and fine sport. It was one more indication as to just how much foxhunters valued hunting in Leicestershire, and the time and effort they were prepared to devote to it.

It had been clearly demonstrated that the Quorn could not act as if it was a backwoods, provincial club, indulging in private internal disputes with little regard to opinion outside. Because of its history, its achievements, and its geographical position, the Quorn is a famous British institution. Even those with the remotest interest in hunting know that Quorn spells foxhunting. The foxhunting world at large, where there is occasionally a somewhat envious doubt expressed about the values of Leicestershire hunting, was reminded that the health of hunting in the greatest of foxhunting Shires is vital to the well-being of the sport as a whole. David Samworth resigned as Chairman in 1993 due to the pressure of work, but the task of achieving a constitution had been completed.

Those who are stewards of foxhunting in Leicestershire have especially heavy responsibilities. On their performance the sport in general will be judged.

Hard on the heels of the resolution of the Quorn row came the attempt by Leicestershire County Council to ban foxhunting on 9000 acres of land owned by the authority. This was soundly defeated. The depth of local pride and loyalty to the Quorn hounds were revealed in a debate at Charnwood Borough Council. There was a small, determined anti-hunting group in the Council, and this had gained new impetus since the row over the fox-digging video. There was a ruling that Councillors who were members of the Quorn Hunt Supporters' Association should declare their interest and not be allowed to speak nor to vote on the issue. Yet anti-hunting councillors certainly spoke, and there was much dispute about this. On a twenty-two to twenty-one vote, victory went to the pro-hunting faction after the Mayor, Councillor Mrs Mavis Mason, cast the deciding single vote. 'I know I have made some enemies as well as friends, but hunting is still a legal pastime,' she said afterwards.

On 14 February the McNamara Wild Mammals (Protection) Bill was defeated by twelve votes in the House of Commons. In both the County Council and Westminster debates the Quorn case was raised. It did not consume much time in either forum, but clearly the resolution of the Hunt's difficulties beforehand was of crucial importance.

Sir Nicholas Bonsor, Chairman of the British Field Sports Society, who achieved the arduous task of winning the battle for hunting in the Commons, was specifically challenged on the Quorn fox-digging issue. He declared that he disassociated himself and the BFSS from the incident, and referred to the disciplinary action against the Masters. He agreed with another Member that the Leicestershire County Council vote indicated that the Council was satisfied with the conduct of foxhunting in that area.

Labour's defeat in the General Election on 9 April was the greatest setback of all to the anti-hunting lobby, since the Conservative Parliamentary Party firmly believes that the issue is one of private conscience and not a subject for government legislaton. Ominously, the Liberal Democrats' annual conference has since adopted an anti-hunting stance, and Labour shows no sign of abandoning its opposition to the sport.

The national battle to ensure that foxhunting survives and flourishes into the twenty-first century has been joined with greater effort and more expertise since the bruising experiences of the 1991–2 season. The Campaign for Hunting has been absorbed by the British Field Sports Society which has produced a new plan for a more effective response to those who would abolish all country sports.

What sort of countryside do the British want? The anti-hunting mole with the video camera was able to operate in the Quorn country because of a relaxed, friendly attitude towards anyone who appeared to be a hunting enthusiast. Inevitably, a more suspicious, security conscious attitude now prevails. Is this in the best interests of a worthwhile quality of life?

The video produced more visits to Leicestershire from Hunt saboteurs, sometimes violent, always threatening and abusive. Attendances of police at meets became more necessary. Country people felt their way of life was being attacked by zealots who delight in using every means available to extinguish not merely country sports, but a life-style.

Hateful elements of class envy appear in many of the attacks; all the more unpleasant because the foxhunting world is open to all who enjoy the sport, far less elitist than many British clubs and organizations with carefully vetted and controlled memberships.

Rightly, those who live and work in Leicestershire are given the premier opportunities to enjoy the country sports for which the county is so suitably endowed.

As described in more detail elsewhere (Chapter Two) the Quorn and the other Leicestershire packs play a huge role in genuine conservation. The county has a large, thriving fox population, and, as mentioned previously, the preservation of the hunting coverts helps to ensure the survival of a great many other forms of wildlife.

The 1991–2 season had many features which foxhunters deeply regret, but from it the Quorn – and the sport in general – has emerged stronger, and better equipped to face the challenges of the future.

The hunting people of Leicestershire demonstrated their love for their sport in 1982 and again in the following year when the Labour group in Leicestershire County Council twice tried to achieve a ban on foxhunting on some 10,000 acres of farmland owned by the Council. In 1982 Captain Brian Fanshawe headed an action committee which lobbied councillors, and held a highly successful public meeting in the Corn Exchange in Melton Mowbray. It was so crowded that an over-flow meeting was held in the car park, with a loudspeaker link from the main hall. James Teacher, then Joint Master of the Quorn, and Captain Ronnie Wallace were the main speakers. On the day the Council debated the matter, all the packs of hounds hunting in Leicestershire, including the foot packs, took their hounds to the grounds of County Hall to demonstrate, backed by hundreds of supporters. It earned huge publicity nationally and locally.

The Council was 'hung', with no overall majority for any party, but the Liberals had the balance of power. The vote proved to be a close run thing: the motion to ban hunting was defeated by just one vote.

Then, early in 1992 the Labour group sprung another surprise motion. Yet with only a week's notice, Leicestershire's hunting fraternity rallied immediately, and showed its strength. Lindsay Symington chaired an action group representing nine Hunts, which achieved intensive lobbying again, and a huge meeting of hunting folk was held in the Fernie country, addressed by Lord King and myself. Lord King said Labour were totally mistaken if they thought there were votes to be gained by an anti-hunting policy. In my own speech I said it was outrageous that Labour should risk damaging livelihods in the county at a time of recession. Seeking to wrench Leicestershire's great traditions from the rural community who still gave field sports immense support and derived recreation and incomes from hunting, was totally unjustifiable and would not be forgiven by the county's electorate. Alan Tacy, a county council tenant farmer in the Fernie country spoke in favour of the tenants' right to make their own decision as to who they welcomed on their land for legal forms of recreation, which included hunting. He praised the value of the Hunts' services in picking up fallen stock. Pledges of support for foxhunting came from Tony Dakin of Leicestershire Wildfowlers, on behalf of shooting interests; Alan Smith, representing 10,000 members of Leicestershire Anglers' Federation; and William Bevin on behalf of the hare hunting packs.

The Leicestershire huntsmen in uniform were among hundreds of hunting folk demonstrating with banners outside County Hall on the day of this debate. Mrs Janet Sturrock, aged seventy-six, a veteran Cottesmore hunting lady, carried a placard saying 'I want to hunt until I'm 100'.

Many of us crowded into the Council chamber for a debate notable for misinformed prejudice from the Labour side. One Labour councillor bawled: 'The real vermin are the men in red coats.'

'We are the landlords', yelled another Labour councillor during a patient expostion form the Liberal Democrat benches that it would be civilized to allow the Council's farm tenants to make their own decisions as to who they invited on their land. It was pointed out that one hundred and five out of one hundred and eight County Council farm tenants had signed a petition seeking that freedom of choice.

Labour did itself no service in dragging the issue into party politics. Hunting folk do not wish to be allied with any one political party. A man's politics are left at home when he enters the hunting field.

Alas, Labour voted en bloc on the issue. The Conservatives opposed the ban, except for one member who spoke with dignity against hunting. A Liberal Democrat amendment confirming the right of tenants to allow or stop foxhunting over land in their care was carried by forty-seven to thirty-four, thus defeating the motion to ban. All but one of the eleven Liberals voted for the amendment.

The Labour motion was carefully timed to occur shortly before the matter was debated in the House of Commons on 14 February. The Leicestershire victory for hunting was one more sign that country people wished to retain their traditional field sports. Alas, the Labour group in Leicestershire merely heightened a town versus country dispute, divisive and damaging to community morale, and not accurate since many in the towns regularly sally forth to the hunting field.

As Brian Toon, the MFHA's official spokesman, said on Radio Leicester: 'If there is so much opposition to hunting where were the antis outside County Hall? They just weren't there. The general public really does not care about this issue. The only people who cared enough to turn up and make their feelings known to Councillors were the hunting, shooting and fishing people.'

8

The Field

When the lady said she felt much better,
the Prince asked politely: 'Are you sure
there's nothing else I can do?' The Quorn
lady replied simply: 'Just kiss me.'

The vast gallery of personalities who have been drawn to Leicestershire to hunt includes the royal, the rich, the raffish and not a few imposters, but in the main the mounted fields are derived from a wide spectrum of British life; people who simply adore the thrill of riding after hounds in a paradise, or as near as they will ever find.

My selection of personalities mentioned here is inevitably subjective, and misses many worthy of a mention in a far more detailed history of each Shires pack. There is no justice in my selection; it should, however, indicate the delightful diversity of the Shire packs' hunting fields. None of these people have been Masters of Foxhounds in Leicestershire but each has contributed something to the legend of Shires hunting. The lure of grass and fences brought money, fame, and talent to the hitherto obscure market town of Melton Mowbray. Many soon discovered that much of fun in hunting with the adjoining Hunts was generated by the sparkling company you met at the covert side even before the first fox went away.

It is often alleged in popular journalism that foxhunting in general stimulates the sex life of its participants, and that nowhere is this more the case than in the Shires. In the commentary he wrote for his fascinating film on the Quorn, *Death in the Morning*, the great television reporter Alan Whicker used a quotation stating 'the night air over Melton Mowbray is alive with the sighs of adulterous love'. This was a reference to Melton Mowbray up to 1939 and it is highly likely that the high jinks of social life in the 1920s and '30s included a fair amount of sexual licence. Similarly, it is all sorts of improprieties that have been attributed to some of those who attended grand house parties in Victorian and Ewardian England.

Disentangling legend from fact is far less exciting in assessing the sex life of the hunting fraternity. Those who take part in risk sports, and are physically fit, tend to be among the bolder spirits when it comes to sexual adventures, but foxhunting is not exceptional compared with other sporting social sets. Its prominence in country life simply means that any improprieties are more starkly apparent. An affair within a tennis club, or a golf club, is less likely to be the talk of the county than in a prominent Hunt because foxhunting in reality is far less exclusive than many other club sports. The earth stopper and the farmer in the market place will have sources of information within the Hunt just as much as a local dowager who gives frequent dinner parties.

Like all other activities involving both sexes, Hunts may go through periodic spasms of notable marital upsets, but then peace sets in for many seasons.

There are many reasons why the hunting field is not an ideal place for a romantic liaison. In a good hunt you cannot guarantee to be near any individual rider, and you will be far too preoccupied with your own salvation to spare much time for anyone else's welfare. When my wife had a fall in the hunting field I seldom happened to be nearby to help her to re-mount. Even though I did my best to keep an eye on her, I just happened to be in the wrong place when she needed me. It was exactly the same when I had a fall. I can think of very few married couples who even tried to stay near each in the hunting field, and the same is true of engaged or romantically involved couples.

I was once riding back to the hunting field after a change of horses with Ulrica Murray Smith when she gestured to a riderless chestnut horse romping in the pastures ahead of us at Lowesby.

'Isn't that your wife's horse?' she enquired.

I hastened to the scene to find my wife lying on the ground, receiving a soothing libation from a gentleman's hunting flask. When she recovered she demanded that we exchanged horses, and never rode the chestnut in

the hunting field again. He was far too small for me, but I had some very good sport on him, despite a number of exciting falls.

I am always amused by the Victorian paintings of hunting couples riding home from the meet together. In reality, horses are usually most unhelpful in conducting an affair. Corned up, fit hunters are all too inclined to kick each other if they stand too close for any length of time, and riding very closely next to someone can involve a painful crack on your ankle from your beloved's heel armed with a metal spur.

Dismounting in the hunting field is something most hunting folk perform as little as possible, mainly because many of us find it exceedingly difficult to re-mount a horse made excitable by others passing it. In romantic fiction the rider casually loops the horse's reins over a gatepost before engaging in a clinch; in reality, the horse breaks the reins and gallops away madly to join the rest of the mounted field, so that romantic stops in picturesque hunting coverts are most inadvisable.

However, love does find a way, and it must be admitted that the modern horse box equipped with fitted kitchen and sleeping accommodation is a new factor in the hunting field, and elsewhere in the equestrian world. I was once invited in the dusk by a delightful lady to 'join me for a little hot soup and sherry' in one of these modern boudoirs on wheels, but before I could reply, my then wife loomed out of the mist to state tersely: 'No, he certainly can't. The horses are cold and he's got to get them home now!'

On the whole, ladies may nowadays allow their husbands to hunt in Leicestershire with little to fear, and vice versa. There is little time, nor opportunity, for anything but the demands of riding to hounds. A good day's hunting tends only to produce an appetite for a hearty meal, and

Tom Firr, the Quorn's great huntsman 872–99): from the painting by Basil ightingale of Firr riding Whitelegs. They said looked like a Bishop and rode like a jockey.

2.   Mr Hugo Meynell, Master and founder of the Quorn (1753–1800): from the painting by Joshua Reynolds. Meynell developed the science of hunting the fox at speed in open country.

Frank Gillard, huntsman of the Quorn 68–70) and of the Belvoir (1870–96): one of greatest of Leicestershire huntsmen who d the Belvoir pack to become the most ght after source of breeding lines in British hunting.

4.   Hugh Cecil Lowther, 5th Earl of Lonsdale, Master of the Quorn (1893–8) and of the Cottesmore (1907–11 and 1915–21): The 'Yellow Earl', a great horseman, a highly knowledgeable foxhunter with a tempestuous temperament, and a great spender.

5. George Barker: huntsman of the Quorn for thirty years (1929–59). The only Quorn huntsman born and bred in the country; he is buried at Thorpe Satchville. He was a tower of strength during the war years.

6. Michael Farrin, huntsman of the Quorn since 1967: promoted as a young man, Michael celebrated twenty-five years as huntsman, and his fiftieth birthday in 1993; a superlative horseman across Leicestershire country.

7. Celebrating its two-hundredth anniversary; the Quorn opening meet at Kirby Gate in November 1953, with George Barker as huntsman. The meet by the Melton Mowbray to Leicester road is traditionally followed by a first draw at Gartree Hill.

. Foxhunting in paradise: the Quorn hounds during a cubhunting morning in 1961. The wealth of well-drained old turf, the undulating terrain, and the well-sited coverts all make Leicestershire an ideal setting for foxhunting at its best.

. Action with the Quorn in 1986. Leading Flat race trainer Barry Hills is jumping a typical Leicestershire cut and laid fence, followed, right, by Nick Connors, son of the late Dr Tom Connors, and Mrs Connors, of Upper Broughton, in the Quorn Monday country.

10. Quorn hounds at an Ingarsby meet in 1989: in the nineteenth century the pack suffered set-backs through being sold when Masterships changed, until Tom Firr's superb twenty-seven years as huntsman, when the pack was retained and never sold again.

11. A highly successful Quorn Mastership: Captain Fred Barker, Mrs Ulrica Murray Smith and Mr James Teacher. Mrs Murray Smith achieved the second longest Mastership in the Hunt's history (1959–85). Captain Fred Barker, after a previous thirteen years in office, rejoined at short notice during the 1991–2 season when the Hunt was hit by the video film crisis.

2.   The fun of crossing the Quorn country: left is the late Dr Tom Connors who nurtured one of the nest stretches of the Quorn Monday country at Muxlow Hill. In front is Viscount Astor.

3.   Major Charles Humfrey, Quorn Hunt Secretary (1976–91) leads the way to the Mayor's eception in Loughborough after the traditional Boxing Day meet in the town in 1986. He is followed y Mr Malcolm Allured, a former member of the Showaddy-Waddy pop group, financier and amateur ace rider Mr Brod Munro-Wilson and former Joint Master, Mr Barry Hercock.

14. Mr Jim Bealby, Joint Master of the Quorn (1985–91) leads the field across country at an end-of-season meet in 1987. Formerly Joint Master of the South Notts, he took charge of the Quorn Monday country and was a highly popular Field Master.

15. Elegance in the hunting field: Lady Wimborne, formerly Mrs Fred Barker, was one of the few to continue riding Leicestershire side-saddle in the 1970s and '80s. She proved that it is a practical form of cross-country riding, retaining her place near the front of the mounted field.

16.   Mr Joss Hanbury: Joint Master of the Cottesmore (1981–90) and of the Quorn (1985–91). He is the only holder of two Leicestershire Masterships simultaneously; a brilliant cross-country rider, he was a popular Field Master in the Cottesmore and Quorn countries. Owner of Burley-on-the-Hill, he is the Squire of Oakham, and is the son of the Belvoir's former Master, the late Colonel James Hanbury.

The Prince of Wales in 1988 judged the Quorn puppy show and is seen with the Joint Master, Jim Bealby, Mrs Bealby and the wheelchair-bound Lord Crawshaw, Hunt Chairman, who resigned in 1990.

18.   Quorn farmers and landowners at a party with the Prince of Wales at Burley-on-the-Hill in 198
Prince Charles has regularly entertained parties of Leicestershire farmers at Highgrove as a gesture o
thanks for the huge pleasure he has derived from riding over their land.

.   The Duke of Rutland's hounds at his ancestral home, Belvoir Castle, after a meet in 1951 when
:orge Tongue was huntsman (1928–56). A great disciplinarian, he was highly effective in kennel
anagement and in hunting the pure-bred English hounds which traditionally form the Belvoir pack
this day.

).   Jim Webster, huntsman of the Belvoir (1956–83); born and bred in Hunt service, Jim was a
alwart huntsman who withstood the rigours of a long career with remarkable resilience, helped by
s dry sense of humour. He was devoted to the traditions of pure English hound breeding.

21. Lord (Toby) Daresbury, Master of the Belvoir (1939–47), son of a previous Belvoir Master, Sir Gilbert Greenall, who became the first Lord Daresbury. A superb horseman and a top-class amateur huntsman, Toby Daresbury moved to Ireland as Master of the County Limerick where he hunted Belvoir-bred hounds with great success. With him is Lady Daresbury, the former 'Boodley' Hilton-Green.

22. Lord King, Chairman of the Belvoir, and a previous Master (1958–72), pictured here in 1977. John King moved from Yorkshire, where he was a Master of the Badsworth, to his estate at Wartnaby, near Melton Mowbray, which crosses the borders of the Quorn and Belvoir countries. A devoted foxhunter, the former Chairman of British Airways has always been ready to speak out publicly for his sport.

23. Lieutenant Colonel James Hanbury, Joint Master of the Belvoir (1947–64), with Mrs Hanbury at a meet at Colston Bassett in 1951. Their son, Mr Joss Hanbury, was to be Joint Master of the Quorn and Cottesmore.

24. Lord Belper: Joint Master of the Quorn (1948–54) and the Belvoir twice (1955–64 and 1972–3). A resident in the Quorn country on his estate at Kingston, Lord Belper was bred and born to Shires hunting and was an excellent horseman, giving a great lead as Field Master in the Quorn and Belvoir countries.

25. Mr John Blakeway, Joint Master of the Belvoir (1983–91), was a successful steeplechase rider. native of the south-west Midlands, he is a natural horseman, and proved a superb Field Master over the Belvoir's grass and fences, making many friends in the country. He is a former Chairman of the British Show Jumping Association and is Honorary Director of the Horse of the Year Show.

26. Belvoir Joint Masters Mr Robert Henson (1978–88) and Mr Charles Harrison (1983–8), both Lincolnshire sportsmen. Their Masterships produced consistently good sport. Robert Henson, son the late Mr Gino Henson, who was a Master of the Blankney, was especially successful in providing fun for the mounted fields in the Vale of Belvoir.

27. The Hon. Mrs Ursula ('Urky') Newton, one of the great characters of the Shires: Honorary Secretary of the Melton Hunt Club, which was founded by her late husband, Lance Newton, in 1956 and has provided many foxhunters with their first experience of Shires hunting, as well as investing thousands of pounds in maintaining the Leicestershire hunting countries.

28. The Hon. Mrs 'Migs' Greenall, daughter-in-law of the late Lord Daresbury, and one of the few pre-war Shires foxhunters still riding to hounds. Her land, near Waltham-on-the-Wolds, is among the best riding country enjoyed by the Belvoir mounted fields.

29. Mr Joey Newton, son of the Hon.
Mrs Ursula and the late Mr Lance
Newton, and a grandson of Lord Rank.
A notable amateur race rider, Joey
Newton was appointed Joint Master of
the Belvoir in 1989. He farms
extensively in the Wednesday country,
and has known the Belvoir country and
its farming community all his life. He
has the support of his wife, Emma, a
keen foxhunter, nowadays
accompanied by their young daughter,
Chloe.

30. Robin Jackson, huntsman of the Belvoir (1983–92), a Scot who formerly hunted the Lanarksh
and Renfrewshire, and then the Grove and Rufford before he was appointed at Belvoir. He soon
proved capable of producing excellent sport on the Leicestershire and Lincolnshire sides of the
country, but gave up Hunt service completely in 1992.

. Arthur Thatcher, huntsman of the Cottesmore (1900–7) and of the Fernie (1907–23), one of the eatest Leicestershire Hunt servants. He was a most entertaining huntsman, being highly popular ith the mounted field, and despite the criticisms of the Yellow Earl, Thatcher was clearly an cellent horseman and a highly-skilled hound man.

. The Cottesmore field near Loddington, in 1960, led by Mr M.D. McAlpine, Joint Master, and ajor Tim Hellyer, Field Master. A large percentage of the Cottesmore following live in the country, uch of which lies in the old county of Rutland, now officially part of Leicestershire.

33. Major C. C. 'Chetty' Hilton-Green, Master and huntsman of the Cottesmore (1931–46). He was a brilliant amateur huntsman, producing superlative sport during the 1930s when the Cottesmore country was largely down to grass. He possessed that 'magic thread' which binds a pack to the wishes of their huntsman.

34. Lieutenant Colonel Sir Henry Tate, former Joint Master of the Cottesmore (1946–58), also served as Hunt Chairman, and nowadays as Hunt President.

35. Major Bob Hoare, Joint Master and huntsman of the Cottesmore (1958–69); famed for his genial approach to foxhunting, and a popular figure in the Cottesmore's long line of amateur huntsmen. He came from the West Norfolk country, and after giving up the Cottesmore, he hunted the South Notts. He was instrumental in raising the BFSS's Fighting Fund for the defence of hunting.

Captain Simon Clarke, Joint Master and huntsman of the Cottesmore (1969–76), a consummate amateur huntsman who came to Leicestershire from the South Dorset country. He first introduced Welsh blood into the Cottesmore pack and provided excellent sport.

The late General Sir Evelyn Fanshawe, talking to Lord Kimball, formerly Marcus Kimball MP, who is a previous Cottesmore Joint Master and amateur huntsman (1953–8). As Chairman of the British Field Sports Society (1964–81) Marcus Kimball was instrumental in saving hunting from abolition attempts in the House of Commons.

38. The Cottesmore mounted field during a day's hunting in the best of its grass country, near Knossington, in 1976. Although still worn, top hats have become far less common in Leicestershire since then. Many more men and women choose to wear modern, insulated headgear, with chin straps

39. Mrs Di Hellyer, Joint Master of the Cottesmore (1976–81) with Mr Edmund Vestey, a landowner in the Cottesmore country, Chairman of the Masters of Foxhounds Association since 1992 and Master and huntsman of the Thurlow. They are seen hunting on a snowy day in December 1987.

. Captain Brian Fanshawe, Joint Master and huntsman of the Cottesmore (1981–92), one of the
ost successful of the Cottesmore's great amateurs. He is seen giving hounds summer exercise,
companied by his former kennel huntsman, John Seaton. Brian Fanshawe bred a superb pack of
ounds which produced sport in most conditions, hunting them with great verve.

. Captain Brian Fanshawe in the hunting field.

42. Mr David Samworth, former Joint Master of the Cottesmore (1976–85), thereafter Hunt Chairman in 1990. He became Hunt Chairman of the Quorn at short notice in 1991, and made a huge contribution in creating the first written constitution for that Hunt.

43. Mrs David Samworth, Joint Master of the Cottesmore since 1991. Rosemary Samworth, a bold cross-country rider who was winner of the Melton Hunt Club Ride four times, is a rare example of a lady Field Master in the Shires, giving a great lead across the Cottesmore's Tuesday country.

44. Walter Gupwell, huntsman of the Fernie (1948–62) with hounds after a meet at Drayton in 1958. He played a great part in helping to rebuild the Hunt's fortunes after the Second World War. His son, Brian, was to become a distinguished huntsman of the Duke of Beaufort's.

Lieutenant Colonel Derek Hignett (1935–7 and 1946–56) and Lieutenant Colonel Lloyd 46–62), highly successful Joint Masters of the Fernie, seen at the opening meet at Gumley in 1953.

46. Lord (Reggie) Paget QC, the Labour peer, who was a keen, lifelong foxhunter, the son of Guy Paget. Reggie lived in the Fernie country and a covert is named Reggie's Folly in his memory. In his will he left money for the field to drink to his memory at a meet, and this occurred after his death in January 1990. In the subsequent hunting one fox ran through his garden at Lubenham Lodge and across the Vale to his covert.

47. One of the greatest Leicestershire Masters of this century: Colonel Tony Murray Smith, Joint Master of the Quorn (1954–60) and of the Fernie (1960–83). He excelled as a Field Master, amateur huntsman, and hound breeder, and made friends throughout the Quorn and Fernie countries.

Bruce Durno, huntsman of the Fernie ce 1962, with his grandson Philip on the dle, and his father, Percy standing by his se. Percy Durno was a distinguished ntsman of the Heythrop.

49.   Mr Joe Cowen, senior Joint Master of the Fernie, since 1972. He is the son of the late Major Denis Cowen who bought and developed much of the finest foxhunting country in the Laughton Hills.

50.   Mr Dick Watson (left) served the Fernie as Honorary Secretary for an extraordinary forty-nine years (1941–90) and was still hunting happily in the 1992–3 season. He is seen with Joint Masters Mr Alan Hinch and Mr Rod Millington who have been in office since 1983, with Mr Joe Cowen.

51. Supporters Clubs are nowadays vital to Hunts. Here, the Fernie Supporters Club in 1973 was presenting a new Land Rover to the Hunt at the puppy show. From left: Mr C. Warriner, Mr J.H. Gilbert, Mr F. Harpham, Mrs R. Beesley, Major S. Holland, Mr B. James; first whipper-in Michael King, huntsman Bruce Durno; Joint Masters Mr Joe Cowen and Lieutenant Colonel Murray Smith; Major Denis Cowen, and Hunt Honorary Secretary, Mr Dick Watson.

52. The Prince of Wales with Mrs Barbara Rich who kept his Leicestershire hunters in her yard in the Quorn Friday country. They are seen waiting to start a day's hunting with the Belvoir in January 1988.

a night's sound sleep. The jollifications of the 'good old days' have given way to harmless rounds of farmers' dances, and other fairly low key social events when non-hunting wives or husbands accompany their hunting spouses just as they do in other spheres of life. It is true that a complete disinterest in foxhunting is something of a handicap at a Leicestershire social event – but the same must be true of a landlubber adrift at yacht club parties during Cowes Week.

In Leicestershire, if we cast back through the history of foxhunters, no visitor can be said to have made more more impact on the scene than William Childe (1756–1854) of Kinlet Hall, Shropshire. He came to the Quorn during the latter part of Hugo Meynell's foundation Mastership, and 'Flying Childe' is given much of the credit, or blame, for introducing the new style of leaping fences in a horse's stride to cross country fast and preferably straight in pursuit of hounds. Nimrod, himself a Shropshire man, and a keen disciple of Childe remarked blandly that he was 'celebrated as having been one of the first to introduce the present spirited method of riding to hounds, and who was a great friend of Meynell.' On the Clee Hills near his home, Childe used to astonish the locals by the speed with which he would gallop down the steepest slopes, giving his opinion that his horse would never fall 'provided the rider gave him his head.' Childe exploited the broad grass acreages in Leicestershire, and the increasing use of thorn fences and timber to enclose farm stock. Better bloodlines, using imported Arabian stallions, gave British riding horses more class, and developed our greatest equine asset, the Thoroughbred horse. The Thoroughbred has the elasticity and agility to attack fences and ditches at a gallop, and the exploits of Childe and his companions not only gave birth to the speed and dash of the Chase in the open, but prepared the way for steeplechasing and hurdling as a new form of racing.

Meynell's friendship with Childe did not prevent him from bemoaning the advent of the young bloods attempting to ride their country straight, for this sometimes meant over-riding hounds. Meynell's famous remark was that he 'had not enjoyed a day's happiness since they developed their racing ideas.'

Soon, to 'go well', to 'be conspicuous in the field' became the accolades appointed to prominent members of the Shires mounted fields, especially by Nimrod who would list these gentlemen as if he were bestowing medals. As well as Childe, he gives the accolades for introducing the 'dashing style of riding to hounds which continues to distinguish our modern sportsmen' to Charles Wyndham and Lord Villiers, Lords Forester and Cholmondeley, Loraine Smith, Ralph Lambton, John Lockley, George Germaine and John Hawkes.

John Moore memorably paid tribute to the early nineteenth century Meltonians in his foreword to Nimrod's *Life of a Sportsman*:

> They were polished and tough, cruel and elegant, brave as lions and thoughtless as butterflies, these foxhunting gentry with their spindly legs and their queer, peaky faces peering out between the absurd high collars up to their ears. . . . The Meltonians had a million faults, among which you may or may not include their absolute monomania for breaking their necks. They were as wanton as weeds, ungoverned wild weeds strangely blossoming in the ordered fields of our history. They were selfish, drunken, socially useless if you like; but when they were asked how in God's name they managed to get across those huge breakneck ox-fences they answered gaily: 'We send our hearts over first, and then follow them in the best way we can.' And, I for one, can forgive them anything for that.

Nimrod has been accused of snobbery, but I note that his lists include 'yeomen and graziers' who wore blue coats instead of scarlet. Thus in a list of those going well when he first hunted with the Quorn he includes 'Joe Deveril of Shoby, Tom Hinton of Hoby, commonly called Gameboy Hinton, Jonathan King of Beilby, Marriot the Melton draper, and Ben Rowland the farrier, to whom Lord Sefton gave a large price for his horse.'

This emphasizes the local basis for the Quorn Hunt's existence. Of course, Nimrod did spend acres of print extolling the distinguished visitors. His selection of crack riders in Lord Sefton's Mastership at the start of the nineteenth century included: Sir Henry Peyton, Lord Foley, Sir Stephen Glynne, Mr T. A. Smith, Honourable Berkeley Craven, Honourable Joshua Vanneck, afterwards Lord Huntingfield, Mr Hawkes, Mr Lockley, the late Lord Forester, Lord Delamere, Mr Bennet, Mr Lindow, the late Colonel Mellish, Mr Charles Meynell, and Colonel Rollestone. Just names, but it is interesting to note how often, down the years the same family names recur in Leicestershire's hunting fields. Foxhunting is so often a sport, an addiction, inherited within families.

Melton Mowbray originally earned its place as a hunting centre simply because it was convenient to hack from there to the meets of the Quorn, Cottesmore and Belvoir. It was essentially a bachelor haunt at first, and the facilities were anything but luxurious in the 1790s when the drift began from Quorn to Melton as a place to stay during the season. Nimrod reported that in 1802 when he first visited Melton 'there was only one inn, and that a very bad one; not one bank, and but a few houses with which a well-breeched Meltonian would be satisfied.' During the first half of the nineteenth century Melton Mowbray became firmly established on the sporting and social calendars and maps. Yet it must never be forgotten that people went there for the serious purpose of risking their necks across country.

'The typical Quornite was no feudal aristocrat, but a young man who had inherited wealth and energy from a recent ancestor and who meant to have as many runs as possible for his grandfather's money,' wrote the Quorn historian Colin Ellis.

Those who hunted from Melton Mowbray by the 1820s were firmly of the opinion that they were the elite of the hunting world. Melton Mowbray swelled with residences, with stables and accommodation for the house servants and grooms. A huge seasonal investment was under way. The Meltonian would rise, breakfast, and mount his covert hack to ride to the meet he had chosen for his day's sport. Harriette Wilson, the courtesan who wrote engaging memoirs, visited Melton in about 1812 and noted that the post-hunting entertainment was pretty dull. She was not amused by Melton Mowbray: 'The members of the Melton Club led what I considered a very stupid life. They were off at six in the morning, dressed up in old single-breasted coats that had once been red, and came back to dinner at six. . . . While they sat at table, it was the constant habit of a few wretched, squalid, prostitutes to come and tap at their windows, when those who were not too sleepy were seen to sneak out of the room. The rest snored and drank till ten, and went to bed till hunting-time again.'

Other reports put a rather better complexion on Melton Mowbray, and it was described by a Captain John Russell, later Master of the Warwickshire, in 1826 as 'the quietest and nicest town possible, and is most tempting in its advantages.' It could hardly be claimed that it was always quiet. In 1837 the Marquess of Waterford and his friends rampaged through the streets of Melton Mowbray one night, possibly celebrating a good day's hunting, and probably well under the influence of a great deal of claret and port. They were armed with brushes and pots of paint, and daubed some of the town's stone buildings bright red, painted the toll-gates, and even gave the toll-keeper 'a coat of red.' They succeeded in adding the phrase 'painting the town red' to the English language, but did not add much lustre to the reputation of foxhunting.

At first the richest foxhunters brought their French chefs, and set up clubs, the most famous and exclusive of which was The Old Club. The founders were Lords Forester and Delamere, with several other friends. They took a house which eventually became the club. One of their diversions was to put up horses for auction after dinner. Lord Alvanley's old house, opposite the George inn, became the New Club, and Sir Harry Goodricke's house became known as Lord Rokeby's Club.

Chiefs of the permanent Meltonians, according to Colin Ellis, were 'the four Ms of the Old Club: Mr Moore (the son of an archbishop), Sir James Musgrave (a jealous rider who lamed Osbaldeston for life), Mr Maxse (a rail-smashing heavyweight) and that charming Irishman and fine horseman, Mr Valentine Maher. They formed the unofficial Committee of the nebulous "Melton Hunt Club" which nominated the Masters, guaranteed the subscription and generally decided the lines on which the Quorn Hunt should be run.'

Among the local hunting folk in the early nineteenth century were some formidable sporting parsons, who included the Reverend John Empson of Saxby, the 'flying parson'; 'Spurting Bullen', the eight-stone Vicar of Eastwell, and in the Cottesmore country, the Reverend William Pochin was left where he fell because 'he wouldn't be wanted 'til Sunday.' The Reverend Mr Bullen hunted until he was ninety, was inclined to wear his surplice over his hunting clothes, and announced the meets as well as the banns every Sunday in church. He would slip back to officiate at a marriage or a burial between hunts on a hunting day. Once when out with the Quorn he was reprimanded for galloping in front of hounds, and told to go home. He explained that was his intention anyway . . . 'only your hounds won't let me. I've a funeral at half-past two. Where shall I find you about four?'

Meanwhile the George and the Harborough Arms, plus numerous lodging houses, were catering for ever growing numbers of Meltonian visitors. In 1826 they were charging twenty-six shillings a week for the livery of one horse at the George.

Soon, the foxhunters began to bring their wives – and other ladies – to Melton Mowbray for the season. The attraction of Shires hunting was widening; it was to cause more than a little social concern when ladies entered the hunting field. Ladies did not hunt regularly from Melton before 1850. One of the first to do so was Lady Grey de Wilton who has been described as the 'uncrowned Queen of Melton for some sixty years'; she lived until 1919. Her father-in-law, the 'wicked' 2nd Earl of Wilton was known as the King of Melton, a great rider to hounds, who played the organ in church, but whose life was described by Lady Augusta Fane as 'a curious mixture, of religion, sport and vice.' Brooksby wrote far more warmly of the Earl when he died aged eighty-one, in 1882: '. . . the King of Melton, the Patriarch of the Quorn Hunt, he had been a leading spirit for fifty years. In his day the neatest and quickest of riders, all his life one of the most courteous of men – we had been brought up to regard him as a model of a sportsman, an example for a gentleman.'

The Earl of Wilton lived at Egerton Lodge, on the banks of the river

Eye which winds through Melton Mowbray. Two Prime Ministers were among the many guests there: the Duke of Wellington who certainly loved his hunting, and Benjamin Disraeli who was no doubt fascinated by hunting society.

If 'Flying Childe' had altered the style of riding, Catherine Walter, better known as Skittles, put Leicestershire on the map as a place where ladies could ride across country with the same dash as men. Born in Liverpool's dockland in 1839, she set up the skittles in a public house as a child, earning her nickname. When her family moved to Cheshire she also learned to ride as a child, one of her many assets she was to employ to great effect. Her beauty, and strength of personality, enabled her to rise as a top-class courtesan, becoming one of the 'pretty horse-breakers' who rode and drove in London's Rotten Row. She started hunting in the 1860–1 season with Mr Tailby's hounds. Her presence caused a huge storm of objection from some, but Tailby defended her right to hunt on the principle that 'the hunting field is open to all. . . . I am not the censor of the morality of the hunting field.'

Skittles stayed at the Haycock Hotel at Wansford, on the Great North Road, now the A 1 – an inn still popular with hunting folk – and tried hard to avoid causing embarrassment in the hunting field. However, Lady Stamford, wife of the then Master of the Quorn, put up the strongest objection, although she was of a similar background, imploring her husband to 'dispatch that improper woman home.'

Skittles immediately turned for home, but on the way the fox crossed the road in front of her, with hounds in full cry. She could not resist joining the field in a splendid hunt, riding brilliantly near the front. Lord Stamford was hugely impressed, congratulating Skittles and muttering 'damn all jealous women.' Skittles earned fame by retorting: 'I don't know why she should give herself such airs; she's not even head of our profession; Lady Cardigan is.'

The rivalry was renewed later at a Quorn opening meet at Kirby Gate when Lady Stamford appeared in a splendid habit in blue velvet, but Skittles outshone her in a scarlet velvet habit. Lady Stamford, much miffed, sent Skittles home, but Lady Grey invited her to change into a less noticeable outfit at her home nearby. Skittles rejoined the hunt, and her revenge was complete when Lady Stamford, unsuspecting, asked the identity of the young lady who had ridden so expertly in front of her all day.

On another occasion Skittles had a fall and left her skirt on the pommel of the side-saddle, revealing herself in petticoats. There was a call for 'a married man' to help her, and one confirmed old bachelor parson was much teased when he vehemently denied that he fell in that category.

The physical risk in foxhunting was one cause of concern when women entered the hunting field. The invention of a side-saddle with a special lower pommel, called the 'leaping head', in France in 1830, gradually spread to Britain. It gave a woman rider a much safer seat, and it is still a feature of the modern side-saddle. The other problem was the danger of the old fashioned habit becoming hopelessly entangled when a horse fell, increasing the risk of severe injury to the entrapped woman rider. In the middle of the nineteenth century the safety skirt was introduced, enabling it to become detached in a case of emergency, although the effect was still extremely modest by modern standards.

After 1850, therefore, far more women could hunt with increased safety whilst preserving the proprieties of the time. No one achieved greater fame as a lady rider in the hunting field than the Empress of Austria, wife of Franz Joseph, the Emperor. She was a brilliant horsewoman and first came to England in 1876 to fulfil her ambition to ride to hounds in the Shires. She first hunted with the Grafton, then went cubhunting with the Belvoir. Accompanied by the dashing horsman 'Bay' Middleton, the Empress explored Leicestershire more thoroughly at the height of the following season, renting Cottesbrooke Park in the Pytchley country. Beautiful, elegant, and a superb horsewoman, she made a huge impression on Victorian hunting folk. She told Middleton as her pilot: 'Remember, I do not mind the falls but I will not scratch my face.' In the Shires she hunted mainly with the Pytchley but visited Ireland, riding the daunting ditches of the Meath with élan. On her last visit to England she hunted from Cheshire, but on this occasion she did not enjoy her hunting so much.

There is no doubt that she was ill-suited to the pomp of royalty in the Austro-Hungarian Empire; she was unhappy in her middle-European world. There was to be much more sadness in her life which ended tragically: she was stabbed to death in Geneva by an assassin when she was sixty, in 1898.

She was highly sensitive, and her trips to Britain and Ireland were marred for her by the gossip attending her friendship with Bay Middleton. Yet there is no doubt that she was sublimely happy, like so many other visitors to the Shires, during the crowded hours she spent in the saddle, riding to hounds. Despite the controversies surrounding her visits, she showed that an apparently delicate female could indeed hold her place in the hunting field, and she unwittingly encouraged more women to accompany their menfolk to the Shires.

Far more appeared in the hunting field in Leicestershire from the 1870s. One of the most notable was the afore-mentioned Lady Augusta Fane, whose book *Chit Chat* gives a far better idea of Shires hunting than many a tome with a more heavyweight title. In this century she would have made an excellent journalist. First visiting Melton Mowbray in 1879 she stayed with Lord and Lady Grey de Wilton. An excellent rider, and having an iron constitution, Lady Augusta stood the social racket in the evenings as well as long hours in the hunting field. She was quite accustomed to hacking well up to two hours or more, to and from her day's hunting. She and her husband stayed at the Old Club in Melton, and caused quite a stir when, on her suggestion, they organized a midnight steeplechase in March 1890, to celebrate her birthday. Lady Augusta was a fervent admirer of Tom Firr, and well aware that she was hunting with the greatest huntsman of the century. But she confesses that she got into his bad books by not inviting him to take part in the 'chase. Captain Warner, the Master, had asked her not to tell Firr about the romp in case he took part and injured himself.

'My lady that was a bit of fun I should have enjoyed,' said Firr reproachfully to Lady Augusta.

Otho Paget recalls the dinner party at the Old Club before the race, when they all dressed in nightgowns over hunting clothes. The course, just outside Melton, was illuminated with railway lamps, as there was no moon. Otho was more than a little peeved because he claimed he never received some amended instructions as to the route, and arrived first at what he thought was the winning post. Victory went to Algy Burnaby, later to be Master of the Quorn, receiving a cup from Count Zbrowski who was one of the first Americans to hunt regularly from Melton.

'I did not say anything but must admit I was very disappointed,' wrote Paget.

The hunting characters in the golden years of the 1880s and '90s appeared regularly in the Leicestershire reports which filled columns in the sporting press. Otho Paget gives special mention to Captain 'Chicken' Hartopp, son of the squire of Little Dalby. The 'Chicken' was a mad prankster, according to Paget, . . . 'his great delight was to blow up something with dynamite, and he had some very narrow shaves of killing himself with that explosive.'

Never mind this lethal eccentricity, 'Chicken' was a great horseman, and that went for Captain 'Doggie' Smith too: '. . . beautiful hands, good judgement and a splendid nerve, he always got the best out of his horses without overtaxing their powers.'

Paget says there was a 'very hard riding crew' who stayed at the Bell in Melton, the best of whom were Mr Alfred Brocklehurst, Mr Buck Barclay and Count Charles Kinsky. The last of these was a Hungarian, and a crack rider even among the best.

Queen Victoria and Prince Albert's visit to the Belvoir hardly established a regular link between Leicestershire and royalty. Their son, Albert

Edward, Prince of Wales, the future King Edward VII, certainly liked hunting, but he rode mainly with the Royal Buckhounds near Windsor. He hunted with the Quorn on but a few occasions, although while staying with Algy Burnaby he sprinkled the gorse seeds at Baggrave to found the covert still bearing his name.

Edwardian society nevertheless embraced Leicestershire as part of its season, although it must be stressed that Melton Mowbray, and the other main centres, Oakham, and Market Harborough, only attracted that section of society capable of jumping fences four days a week in the depths of an East Midland winter when the cold can be biting, and the winds extremely keen, even if the total rainfall is notably less than the west side of Britain.

Oakham, county town of Rutland with its motto *Multum in Parvo*, essentially grew in the nineteenth century as a centre for the Cottesmore, although the Belvoir Wednesday country and Quorn Friday countries were within easy reach on a good covert hack. The hunters would be sent ahead, whilst the hunting folk followed on their hacks to mount their first horses near the meet, or the first covert to be drawn. The groom would then join the cavalcade of second horsemen with the horses to be ridden in the afternoon.

As in Melton, the side-streets were alive with the sound of hunters' hooves on the cobbles in the mornings during the season. Livery stables, farriers and saddlers catered for a huge influx of horses brought from all over Britain, many transported by rail in the autumn.

Foxhunting played its part in making country living in late Georgian and Victorian Britain more sociable, exciting and attractive to visitors. Market Harborough, at the southern end of Leicestershire, benefited most of all, since it was more accessible to London and the Home Counties and it was an especially convenient centre for the Fernie and Pytchley countries.

G.J. Whyte-Melville's novel *Market Harborough*, published in 1861, used that town as the centre from which his hero, Mr Sawyer, visited the Shires hunting fields for the first time, but the author did not paint an inviting picture: 'Market Harborough, though perhaps the best headquarters in the world for foxhunting, can scarcely be termed a gay or very beautiful town. On a wet, drizzling afternoon in early winter, when twilight begins somewhere about a quarter to three, with no movable object visible save a deserted carrier's cart, and a small rain falling, which dulls the red brick houses while it polishes the paved and slippery streets, it is, doubtless, a city suggestive of repose, not to say stagnation.'

This is less than kind to a town which today is a designated conservation area, and its Georgian high street earns it the compliment of retaining 'an air of well-bred elegance' in the AA's guide to county towns and villages.

Yet, when the twentieth century's Indian summer of privilege, wealth and fashion descended on Leicestershire as a place to stay for the winter season, it was Melton Mowbray which remained the major attraction. Royal patronage put the gloss on Melton's reputation as the most fashionable foxhunting centre. Edward, Prince of Wales, who was to be Edward VII so briefly before abdicating, embraced foxhunting in Leicestershire, relishing the hunting field in the 1920s and '30s and thoroughly enjoying the social life of Melton Mowbray. He first hunted in Leicestershire in 1923, taking a suite at Craven Lodge, a hunting box of Mr Craven in the previous century, but run between the wars as a club by Major General John Vaughan. It was the focal point of the whirl of social activity in the town during the winter months, and above all it was the 'done thing' to be invited to the dinner parties and dances given by the Prince. His brothers, Prince George (Duke of Kent) and Prince Henry (Duke of Gloucester), also stayed at Craven Lodge and hunted, although not so frequently as the Prince of Wales. The Duke of York, who was to succeed his brother to become King George VI, hunted sometimes from Melton, but after his marriage to Lady Elizabeth Bowes-Lyon in 1923 he took a hunting box at Naseby Woollies in the Pytchley country for several seasons.

Although not an especially polished horseman, the Prince of Wales was bold across country; he 'went like a bomb' according to Ulrica Murray Smith. Apart from his hunting, there was some public controversy about his riding in point-to-points, and he was forbidden by King George V to ride in steeplechases again after a heavy fall when he was concussed during a point-to-point at Arborfield, Berkshire.

He was justifiably popular in the hunting field where even royalty do not shine unless they 'go well.'

'No man loved it more, nor went better,' according to Guy Paget (*Bad 'Uns to Beat*). He tells of the Prince breaking his collar bone in a fall near Houghton, in the Fernie country when it was hunted by Arthur Thatcher.

> Arthur shouted at him, but he would go on; he'd been leading the field for ten minutes; you know the place, a real terror. Arthur jumped it lower down and got over, so did I. Ewart Levy was first to get to the Prince, and Arthur turned to me: 'No need to stop, he's in good hands. . . .
>
> I was with the Prince on one occasion down by the Coplow. We had met some rails leaning away from us, pretty big hounds circled round and met them the other way. Arthur Thatcher called out to the Prince: 'You can't jump there, sir. Come round with me.'
>
> 'No,' he replied. 'I funked 'em last time, and you got over.' And over he got.

In Melton Mowbray the Prince was remembered by an old resident (*Melton Mowbray as I Remember It*) as attending all sorts of local social events, as well as the parties for the elite. At the Corn Exchange 'he used to dance with the town girls as though he lived in Melton. He would go to the church for the church parades. If there was any anxiety about the river coming in he would go down to see how the water was rising so that Melton didn't get flooded, although he couldn't do anything about it, but he was interested.'

Such memories give an insight into the Prince's genuine popularity among most of the populance, even if he ran foul of the establishment through his wish to marry Mrs Wallis Simpson – and he first met that lady in Melton Mowbray, at Burrough Court, the home of Lord and Lady Furness. His previous love for sixteen years, Winifred May Dudley Ward, wife of the MP for Southampton, was a Nottinghamshire personality well-known in the Melton hunting set. Her father was a rich industrialist, Charles Birkin, of Radcliffe-on-Trent.

It cannot be said that the Prince of Wales was unaware of the more raffish side to Melton foxhunting. Nor can it be pretended that the image of the sport was altogether assisted by the Melton fast set; they tended to confirm the worst suspicions of those who opposed hunting the fox. There were plenty of comparatively humble origins and means drawn to Melton Mowbray simply because they loved the sport, and wished to test their horsemanship across Leicestershire's grass and fences. Yet the image of wealth, privilege and excess in the 1920s and '30s was one which foxhunting has had to redress throughout the post-war years when it has been fighting for its survival against abolitionist attempts in Westminster.

Edward, Prince of Wales, known to his friends as David, recalled the hunting fields around Melton Mowbray thus, in his autobiography:

'Intermixed with the local landed gentry . . . was a lively sampling of dashing figures; noblemen and their ladies; wealthy people who had discovered that the stable door was a quick if expensive short-cut into society; a strong injection of Americans from famous East Coast Hunts; ladies whose pursuit of the fox was only a phase of an even more intense pursuit of romance . . . good riders on bad horses; bad riders on good horses.'

There was ample room for the wealthy visitors. As well as at Craven Lodge, there was comfortable hunting box accommodation at Wicklow Lodge, Sysonby Lodge, Stavely Lodge, Hamilton Lodge, Warwick Lodge and Wyndham Lodge. The Maharanee of Cooch Behar used to stay at the Spinnies in Thorpe Road and later at Staveley Lodge. Another notable hostess was Lady Irene Curzon, eldest daughter of Lord Curzon, then

Viceroy of India. While she was hunting from Melton she was created Baroness Ravendale.

Tycoons as well as aristocrats abounded at Melton during the season. At Warwick Lodge Mr Ambrose Clarke, of the Singer sewing machine empire, stabled fifty hunters, and at nearby Thorpe Satchville, Mr Lowenstein, a millionaire financial advisor, kept a large yard of hunters and used to give investment advice to his friends in the hunting field.

According to Simon Blow (*Elysian Fields*): 'One day a client was furious because the shares had not risen as expected and he went for 'Low' with his crop. Immediately afterwards the shares rose, but the client had already sold.'

Fancy dress balls, pageants and other jollifications filled the Melton Mowbray season off the hunting field. Outdoors, apart from the hunting, the Melton steeplechases at Burton Lazaars were a great attraction; earlier they had been attended by Lord Lonsdale in his yellow coach, drawn by chestnut horses.

The annual influx of visitors brought prosperity to some in a town famous otherwise for its pork pies and Stilton cheese. Memories of some lifelong residents put the social scene into a different context. Mrs Lucy Skinner (*Melton Mowbray as I Remember it*) recalled that her brother, Mr Jack Oakley was a tailor in Nottingham Street: 'He made livery for servants' breeches and hunting pink jackets for the gentry; incidentally, he was kept waiting months before the bills were paid, but as there was very little industry in the towns the shops were glad of their patronage, however long they waited for their money.

'. . . I am sorry that Melton has lost so much of its charm and character, but at least the people living here are more prosperous. There was a lot of hardship and poverty; it wasn't all beer and skittles, although there were forty public houses.'

Another old resident, Mr Shilham, remembered working for W. Rowell and Son 'Bootmakers to Royalty'; he worked from half-past eight in the morning until eight at night, for seven shillings and sixpence a week: 'Most of my time was spent in the cellar, where I had a bench and that was where I cleaned shoes and boots, and when hunting boots came from the workshop, instructions were to make them look like a mirror. Two to three hours were spent on these boots; spit and rubbing with a deer bone was hard work, then safely wrapped, I would have to take them to the big hunting lodges.'

In the post-war years the Lodges have become public offices, flats, or have been demolished. Melton Mowbray is still a pleasant market town, but it is semi-industrial; it has a new coal mine above at Asfordby, and near the town centre is a large pet food factory. There is light engineering

and other industrial enterprises. In the shopping centre there are still pork pies and Stilton cheese to be bought, but a Tandoori restaurant indicates the cultural mix of modern Leicestershire which has a large post-war element in the community of Asian origins. Melton Mowbray people are warm, friendly and welcoming, but their town has moved far away from the days when the 'Hunting toffs' made their annual migratory visits. Hunting folk from outside the county no longer make Melton, Oakham and Market Harborough their winter bases in the pre-war manner. Americans and other overseas visitors often choose country hotels well outside the towns, such as Stapleford Park or Hambleton Hall, when they visit the Hunts.

Yet there are Melton folk who do not ride, but regard following hounds on bicycles and in their cars as their winter recreation. The town's regular horse sales are popular, although top-class hunters are far more likely to be bought privately nowadays. In recent years Melton Mowbray has revived the practice of the New Year's Day meet in its market place, with the Quorn, Cottesmore and Belvoir taking this fixture alternately. There is always a huge, enthusiastic gathering of local folk at the meet and many follow hounds for the rest of the day.

Ulrica Murray Smith in an article in *Horse and Hound* listed some of the most notable personalities who visited Leicestershire in the 1930s for the sake of the sport:

Riding side-saddle, Mrs Fred Cripps and her sister Mrs Colin Buist. Lady Fortescue, and Mrs Jack Harrison were all superb. Monica Sherriff and Olive Partridge were first-class astride.

A sight never to be forgotten were the 'Twinnies' (the Miss Wilsons) with the Cottesmore, in grey habits, with very low, flat top hats, riding to the meet or homewards, one always a hundred yards in front of the other. . . .

Reggie Farquhar (Sir Peter's younger brother), was a beautiful horseman, very courageous, with an eye for the quickest way. He and his wife Betty, who looked very smart side-saddle, lived in Gaddesby.

Donnie and Leila Player were a great asset to any hunting field. They lived at Little Belvoir, and then built Friars Well, Wartnaby, where John King who did so much for the Belvoir during his years of Mastership, now lives. Donnie, Jackie de Pret, Hugh Lloyd Thomas, Flash Kellet, Geoff Harbord and Anthony Head were all immaculately turned out, magnificently mounted and went like hawks.

Lady Fortescue's daughter, Lady Margaret Fortescue, was one of the last side-saddle riders in Leicestershire, coming up every season from her home near Barnstaple, Devon, to take a hunting box at Thorpe Satchville. She continued to ride superbly across country until injuries in a bad fall caused her to retire from the hunting field in the mid-1980s.

One who hunted with the Leicestershire packs before the war and continued until the 1991–2 season is the Honourable Mrs Ursula ('Urky') Newton, daughter of Lord Rank. Her late husband, Lance Newton, in 1959 founded one of the most enduring and useful hunting institutions in Leicestershire: the Melton Hunt Club, not an exclusive body, but one which has enabled many hundreds of people to experience hunting with the Shires packs at a reduced cost. Each member is allowed two caps to the Leicestershire Hunts at approximately half the usual rate. For example, in the 1991–2 season a Quorn or Belvoir cap was on a Melton Club ticket £50 in their best country; and a Cottesmore cap £45. From its fund-raising functions, including an excellent sponsored ride, the Club makes annual donations to the Hunts for improvements to their hunting countries, and has therefore contributed thousands of pounds to rural conservation.

After Lance's death in 1969 Urky continued to run the Club with huge efficiency and devotion, the same qualities being equally applied to her work for the Pony Club and point-to-pointing. The Melton Hunt Club runs its own immensely successful point-to-point at Garthorpe, the course to the east of Melton Mowbray where the Quorn, Cottesmore and Belvoir hold their fixtures. The Club's most famous annual attraction is its annual cross-country ride, which is really a race but is called a 'ride' because the

Jockey Club used to be sensitive about racing outside its Rules. Fields of up to seventy ride a course of about four miles across natural Leicestershire country, held each year alternately in the Quorn, Cottesmore and Belvoir countries. Most of us who think we can cross country on a horse have tackled the ride at various times, and it is tremendous fun. Unfortunately, in recent years it has been switched from a spring to an autumn fixture because the ground usually rides better at that time. This means that regular hunting folk in Leicestershire are less likely to risk their precious hunters in the ride at the start of the hunting season. Yet the ride is still well supported by intrepid hunting folk from all over Britain. The 1992 ride was held in unusually wet conditions in the Cottesmore country, starting from Barleythorpe. I liked to think Barleythorpe's famous former resident, the Yellow Earl, would have approved – and I am sure he would have enjoyed the excellent day's hunting afterwards, provided by the Cottesmore hounds, hunted by Neil Coleman, on the grass and fences above Barleythorpe.

Although still prominent as an organizer, Urky is much missed in the hunting field; she hunted with all the Melton packs regularly every week for many years, and recalls starting her hunting career in Leicestershire by bringing her horse with her when she stayed at the George in Melton Mowbray. She was an immediate Leicestershire convert, and as a resident ever since she has made a huge contribution to foxhunting in the county in so many ways, not least by purchasing land and coverts in the three hunting countries adjoining Melton and maintaining them beautifully for sport. It is good to see her son, Joey, making such a success of his Mastership of the Belvoir, often accompanied in the hunting field by his wife Emma, and their daughter, Chloe.

Apart from all her good works, those of us who have enjoyed hunting teas at Urky's hospitable home at Saltby are especially in her debt.

Another great hunting lady is the Honourable 'Migs' Greenall, daughter-in-law of the late Lord (Toby) Daresbury. A highly popular figure in the hunting field, Migs maintains her land at Waltham-on-the-Wolds beautifully for the Belvoir, and is another who has entertained so many foxhunters after hunting.

I have no intention of listing all those I consider 'go well' in the modern hunting field, but certain personalities in modern Leicestershire stand out because of their huge commitment to the best interests of foxhunting. There was much sadness in November 1992, when Dr Tom Connors, of Upper Broughton, died. He arrived in 1949 in Leicestershire from his native Ireland with a suitcase and saddle to join the medical practice in Long Clawson. Soon his brothers in County Waterford were sending him good Irish hunters to ride; people admired them in the hunting field, and Tom Connors started an extraordinary career as family GP and horse dealer. His horses were eagerly sought in Leicestershire, and in hunting countries all over Britain. Tom adored his hunting and all his life rode young, imported Irish horses with great dash and style across Leicestershire. He had immense charm and managed the almost impossible feat of making friends with most people who bought his horses. In the Vale of Belvoir he was renowned for dashing to and from his surgery to the hunting field, and for more than forty years he saved lives during hunting by giving immediate aid and diagnosis to those more seriously hurt in falls. He had a marvellous reputation with country people as a caring family doctor. His most enduring memorial is the land he bought and nurtured around Muxlow Hill: a beautiful stretch of old turf, fenced with inviting thorn hedges. A ride across Dr Tom's at Muxlow Hill is always a highlight of a Quorn Monday in the Hickling area; across the Melton road the superb grass and fences on Bob Chaplin's farm complements the ride, especially when a fox goes away from Curate's and runs towards the Broughtons.

Fortunately, Tom's son, Nicky and his wife, Helen, have farmed the land at Muxlow and continue the horse dealing business after Tom's death.

One of Tom's best friends was the late Captain George Rich who was a much esteemed horse dealer at Thorpe Satchville. Bred to hunting, he was a marvellous lightweight across country, and had a great eye for a horse. I kept a horse with him for one season, and it was one of the most enjoyable I can recall. George's wife, Barbara Rich, has maintained the livery and dealing business at Thorpe Satchville, her clients for some years including Prince Charles, Prince of Wales. She is in much demand as a judge in horse classes at shows up and down the land and hunts regularly with the Leicestershire packs.

Probably the last foxhunter in the post-war years to hunt regularly with the Quorn, Cottesmore and Belvoir every week throughout the season was George Coombes, who deals in horses with much success near Great Dalby. He has curtailed his hunting somewhat, but still hunts regularly with the Quorn.

Another veteran horseman of considerable note is Noel Pegge, who was a lifelong livery owner and dealer at Somerby in the Cottesmore country. Now retired from the business, he still lives in Somerby and hunts regularly on Quorn Fridays and Cottesmore Tuesdays, crossing the country with the neatness and skill of a top-class natural horseman. His wife, Grace, is the mother of the Cottesmore Joint Master, Rosemary Samworth.

One of the best known personalities in the Leicestershire hunting world is Lieutenant Colonel Sir John Miller, former Crown Equerry, the official in charge of the Queen's coach horses at the Royal Mews and elsewhere. In the hunting field, Sir John has long been distinguished by his iron nerve and his determination to take his own line across country – not always entirely in accord with the wishes of various Field Masters in the past! He made a major contribution to foxhunting by encouraging and introducing the present Prince of Wales to take up the sport in 1975 when he was aged twenty-six, a comparatively late starter as a foxhunter. His debut was with the Duke of Beaufort's, but he soon came to Leicestershire, beginning with a low-key visit to the Cottesmore, meeting at Sir Henry Tate's home at Withcote. Soon he was hunting with the Quorn and the Belvoir as well, and learning the art of riding across country in a crowd. The 1970s were a boom time for the Leicestershire packs, with so many visitors seeking hunting that waiting lists for subscribers were maintained.

The Prince earned widespread approval for his approach to foxhunting. It was far removed from the social implications of the exploits of the previous Prince of Wales in Leicestershire. Prince Charles showed that he is a natural country man, deeply interested in the environment, wildlife and the people who live in the countryside. He made friends quickly with farmers and Hunt staff in Leicestershire, and has maintained these friendships quietly and resolutely, no matter how many other distractions and pressures have entered his life.

'I have met more farmers, and more ordinary British blokes than in any other exercise or sport that I have ever done,' he said in an amusing after dinner speech on foxhunting. With tongue in cheek he confessed he found it difficult to recognize some of the Leicestershire lady foxhunters at the dinner because they were wearing less make-up than in the hunting field! He understood from the start of his hunting career that the sport can only take place with permission of farmers and landowners, and has for some years demonstrated his own warm gratitude by arranging annual visits for Leicestershire farming families to his home at High Grove in Gloucestershire. He takes a keen interest in hounds and hound breeding, and has judged at the Quorn and Belvoir puppy shows, at the former with Captain Ronnie Wallace and at the latter with the late Lord Daresbury.

Prince Charles rode amid the hurly burly of the mounted fields in Leicestershire, and increasingly went ahead of the field to ride with the huntsmen, Michael Farrin at the Quorn, Robin Jackson at the Belvoir, and Captain Brian Fanshawe at the Cottesmore. Undoubtedly, the Prince enjoyed the ride and the experience in Leicestershire was seen to improve his horsemanship considerably, since he had previously spent most of his time in the saddle playing polo which makes different demands. Some of us were concerned that he did not buy a large stud of hunters, but rode Candlewick, a mare bred by the Queen for eventing, and tended to borrow other horses. Inevitably, he had a few crashing falls, but showed himself to be extremely tough and resolute, always re-mounting immediately and kicking on with the best over more fences. One horse he rode frequently was Highlight, a Thoroughbred mare owned by Mr Geoff Brooks, a born and bred Leicestershire farmer at Widmerpool, and one of the Quorn's keenest supporters (Chapter Six). Geoff has always believed in taking to the hunting field the stallions he stands on his farm; it is performance testing and it works. The stock produced are sound, and they make excellent hunters. Highlight was only five when Geoff was hunting her with the Quorn. Sir John Miller liked the look of her and asked if she was for sale. Geoff is not a dealer, but he has always been willing to lend a good horse to a friend. Soon, Highlight became a spare ride for Prince Charles, and then he rode her regularly, taking her all over Britain as well as hunting with the Quorn; they formed a happy partnership. Like most good mares, Highlight was an exceedingly safe ride across country; she would sort out a route across any fence in her path, and although she was eighteen hands high she rode much smaller and was beautifully balanced. (I write this with firsthand knowledge, having had some excellent days on the mare.) She was retired at the age of twelve and has since been at stud on Geoff's farm, producing several excellent foals.

Prince Charles's assessment of hunting in Leicestershire for the first time is similar to that of many newcomers:

'It is like the start of the Grand National. I had never seen anything like it, everyone pushing and shoving. It was terrifying to start with . . . going for a fence you get knocked over. Now I know nearly everyone, and I know how to cope. Initially, if you are not used to it, and you haven't much experience, it is terrifying. I wouldn't recommend anyone to go near it until they have done a lot of hunting and riding elsewhere.

It says much for Prince Charles's determination that he overcame all these problems, and is nowadays a top-class rider across country.

There is plenty of cause for laughter in the hunting field. This fact seems to have escaped some people who leave their sense of humour behind, but Prince Charles is certainly one who appreciates the quirky elements in the Chase, as real today as they were when Surtees captured them in his comic novels.

A Quorn story involving the Prince which has become something of a legend, concerned a Leicestershire lady who was lying prostrate in his path after a fall. The Prince considerately dismounted, enquired about her condition and offered her a refreshing sip from his flask. When the lady said she felt much better, the Prince prepared to re-mount his horse, but asked politely: 'Are you sure there's nothing else I can do?' The Quorn lady replied simply: 'Just kiss me.' (In some versions of the story, the lady then received a peck on the cheek; in other versions she did not!)

On another occasion, hunting with the Belvoir, the mounted field reached a place where there was only one practical jumping spot in a wired-up hedge. Prince Charles, amid the mêlée of surging horses and riders attempting to jump the place at once, was baulked by queue jumpers repeatedly. As he turned his horse to trot to the back of the queue yet again, he sighed: 'Ah well, I can't do anything about it. I just wasn't brought up to barge.'

Whether it was a tree planting in Long Clawson, a visit to a dairy, or a call in a farmhouse to enquire about a farmer's health, the Prince showed a depth of concern and interest in the community in Leicestershire. He set an excellent example for some who visit the Shires packs from outside, only to flit away at the end of a day's hunting, and take no interest in the country between hunting seasons. It is perfectly possible to know the identities of farmers and landowners and to make friends with them, if you are a subscriber living outside Leicestershire.

It was notable that the Quorn and Belvoir huntsmen were among the Prince's friends from the hunting field invited to his wedding. A decade later, whatever nonsense was published about the Prince of Wales in the newspapers during the royal family's *annus horribilis*, as 1992 was described by the Queen, there can be no shred of doubt that the Prince has an especially loyal following in the Leicestershire rural community where he has supped in many a farmhouse kitchen and is known and liked as a true friend of all that is best in country life.

Foxhunting in Leicestershire has never been cheap, but far more people hunt nowadays with one or two horses at most, compared with the huge strings kept by the pre-war Meltonians. Very few people hunt four and five times a week, picking the cream of the country in three or four packs, as they did in the 1920s and '30s.

Men and women from a huge variety of professions and jobs fit in their precious days' hunting with many other responsibilities. Ironically, travel by the very motorways which have spoilt hunting countries and the use of horse boxes has solved the transport problems which made Melton Mowbray, Oakham and Market Harborough foxhunting centres.

'Where are the characters nowadays?' is a commonplace question in many areas of British life. The truth is that we and our friends are the 'characters' and some of us will be remembered in just the same way as the more quirky personalities of the past.

Dipping more or less at random into my own memories of notable personalities hunting in Leicestershire in the last quarter of a century, from the racing world there was Willie Carson, the great Flat jockey, who told me once: 'I like it up here so much that I sometimes come for a day's hunting and stay all week!'

Lord Manton, a former Senior Steward of the Jockey Club, hunted with the Quorn for many years and is represented nowadays by his son, the Honourable Milo Watson. Major Dick Hern, the distinguished trainer, kept his horses with George and Barbara Rich and adored his hunting until it was so tragically cut short by the fall during a Friday country hunt in which he received injuries which rendered him a wheel-chair bound paraplegic. Dick's achievement in overcoming this handicap to continue his superb career as a top-class Flat trainer is an example of a true horseman's grit.

Barry Hills is another trainer who adored hunting in Leicestershire; his wife, Penny, was a Quorn girl. Mimi Van Cutsem, a notable Newmarket racing personality, kept her horses with Noel Pegge at Somerby to hunt in Leicestershire; she has since married Billy Abel-Smith and hunts in Virginia.

From the world of showjumping, no one was more noticeable than Douglas Bunn, the founder and owner of the All England Jumping Course at Hickstead. Duggie used to helicopter up from Sussex, but the fog or the wind, or some other weather phenomenon, all too often made him late or miss a day's hunting altogether. He bought land at Hickling, rode superb horses and insisted on wearing his cap and blue coat as Master of the Mid Surrey Farmers' Drag Hounds. Duggie also kept his horses at the Rich establishment at Thorpe Satchville and much enjoyed those happy post-hunting teas and suppers at Barbara's table.

Paul Mellon, the famed American sportsman, art collector and philanthropist has happy memories of Shires hunting. American foxhunters devoted to Leicestershire in recent years have been John Bowles from California, the Bostonian Russell Clarke and Fife Symington from the Green Spring Valley Hunt, Pennsylvania.

Just to emphasize the breadth of Leicestershire's hunting field, it is worth noting that show biz has in recent years been represented by such as Mickey Dolenz of The Monkeys pop group, and the Quorn has a devoted subscriber in Malcolm McLured, formerly drummer with Showaddy-Waddy.

Legal luminaries are to be found widely in foxhunting. None was better known in Leicestershire than late Lord Diplock, a man small in stature but huge in determination, he hunted with the Cottesmore and revelled in jumping as many fences during a day's hunting as could possibly be managed. When it was his turn to be the official gate shutter he was known to shut gates after the mounted field had passed and then jump the gate. He kept his horses with Michael Stokes at Wansford.

When it comes to elegance in the hunting field, I shall always think of the late Major Stephen Eve, who hunted with the Cottesmore; his top hat was set at a certain angle and he sometimes smoked a cigar during a pause in the day's sport.

Among the great 'goers' across Leicestershire in my time, I think particularly of the Chatterton brothers, Michael and Roger, who help to maintain a cheerful atmosphere in the Belvoir hunting field. Michael and Adrienne Bell, Charlotte Rodriguez riding side-saddle, and Steve and Carol Taylor, are others among the Belvoir front flight. It was good news that Steve Taylor, a former National Hunt rider, was joining his brother-in-law, Joey Newton, in the Belvoir Mastership in the 1993–4 season.

One who added considerably to the pleasures of hunting with the Quorn and Belvoir was the late Colonel Humphrey Mews, formerly of the King's Troop RHA and at one time a private secretary to the Prince of Wales. Humph would dash up to Leicestershire on a motor cycle, or he would bring his horses up from Northampton in his specially designed trailer. He was always cheerful and full of charm in the hunting field, on good days or not so good and he has been much missed since his untimely death from a heart attack whilst attending the Cheltenham Gold Cup in 1990.

Undoubtedly, the subscriptions from those who live outside the county have long made it possible to run the major Leicestershire packs on a large scale. The addition of VAT to subscriptions and many other hunting costs are an additional burden, but undoubtedly the recession of the early 1990s has hit outside subscribers harder than any other factor in the post-war years. The heavy losses incurred by many deriving incomes from Lloyds of London was another major blow which caused a substantial reduction in the number of outside subscribers during the 1992–3 season.

There was some concern among Hunt Committees about loss of income, but Leicestershire hunting has withstood financial depressions in the past and there was every reason to suppose that it would be resilient enough to come to terms with the recession hitting so many aspects of British life in the '90s. In 1910 a full season's subscription to the Quorn was £40. In 1992, an outside subscription for the season to the Quorn cost about £1,000 for each of the Melton days, Monday and Friday, but £2,000 per season, involving many days hunting from September to March, compares very well with the cost of top-class fishing or shooting. Although the private costs of a foxhunter in maintaining horses tip the balance considerably. Livery for each horse in 1992 was about £80 per week, plus local transport to meets, shoeing and veterinary costs. The

Belvoir was charging only a few hundred less for the possibility of hunting up to four days a week and the Cottesmore subscriptions were similar. Those living inside the hunting countries pay at a lower rate, with further reduced rates for farmers and landowners. A top-class quality hunter up to weight was selling for £6,000 at least. Yet many were enjoying Leicestershire in the 1990s on horses costing far less; discarded horses from the competitive sports, or horses with a physical 'if', which fetch low prices in the market. Thoroughbred blood is still essential for the horse which will carry you best over Leicestershire, but by the early 1990s there was a wide range of horse flesh in the hunting field, even including some of the Warm Blood cross-breds from the Continent. Speed was somewhat less important than in the old days of permanent grassland everywhere, but jumping ability was as important as ever. Accuracy in jumping was especially desired, since horses have to jump on a narrower front in taking on timber and hedges nowadays.

For every smart horse box at the meet, there are plenty of ancient diesel boxes just as suitable for taking farmstock to the market in the early 1990s. Whether they were outsiders or local folk, many in the modern hunting fields maintain their sport only by making severe sacrifices on other costs and by putting in a great deal of hard work in keeping their own horses. This is as true of Leicestershire as elsewhere.

Is it all worthwhile? Foxhunting as I have remarked above, is an addictive sport, and many a newcomer to Leicestershire will have shared the same feelings as Whyte-Melville's hero, Mr Sawyer, after his first good run across Leicestershire: 'He had never felt so keen in his life. He would never hunt anywhere else. He could ride with any of them, he thought; he was determined to be as well mounted . . .'

For as long as those in the mounted field experience the same feelings after their first taste of Leicestershire, it is unlikely that its magic will wane.

9

Hounds for Elysian Fields

They need plenty of hunting, but they
are biddable and they have what Sir Peter
Farquhar called 'fox sense'

In seeking evidence of the individuality of the Leicestershire Hunts you need do no more than look carefully at the hounds maintained in each Hunt kennels. Each pack has been bred and cherished in separate establishments, by Masters with different backgrounds and sometimes widely differing objectives. There are considerable differences between the hounds hunted in each hunting country, despite their close proximity.

It has been said that if you wished to study the marriages, and sometimes the marriage break-ups, of Masters of Foxhounds you should study the Foxhound Kennel Stud Book. When a Master changes his Hunt he often takes hounds with him and sudden appearances of outcrosses in the hound breeding in long established kennels may well be due to the arrival of a new Master. However, the vast majority of changes in breeding are entirely in the realm of sport in the hunting field; hound breeding is an immensely successful science. The modern foxhound has none of the appalling conformation faults of too many dogs bred for fashion and showing. It is a true working animal, bred for stamina, speed and intelligence; capable of running up to one hundred miles in a day. Its qualities

of sustaining a scent – known simply as 'nose' – its voice, essential in telling the huntsman that a fox is found and its ability to work with fellow hounds as a pack, make it a remarkable example of careful breeding for the past two centuries.

In Leicestershire there is every need for a pack which can hunt fast and accurately in the open, whilst remaining biddable to their huntsman. All the countries have areas of dense woodlands and these tend to be hunted by the doghounds, although the Cottesmore bitch pack has to cope with considerable woodlands at Owston close to the grass country.

Continuity is a major asset in successful hound breeding, and the hereditary ownership of the Belvoir pack by succeeding Dukes of Rutland achieved this from one generation of Masters to the next. The present Duke of Rutland is just as insistent as his forebears that the Belvoir continues to be bred on pure English lines. The traditional Belvoir tan colouring – largely black, with tan and some white – sets it apart from most other packs throughout the British Isles. Only the Brocklesby and the York and Ainsty South claim to be absolutely pure English bred and in Ireland the County Limerick has this distinction because the hounds are a branch of the Belvoir pack, taken to Ireland just after the war by the late Lord (Toby) Daresbury when he completed his Belvoir Mastership. Because the pack was not sold as Masterships changed, the Belvoir kennel established a reputation as the main source of foxhunting blood at its best in the nineteenth century. Many packs throughout Britain sought to use Belvoir lines, especially those in the Midlands. All too many of these direct lines have been lost in other kennels, due to outcross breeding,

but the Foxhound Kennel Stud Book still provides ample evidence of the huge influence of Belvoir blood, despite the twentieth century swing of fashion against the pure English hound.

The foxhound was far more varied in type in the eighteenth century than today. Improved communications in the nineteenth and twentieth centuries made it possible to send hounds further afield to sire or to conceive in distant hunting countries where the bloodlines were known to be valuable. The fashionable image of a foxhound therefore became much nearer the norm in most English Hunt kennels, although significantly the Welsh retained their own breeding, their hounds usually being rough, or broken coated, white or lemon coloured, with a tendency to domed heads, great voices and scenting ability, but according to their critics too much independence as individuals in the hunting field; not possessing the stricter team spirit of the more closely bred English hounds. The Welsh hound would be doing his own thing on the far side of a valley while the English hound often had to be more biddable to a huntsman in a more intensively farmed vale.

The Dukes of Rutland, the Earls of Yarborough and the Earls Fitzwilliam were all possessors of long established kennels where the breeding was especially valued by other Hunts. Not only the Belvoir tan, but the so-called Belvoir type became a cult for many hound breeders.

Daphne Moore, the student of hound breeding has described the Belvoir hound at its most extreme, at the end of the nineteenth century, as 'standing woodenly on four legs like bedposts terminating in round club feet; wide barrel ribs pushing forward a shoulder which was placed perpendicular with the ground.'

The foxhound of the mid-nineteenth century had been light-framed and more racy. Later in the century the pendulum was swinging too far in the

direction of bone and substance in an animal expected to run up to one hundred miles in a day's hunting, matching the agility and brainpower of one of nature's most cunning and active mammals, the fox.

The fashionable hounds of huge substance were known as the 'Peterborough type', or more derisively as 'Shorthorns', comparing them to the girth and stance of beef cattle.

After the 1914–18 Great War, some younger Masters of Foxhounds expressed dissatisfaction with the Peterborough type based on what was thought to be the Belvoir model. They set about making a change by introducing Welsh blood as an outcross. It caused a huge row in English foxhunting circles, so bitter at times that families were split and friendships ended.

At the Belvoir kennel many decisions on hound breeding were made by the long series of professional huntsmen, although the Dukes of Rutland certainly took the closest interest in the pack and maintained overall control. The huge popularity of Belvoir hounds meant that Masters from all over Britain sent bitches to the Belvoir stallion hounds. Otho Paget wrote tactfully: 'Belvoir blood, which had always been appreciated by other kennels, became in such demand that the stallion hounds were used rather too freely.'

Much admired throughout the foxhunting world were the doghounds Dexter, Gambler and Fallible, bred by the Belvoir's popular huntsman Frank Gillard; and Ben Capell followed with other notable sires using the same lines.

Captain Charlie McNeill, who was Master of the North Cotswold (1901–6) and the Grafton (1907–13) wrote to *The Field* complaining that if the best Belvoir stallion hounds sired as many litters as they were shown to have achieved in the stud book, they could not have done much hunting. There was an angry response from others who said it was an impertinence to attack another Master's management of his kennels, and in any case the Belvoir was performing a kindness in allowing bitches to be sent to their sires. The Captain retorted that the Belvoir was a national institution, that hound breeding was of national importance and therefore he was thoroughly justified in raising the matter. The debate wrangled on for some weeks, but reached no conclusions.

In Leicestershire there was criticism from some that the doghound pack was not performing at its best, and the 'experts' joined in the criticism that perhaps this was because they were indeed doing too much work at stud! Some claimed that the doghounds were inclined to finish the day well in time for tea and according to a witness quoted by Guy Paget, always less reverent than other hunting writers, they were 'home for lunch the day I went out.'

Mr Chandos Pole of the Meynell (Master, 1881–8) is said to have called them disparagingly a 'very beautiful summer pack'.

There is a huge contrast in views on the Belvoir kennel from the two

amateur huntsmen who hunted them in this century as Masters, Major
Tommy Bouch (1912–24) and Lord Daresbury (1934–46). As recounted in
the Belvoir's history, the former endeavoured to introduce some outcrosses,
but was firmly overruled by the Duke of Rutland, while the latter was a
disciple of the purest English blood all his life, taking Belvoir hounds to
Ireland later to form his own pack at the County Limerick kennel.

Having hunted with the Belvoir for over twenty years, I would attest
that the modern Belvoir hound produces superb sport and I have also had
marvellous sport with pure English hounds in the County Limerick country

which offers hounds such a different challenge, with its huge banks and ditches. In the Brocklesby country I have been extremely impressed by the English pack still maintained in that kennel by the Earls of Yarborough and their forebears since the early eighteenth century.

It seems likely the modern Belvoir hound is somewhat smaller than the hounds which excited such controversy at the beginning of this century. They are somewhat more boxy in conformation than the so-called modern foxhound; the Belvoir hound is still straighter in front than many others. Yet among the most important factors for a huntsman in producing consistent sport is the ability of his hounds to hunt together as a pack and the Belvoir certainly do this well. They are very exciting to ride behind when they surge out of one of their famous coverts in the Vale of Belvoir and the persistence and fox catching abilities of the doghounds in the ploughs on the Lincolnshire side are manifest. They have the drive which is essential in a pack of foxhounds if it is to be followed by reasonably well-bred horses across a grass country.

It is a pity that more foxhunters elsewhere have not seen English hounds at work. Post-war hound breeding has been dominated by kennels of the 10th Duke of Beaufort at Badminton, and by Captain Ronnie Wallace's at Heythrop and latterly the Exmoor. These are superb hounds and they have for many years scooped most of the doghound and bitch championships at Peterborough Royal Foxhound Show, the annual holy of holies held by the foxhunting world in conjunction with the East of England Agricultural Show in mid-July. You will not see Belvoir, nor any other English hounds exhibited at Peterborough nowadays. Modern foxhound judges are so attuned to the modern hound that presumably they would find it difficult to judge them in company with English hounds which

are so different. I have seen this problem arise at the Irish Foxhound Show at Clonmel and at Dublin where the County Limerick hounds were entered but were constantly put down when judged against the 'modern' hounds of such packs as Major Victor McCalmont's Kilkenny or the County Tipperary originally 'modernized' by Evan Williams. Although the Limerick often won group prizes because they are so well matched.

The late Sir Peter Farquhar, father of the current Joint Master and huntsman of the Duke of Beaufort's, Captain Ian Farquhar, was one of the leading prophets of change, describing the English foxhound just after 1918 as 'too big, not active enough, lacking drive and intelligence, and short of tongue.'

Mr Isaac ('Ikey') Bell, an American born MFH and hound breeder in Britain and Ireland was a great innovator and used Welsh lines widely in the 1920s and '30s. When the 10th Duke of Beaufort took over as MFH of his own pack in 1924 he used Welsh blood via Ikey's hounds at the South and West Wilts.

Once Badminton had used Welsh infusions, many other Hunts followed suit. The trend has continued ever since, with a fresh leaning to further Welsh outcrosses, led by Sir Newton Rycroft in the New Forest pack in the 1960s. There were clearly good reasons for the outcrosses of Welsh blood effected earlier this century. Yet if those who made the change in breeding were entirely correct, surely the present day English hounds would be showing vastly inferior sport to the others? This is emphatically not the case, as the performance of the Belvoir hounds indicates, providing top-class sport on grass, plough, or in woodlands.

As I have stated, so far has the pendulum of foxhound breeding swung nowadays that only the Belvoir, the Brocklesby and the York and Ainsty South claim to have 'pure' English packs, but I should add that there are other packs which have a distinctly English appearence, even though they cannot claim to be free of outcrosses. Among the others bred very much on English lines are Sir Watkin Williams Wynn's; significantly, they produce excellent sport in their superb Welsh Borders country of grass and fences, nowadays hunted by Gerald Gundry's son Robin.

In recent seasons the Belvoir's use of stallion hounds from outside their kennel have included the following: Blankney Lincoln ('83), Brocklesby Actor ('86), Brocklesby Colonel ('84), Limerick Lancer ('84) and York and Ainsty South Playboy ('82).

In Leicestershire the Belvoir continued to have great influence on its neighbouring packs until after the Second World War.

Tony Murray Smith did not effect a dramatic change during his Mastership (1954–60) but there was a cautious start of a new direction in the Quorn kennel at that time. It is doubtful that he would have gone as far as the changes wrought since in the Quorn hounds; for at the Fernie he later evolved a modified English hound rather than a completely new stamp.

David Keith (1965–72) went somewhat further away from Belvoir breeding in the Quorn kennel. Then the Quorn breeding was for many years largely handed over to Captain Ronnie Wallace who inevitably introduced a great deal of Heythrop and Badminton blood which effectively 'modernized' the Quorn hounds considerably.

The colour of a hound is not significant at all in terms of its performance, nor is it ever judged on colour at puppy show nor in a full-scale hound show. However, one effect of the influence of the Greenjackets (Beaufort, Heythrop, whose Hunt staff wear green instead of scarlet) was to lose the Belvoir tan colour in the Quorn kennels, except for occasional usage of Belvoir stallions which has continued until today.

In recent seasons the Quorn has used the following stallion hounds: Berkeley Albion ('86), Berkeley Douglas ('86), Exmoor Dunkery ('84), Berkeley Freshman ('84), Zetland Hawksby ('87), Belvoir Tractor ('86), Duke of Beaufort's Palmer ('83), Limerick Lancer ('84), Heythrop Wildboy ('85), Heythrop Herdsman ('85) and Heythrop David ('85).

From 1992 the breeding of the Quorn hounds was being handed over to Captain Ian Farquhar at the Duke of Beaufort's. The route towards far more Welsh blood in the Quorn kennel during the 1990s was almost inevitable.

The Leicestershire packs traditionally used their bitch packs in their grass country, and the separate doghound packs on the more arable or woodland side of the country. The Belvoir, Cottesmore and Quorn still broadly follow this pattern, although the march of arable into the so-called fashionable hunting days has blurred the situation somewhat. However, the tradition is soundly based on the different characteristics of the male and female foxhound. The male is persistent and 'doggy' in his approach to hunting. Doghound packs tend to be more dour and do not like huntsmen lifting them off the line unduly, tending to become less co-operative if they suffer too much interference rather than sympathetic help from the huntsman. Their greater physical bulk and strength also helps them in hunting in plough and dense woodland. Bitch packs can be more volatile, but they are credited with being more generous and forgiving if the huntsman has to lift them from the line, or halt them because it impractical to hunt a line further. A good bitch pack should be fast, accurate, of good voice and with plenty of drive, but biddable to a huntsman's directives by horn and voice.

The Quorn therefore hunt their bitch pack on Mondays and Fridays on the Melton Mowbray side where there is open grasssland and fences and the doghounds on Tuesdays and Saturdays, in Charnwood Forest or the more constricted country to the west on the Donington side.

The Belvoir hunt their bitches on Saturdays and Wednesdays on the Leicestershire side, which includes the Vale of Belvoir and the country on the hill above it to the south and the doghounds on Tuesdays and Fridays on the far more arable Lincolnshire land. The Cottesmore bitches hunt Tuesdays and Saturdays, which includes their greater stretches of grass and their doghounds, which in fact nowadays include some bitches, on Mondays and Thursdays, again including the eastern, Lincolnshire country.

The Fernie, since cutting their days to mainly two days a week, Wednesdays and Saturdays, having lost so much country around Stoughton due to the Co-op ban, do not run two distinctly separate packs.

All Hunts keep more hounds than they put into the hunting field, since they need brood bitches to produce the next generation and hounds which may be temporarily unfit for work, plus the unentered hounds which are 'walked' by members of the Hunt: brought up on farms during their first year of life until returned to the pack to be 'entered' into the pack for work in the second year. The abundance of farmers and other enthusiasts willing to walk hounds in Leicestershire is one more testimony to the continuing popularity of the sport in the county. Foxhound puppies can be hard work as well as fun; they need considerable supervision and they have huge appetites. The huntsman visits the walks to see how the young hounds are progressing. This early experience is vital; it sharpens the growing hounds' intelligence through being closer to a domestic environment and the individual attention they receive promotes their growth and early development.

The annual puppy show run by each Hunt is a vital date in the hunting calendar. The young hounds are judged by visiting MFHs and professional huntsmen and prizes are awarded to those who walked the winners. Speeches and presentations are made at large-scale tea parties given to the puppy walkers and other farmers and supporters. It is quite a heavy financial outlay for the Masters nowadays. Various solutions are found in accommodating tea parties for several hundred people. The Belvoir resolutely continues to use a marquee, but the Quorn has used its ultra-modern stable block for the tea party, while the Cottesmore's venue has varied from the dining room at Ashwell prison to a large steel barn owned by Mr Joss Hanbury at Burley-on-the-Hill.

Following the progress of the hounds they have 'walked' when they see them hunting with the pack later in their career is fascinating, and it helps to cement the support and interest from a wide cross section of the rural community who make a huge contribution to the sport. No wonder people in country areas speak so often of 'our hounds' with such pride.

When Tony Murray Smith took the Fernie Mastership in the early 1960s, he introduced Heythrop and Beaufort blood into the traditional English pack and they nicked in well with the earlier breeding. He was also able to introduce an American tail female line which is still flourishing to this day, through a hound called Darkness from the Green Spring Valley Hunt in Maryland, USA. The former Master of the Green Spring Valley, Mr Fife Symington, was a keen foxhunting visitor to Leicestershire. He was given a couple of bitches from the Quorn kennel by Tony Murray Smith, and in return Fife Symington presented a couple of doghounds and a bitch from the Green Spring Valley, the bitch going to the Fernie.

In recent seasons the Fernie has used as stallion hounds South Shropshire Crocket ('87), South Shropshire Crawford ('88), South Shropshire Crackshot ('88), Brocklesby Actor ('86), Sir Watkin Williams-Wynn's Somerset ('86) and Heythrop David ('85).

The Cottesmore kennel shows most evidence of Welsh outcross influence among the Leicestershire packs. Two notable amateur huntsmen were responsible for this: Captains Simon Clarke and Brian Fanshawe. Simon Clarke (Joint Master and huntsman 1969–76) introduced several new female lines from the Duke of Beaufort's and South Dorset kennels into the Cottesmore. Their successes at hound shows backed up the fine results he achieved in the hunting field. He also used New Forest Medyg ('69), probably the most influential source of post-war Welsh blood in many kennels. Medyg was bred by Sir Newton Rycroft out of a New Forest bitch, Traffic ('65) and sired by the Welsh doghound Miller ('65) from the Plas Machynlleth Hunt. He proved to be remarkably pre-potent, stamping his image and hunting qualities on all his progeny. The 10th Duke of Beaufort used Medyg with much success in the Badminton kennel.

Like all great huntsmen, Brian Fanshawe was much concerned to breed a pack of hounds to suit him and during his Mastership the Cottesmore pack saw major changes. He used Welsh lines through the stallion hound North Cotswold Craven ('78), going back to the Curre stallion hound Saucy ('47) who was used in the North Cotswold kennel by Brian Fanshawe's parents, Major and Mrs R.G. Fanshawe. He also introduced Welsh blood from the kennel of his cousin Ian Farquhar at the Bicester and Warden Hill. The stallion hound used at the Cottesmsore was Bicester Granby ('88).

Broken coated, somewhat whiskery hounds were seen for the first time in the Cottesmore pack after the Welsh outcrosses were introduced. Not everyone in Leicestershire liked the look of the Welsh 'woollies', but they had to admit, and did so that they hunted like dingbats for Brian. He was especially pleased with the Carlow line which he had maintained in his various packs since 1963. Some forty per cent of the Cottesmore pack have Carlow blood on the bottom line, and it is elsewhere in the hound breeding.

'They are terribly easy to handle, nearly like pet dogs,' Brian would say with great affection. 'They need plenty of hunting, but they are biddable and they have what Sir Peter Farquhar called "fox sense".'

It can be seen from the use of stallion hounds from elsewhere, that Brian Fanshawe has drawn heavily on some of the best proved foxhound breeding as well as the Welsh outcrosses which are a comparatively minor element. In recent seasons the Cottesmore hound list includes the following stallion hounds: the Duke of Beaufort's Palmer ('83), Exmoor Dancer ('84) and Cotswold Grampian ('85) as well as the above mentioned Bicester and Warden Hill Granby ('88).

Foxhound breeders can be proud of their product in the late twentieth century; as mentioned previously it bears none of the appalling faults of too many domestic dogs, bred solely for appearence and fashion. The foxhound is a remarkable working animal.

Breeding is by no means the only factor in achieving success in the hunting field. Although the lines of breeding are important, the element which sets apart a great huntsman is his skill in handling the pack in the hunting field, his ability to use what Ronnie Wallace has called 'the invisible thread' of communication between himself and his hounds. However, like a good horseman, the great huntsman benefits enormously if the animal he is working with is of top-class quality and suitability for the task ahead.

Old Meynell would no doubt be appalled at the change in the terrain of Leicestershire if he were to return today, but he would soon be cheered by the remarkably high standard of the modern hounds still hunting his paradise, and by the skill and dedication of the current Leicestershire huntsmen and their supporting staff.

The foil caused by fertilizer dressing on arable land and by diesel and petrol fumes on the roads, are huge drawbacks in modern hunting. The modern hound's abilities in overcoming such challenges are evidence of the triumph achieved by all who contributed to its breeding over the past two centuries.

10

The Fernie

Wonderful going – mile upon miles of beautiful grass, that, even after a week's rain,
hardly shows the mark of a horse's foot,
and yet seems to have all the spring and
elasticity of highly tempered steel

Born out of a boundary dispute, the Fernie hunts some of the most delightful country in the whole of the British Isles. After my first visit I ceased to wonder why those who lived and hunted there wished to create their own Hunt from the country which was originally part of the Quorn territory.

The Harborough country, as it has been called, is certainly among the most beautiful and varied in Leicestershire. Market Harborough became a great hunting centre, with its easy proximity to the Pytchley, Fernie and further north the Cottesmore and Quorn. It has been said that Harborough was a town of much historical importance and interest long before the late eighteenth and early nineteenth century development of foxhunting gave it extra prominence, whereas Melton Mowbray was elevated to greater importance from a tiny market centre simply because of foxhunting. Certainly the Harborough area is an exceedingly pleasant place to live; its accessibility to the south and London no doubt increased its attractiveness ever since road and rail travel improved.

Thus, although attracting short-term visitors, the Fernie has long had the benefit of keen foxhunters who live in the country. This has produced stability in long-term Masterships and Hunt officials.

There is a charm and ease born of confidence in the Fernie country which I have always found congenial. Its pasture land even at the end of the twentieth century is still superb; there has, of course, been a huge increase in arable farming, as elsewhere in the Midlands.

From the riding point of view the Fernie has relied heavily on made Hunt jumps far more than its neighbours to the north; this is due to a practice of using barbed wire oxers behind fences to keep in stock which became all too popular locally. However, the Fernie proved simply to be ahead of its time, for the practice has spread widely, and the Fernie Hunt jumps are particularly well constructed, broad and of stout build. A horseman can 'get about' in the Fernie country, and if he wishes to frighten himself there are ample opportunities; indeed the presence of the many Hunt jumps can easily cause the unwary to be taken by surprise when suddenly confronted with some obstacle far more difficult, which is certainly not a specially constructed Hunt jump!

As one who likes to look about during a day's hunting, I find the Fernie terrain especially beguiling. There are beautiful views in so many parts of the country, especially the Laughton Hills.

During all my travels for *Horse and Hound* over the past twenty-one years as hunting correspondent, I have certain days which come more easily to mind, and I shall never forget my visit to the Fernie on 25 February 1977, when hounds ran all day over the cream of the country. The afternoon hunt, from John Ball was a run of sixteen miles, with a six mile point in two hours fifteen minutes. I was fortunate to be among the few to be there at the finish. Here is an extract from my Foxford's Hunting Diary record of the day in *Horse and Hound*.

We changed horses and I mounted one of the cleverest little hunters it has been my good fortune to ride in the hunting field. It was barely sixteen hands and is normally ridden by the whipper-in (Michael King); a smallish mount for a six foot two inch hunting correspondent, but I was never conscious of this, and the little horse gave me a grand ride throughout, no matter how big the fences nor how demanding the pace.

I have always wanted to see a fox go away from the famous John Ball covert in the Fernie country. . . .

It was a wonderful moment when Bruce Durno put his hounds in at one end and they were soon speaking. There was one of those splendid holloas which make the hairs stand up on the back of your neck, and suddenly we were galloping along the top side of the covert to come round the far end and be confronted by a wonderful sight – a classic 'gone away'.

The Fernie hounds were running beautifully together over the grass with a wonderful head, and the pace was fast enough to make you sit down and ride, but not too fast to spoil the pleasure of jumping the delectable variety of timber and fly fences criss-crossing the downhill grassy slopes ahead.

The fox made a big left-handed circle by Furnivals and Saddington nearly to Fleckney and back to the John Ball covert. We had some road work in the middle of this run, but it had been a wonderful ride and it seemed almost too good to be true when hounds pushed their fox straight through the covert and across the grass again.

He ran left-handed this time to cross the Mowsley road by Foxons Farm, over the Laughton brook and between Gumley and Laughton up to Bunker's Hill. Then the line continued along the hills and right again by Laughton Village, Gumley covert and Lubenham Lodge, but this time crossing the canal and going on with Gartree Prison on the right.

At this stage hounds were hunting better than ever; it was a joy to watch them making the line good and putting on the pressure.

But the fox just got to ground by a few yards in the badger holes below the A 6 on Gallow Hill. It had been a wonderful hunt to ride and to watch hounds all the way, and I am so grateful to all concerned for having had the opportunity to take part in it.

As recorded in the early history of the Quorn (Chapter Four) Sir Richard Sutton was so enthusiastic a Master that he took over the Donington country to the west as well as the Quorn, hunting two days a week for two seasons. It was a huge commitment, since the Quorn country then stretched south as far as Market Harborough. In 1854 Sir Richard decided to reduce his scope by having the Harborough end of the country hunted separately by his sons, Dick and Frank. There was a story that he told them he was sick of having his hounds over-ridden and therefore they had better take twenty couple of hounds and go to break their necks over the Skeffington Vale ox-fences. Alas, in November 1855, Sir Richard died before anything had been negotiated about the exact arrangement under which the Harborough country was being hunted separately.

During the 1855–6 season Mr Richard Sutton's hounds met four days a week between Harborough and Melton, a superb stretch of country; and his brother Mr Francis Sutton's hounds met three times a week, between the Soar and the Wreak and one day on the Charnwood Forest.

Lord Stamford took the Quorn in 1856, thereby preserving that great hunting country as an entity, but the Harborough country had been given up by Mr Richard Sutton, and his brother ceased to hunt his stretch of Quorn country.

Into the breach in the Harborough country stepped Mr W.W. Tailby of Skeffington Hall. He formed a pack which became known as the Billesdon Hunt. Billesdon sits by the A 47, the Leicester to Peterborough road, nowadays on the border of the Fernie and the Quorn Friday country to the north. It is still an area which delights the foxhunter's eye; I always enjoy driving a car along the road south to Market Harborough from Billesdon, let alone riding the country sometimes with the Fernie. Fortunately Mr Tailby kept a marvellous journal from 1856 until four years before his death on 5 January 1914, when he was only a fortnight short of his ninetieth birthday. I commend the diary as reading for enthusiastic foxhunters, especially those with a love for Leicestershire. What a man! Known as 'Little Tailby', he was slight of stature, but rode large horses well above his weight. He had a mercurial temperament, and was either 'up' or 'down', but he had tremendous fortitude and stamina. Born on 18 January 1825, at Humberstone, William Ward Tailby was thirty-one when he founded the Billesdon Hunt. He suffered some terrible falls in the hunting field, although considering his longevity the number of falls was not an undue proportion of the number of days he hunted. He was that somewhat rare individual, a hard-riding hunting man who took on the country with iron nerves all his long life, but at the same time he was an exceptionally keen hound man, and it bothered him greatly if the field indulged in over-riding or pressing hounds. He was said to have resorted to holding on the cantle of the saddle to stay in the plate when jumping the biggest places. When over seventy he was thrown at a gate, his horse rearing up and falling back on him, breaking his thigh, and he lay in the open for several hours until he was found.

His Mastership, and the high standard of sport he achieved, gave the future Fernie country a special place in the affections of foxhunters who liked to see hounds well hunted, whilst enjoying a great ride.

There is no doubt that a Hunt with a genuinely hard-riding Master, who tends always to employ a huntsman of the same ilk, has a drive and persistence which is reflected in the hound work, and the length of runs achieved. Mr Tailby's produced some truly phenomenal runs. He hunted a much larger country than the present Fernie country, having astutely borrowed a huge chunk of the neighbouring Cottesmore as well. This has been one of the most important areas of the Cottesmore ever since it was returned to them in 1872. The country from the Whissendine down to Billesdon was loaned by the Cottesmore on condition that it must be returned if requested by a member of the Lowther family.

In *Horse and Hound's* 17 January 1914 issue there is a tribute to him following his death, which recounts that in 1886 he was writing in his journal after a bad fall in which he broke three ribs that he was 'seriously thinking of giving up the game.' Yet twenty years later he was still riding out with hounds! What runs the Billesdon hounds achieved during his Mastership! Tailby's first huntsman was Tom Day who had whipped-in to the Quorn, but the following season he engaged Jack Goddard who stayed nine years. Tailby disapproved of Goddard's tendency to lift hounds off a hunted fox to go to a holloa on a fresh fox. In 1863 Goddard went to the Quorn, and was replaced by Frank Goodall from the Cottesmore. He hunted the Billesdon hounds until 1872, and Tailby's diary records the cream of the sport during that period. Among the many extraordinary hunts achieved was a run over twenty miles after hounds met on 26 February at Saddington. They had a good fifty minutes' hunt from Jane Ball, catching their fox, and then hounds were put on the line of a fox seen running past Walton Holt. They ran to Bosworth village, past Welford, to the Hemplow Hills, Stanford and over the River Avon – an ugly place where one man nearly drowned his horse, wrote Tailby – over the Rugby and Leicester turnpike, to Coton House, on to Cosford, and on to Bruntingthorpe where hounds had to be stopped after a run over two hours two minutes, with all the horses dead beat. They had run through the Pytchley and Atherstone countries and reached the borders of the North Warwickshire. Tailby concedes that they probably changed foxes on the way. They had to take a special train from Rugby to Leicester for horses and hounds, arriving home at nine at night. Alas, the huntsman's horse had to be left at Rugby where it died the next day, testifying to the severity of the run.

Tailby's hounds produced tremendous runs in what is now the best of the Cottesmore country, swooping from the present Fernie borders down to Launde, and on to the delightful country above Braunston, then going on to Whissendine to the north east, or Somerby and the present Quorn borders to the west.

Tailby was much cast down to lose the Cottesmore country and threatened resignation, but he changed his mind, and hunted hounds himself from 1872–6. He continued to produce good sport, but appeared to be having considerable trouble with his mounted field who, he complained, upset him by holloaing, shouting and interfering with hounds. It is possible there was some dissension in the country because of the Quorn boundary row of 1878 which was already brewing. Tailby was not a man to compromise or make peace easily, and the atmosphere became worse. He put on Dick Christian to hunt the hounds, but he was past his prime by then, and in 1877 Tailby engaged Richard Summers as huntsman. He wrote bitterly in his diary that Summers 'did everything right' but was still criticized by some elements in the mounted field who claimed he was slow and could not ride. 'All this was gall and wormwood, and it worried me so much that I decided to give up the country,' recorded Tailby.

Discord over his successor broke out as soon as Tailby's resignation was known. This was compounded in 1878 by a major problem: the Quorn's Mr Coupland wrote politely to request that the Billesdon country be returned to the Quorn. Mr Coupland wanted to move from the kennels at Quorn, set up new kennels in a more central position and hunt the Harborough country as well as the Quorn. The Great Hunt Row which this provoked, was to roar and then rumble on well into the next century. At its height friendships were broken, family rows erupted, and some members of the Quorn Hunt wore 'ratcatcher' when they chose to visit the Billesdon country – sometimes being ridden at or into by irate members of that Hunt. If television and the rest of the media had been in existence, there is no doubt that the dispute would have proved even stronger meat for broadcasting and press than the Quorn Hunt row of January 1992.

The great lesson which became starkly apparent was that no matter how Masters may pontificate, or Committee members huff and puff, in foxhunting the heart of power is in the hands of the landowners and farmers over whose land hunting is proposed. If they will not have a Master, or a particular pack of hounds, there is nothing that the Hunt can do about it. More than enough of the local landowners and farmers in the Billesdon country wanted their next Master to be Sir Bache Cunard, aged only twenty-seven, having succeeded to the baronetcy in 1869 when he was aged eighteen, and residing at Hallaton Hall and later at Nevill Holt. He proved to be an excellent Master in every way, especially in the vital department of making friends with the farmers. His Mastership proved crucial; if he had been a failure, the Quorn's case for resumption of the country it had formerly hunted could well have proved irresistible. Mr Coupland on behalf of the Quorn had not desisted, but he referred the matter for arbitration to the only ruling body existing at that time, the Masters of Foxhounds Committee at Boodle's, the London Club. This caused more than a little mystification among some Leicestershire farmers. 'Who is Boodle?' they asked in some puzzlement. Meanwhile Mr Coupland agreed that Sir Bache Cunard could hunt the Harborough/ Billesdon country until such arbitration was achieved. When it came, early in 1879, the Boodle's decision caused even more uproar. The Committee was of the opinion that the Harborough country was still part of the Quorn and Mr Coupland had every right to hunt it. It was to be hoped that those on the Billesdon side would support him. A meeting of tenant farmers on the Billesdon side sent a letter to Mr Coupland protesting at Sir Bache being turned out after building new kennels, and they threatened prosecutions for trespass against Mr Coupland if he attempted to hunt their country with the Quorn hounds. Feelings ran high on both sides of the border. The Earl of Wilton on the Melton side was one of the leading hawks in the Quorn's battle to regain its country. Conciliation was at last achieved in the middle of 1879 by the powerful Earl Spencer, 'ruler' of the Pytchley country. He sent Mr Coupland a communication signed by forty Masters and ex-Masters. This agreed that Mr Coupland had established his right to that part of the Quorn country formerly hunted by Mr Tailby, but they suggested Sir Bache should continue to hunt it, on that understanding that it should revert to the Quorn on his retirement.

There was further huffing and puffing, but the Quorn Committee agreed to settle on these terms, and a sort of peace broke out, but the dispute was not forgotten, nor forgiven by some, for many a year.

Sir Bache Cunard reigned for a decade, and achieved much in ensuring that the country Tailby had hunted, minus the Cottesmore portion, was totally viable as a complete hunting country, paying much attention to covert maintenance. It must be remembered that when Mr Tailby had taken the country he had described it as 'derelict' and he hunted far beyond the boundaries of the present Fernie, presumably selecting the most suitable country, and somewhat neglecting the rest.

Richard Summers remained as huntsman for two seasons, but in 1880 Will Grant came from Lord Macclesfield as huntsman; he had been second whip to Goodall during Tailby's time. Cunard built his kennels at Medbourne, and they were used throughout Mr Fernie's Mastership, and for one season by Lord Stalbridge. The present kennels were built at Great Bowden in 1923 and first used the following year. Sir Bache Cunard moved to Nevill Holt, where his family resided for nearly fifty years, in order to be nearer the kennels. He resigned as Master in 1888, but he remained closely connected with the Hunt until his death in 1925.

The Hunt's future as a separate entity was to be assured by a great Mastership which, in effect, made the Quorn's claims even more irrelevant, since they established still further the solid support of the farmers and landowners behind the Hunt which was to bear the name of the new Master, Charles Witherington Bruce Fernie. Continuity is a huge asset in foxhunting, and the Hunt was to have the benefit of this for the next thirty years. He was allowed to take the Mastership on giving a written agreement to the Quorn Committee that the country should revert to them on his own retirement. However, in 1909 Viscount Churchill negotiated a permanent arrangement whereby the Quorn Committee agreed to recognize a local committe which would select and appoint new Masters when the occasion arose, subject only to formal confirmation by the Quorn. When Mr Fernie died ten years later, he left his hounds to the country on the condition that the Quorn surrendered any claim to it. The embers of the old dispute had died down; the Quorn Committee was pleased to meet the Fernie at a joint meeting in Leicester. This resulted in 'Mr Fernie's hounds' becoming officially 'The Fernie Hunt'. The Quorn Hunt Chairman, Mr John B. Cradock, confirmed the Quorn's relinquishment of all claims and rights in a letter dated 17 January 1920. At the Fernie Committee meeting on 17 May 1921, it was decided to call the hunt 'Fernie's Hunt', but by the end of the 1930s the final 's' had been dropped, and the Hunt is usually referred to simply as 'The Fernie'.

Mr Fernie was born in Hertfordshire but had Scottish relatives and began his hunting with the Linlithgow and Stirlingshire. It was related that at twenty-eight his doctors told him he was seriously ill and did not have too many years of life left to him. He resolved to live life to the full, and took Keythorpe Hall as a residence in the Fernie country, hunting there regularly before taking the Mastership. Hunting appeared to assist his health, for he thrived in Leicestershire, and in 1900 married a local hunting lady, Edith Hardcastle, younger daughter of Thomas Hardcastle of Blaston. She was an exceedingly keen foxhunter, and was to succeed her husband in the Mastership.

Mr Fernie first appointed Charles Isaac as his huntsman; he had been with the Pytchley for thirteen years, finishing there as first whipper-in. He was Cornish bred, and had enjoyed hunting since his boyhood; he was a natural huntsman, and gave Mr Fernie a great start to his Mastership, helping him to renovate old coverts and planting new ones; including Mowsley, Peatling and Tamborough Hill.

In 1907 Arthur Thatcher was appointed Mr Fernie's huntsman. Thatcher (Chapter Fourteen) had been huntsman to the neighbouring Cottesmore since 1900, but he had been with the Fernie previously as a whipper-in. Anyone who has read the Earl of Lonsdale's celebrated three-thousand words letter chastising Thatcher for his performance as a huntsman, as referred to in the Cottesmore history, will appreciate that Thatcher was unlikely to be altogether happy in that kennel with the Yellow Earl as his Master! Despite Lonsdale's low opinion of him, Thatcher was a remarkably good huntsman. Some Leicestershire foxhunters said that for sheer fun they preferred hunting with him to anyone, even the great Tom Firr. Thatcher was quick of decision and action; he could seize the opportunity of a hunt quickly, and thereby suddenly increase the pace. Some criticized him as being too artful; for many others he was simply a great opportunist. He was hunting hounds when the great Horninghold run occurred after the meet at Blaston on 25 February 1911. 'The Quorn had a great run yesterday,' Thatcher said to Mr Fernie. 'I think we shall have a better one today.' Indeed, hounds found in Hegg Spinney, ran as if for Stockerston, turned left and crossed the Eye Brook, hesitated below Beaumont Chase, and then raced up the hill, skirting Wardly Wood. On the outskirts of Uppingham the fox crouched under a wall, and hounds jumped over him, but he got up almost among the hounds and began a great run northwards into the Cottesmore country, heading for Glaston, running to Brooke, and nearly to Oakham Pastures. He then swung back southwards to Preston, running below Manton Gorse, then set off towards Orton Park, above Braunston. Hounds raced through this covert, although it is likely they changed foxes here, running to Knossington Spinney, back to Lady Wood, then Cold Overton, and on past Owston Wood to Marefield. Thatcher managed to change horses at Knossington. Veering right, the fox ran to Burrough Hill, checking near Peake's Covert, and then doubling back to Somerby, on to Orton Park, with a great storm blowing, and down to Braunston where most of the pack marked at a stick heap. Thatcher then saw some hounds feathering along a furrow, and brought up the rest of the pack; they killed their fox dead beat in the open. Only six in the mounted field completed the run, besides Thatcher and two whippers-in.

The run covered about thirty miles in three hours and twenty minutes, with a furthest point of just under nine miles, from Horninghold to Peake's.

In 1907 Mr Fernie had suffered a severe fall from which he never fully recovered, and for physical reasons he had left the field during the early part of this run. Thatcher gave him a full report in the billiard room at Keythorpe. Mr Fernie was pacing around the billiard room.

'I'd have given you anything if you'd killed that fox,' he said. 'They tell me you lost him.'

Legend relates that Thatcher simply handed him the fox's mask and brush.

Despite the depredations wrought on the landscape since then, the above run would be perfectly possible today, and much of the country crossed is still down to grass, especially that beautiful, unspoilt hillside above Braunston. The coverts named are still in existence, and still drawn by the Cottesmore. I have hunted over all the country described in recent seasons, albeit in segments rather than the whole run described.

The Fernie continued hunting throughout the First World War, although on a much reduced scale. Like the other Shires packs, the Fernie experienced the same upsurge of enthusiasm for foxhunting from the men and women who returned from the horrors of that war.

Mr Fernie died in 1919; a cause of much mourning in the country. His widow continued in office for the 1919–20 season, and the following one. She was joined in 1921 by Mrs Faber as Joint Master, but rising costs and higher taxation led to Mrs Fernie's resignation, although the Hunt had reduced fixtures from three to two days a week, and an occasional bye-day.

An outbreak of foot and mouth disease in cattle halted hunting for the rest of the season, and was to plague the area again all too soon.

The agricultural depression may well have been a cause of the lack of local candidates for the Mastership. For the first time, the Hunt advertised for Masters; there was only one applicant, Lord Stalbridge, who had been Master and amateur huntsman of the South and West Wilts from 1911–23. Leicestershire in general, apart from the Cottesmore in later years, has never been especially enthusiastic about amateur huntsmen, believing them too inclined to do their own thing, rather than concentrate totally on entertaining the field. Lord Stalbridge did not lack enthusiasm for the challenge awaiting him. He was to write (as part of an Introduction to Charles Simpson's *Harborough Country*): 'What a country it is! The cream of High Leicestershire! And what more can you want?' When he took the Mastership the kennels were still at Medbourne where they had been built by Sir Bache Cunard, but the Committee purchased Mr Stokes' stables at Great Bowden and built new kennels there. Lord Stalbridge described them as 'the best and complete, up-to-date establishment in the kingdom.'

He wrote glowingly of the Fernie.

Wonderful going – miles upon miles of beautiful grass, that, even after a week's rain, hardly shows the mark of a horse's foot, and yet seems to have all the spring and elasticity of highly tempered steel.

There is a sting in it, riding a good horse and jumping the big black fences clean from field to field of perfect turf, that once felt can never be forgotten and, in my humble opinion, can never be felt so completely as in Leicestershire.

There is, of course, also the pace: the fields are large, the going perfect, nothing to stop hounds, and the scent good on the whole, and so hounds travel on at a great pace, and keep going, whereas the horse has always the ridge and furrow to contend with and, be his shoulders ever so good and his conformation perfect, no horse can gallop at any great speed over ridge and furrow, although it is wonderful how they get across it when they get accustomed to it.

Lord Stalbridge averred that the 'Fernie fences are not to be trifled with,' although he conceded that double-oxers were now rare. He admitted, however, that 'it is the hardest country to hunt a fox in that I have ever come across.' His testimony is especially interesting, being a starkly honest account of someone who clearly found more problems than he had expected on coming from a provincial country. His Lordship said the foxes were 'extraordinarily stout', and the coverts 'were all against the hounds', being 'so thick that foxes will not leave them unless properly rattled cubhunting. . . . He complained that hounds tended to stop drawing because they were afraid of being left in covert when the huntsman went away with three or four couple on the line of a fox.

Altogether his detailed explanation of his problems seem to indicate a lack of the 'invisible thread' which great huntsman possess in communicating with and controlling their hounds. He found it difficult to kill a fox in a galloping country because the fox could see a long way ahead, and was inclined to turn back through a fence if it saw someone on the next ridge perhaps two more miles away. Then hounds would flash on well beyond the line, reported Lord Stalbridge ruefully. Perhaps if he had seen the great Leicestershire huntsmen at their best he would have realized that the shortcomings he experienced lay not in the country, or the coverts. Writing in 1926, he indicates that modern developments were beginning to cause extra problems for huntsmen. He complained of tarred roads, the smell of a motor car, artificial manures . . . 'to say nothing of the unemployed on bicycles and ladies in limousines.'

No doubt, words would have failed Lord Stalbridge if he had to contend with the volume of today's 'unemployed and ladies in limousines,' to say nothing of articulated lorries, miles of plough prairies and barbed wire everywhere. His arrival in the Fernie country meant the retirement of Arthur Thatcher, although he carried the horn again for the South Atherstone for the two seasons 1930–2.

More foot and mouth disease outbreaks between 1923–6 somewhat marred Lord Stalbridge's Mastership, causing all too many hunting stoppages. Things became so bad during the 1923–4 season that some members, hungering for a ride over grass and fences, organized paper chases in lieu of foxhunting, causing some raised eyebrows and critical comment in the sporting press.

Major Wernher, later Major General Sir Harold Wernher, had joined the Mastership in 1924. When Lord Stalbridge resigned in 1928, Sir Harold offered to continue with Mr A.C. Edmonstone as Joint Master. Charles Edmonstone had an outgoing personality and was especially popular with the farmers. He rode with very short stirrups, jockey style, and crossed the country at top speed with an iron nerve. The Committee, perhaps significantly, accepted this offer rather than another which would have involved an amateur huntsman again. The new Mastership engaged the professional Bert Peaker who had started his career as second horseman to that genius, Frank Freeman at the Pytchley; a marvellous model for an aspiring huntsman to observe. Peaker survived service throughout the war, and was a whipper-in at the Heythrop, the Southwold and the Whaddon Chase before hunting the Crawley and Horsham from 1925–8. He proved to be one of the best huntsmen ever to carry the horn in the Fernie country, maintaining the role effectively for the next twenty years.

Foot and mouth restrictions hit the country yet again in the 1927–8 season, and again in 1932–3 when twenty-eight days' hunting was lost. At that time restrictions on animal movements were imposed throughout a fifteen mile radius of an outbreak, which was crippling to foxhunting.

Mr Edmonstone retired in 1934, but the indefatigable Sir Harold Wernher continued, with Commander F.J. Alexander who had been appointed Joint Master two years earlier.

Sir Harold resigned the following year, to be succeeded by his wife, Lady Zia Wernher, a Russian aristocrat, and by Captain Derrick Hignett who stayed in office for two years, but was to play a vital role again after the 1939–45 war. Hignett was a Seventh Hussar who came to Leicestershire as Adjutant of the Leicestershire Yeomanry, and stayed on when he bought East Langton Grange. He recalled his pre-war Mastership as having been achieved at 'an horrendous financial cost.'

Sir Julian Cahn, Master of the Woodland Pytchley for two seasons, was appointed in 1937 and provided a somewhat controversial Mastership, although those with a sense of humour enjoyed some of his eccentricities. Ulrica Murray Smith opined that 'the meet was the only part of a day's hunting which he really enjoyed. He would only stay out for an hour or so and then retire into the back of his Rolls Royce, where he would find a three-course lunch ready for him, including an orange soufflé, which apparently was his favourite dish.

'Out hunting Sir Julian Cahn had riding with him a man carrying an axe, ready to demolish any obstacle in his Master's way, but if the worst came to the worst and there was a ditch, the Master would dismount, the groom would jump the horse over, and Sir Julian would remount.'

The riding performance smacked more of Jorrocks than of Osbaldeston, but it indicates just how versatile is the hunting field in accommodating people of differing ambitions. However Sir Julian clearly paid a great deal of cash not to jump fences in one of the best hunting countries in England, and he was thereby subsidizing everyone else's fun.

A small executive hunted the country during the Second World War: Major Wardy Gillilan, Sir Harold Wernher, Brigadier General Jack, Major Guy Paget and Mr J.T. Forsell. They were soon hit by major difficulties. Funds were so short that in 1941 they considered selling the Hunt property, but there were no buyers. A stroke of good fortune was the appointment in 1941 of Mr R.G. (Dick) Watson as Honorary Secretary – a post he held with great distinction and devotion for a remarkable forty-nine years. He was still hunting in the 1992–3 season, probably the only foxhunter who has hunted regularly in Leicestershire in every decade of this century, having first hunted with the Fernie as a child in 1909. He began hunting as a subscriber in 1919, the year of Mr Fernie's death. Between the wars, Dick Watson combined his successful career as a solicitor in Market Harborough with foxhunting in the winter and cricket in the summer, captaining the Leicestershire second eleven. He found time to run his farm and breed hunters; he has hunted five generations of his own stock. Always courteous, cheerful and welcoming, and ever efficient, Dick Watson is the model of an ideal Hunt Secretary; his contribution to the Fernie is incalculable.

Mr J.T. Forsell of Winkadale, near Bushby, was appointed Acting Master in 1941, and played a significant role in keeping the Hunt going. He was Chairman for the last eight years of his life, to 1955 and a much revered county figure as a JP and County Council Alderman. Bert Peaker worked prodigiously to keep wartime hunting a reality, maintaining fixtures, and hounds killing foxes, as directed by the Ministry of Agriculture; on their instructions hunting ended on 31 January.

The ten years 'reign of the Colonels' immediately after the war was a vital service to the Fernie, enabling the Hunt to make the transition to the better times ahead economically in the post-war years. Colonel Derrick Hignett and Colonel Pen Lloyd were appointed in 1946. Alas, Peaker died suddenly in 1948, and was replaced by Walter Gupwell who was with the Galway Blazers in Ireland. The whipper-in George Dimblebee would have been the first choice, but he proved unable to pass a driving test, which was regarded as essential for the huntsman! Gupwell had been huntsman of the great Yorkshire pack, the Middleton, before the war and served in the war in the Royal Veterinary Corps. His son, Brian, was to earn esteem as huntsman of the Duke of Beaufort's from 1967–84; he whipped-in to his father at the Fernie in 1955 after the whipper-in Fred Sallis was out of action. He was to hunt the Fernie hounds for fourteen years, much supported by Colonel Pen Lloyd. In the 1952–3 season hounds killed thirty-one and a half brace, the highest number since the war. However, Joe Cowen remembers Gupwell as having a volatile temper, and 'never much of a hound man, but he was a very forceful and brave horseman who crossed the country as well as anyone at a time when it was difficult to get about, before the country had been properly re-opened.'

Bob Buswell whipped-in, with Bill Jones remaining as second whip. Later Harvey Andrewes, Fred Sallis and the young Bruce Durno whipped-in.

Although plough was encroaching, there was still plenty of grass; more young people were returning to the Chase, and the bleak 1940s and

'50s were giving way to more spacious times when foxhunters could again migrate to the heaven of the East Midlands old turf.

Derrick Hignett had emerged from the war as Lieutenant Colonel, having been involved with special activities connected with Intelligence. He resigned from the Mastership in 1956, remaining a staunch supporter of the Hunt, serving as Chairman of the Committee for many years; he appeared in the pro-hunting demonstration outside Leicestershire County Council offices in 1992 when he was aged ninety. Joe Cowen pays tribute to Derrick Hignett thus:

> Nobody was better at smoothing down ruffled feathers or charming people who might otherwise have been upset. He cut a superb figure on a horse and went well across country, as a good Field Master. In 1955-6 he had a number of falls, after the last of which he gave up riding forever at the age of fifty-six, and with it the Mastership. He was the ideal candidate to step into the vacant Hunt Chairmanship after the resignation of Adam Levy a year later, and it was a role in which he was able to use his talents for the next twenty-five years, until he handed over to Tony Murray Smith in 1983. It was a role Derrick filled with distinction, with aplomb and in his own inimitable manner. He first came on to the Hunt Committee in 1935, and remains on it in 1993.

Pen Lloyd is remembered as a somewhat flamboyant character with immense energy; he was chairman of Leicestershire County Council, and held many other offices and business appointments. He cheerfully bore the financial burdens of Mastership for sixteen consecutive seasons, 1946–62.

'He was always a supporter of what others were trying to do, and never a critic; always an enthusiastic proponent of new ideas, and particularly of young people. He remained young at heart to the end of his days,' Joe Cowen recalls.

Pen Lloyd was joined in the Mastership by Captain Bertram Currie of Dingley Hall, an immensely wealthy man who owned Dunbeath Castle and estate in Scotland, and was a keen yachting man. He was much liked and a generous supporter of the Hunt. The other Joint Master was Captain W.A. (Robin) Gillilan, who stayed in office from 1957–62. He was brought up in Great Bowden, and his father, Wardy Gillilan, had been Hunt Chairman. Robin lived at weekends in a cottage at Great Bowden, and worked hard in the country, building up excellent relationships with the farming community.

As reported in the Quorn history, the arrival of Tony Murray Smith in the Mastership of his home country in 1960, presaged a long period of stability and progress for the Fernie. His influence on hound breeding and all other matters pertaining to the Hunt over the next two decades was entirely beneficial. The vagaries of the Chase are such, that Tony's Mastership started with a severe set-back: he broke a leg just before the end of cubhunting in the 1960–1 season, and could not hunt again in that season, but undaunted he became the Fernie's first amateur huntsman since Lord Stalbridge, in the 1962–3 season, hunting hounds with much success until 1966 when Bruce Durno took over. One of Tony's many qualities was generosity of spirit; a certain jealousy has alas marred all too many other sporting careers in foxhunting. Tony could enjoy someone else's success, could be supportive and quick to praise. When I was fortunate to enjoy the great run in 1977, described above, Tony was not out on a horse because he had bad back trouble. When I returned to his delightful home at Gumley for tea, his pleasure at the performance of hounds could not have been greater if he had been hunting them himself, and his interest in every yard of the run was intense.

Bruce Durno has proved to be one of the most durable and best liked huntsmen in the history of foxhunting in the Shires. He was born into the profession, being the son of the much admired huntsman Percy Durno who hunted the Heythrop with distinction from 1937–52, continuing thereafter as a loyal and much valued kennel huntsman for Captain Ronnie Wallace. He was taken on as kennel huntsman for four seasons in which Tony Murray Smith hunted hounds, and then succeeded him as huntsman in 1966, remaining in that role ever since. Bruce is a quiet huntsman; his technique is like dry white wine: somewhat unassuming until you have hunted with him for some time, and then you learn that his hound control, and his rapport with the pack mark him down as a special exponent of his craft. His horsemanship is similarly lacking in flamboyance; he seems to slip unobtrusively across the country, masking his skills with the apparent ease with which he tackles any obstacle in his way. Since 1966 he has had seven whippers-in, including the present incumbent, Nick Cooper. The others have all graduated as huntsmen of good calibre in their own right: Pat Langrish (Tynedale, and late of the North Staffs), 1964–73 at the Fernie; John Goode (Crawley and Horsham) 1971–2; Michael King (Fife, and late of Flint and Denbigh) 1973–7; Ian Higgs (Worcestershire and late of West Norfolk) 1977–81; Peter Collins (Seavington) 1981–87; and Derek Hopkins (West Pytchley) 1987–92. The Fernie can indeed be seen as a marvellous school for huntsmen during Bruce Durno's long tenure carrying the horn.

Tony Murray Smith's Joint Master from 1962–5 was Major Robin Collie, a great sportsman, and fearless horseman. Tragically he lost his life in the Melton Hunt Club Ride in 1959 when his son, Andrew, was the winner. Andrew, a natural horseman, and his wife Jane live in the Cottesmore country, and hunt enthusiastically with the Shires packs.

As well as Captain Gillilan, Mr Archie Clowes and Captain Brian Bell were Joint Masters with Tony Murray Smith, and he was joined in 1972 by Mr Joe Cowen who remains in the Mastership today, the longest serving MFH in Leicestershire. His family was associated with the Braes of Derwent Hunt for more than a century, but his father, the late Major Denis Cowen moved to Market Harborough when Joe was a child. Major Cowen, a successful land agent, was for many years Vice Chairman and Honorary Treasurer of the Fernie. The Cowen family own some of the finest country in the Laughton Hills, and it is due to their devotion to the Hunt that so much of the terrain around the famous John Ball covert remains permanent grass.

Denis Cowen made judicious land purchases of an area around Saddington and Mowsley initially, and between 1965 and 1985 put in immense hard work in creating and maintaining his land as some of the best hunting country in Leicestershire, with its superb grassland and fly fences. He was never a front man, but above all he was a successful manager, and had an abhorrence of public relations work which he left to others. Neither did he sing his own praises; he just got on with the job in hand. From 1951 he played a vital role in the management of the Hunt, creating a stable financial base. In the mid-1960s there was a Hunt debt of some £3,000, a considerable sum them. Denis Cowen organized a special subscription to pay it off, and from then on kept tight control of the budgeting and financial control of the Hunt, building up healthy reserves. He was a great friend of Pen Lloyd and Dick Watson, with whom he always acted in close concert. When Tony Murray Smith hunted hounds Denis Cowen was Field Master, and they made a strong team to drive the Hunt forward from 1960 to the present day.

Denis Cowen was especially apt at placing the right people in the right roles, such as Leonard Smith in charge of the point-to-point, or Archie Clowes controlling the Fernie fairs which proved very successful money raising enterprises. The work in the country was supervised by a paid field secretary until Joe Cowen took over this task in 1973. Just after the war the job was carried out by Charles MacNaughton, and by Father Claud Beasley Robinson, a remarkable character who was Colonel Pen Lloyd's brother-in-law. Robinson was an Eton housemaster, and later became a monk; he was also a fearless rider to hounds, wearing a top hat and a red coat.

Major Michael Grissell was field secretary for five seasons, to be succeeded by George Thorneycroft who handed over to Langton Waller in 1957. Over the next twelve years Langton performed great labours in making the country far more rideable, building numerous strategic Hunt jumps, the work being expanded in the 1970s. Lindsay Symington then acted as a co-ordinator of works until Joe Cowen took over, with Herrick Sanderson making a great contribution to the work.

Hunt visitors are usually impressed by the quality of the fence construction. All are soundly built, and many are wide enough for the Hunt to cross them on a broad front. There are fine stretches of well laid hedging as well as the substantial timber, built to last no matter what stress they receive from horses.

Harry Sheffield arrived with Tony Murray Smith from the Quorn to act as terrier man until he was succeeded in the late 1960s by Bernard James who remains to this day. Denis Tompkins was kennelman from 1948–85, to be succeeded by the present kennelman, John Mattock.

From the late 1940s Percy Wood was the stud groom, succeeded by Tom Crofts. From about 1968 Tony Murray Smith made an arrangement with Liz Powell to run a livery yard in the Hunt stables and to keep the Hunt horses at livery. On Tony's retirement, Liz moved to her present livery yard in Lubenham, and was made an honorary member of the Hunt. Since 1984, Tony Rogers took over management of the Hunt stables with much success.

When the Hunt kennels moved away from Medbourne in 1924, the Hunt bought Nether House, outbuildings and other property at Great Bowden, where the huntsman and other staff lived. After the war the old stable yard, unwieldy to work, was sold, and Nether House and outbuildings were also sold after a disastrous fire in the house in the early 1950s. As a result of all these transactions the Hunt establishment became settled with an excellent huntsman's house, three good cottages, with a further one in the village, an excellent stable yard, good kennels erected in the 1920s, and a five-acre paddock, all situated conveniently on the edge of Great Bowden village, and comparatively inexpensive to maintain compared with the huge nineteenth century 'workhouse style' Hunt kennels still existing in some other Hunt countries.

In 1982 the Fernie was hit by the political attack on foxhunting in general. The League Against Cruel Sports influenced members of the Co-operative Party who worked to persuade the Co-operative Wholesale Society to ban hunting on some 50,000 acres of farmland which it owned throughout Britain. The CWS made this decision, then firmly refused to listen to representations, nor even to receive a huge petition against the ban from many of its rural customers. Worst hit was the Fernie country, which immediately lost access to some 5,000 acres around Stoughton on its northern boundaries, just south of the city of Leicester. This included the loss to the Hunt of fifteen coverts. Fernie foxhunters, and fellow field sportsmen, did not give in without a spirited campaign, which included holding a fringe meeting at the CWS annual conference in Brighton. Publicity was helped by the enthusiastic participation of the late Jimmy Edwards, the moustachioed comedian who was a keen hunting man, and was indeed Joint Master of the Old Surrey and Burstow. Some keen foxhunting milkmen employed by the Co-op were among the protestors against the ban. The CWS refused to budge, and the ban remains in force today.

Joe Cowen proved then, as in other battles for hunting, to be especially effective as a speaker on behalf of the sport. I heard him give some particularly worthwhile radio broadcasts during the CWS battle, making his points calmly and lucidly. He was equally effective during the Leicestershire County Council campaigns on the hunting issue.

The immediate effect of the CWS ban from 1982 was to reduce the Fernie's fixtures from three to two per week. Worst affected were many young people from the outskirts of Leicester who used to hunt on the Co-op land close to their homes on Saturdays. Their weekend recreation was ruined overnight by a decision taken purely on a doctrinal basis with no proper consultation nor consideration of the interests of the local people. Extraordinarily, organized shooting has continued to be enjoyed on the CWS estates in the Fernie country, although foxhunting has been banned, and foxes have been 'controlled' by methods less open to examination than organized foxhunting by a registered pack of hounds.

When Tony Murray Smith resigned from the Mastership after twenty-three years in 1983, there was much regret; it was the end of the second longest Mastership in the Hunt's history, exceeded only by Mr Fernie himself, and one year longer than that of Mr Tailby. But the luncheon given at Burley-on-the-Hill to mark the retirement was a cheerful affair; Tony remained closely in touch with the Hunt, and with the breeding of the hounds.

Joe Cowen was joined in the 1983–4 season by Mr Alan Hinch and Mr Rod Millington, both of whom farm in the country. They have formed a most effective Mastership, noted for their cool, calm approach to the sport, and their careful stewardship of the country. Landowners and farmers have clearly had every confidence that these three Masters are more than competent to ensure that crops, stock and fences are most carefully protected during the hunting season.

The Fernie continues to make a huge contribution to the sporting and social life of the Harborough country, part of the heart of hunting England.

11

The Belvoir in the Eighteenth and Nineteenth Centuries

Throw your heart over first

Belvoir spells fun. It can be exceptionally vigorous fun. I once described a Saturday with the Duke of Rutland's hounds on the Leicestershire side as 'rugby on a horse'. This is an unfair over-statement, but I was trying to convey that riding with the Belvoir can be, at times, as competitive as any foxhunting I have ever encountered, and at times calls for extra physical robustness. One reason for this, I am sure, is that the Belvoir is the only Leicestershire pack which hunts its most rideable country on Saturdays. This means that young men, otherwise engaged in work, can hunt over the best of the Belvoir country at least once a week. More important are the Belvoir's hunting farmers; they are bred to the sport, know the area intimately, and they have inherited a tradition that to hunt with the Belvoir you must be a goer, no matter what challenge lies ahead. Many come from over the border in Lincolnshire, one of the most sporting of counties in Britain. Even the children who hunt with the Belvoir seem to exhibit a verve which I have not seen excelled elsewhere.

There is a strong, masculine element in the Saturday mounted field, although the Belvoir ladies are by no means over-shadowed, and many of them cross the country as well or better than the men.

The Belvoir hounds, one of the last of three packs in the United Kingdom claiming to be pure English, have a rugged masculinity about them too – although of course it is the bitch pack which hunts the Leicestershire side. Their traditional foxhound colour – Belvoir tan, which means black, tan and some white – presents a formidable dark smear on the landscape as they surge across it during a hunt. The closeness of their breeding makes them work together as a pack exceptionally well; when they go, they generally go together with a singleness of will.

I confess to considerable bias in favour of the Belvoir; I have had some of the greatest fun in my foxhunting life with these hounds. If I were to be given the choice of one last day anywhere, on a good horse, before hanging up my boots, I would choose a Saturday on the Leicestershire side – and I would hope to see the Belvoir bitches running hard from Clawson Thorns, that marvellous covert overlooking the Vale of Belvoir, above the village of Long Clawson.

I would love to experience again the down hill gallop over grass and fences past Mill Farm, then right handed and past the village, to jump the fences alongside Canal Lane, and down to Hose Thorns. If I could negotiate the in and out of the green lane approaching Hose Thorns from the south, then I would be happy to clear the delectable line of fences beyond and see hounds catch their fox just before the covert.

Perhaps because I was brought up in a deep riding vale country in Dorset, the Portman, I have always relished the Vale of Belvoir. It rides lighter than Dorset, but the Belvoir thorn fences, guarded by ditches, need the same degree of firm riding. It pays to hold on and keep kicking; it is a country which needs attacking, especially when the ground is wet and holding.

The old maxim that you should 'throw your heart over first' applies nowhere more accurately than the Vale of Belvoir when hounds are running, and you may be approaching a fence with scores of riders around you.

John Blakeway, former Joint Master, and one of the best men across the country I ever saw, declared that the bravest Belvoir riders are those who ride in the middle rank. The front rank have no one in front to baulk or crash into them, but the later ranks have the added risk of being brought down by refusers or those running out. As a second rank man I have certainly experienced this, but after the first fences this is far less likely, and the very best rides I can recall were those when I was fortunate to secure a position on the flank, reasonably well out of trouble.

There is a great spirit in the Belvoir. Those in the mounted field are genial, warm hearted, and come hunting with the expectation of enjoying themselves. I have been especially fortunate to enjoy hunting with these hounds during periods when the Field Masters were all worthy of the greatest respect; they gave a great lead and helped to foster a happy atmosphere. It is exceedingly difficult to communicate some of the fun afterwards, but it was real; no one can take away the pleasure one has experienced with that great Hunt.

Mr Frederick Stone Stanley who contributed personal recollections to T.F. Dale's history of the Belvoir at the end of the last century, declared that 'the Belvoir country has been very much spoilt and altered since I have known it (1858–88) by railways and ironstone tramways, and I think the same remark would apply to a large part of the Quorn country, and as far as I can see I must own that I think the Cottesmore country to be the best hunting country that I know of in the Shires. . . .'

It is a stark example of the way hunting countries experience changing fortunes; the ironstone tramways and nearly all the railways have been closed in the twentieth century, and the Belvoir Hunt has for many years used these railway tracks as highways across the landscape, often enabling large tracts of arable land to be bypassed. The cuttings and embankments so carefully built in the last century, only to be abandoned in this, are clothed with large areas of bushes and other growth which are ideal fox havens, and they have been drawn as additional coverts, an important factor in enabling the fox population to increase far beyond that which existed in the late nineteenth century. The Vale of Belvoir and some of the hill country to the south was then so denuded of large natural coverts, that the Hunt built artificial earths in small coverts. This tended to result in short hunts of about twenty to thirty minutes because the fox was so soon in the open after being found by hounds. Fortunately on the Lincolnshire side there were, and are, large woodlands, giving hounds plenty of time to draw at length, and strong foxes provided long, persistent hunts over the Lincolnshire ploughs. The subsequent growth of the fox coverts on the Leicestershire side, planted in the latter part of the nineteenth century, plus the appearance of self-sown new coverts along the railway lines, and the abandoned Grantham canal, have produced increased habitats for foxes and other wildlife in the twentieth century. Foxhunting would be vastly more difficult without the abandoned railway lines. At Old Hills, just north of Melton Mowbray, warning signs are erected to alert the public to the danger of subsidence caused by old ironstone mining. There are strange and sudden dips in the ground, caused by the old mine works. Fortunately, Old Hills covert remains a potent source of foxes, and the Belvoir continues to draw the covert, and the adjacent abandoned tramway tracks, enjoying some of its best sport in the area now abandoned by mining exploitation.

Continuity, provided by the Dukes of Rutland, has been the key to the

Belvoir's success. While the Quorn changed Masters all too frequently after Meynell, and the Cottesmore had its Mastership uncertainties, there was never any doubt as to who would be at the helm of the Belvoir. True, some Dukes were less keen on the Chase, and used stewards to run the Hunt, but the basic stability provided by the Dukedom greatly benefited the hunting country and the hounds. Materially, it provided a permanent site for kennels and Hunt stables at Belvoir Castle, avoiding the considerable problems encountered by the neighbouring packs at varying times in their histories.

Because the pack was not sold as Masterships changed, the Belvoir kennel established a reputation as the main source of foxhunting blood at its best in the nineteenth century. Many packs throughout Britain sought to use Belvoir lines, especially those in the Midlands. All too many of these direct lines have been lost in other kennels, due to outcross breeding, but the Foxhound Kennel Stud Book still gives ample evidence of the huge influence of Belvoir blood, despite the swing of fashion against the pure English hound.

In Ireland, the County Limerick is an all-English pack because Lord Daresbury took Belvoir hounds there after the war and maintained the breeding. The great 'modern' packs of hounds are superb in their performance and have all the qualities needed in foxhounds. I am sure, however, that some of the packs which attempted to follow 'modern' breeding without the presence of its great exponents in their Masterships, would have been far wiser to stick to English hound breeding, perhaps with minor modifications. They would have packs of hounds of one recognizable type, instead of mixtures of types which do not always work well together. Looking round the foxhunting world to see who breeds good working hounds and simply breeding from their sires is somewhat like getting in a West End interior decorator to take over the furnishings of a new house. It looks good at the beginning, but is it really the house owner's choice?

Hounds should be bred for their country, preferably with the major decisions being taken by the huntsman who is to handle them.

Has the foxhound breeding pendulum swung too far the other way? Surely there should be far more than three British packs containing pure English blood? However, before anyone enters the argument they should come to the Belvoir and Brocklesby countries to see how these hounds fare in all conditions. I have heard arguments against pure English hounds by pundits with great knowledge of hounds and hound breeding, but they have not ridden behind the Belvoir bitch pack in a good hunt. Handling of hounds by their huntsmen is vital and fortunately the Belvoir and Brocklesby are still exceedingly well hunted today.

Continuity gave the Belvoir enormous advantages from the outset: three Dukes of Rutland employed only six huntsmen in one hundred and twenty years: from the 5th Duke, born in 1778, to the seventh Duke, born in 1818.

Like all the aristocratic hunting families, the Manners, who were to become Dukes of Rutland, originally enjoyed hunting the stag. The fox was considered a much inferior beast of the chase until the great forests of

England were largely cleared, and as we have seen in the story of Hugo Meynell, foxhunting began to make great strides as a popular sport in the late eighteenth century.

Hounds must have hunted from the site of Belvoir Castle since it was founded near the end of the eleventh century by a member of the Norman aristocracy who took over so many Saxon manors. The Normans were ardent hunters, and brought organization to the Chase as they did to so many other aspects of English life.

Tally Ho, the most famous English foxhunting cry, came from the Norman hunting vocabulary: 'Ty a hillaut' was the warning that a deer had roused himself. Stag, fallow buck and boar long continued to be the main quarry in England after the Conquest.

The first Earl of Rutland, Sir Thomas Manners, began rebuilding Belvoir Castle on its hilltop site west of Grantham in 1528, two years after he was created an Earl. It had been badly damaged in a battle in the previous century.

Worse was to follow in the seventeenth century when, as a royalist garrison, the Castle was demolished during the Civil War in 1649, by consent of the 8th Earl who was a Parliamentarian. He retired to the family's other great home, Haddon House in Derbyshire. He rebuilt Belvoir as a mansion, but the family did not regard it as their premier home until the early eighteenth century.

The 9th Earl was created the first Duke of Rutland in the second year of Queen Anne's reign, 1666, and he was known to be especially fond of buck hunting. His deer roamed over the Vale and the wooded hill country. As happened elsewhere, farming became more important, and deer were reduced and scattered because of their predatory attentions to farm crops. Hunting men began to look towards the fox as an alternative quarry capable of providing surprisingly good sport in a run in the open.

Kennels were therefore a permanent part of the Belvoir establishment, although doubtless rebuilt many times. The present kennels date from 1802, and we will describe them in more detail later. The Castle itself was to achieve its present romantic outline as late as the early nineteenth century when the 5th Duke raised the present buildings which seem to float above the treetops, the battlements giving superb views over the Vale of Belvoir lying below to the north and west.

The 3rd Duke (1696–1779) transferred the family home to Belvoir and built a lodge in the deer park at Croxton as a place to relax and enjoy the fishing. Fortunately, foxhunting became his prime passion and he is credited with the formation of the Belvoir Hunt as a pack of foxhounds from 1750.

As we see in the history of the Cottesmore (Chapter Thirteen) prior to that, John, first Duke of Rutland shared a pack of hounds on a part-time basis with the Earl of Cardigan, the Earl of Gainsborough, Lord Gower and Lord Howe. The Duke of Rutland was therefore hunting foxes on his estate much earlier than 1750, but the boundary agreements with Mr Meynell of the Quorn, and Mr Noel of the Cottesmore, ensured a definite shape to the Belvoir country; a process occurring elsewhere as Hunts emerged from loose arrangements made by aristocrats and squires.

Meynell was evolving the modern science of hunting the fox in the open in the neighbouring Quorn country, but the Duke of Rutland's and the other aristocratic packs during much of the eighteenth century were still employing the old methods. These entailed hunting the line of a fox slowly and patiently back to his earth; the dash of the fast hunt above ground no doubt occurred sometimes, but it was the exception. It was the bell-like chiming of the hounds and their patient work which delighted the followers. Enclosure of land had not yet arrived to such an extent to make it necessary for fences to be taken at a gallop. Craning and jumping from a standstill over occasional inconvenient upright obstacles, but mainly over ditches, was the technique in crossing country.

The third Duke's son, John Marquis of Granby (1721–70) loved fox-hunting as a pastime, but his life was dominated by his great career as soldier and statesman, earning him much fame, popularity and glory on many a foreign field of battle. He was made Colonel of the Royal Horse Guard (the Blues) in 1758. He is credited with being the first Master of Foxhounds to lead a cavalry charge in battle. His success in public life added lustre to the Belvoir hounds who were becoming increasingly popular among foxhunters who were already using Grantham as a base for their winter's sport with the Duke's hounds. His death in 1770 predeceased his father by nine years. The Marquis's eldest son, Charles (1754–87) was to succeed as the 4th Duke. His marriage was of crucial importance to the Hunt, since his wife was the beautiful Mary Isabella Somerset, daughter of the 4th Duke of Beaufort. It need hardly be stressed that the Dukes of Beaufort have been the among greatest foxhunters in the land, and the 10th Duke is Master of the family pack at Badminton today. The Duchess came from a marvellous sporting household at Badminton, and it was a time of great change. In 1762, Isabella's brother, the 5th Duke of Beaufort made the celebrated discovery that foxhunting was fun by throwing his hounds into Silk Wood, near Badminton, after a poor day's deer hunting. A great hunt ensued on a fox, and thereafter the Badminton hounds were steadied from deer to fox.

Hunting was just an element of the 4th Duke of Rutland's full life in which literature, politics and the pleasures of the table played a great part; he was a big spender. In 1784 he was nominated Lord Lieutenant of Ireland. He was in Ireland for three years, and a committee took over the Belvoir hounds during that time, headed by Mr Thomas Thoroton, Lord George Cavendish and Sir Carnaby Haggerston. They appear to have been meticulous in keeping the Hunt accounts. The huntsman was a John Smith, and according to a surviving balance sheet of the Hunt for 1786, he was paid forty-nine pounds fourteen shillings per year – plus three pounds nine shillings for 'boots, cap, wipp etc.'. The total cost of the year's hunting, including much labour, forage and flesh bills of forty-nine pounds seventeen shillings and threepence for the hounds, was one hundred and seven pounds eleven shillings. Attempts to translate these sums into modern currency would indicate that hunting the Belvoir country was certainly an expensive enterprise over two hundred years ago. The Hunt servants' livery was a blue coat with red waistcoat at that time; there was only one so-called 'wipper in'; the Hunt employed four men and used eleven horses. Hounds were kennelled at Wilsford and the stables were in the Park at Belvoir.

When the 4th Duke died in 1787 his eldest son, John, was only nine years old. This meant that for some years the Hunt was managed on behalf of the Dukedom by dedicated foxhunters to whom the sport was of primary interest. It is not surprising therefore that great progress was made in hound breeding, in developing the coverts and in ensuring that the Hunt was to become a worthy rival to the Quorn.

A new Master was appointed, and he proved to be a splendid choice: Mr Perceval, brother of the tragic political figure Mr Spencer Perceval, MP for Northampton and Prime Minister of Britain from 1809–12, being the only British Prime Minister to be assassinated. Perceval MFH proved to have considerable organizational abilities, and knew what was necessary to produce good sport. He took up residence at Croxton Park, and kennelled the hounds there. He quickly appointed a new huntsman, Newman, first of a great line of Belvoir huntsmen who were to maintain such high standards. He introduced some useful blood into the kennels from his neighbours in the Midlands: Lord Monson's, Lord Fitzwilliam's, and Lord Spencer's Pytchley hounds, then hunted by the great Dick Knight. However, Perceval's best coup was to use the Manners family's relationship with the Dukes of Beaufort. Blood from the Badminton kennel was used liberally in the Duke of Rutland's pack, and with great success. The Beaufort hounds showed considerable signs of descent from the northern hound, it is said. They stood about twenty-five inches, had great power, and were claimed to be 'rather long in their coat'.

It is probable that the Belvoir began to extend their hunting from two to three days per week at this time. By the time the 5th Duke (1778–1857) reached manhood, much had been achieved in improving his inheritance of the Belvoir hounds.

The great Belvoir doghound Rallywood (1853) is among the most famous in foxhound pedigrees. He was sired by the great Brocklesby Rallywood (1843) but according to the Belvoir's historian, T.F. Dale, there is in his pedigree a bitch, Songstress (1816) whose dam, Costley (1804) was by Beaufort Champion – and the dam, Transport, was also of Beaufort blood.

The 5th Duke developed into a keen foxhunter; he received advice and encouragement from his uncle, the Duke of Beaufort, as well as the strong team producing increasingly good sport in the Belvoir country. He took over the Mastership of the Belvoir in 1804, and engaged 'Gentleman' Shaw as his huntsman; who had made his name as huntsman in the country now known as the Bicester. It would appear that Shaw was more in the mould of huntsman and entertainer than his predecessors. He was quick and bold in his casts, which did not always succeed, but on a fair scenting day he could show a great deal of sport, no doubt greatly pleasing his keen young Master. He was a bold horseman, and exhibited the drive and dash which was to make Leicestershire such a Mecca during the forthcoming century.

In 1805, with Shaw as huntsman, the Belvoir achieved a great run which did much to cement his reputation. After meeting at Waltham on 10 December, after a light snowfall, hounds found at Jericho covert and ran towards Redmile, but swung towards Bottesford, crossing the Nottingham road, and the river Devon. They passed Normanton on the right, and Kilvington on the left, made for Staunton, but ran to Cotham, Long Bennington, Allington, towards Sedgebrook and Barrowby Thorns. They passed Gonerby and ran to the wharf at Grantham where the fox ran the towing path and crossed over the bridge. He crossed the Melton road, ran past Harlaxton Wood, to Straxon, Great Paunton, past Bassenthorpe, and then ran towards Burton Slade Wood. At this point, with only five or six riders still in the hunt, it was decided to stop hounds because the horses were cooked. This was a hunt with a furthest point of eighteen miles, in a time of three hours; hounds never entered any covert except Sir John Thorold's plantation.

Long runs were by no means the only way in which the Belvoir hounds excelled themselves. They became known for their ability to burst a fox in a 'quick thing'. Nimrod thought a great deal of Shaw, and tells a story of a Belvoir run which lasted twenty-two minutes, and in which all the field were beaten by the pace, except a Mr Storey on his blood horse.

Shaw retired from the Belvoir in 1816 with his health broken. He may not be the greatest of all the Belvoir's huntsmen but he was the man carrying the horn when the acceleration of the nineteenth century Shires hunting style began.

He was succeeded in 1816 by an excellent whipper-in who had served apprenticeship under him, Thomas Goosey. The season beginning with calamity when Belvoir Castle was severely ravaged by fire, some of its most valuable pictures and furniture were destroyed. The fire appeared to have started through extensive building works on the Castle, but the Duke resolutely resumed the work afterwards.

Goosey had a poor first season; scenting conditions were atrocious, but he proved to be an excellent huntsman throughout a golden period of Belvoir sport. Landowners and farmers were prospering before the repeal of the Corn Laws and there was money to spare for hunting and other entertainments.

The Meltonian set, basing itself on Melton Mowbray, expected to hunt with the Belvoir as part of their extraordinary winter programme of intensive sport. Princes, peers and foreign nobility were among the throng of visitors. John, the 5th Duke and his Duchess kept court at Belvoir on a munificent scale; guests who were invited into the Belvoir circle were indeed privileged.

It is probably significant that Nimrod never penetrated the Belvoir set, and therefore we read somewhat less detailed information about the Belvoir Hunt in his reports than his beloved Quorn.

Elizabeth, wife of the 5th Duke, a daughter of the 5th Earl of Carlisle, was a formidable but kindly hostess. It is extremely unlikely that she would have welcomed the publication of Nimrod's candid reports from inside her household; although hunting was his passion, he was a natural diarist on all aspects of the Chase, and would no doubt have made a fortune as a scribe in the tabloids if he had lived in the twentieth century. The Belvoir set would have been mouth-watering material for a nineteenth century Nigel Dempster: it included the celebrated dandy Beau Brummell, the Prince of Wales, the Duke of York, the Duke of Argyll, the Marquis of Lorne, Lord Alvanley, Lord Jersey and many another aristocratic exotica. Beau (George) Brummell was not noted for his prowess in the hunting field, but he was a fair horseman, and appeared in the hunting field, exquisitely turned out. He was once known to have been among the few finishing a hard hunt, but this must have been a rare experience for him.

When it came to prowess in the hunting field, few could match Cecil

Forester, the first Lord Forester, brother-in-law of the Duke of Rutland. Forester was the son of the Duke of Rutland's sister, the Lady Katharine. He was a brilliant horseman, equalling Mr Childe of Kinlet, credited with introducing the new brand of dare-devil cross-country riding into Leicestershire (Chapter Eight). He took over the management of the Belvoir hounds soon after the death of the Duchess Elizabeth in 1825, but Cecil Forester was by then suffering ill health. Changes were on the way in the hunting field, reflecting the major political moves in the social and political fabric of Britain. The forthcoming repeal of the Corn Laws and the Reform Acts were to erode the power and to some extent the wealth of many landowners and farmers. The changes were to cast something of a shadow on the ducal splendour at Belvoir Castle. The 5th Duke continued to entertain lavishly, to enjoy a wide circle of eminent friends who came to Belvoir with the common bond of a love of the Chase, but he was to relinquish his personal leadership of the Hunt.

Cecil, Lord Forester, had died in 1828, but his son, John George Lord Forester, was to be given the honour of Mastership of the Belvoir only two years later. The 5th Duke felt the time had come to hand over the responsibility, and he knew that Cecil's son had inherited all the qualities necessary to make a success of Mastership. These changes were made quietly but firmly at Belvoir by benevolent dictatorship; there were none of the all too public upsets which sometimes occurred in the Quorn and Cottesmore when Mastership changes had to be made by committees. It would be amazing if all the Dukes of Rutland shared a passion for the Chase at the same high voltage, but they have invariably showed great wisdom in choosing wisely when they decided to pass on the burdens of running the Hunt to other shoulders, whilst keeping a firm hold on the ownership of the hounds and of the Hunt kennels and stables.

George, second Lord Forester, certainly had a passion for foxhunting at the highest pitch and retained it all his life. His Mastership (1830–42) was based, according to the *Sporting Magazine*, on an arrangement whereby the Duke of Rutland lent the hounds, kennels and stables, and gave £1,200 a year towards expenses. It was a practical example of the English aristocracy's ability to adapt to change, whilst retaining control. For the Belvoir was still ducal, but it was also taking the first step towards becoming a subscription pack. Forester took a subscription of £1,000 a year from the Grantham side of the country, and found the rest of the expenses himself. It should be noted that the Belvoir historian T.F. Dale considered that the magazine may have been inaccurate; he cannot find any other authority for the reported arrangement.

However, the Belvoir certainly became a subscription pack in due course, whilst owing its existence to the immense generosity of the

Dukes of Rutland, and this has remained the case to this very day when the hounds, Hunt kennels, stables and site remain the property of the Duke. And of course, much of the hunting takes place on the Rutland estates.

Thomas Goosey must have been a tough old stick; he rode as hard as ever, but fortified himself with prodigious infusions of alcohol, without apparently faltering, nor showing signs of drunkenness. He could drink a bottle of brandy at a sitting, and is reported to have imbibed thirteen glasses of hot whisky and water on one cold day without being any the worse for it. His politeness in the hunting field was legendary. He told one thruster: 'You jumped on that hound, sir, and I beg leave to say that you buried him as well.' Inevitably, increasing age meant that Goosey was losing his edge of quickness in the hunting field, although he was a superb kennel huntsman, and his hounds were superbly conditioned and entered.

The continuity and careful breeding of the Belvoir hounds had now established them as an invaluable source for all other Hunt kennels, and their blood was in great demand.

Lord Forester had certainly taken over a pack in great heart, and they enjoyed splendid sport. Yet even in the nineteenth century hey day of hunting, there could be considerable problems with the occasional hostile landowner. These rows had nothing to do with an ideological opposition to foxhunting; they were far more likely to spring from private feuds.

In 1810 the 5th Duke of Rutland's kinsman, Sir William Manners believed that the Duke had robbed him of what the baronet regarded as his due electoral influence at Grantham. He retaliated by stopping the Duke hunting over his land, and got thirty-five farmers to bring actions for trespass against the Hunt. The Duke compromised rather than lose sport, and the wave of actions for trespass subsided.

The Belvoir and the Cottesmore had a major upset with Lord Harborough at Stapleford, in the country of the Cottesmore, but often run over by the Belvoir. He opposed the Hunts and lined his coverts with dog spears to prevent them being drawn. This caused considerable frustration to both Hunts because hounds often had to be stopped when running hard in some of their best country around the village. After his death, his widow re-opened the coverts to the Hunts and her second husband, Major Claggett, was a great supporter of foxhunting. As so often happens, when a Hunt loses territory in one area it gains it in another.

Goosey retired in 1835 after twenty-six years as huntsman, receiving a silver cup and a testimonial of deepest gratitude. He died at Knipton and was buried in the village churchyard, very close to the ancestral home of the family he had served so faithfully.

Lord Forester replaced Goosey with William Goodall who had been second whipper-in. More than a few excellent huntsmen have made this leap in their careers. During the next seventeen years Goodall was to establish a huge reputation; some said he was only second to Tom Firr, but they tended to say that about any exceptional huntsman. William was the grandson of Stephen Goodall, reputed to be the heaviest professional huntsman ever to sit on a horse; yet he hunted hounds with much success for Mr Corbet in Warwickshire. Whilst still young, William worked first in stables, and rode as a second horseman, no doubt achieving the equestrian skills which later adorned his career. Yet he was primarily a devoted hound man, and first learned his craft as second whipper-in to Tom Wingfield in the Bicester country. As always, it was his pleasing character and willingness to learn which impressed his employers. Lord Forester had a high opinion of him from his first season in 1837 with the Belvoir as whipper-in.

Whilst the Masters retained overall control, at the Belvoir kennel the professional huntsmen had a considerable influence on the breeding of hounds. One of the virtues of maintaining a consistent hound breeding policy enabled the huntsmen to avoid major mistakes through injudicious outcrosses, whilst at the same time enhancing performance through decisions based on his own observation of his pack at work. Goodall introduced the great Rallywood into the Belvoir kennel from the Brocklesby, as referred to above, thereby securing one of the most influential foxhound sires in the nineteenth century. He appeared to have the invisible thread of communication with his hounds in the field, and an instinctive feel for the right choices in breeding his pack which mark out the great hound man. Meanwhile Lord Forester exercised control in ensuring that hounds were of correct conformation. Goodall was of high intelligence, and kept an excellent hunting diary; copies of his correspondence also show him to be of well above average literacy in the nineteenth century working class.

In 1843, Albert, the Prince Consort hunted with the Belvoir from their meet at Croxton Park on 5 December. Queen Victoria was not enthusiastic about foxhunting, although certainly not opposed to it. However, she had not been amused by the visits to Leicestershire by the Empress of Austria. She was always concerned about any risk taken by her beloved Albert, although the Prince was a competent horseman and much enjoyed hunting with staghounds and his own harriers. Significantly, the Queen decided to accompany her husband to the Belvoir country. It must have been a momentous occasion for the Hunt. Queen Victoria attended the meet, accompanied by the dowager, Queen Adelaide. They arrived at the meet in a carriage and four with the Duke of Rutland, escorted by outriders in livery. Carriages lined the route for nearly a quarter of a mile, and some eight-hundred people attended the meet on horse, with thousands on foot. Hounds were brought to the carriage window for the Queen's inspection. After a procession through Waltham, the Queen's carriage was halted on the high ground looking across to Melton Spinney. It is incredible, with the accompanying crowds, that any sport was achieved. However, hounds found a brace and a half in the Spinney, and pursued one to Clawson Thorns where he was headed by foot people and ran back to Melton Spinney, hounds catching him one field before the covert. After several abortive draws, hounds found in Newman's Gorse, near Waltham, and ran to Sproxton Thorns – a distance of less than a mile, but at top pace, and the Prince was among the leaders of the field. Both his equerries had falls which caused some amusement. The Duke of Rutland, Lord Forester and the Hunt staff must have been much relieved that the day concluded without harm to the Prince Consort who declared himself well pleased by 'a capital run'.

Queen Victoria in a letter to King Leopold, reported: 'One can scarcely credit the absurdity of people but Albert's riding so boldly has made such a sensation that it has been written all over the country, and they make much more of it than if he had done some great act!'

Lord Forester ensured that the Belvoir hounds now hunted five days a week; some sixty couples of hounds were kept in kennel. There were additional kennels at Ropsley to assist the huntsman when hunting the Lincolnshire side to avoid long rides back to Belvoir.

Nevertheless, it was a tough regime. Goodall's strength was tested with long runs, and late returns to kennels in the dark. There were no arrangements for him to eat during these long days, and arduous hacks home, and the task was clearly taxing to his health. T.F. Dale, and other accounts, describe Goodall's reign as huntsman as a 'golden age' for the Belvoir. The country was wild and natural; it was well foxed; as yet it was not marred by the railways which were to cause such dismay later in the century.

Lord Forester married in 1856, and the following year the 5th Duke died in his eightieth year. The succession of the 6th Duke, Charles (1815–88) seemed to promise much, but in the remainder of the nineteenth century the combination of talents in the Hunt during Lord Forester's regime, and the special suitability of the environment were never to be outmatched. However, there was much good sport yet to be achieved.

Charles, Duke of Rutland took the Mastership soon after he succeeded to the title in 1857, and undertook to hunt hounds at his own expense, and did so for more than twenty years. He was a fearless horseman, and like all good riders when he had a fall it tended to be a bad one. According to some accounts, his ill health in later life was due to some heavy falls in the hunting field. In 1863 during a run from Casthorpe, he had a serious fall on his head when jumping a stake-and-bound fence; after that he was physically incapable of riding close to hounds during a fast run. Gillard's career ended after the effect of head injuries; Tom Firr suffered a similar fate with even worse head injury effects. (Reading hunting histories, I find all too frequent references to Masters and huntsmen being permanently incapacitated by head injuries. They recovered from horrendous fractures of limbs, but serious head injuries seldom heal completely. It would be instructive to know just how many in the mounted fields have suffered similarly over the past two-hundred years. It is regrettable that in 1992 foxhunting remains the only sport involving high risk equitation in Britain where the ruling body does not make the wearing of modern safety headgear, with insulation and chinstrap, mandatory either for Hunt staffs or those who follow them across country. It will doubtless happen in due course, if only because of the pressure of insurance risks.)

In his youth the 6th Duke of Rutland had jumped the Croxton Park wall on the south side where the wall was five foot high, with a considerable drop. He also jumped the river Witham between Great Ponton and Grantham at a very wide place, and swam the Nottingham and Grantham canal on horseback. According to the reminiscences of Frederick Stanley: 'One of the reasons for the Duke's great popularity as a Master of Hounds was that he never swore at his field, nor used any bad language to them, but if he called them to order he did so in a determined manner, and on some occasions, when he was not listened to, he threatened to take the hounds home.' I like the stories about the Duke's experiences with a horse dealer and farmer, Mr Tomlin, known as 'Cap' Tomlin because he wore a huntsman's cap. It throws an endearing light on the Duke's tolerance and happy relationships with local folk. On one occasion he saw Tomlin galloping down a hill and jumping a deep wide brook near Croxton Park. The Duke, then Lord Granby, admired the performance and later bought the horse which Tomlin assured him was a 'fine hunter'. The first time he rode it he found he could not hold the horse which bolted immediately and had to be galloped round a deep ploughed field before to be stopped. He sold the horse for a song, and found out that Tomlin had himself been run away with when jumping the brook!

Goodall retired as huntsman in 1859, and his first whipper-in, James Cooper, was appointed in his place. Jem Cooper was a Scot, from Fife; a strong, wiry man, and a great horseman. He served as the Belvoir's huntsman with distinction until 1870. He achieved many fine runs, and trained some excellent whippers-in who went on to become top-class huntsmen. He was undoubtedly a highly competent huntsman, but was not noted as one of the 'greats' in Leicestershire history. The physical toll of hunting hounds in the nineteenth century must have been considerable; failing health was one of the reasons for his retirement after only eleven years. Among his whippers-in had been Frank Gillard – and he returned to the Belvoir to create new legends. He was born in Devon in 1838; his father was kennel huntsman to a pack near Exeter. Gillard started Hunt service with a pack of harriers at Monkleigh, North Devon, moving to the Stevenstone as second whipper-in. In 1860, he joined the Duke of Rutland's as whipper-in. He recalled hunting five days a week with the Belvoir, and the sixth visiting a neighbouring pack! Seven years later he was promoted kennel huntsman to the South Notts where John Chaworth Musters was Master, a great opportunity to study venery under a fine amateur huntsman. He then went to the Quorn when Musters took that Mastership, and in 1870 was huntsman of the Quorn under the new Mastership of Mr Coupland when Cooper resigned as huntsman of the Belvoir. The Quorn were not anxious to release Gillard, but after a personal request from the Duke, Mr Coupland graciously released the huntsman, and he moved to the Belvoir establishment where he was to carry the horn with huge success for the next twenty-six years. He had great stamina, but as we shall see, his constitution was taxed by duties far outside those normally allotted to a professional huntsman. Perhaps he was the victim of his own talents. He established from the start an excellent relationship with the 6th Duke.

At the Belvoir Hunt kennels today, the 'Duke's Room' remains much as it was when Frank Gillard would show the 6th Duke the celebrated sires and favourites of his pack. Long discussions would take place over a railed guard erected to prevent hounds touching the Ducal Master's gouty leg, aggravated by severe accidents in the field. Nowadays, the room is maintained as a fascinating miniature museum of the Belvoir's past, with pictures, documents and foxes' masks adorning the walls.

According to Frank Gillard's biographer, Cuthbert Bradley: 'The noble Master placed the greatest confidence in Frank Gillard's abilities, leaving it to him to carry on the correspondence and business generally of the Hunt. The whole internal machinery of so vast and important a Hunt as the Belvoir was practically worked by one man for a quarter of a century, and on such good lines that the kennel occupied the premier position by general consent.'

It sounds as if Gillard did much of work which would nowadays be regarded as the preserve of the Hunt Secretary. Some evidence of the Duke's reliance on his huntsman is the account of the visit of the Empress of Austria to the Belvoir in 1874. It was her first day's hunting in England, and they changed the meet to eight in the morning at Three Queens to suit Her Majesty. It was a cubhunting morning at the end of September.

Gillard took care to provide some sport in the open: finding in Herring's Gorse, hounds produced a nice spin by Saltby to Hungerton, and finding again at Sproxton Gorse they ran hard over what was then heathland to Denton where they caught their fox after a sharp twenty-five minutes. The Empress was a natural horsewoman and rode well; she was given the brush at the end of the second run, and returned to kennels to inspect all the hounds, the Hunt horses, the gardens and the Castle. The Duke was away, but deputed Gillard and his wife to be hosts to the Empress for luncheon in their parlour. Poor Gillard drenched the Empress when he attempted to open a fizzy bottle of soda water, but she laughed it off. She chatted happily with the huntsman and commissioned him to buy her a complete pack of beagles, the best that money could buy; this must have been a lucrative commission for Gillard. His son, Frank, took them over to Austria and had a marvellous week, being entertained in the royal entourage at Vienna.

In the 1875–6 season the expense of hunting the pack five days a week began to pinch in the agricultural depression. The Duke suggested cutting the fixtures from five to four days in a week. Gillard begged that this decision should not be taken. The solution was found by gentlemen of the Hunt who held a meeting at Belton Park, with Lord Brownlow in the chair. He volunteered a subscription of £1,500 a year to meet the poultry and damage funds, with the proviso that Gillard was not to be interfered with, and responsibility rested with him, as the Duke was not in the field. The Hunt thereafter continued on an even tenor at five days a week.

Gillard is accused in Guy Paget's book, *Bad 'Uns to Beat* of 'doping' foxes, that is hunting foxes which had been doused in strong smelling liquid to enable hounds to hunt them all the more effectively; the implication is that such foxes had been 'put down' in coverts from bags. Since Paget interviewed old hunting folk who had hunted with Gillard such accusations need not be dismissed lightly, but Paget quotes an unnamed Belvoir old-timer who blames such hunting crimes on the huge pressure that Gillard was under, especially towards the end of his long, arduous career. Paget says Gillard even had to buy the horses, manage the horses, act as his own Field Master (an incredible burden) settle all claims, organize the earth stopping, and arrange the meets.

According to Paget's informant: 'Poor Frank were, like a lot of his hounds, fair worn out towards the end.'

It should be remembered that these seasons were before the Masters of Foxhounds was formed to put in writing a code of conduct for hunting the fox which expressly forbade such practices. Although Surtees, and such great huntsmen as Colonel Cook, were sternly warning against the practice of hunting 'bagmen' much earlier in the nineteenth century. These were times when public sensitivities about animal welfare were far more blunted than today, and when it is quite feasible that an ageing professional huntsman might well have been tempted to take short cuts in endeavouring to provide consistent sport for wealthy, well mounted riders to hounds.

However, Gillard certainly had a reputation, and a warm following of admirers. It is unlikely he would have achieved this if he were consistently seen to be cheating against the precept that the fox is a wild animal to be hunted in its natural environment without artifice. In the late twentieth century, organized foxhunting's only hope of survival is to stick meticulously to the code laid down by the MFHA, and that body is rightly determined to exercise the strictest discipline by expelling Masters proved to have broken it.

Cuthbert Bradley quotes Gillard as saying that he hated digging foxes: 'I should say that after 1 November in each year, for the last twenty years, not more than a brace in a season have been dug out. In the cubhunting season, however, when foxes go to ground like rabbits, it is ruinous to a pack of hounds, but to help them to get a fox out not only makes them keen in their work, and steady from riot, but it thus teaches them to mark their fox to ground.'

In his last season the Belvoir pack killed thirty-nine and a half brace of foxes, making a total of 2,709 during the twenty-six years of Gillard's term as huntsman, ending in 1896.

The 6th Duke died on 4 March 1888, after holding the Mastership for thirty years. Hunting stopped for eight days, and there had been forty days lost through frost, but they had hunted 1,090 days, and killed forty-two and a half brace.

Lord John Manners, 7th Duke of Rutland, was the brother of his predecessor, and was aged seventy when he succeeded. Gillard continued to run the Hunt, and it is clear that his burdens increased. Despite the toll of the years, and the falls, Frank rode at a spry eleven stone eleven pounds in his twenty-first season, and had his son Frank to turn hounds to him. At last he had the assistance of a Field Master, Lord Edward Manners, MP for Melton, the Duke of Rutland's second son.

In 1891 the Hunt was reduced to a four-day-a-week pack, the agricultural depression forcing the 7th Duke to cut costs somewhat. In the 1895–6 season, the aged Duke finally decided to give up the Mastership, severing at last the Manners family's direct link with the pack they owned. It was a momentous occasion in the history of Lincolnshire and Leicestershire.

Lord Brownlow, Lord Lieutenant of Lincolnshire, chaired a meeting at Grantham, to express regret at the retirement and to form a commitee to make new arrangements.

It had been a fine, open season, and Frank Gillard's last day hunting hounds in Leicestershire, 25 March 1896, saw a brilliant run of one hour and twenty minutes from Burbidge's, ending with a kill in Ranksborough Gorse in the Cottesmore country, near Oakham. He hunted hounds twice more on the Lincolnshire side, riding an old favourite, Farewell, at his last meet. Farewell was a half-brother to Playfair, winner of the Grand National, which indicates the quality of horses ridden by the huntsman of the Belvoir. The Duke gave Frank the horse as one of his retirement presents; a testimonial from the Hunt raised nearly £1,300.

I particularly like Frank Gillard's remark in the preface to his biography: 'The memory of my hounds is very dear to me; their individuality has left a lasting impression on my mind like those of human friends, which only death can cancel. It was beautiful to have to hunt such hounds!'

12

The Belvoir in the Twentieth Century

'Gone Away' blows triumphantly, and the
pack tumbles out of covert, almost gliding
over the grass

There were many offers of would-be Masters for the Belvoir; the Committee chose to appoint Sir Gilbert Greenall, an energetic and exceedingly successful Cheshire brewery. It was something of a radical choice in 1896; there was some tut-tutting that the Belvoir Mastership had gone to 'trade'. It proved to be an inspired choice. Many of the Belvoir's best years lay ahead, thanks to Gilbert Greenall – and later to his son, Toby, one of the greatest foxhunters of the twentieth century, and certainly one of its most interesting personalities.

Gilbert Greenall was the inheritor of Greenall Whitley and Company, which started in the mid-eighteenth century as just one of a number of brewing enterprises in the North West, but became the largest regional brewer in the United Kingdom. The family enterprises were based at St Helens and Warrington, and its fortunes were hugely successful by the end of the nineteenth century. Sir Gilbert was only twenty-nine when he was invited to be Master of the Belvoir. He had hunted with the North Cheshire and served in the Cheshire Yeomanry. His father, Sir Gilbert Greenall, the first Baronet and MP for Warrington, was a formidable Parliamentarian and businessman. Young Gilbert Greenall resolved to be non-executive chairman of Greenall Whitley, and devoted himself largely to horses and country life. Having inherited his father's organizing talents, and energies, not only did he take on one of the largest Hunts in Britain, but he became honorary director of the Royal Show for twenty-five years, saving it from near collapse, and ensuring that it became Britain's premier agricultural show. He bred bloodstock with much success, winning the Oaks in 1921 from his own stock, and he bred and produced hunters, hackneys, cattle and pigs with equal enthusiasm. He was to be created a baron, the first Lord Daresbury, for public services in 1927. It was not surprising that his powers of management and organization were brought into play in his Mastership of the Belvoir, backed by a deep and generous purse. He was reported to have paid £18,000 to Mr John Henry Stokes of Bowden for the Hunt horses. In his first year he built a superb new stable yard at Woolsthorpe to hold seventy horses. There was a riding school, valeting rooms, a forge and cottages for the grooms – all built in seven months, the bricks still smoking from the kilns. Sir Gilbert even had a special railway siding built to improve communications and deliveries, ensuring that the Belvoir hounds could travel by rail to their Lincolnshire meets, changing trains at Bottesford.

The Hunt staff were all to wear leathers instead of cord in future, and one man was employed full time during the season to keep the leathers clean. The quality of horse flesh in the Hunt stables had never been higher.

Greenall appointed Ben Capell as huntsman to succeed Frank Gillard, and Capell displayed the usual durability of Belvoir huntsman, carrying the horn for the next sixteen years. He had learned much of his skills whipping in to none other than Tom Firr at the Quorn. He knew all about the skill of producing sport to amuse a Leicestershire field, as Cuthbert Bradley noted: 'Ben Capell is a Leicestershire huntsman bred and born, his methods of conducting a hunt being in keeping with modern ideas.' Cuthbert notes that under the generous Greenall regime, the Belvoir huntsman seldom rode the same horse for more than three seasons, observing that 'the constant change on to new mounts in the full vigour of life has probably reduced the average of falls taken by the Belvoir Hunt staff to a minimum.'

After his Quorn experience, Capell went to the Blankney with Lord Lonsdale when he took them for the 1885–6 season. Capell remained and hunted the Blankney with much success; in those days it was similar to much of the Belvoir country, and doubtless this greatly influenced his appointment. His eldest son, Nimrod, was to hunt the Belvoir for four seasons in the 1920s.

Capell's first whipper-in was Jack Hewitt, who was to succeed as Belvoir huntsman, and the second whipper-in was Herbert Norman, later to become first whipper-in and kennel huntsman to the great Chetty Hilton-Green at the Cottesmore.

In 1912 Sir Gilbert decided to give up Mastership; he had so many other interests, and he had certainly invested hugely in the Belvoir's future. His son Edward, better known as Toby, was to reap the benefits in the last golden decade of hunting on grass, the 1930s. Meanwhile Sir Gilbert was succeeded by a Master who was determined to prove that hunting is for fun: Tommy Bouch, formerly Master of the Atherstone with Lord Huntingdon. He had hunted the County Galway and the Tipperary in Ireland previously. According to Guy Paget, Tommy 'didn't care a damn for appearances, but was all for sport.' His Joint Master for two years up to the Great War was Lord Robert Manners, and the huntsman was the former whipper-in, Jack Hewitt for just one season, to be succeeded from 1913–19 by Dick Woodward. Bouch had his own pack of hounds, anything but handsome and largely from all-sorts assembled in Ireland, with which he hunted the Lincolnshire side of the country and achieved excellent sport. He took a great interest in the pure-bred English hounds and worked hard to try to rectify some of the breeding problems described above. However, any attempt to introduce a Welsh outcross into the pack was sternly resisted by the Duke of Rutland and his family, as recounted by the present Duke at the end of this chapter.

As a huntsman or as Field Master Tommy Bouch took some following. He was exceedingly bold across country, and used to say that if you went fast enough at wire, you generally got over it or it broke. Barbed wire had become something of a problem, even in Leicestershire. Gilbert Greenall had devised an area plan for representatives of the Hunt to take down as much wire as possible at the start of the season, and erect it again in the spring. It is the use of wire as a single strand oxer, guarding a ditch and a fence, which catches out the unwary horseman. It is difficult or impossible to see on the approach to a fence until your horse hits it on landing; all too often it will give you and horse a nasty fall, probably cutting the horse as well. Barbed wire, an American invention, was to become an increasing nuisance throughout the twentieth century. The older generation viewed it with horror; the new intake accommodated to it, and continued to have a lot of fun.

Major Bouch served in France during the First World War, but he retained his Mastership, and ensured that the Hunt kept going. Since the Dukes had given up hunting on their previous scale as Masters; the focus of the Belvoir had shifted somewhat, despite the kennels still being located in the Castle grounds.

Paget remarks that fewer of the landed gentry in the country hunted after the First World War. Yet the return of hunting visitors to Melton accelerated again, as related in the Quorn history. They expected to hunt four or five days a week in the late '20s and '30s. The new Prince of Wales, to be the ill-starred Edward VIII, joined the throng hunting in the Shires, and the Belvoir shared fully as a host pack for visitors who came up for the season.

Fortunately, the tradition of farmers hunting with the Duke's hounds has continued throughout its history, so that the links between the mounted field and the country have always been exceedingly strong.

Major Bouch had spent a great deal of capital during twelve years of devoted service to the Hunt, including the invaluable task of ensuring continuity during the war. The Mastership was taken up in 1924 by Captain Marshall Roberts, who came from Holm Pierpoint, near Nottingham. He had been badly injured while serving in the Grenadier Guards in the Great War. He was a wealthy man and spent most generously on the Hunt, renting Easton Hall, home of the Cholmeley family. However, he was unfortunate in his choice of huntsman: Ben Capell's son, Nimrod, who had served nine seasons at the Quorn as whipper-in, and latterly as kennel huntsman. He had suffered a bad fall which kept him out of Hunt service for three years, and then joined the Belvoir. Not every former whipper-in makes a top-class huntsman, and Nimrod was not able to match his father's performance in that role. The Mastership lasted only until 1928 when Major Charles Tonge, of Barrowby, and Mr Peter Ackroyd, of Woolsthorpe, took over for two seasons. Major Tonge was a most knowledgeable and devoted foxhunter; he had been a Master of the Newmarket and Thurlow from 1919–27. He married a lady from the Belvoir country, the grandaughter of Colonel Bobby Swan, who lived at Barrowby, and was a Chairman of the Hunt Committee, and the point-to-point Committee; he was Field Master from 1921–4.

Charles Tonge continued Tommy Bouch's practice of hunting hounds himself two days a week on the Lincolnshire side. His brother, Maurice Tonge, although not a Master, contributed hugely to the Hunt's finances. He paid a third of the Hunt's running costs, and a third of the capital spent on the eighty horses kept at the hunt stables at Woolsthorpe where there were twenty-three grooms managed by a stud groom, Mr Glass. The Hunt's running costs at that time were some £15,000 to £20,000 per season – a very considerable sum in the 1920s.

Apart from his major expenditure and his management, Major Tonge performed a great service for the Belvoir in appointing as the new huntsman, one of the most effective in Belvoir history, George Tongue from Essex. He was born at the Grafton Kennels, and started in Hunt service with the York and Ainsty as a second horseman. Before the Great War he moved to the Essex and became second whipper-in. George had a great reputation for toughness, and his war service was certainly evidence of this: he was awarded the DCM for gallantry under heavy shell fire near Ypres, as a sergeant in the RFA. He returned to the Essex Hunt, and in 1923 he joined the East Essex as huntsman, showing great promise. The Hunt servants who served under him at Belvoir for twenty-eight years, from 1928–56, speak of him not merely with respect, but awe. Perhaps it was partly due to his military experiences, but he certainly believed in discipline and knew how to exert it effectively.

Dick Perkins, later huntsman at the Rufford Forest, recalled the Belvoir Kennels as being 'very hard on Hunt servants before the war, they had only oil lanterns. It was an unhandy kennel in which to work, with the boiler house on one side of the yard and the feed houses on the other side, and it was surrounded by those Belvoir Woods into which hounds always seemed as if they must escape!'. Dick served under George Tongue from 1927; despite the hardships he paid great tribute to the quality of his training.

The vital role of a kennel huntsman or professional huntsman is to ensure that hounds are really fit to hunt. Few realize just how much sport is spoilt by packs not being sufficiently exercised and conditioned by the huntsman long before the season gets under way.

Ken Anyan, later huntsman of the Blackmoor Vale, recalls the 1930s with the Belvoir where he was second horseman to his brother Frank who was then first whipper-in to George Tongue. There were more than one hundred and eighty-nine second horses out with the Belvoir on Wednesdays and Saturdays at that time. There were seldom less than sixty horses kept in the Hunt stables at Woolsthorpe, with thirty men to look after them. 'What a cavalcade they made out exercising in the mornings,' Ken recalled.

'One early cubhunting morning, I was taking horses to the kennels with the other second horsemen when I heard a splash in front of me. The leading horses had gone into the lake in the park at Belvoir in the dark!'

Major Tonge continued in the Mastership until 1931 with Colonel Gordon Colman, whose family firm made the famous mustard. He had been Master of the Surrey Union from 1904–10, but had married a Leicestershire lady, Peggy Brocklehurst whose family home was near Thorpe Arnold. She and her husband made their Leicestershire home at Burton Lazaars. He was a particularly keen hound man, and co-operated with Tonge in the hound breeding, succeeding in producing a smaller, lighter pure English hound than had been seen in the kennel during the time of Gillard and Capell senior.

Colman, on joining the Belvoir Mastership in 1930, managed the Lincolnshire side of the country, and in 1934 he was joined by the Honourable Edward (Toby) Greenall, second son of the first Baron who was previously Master as Sir Gilbert Greenall. Toby did not merely enjoy foxhunting; it was his lifelong passion. He was a rare combination of superb rider and keen hound man; he was to hunt his own hounds in Ireland as Master of the County Limerick after the war. Hunting had already meant tragedy to Toby: his first wife, Joan Sherriffe, of Goadby Marwood in the Belvoir country, had died in March 1926, only seven months after their marriage, from injuries received in a fall while hunting with the Quorn. Two years later, in 1927, he remarried and had a son, Edward. Toby had become heir to his father's title, because his elder brother, Gilbert had died in a car accident while driving to Windsor for duty with his regiment.

In 1934, Toby was thirty-two years old, and a seasoned foxhunter; he was a superb Field Master and chose to wear a top hat rather than a cap when filling this role with the Belvoir. 'If anyone in the field could not recognize me in a top hat he had no business hunting with me,' said Toby with a smile. He had a most engaging, dry sense of humour which saw him through life's vicissitudes and disappointments.

He had a profound admiration for the pure English hounds of the Belvoir kennel, and when he went to Ireland he took a draft with him, setting up a pure English kennel at Clonshire, County Limerick. He proved that the English hounds could hunt just as well over the banks and ditches of Ireland as they could on Leicestershire's much tidier pastures. He admitted cheerfully to extreme prejudice on the subject, describing the modern Welsh cross foxhounds as 'barking dogs'. He would say they were 'self hunting hounds', bred by slow amateur huntsmen for their own use, but not fit for a top-class professional in a real galloping country. After a judging session by two young English disciples of modern breeding at the Irish Hound Show, at Clonmel, Toby remarked cheerfully: 'It's a good thing they didn't give a prize to one of my hounds because I should have to shoot it.'

No one could ever take the slightest offence at his strictures; they were murmured rather than declaimed, and he always had a twinkle in his eye. He was a true countryman, and the farmers loved him both in Leicestershire and Ireland.

He extolled the drive of the English foxhound, and its ability to hunt with its brothers or sisters as a united pack. In Leicestershire he would ride as many as three horses a day to ensure that he remained at the head of the field. The Belvoir's sport in the 1930s was superb, and attracted huge mounted fields.

Toby Daresbury and Gordon Colman were both excellent organizers, and they ensured that the coverts were well maintained, and the country kept in good order. In George Tongue they had a tough, single minded huntsman, able to take the strain of a taxing regime. Toby's method of control of the field was firmness applied with a mild manner. If a thruster jumped a fence ahead of him when hounds were not running he would affably invite that rider to jump the fence back the other way; sometimes an entertaining spectacle for the rest of the field. The six years of his Mastership up to the start of the Second World War flashed by all too quickly. As well the hectic round of hunting fixtures at least four days a week, the foxhunting set made merry in the evenings (Chapter Eight).

One of the 'sensations' which hit the social news columns of the newspapers was a knuckle fight between Toby Greenall and the Master and huntsman of the neighbouring South Notts, Captain Billy Filmer-Sankey. It was probably about the Hunt boundary because Filmer-Sankey used to cause much mirth when he would ask his field: 'Hands up who'd like to draw the Belvoir today?' According to a contemporary newspaper account of the encounter, by Blackberry Hill fox covert on the border of the South Notts country: 'Filmer-Sankey wore a low-neck jersey, flannel trousers and tennis shoes. But Greenall contemptuously retained his collar and tie. They set to it with a will. Weight and experience were in Greenall's favour and he looked to be winning when Filmer-Sankey landed a punch between "wind-and-water" in the Derby Kelly. Though Mr Greenall's heart was willing, previous digestive trouble had made his stomach weak. The fight was ended.'

Toby was renowned for meeting all kinds of disaster with equanimity. After falling in the River Smite in the Belvoir country, Lord Daresbury was given a bottle of whisky by a farmer. To the farmer's amazement Toby poured one half of the whisky into one hunting boot and the rest into the other. 'That will really keep me warm,' he said.

It is related by Captain Ronnie Wallace that when staying with Toby and Boodley at Clonshire, County Limerick, there was an occasion at breakfast; 'the second morning after a Hunt ball when Boodley had failed to negotiate the bridge over a big river when coming home.

'Toby peering over his spectacles, said: "Darling, I haven't seen the Mercedes the last two days." She replied: "To tell you the truth it's in the (river) Maigue." "Indeed," commented Toby.'

When war came Toby Daresbury served in the Lifeguards, but also kept the Belvoir hounds operative, often hunting them himself, and proving to be a natural huntsman. During the war years, as in the First World War, the loyalty and backing of the current Duke of Rutland ensured that the Belvoir hounds, and therefore the Hunt, had stability and security, with the kennels guaranteed in the park of Belvoir Castle.

One of Lord Daresbury's whippers-in was Miss Meriel ('Merry') Atkinson, daughter of a doctor in the Belvoir country. Of diminutive stature, but with a great heart, and an iron nerve, she was a most engaging personality, totally dedicated to the world of horse and hound. Merry, who never married, was highly successful in rearing young horses and hounds. On one occasion after a fall in Ireland she climbed on to a wall, and shrieked 'pony, pony, pony' to her home bred horse which had careered after hounds. The animal promptly turned round and cantered back for her to re-mount. She was said to have been capable of stopping the Limerick hounds by calling 'puppy, puppy, puppy' but I cannot vouch for that. She joined Toby Daresbury's establishment in County Limerick and whipped-in to him during his Mastership from 1947–77; he hunted hounds himself until 1971, handing over to the brilliant professional Hugh Robard who still hunts these hounds with much success, and manages the country.

Toby Daresbury's second wife, Josephine, died in 1958, and he married in 1966 the renowned hunting personality referred to earlier, the Lady Helena 'Boodley' Hilton-Green, a daughter of Earl Fitzwilliam and a former wife of 'Chetty' Hilton-Green of Cottesmore fame (Chapter Fourteen). Only four years later 'Boodley' died in a fall while hunting with the Limerick. Toby Daresbury continued to hunt until near the end of his life, dying in February, 1990, aged eighty-seven. Leicestershire hunting folk attended a special memorial service to him in Melton Mowbray. As one of those fortunate to enjoy his hospitality at his home at Askeaton, County Limerick, I would pay tribute to the memory of a truly great foxhunter, an entertaining companion in the hunting field and at all other times. He fully understood that hunting only survives through goodwill and ensured that this prevailed in both his long Masterships. He remained closely interested in the fortunes of the Belvoir for all of his life and was much honoured when invited to judge a new Belvoir entry with Prince Charles, the Prince of Wales, who had then become a keen member of the Belvoir's mounted field.

The Belvoir found one of its most popular Masters to succeed Toby Daresbury in 1947: Lieutenant Colonel James Hanbury of Burley-on-the-Hill in the neighbouring Cottesmore country, father of Joss Hanbury (see Chapter Fourteen). One of the most genial of personalities, James Hanbury continued the Belvoir tradition that hunting must be for fun. Everyone who hunted during his Mastership speaks of him with much fondness. Ulrica Murray Smith recalls: 'James was very easy going as a Field Master. He was never in a bad temper, always enjoyed himself, went well, and was fun to hunt with always.' His Joint Master for two seasons was Lieutenant Colonel F. Bowlby; for the next season Major James Seely; from 1953–4 Major C. Pretyman, and from 1955–64 Lord Belper, former Joint Master of the Quorn (Chapter Six); Lieutenant Colonel Hugh Beddington was also Joint Master from 1956–64, dying in office; and from 1958–64 Mr John King was part of this Mastership. He was to continue in office with Lord Belper until 1966, remaining in office as sole Master until 1971, and then joined for one more season by Major General Wildbore-Smith. John King was Joint Master of the Yorkshire pack, the Badsworth from 1949–58, and came to Leicestershire on buying the Wartnaby estate at the very cross-roads of the Quorn and Belvoir, atop the hill, west of the Melton Mowbray to Nottingham road, which swoops down into the Vale of Belvoir. Knighted in 1979, and made a life peer four years later, Lord King is one of the best known and acclaimed business supremos in Britain, largely due to his success in reviving the fortunes of British Airways before and after it was privatized. He had already made a great career in business with his engineering companies, Babcock and Wilcox and Babcock International. Fortunately, despite his heavy business preoccupations, he has always found time for the Belvoir Hunt, steering its fortunes as its Chairman since he gave up the Mastership. He is passionately committed to country sports and the environment in which they take place. When I was a member of the Belvoir Committee I recall Lord King, then Chairman of British Airways and with multifarious other commitments, spending a considerable time discussing the price and availability of split rails for Hunt fencing. At a quiet country inn near Belvoir Castle he greets his old friends, the Belvoir farmers at committee meetings, and clearly finds considerable relaxation in steeping himself in the cares of the Hunt, although he would say with mock seriousness: 'Being Chairman of British Airways is nothing like as difficult as being Chairman of the Belvoir.' As Master of the Belvoir he proved that he knows only one way to run any enterprise – successfully. Yet his reputation for toughness in business dealings was not by any means mirrored in his Mastership which was characterized by considerable fun and good humour in the hunting field, and a great many quiet acts of kindness and generosity to individuals throughout the hunting country, especially those in the farming community. Although, it must be said, that John King's displeasure if things are not done correctly, is a powerful incentive to ensuring that everything runs smoothly in his enterprises; inevitably, his nickname is King John to some.

It has been an enormous advantage for the Belvoir to have a chairman of such calibre, bestowing stability and continuity. No one need have any doubt who will make firm decisions and sort things out if troubles afflict the Belvoir. John King believes that foxhunting flourishes with good organization, goodwill and not too much democracy, provided the management is effective, and he certainly ensures that is the case. As a foxhunter in the field he was a great goer, riding powerful horses which would not turn their heads. For many years his horses were at livery with Tom Barlow, and they were always kept fit to stay at or near the front of the field throughout any run. I can hear him now, saying to his huntsman in the hunting field: 'Come on, Jim, do something to astonish us.'

Lord and Lady King have given up riding to hounds nowadays, but they remain intensely interested in the Hunt and give meets at Wartnaby to the Belvoir and Quorn, their estates lying in both countries.

Lord King was exceedingly loyal to the huntsman throughout his Mastership, Jim Webster, who took over when the formidable George Tongue retired in 1956. Jim had whipped-in to George for five seasons previously, and was thirty-three when promoted to huntsman. He is one of the great characters of the foxhunting world, with a sense of humour which helped him to survive and flourish during a remarkable twenty-seven years in one of the toughest roles in sport of any kind. Probably his greatest asset was that if anyone can claim to be born to foxhunting it is Jim Webster. His great grandfather and grandfather were successively huntsmen of the Lanarkshire and Renfrewshire, and his father, Arthur Webster was huntsman of the Essex Union until he retired in 1951. Jim's brother Clarence became huntsman of that great sporting country, the Warwickshire from 1958–82. The brothers had both whipped-in to their father before moving on to make their careers elsewhere.

'He was a great schoolmaster, but I was jolly pleased to get away from him,' Jim recalled.

Just before the war, Jim had two seasons as second whipper-in to George Tongue at the Belvoir, before Jim saw war service with the Essex Yoemanry. He took part in the D-Day landings and finished the war in occupied Germany. After the war he whipped-in at Sir Watkin Williams-Wynn's and the Cheshire, both grand countries still, before returning to the Belvoir.

As one who hunted during the latter part of Jim's long stint at Belvoir, I certainly owe him much for a great deal of fun. He was extraordinarily imperturbable, never seeming to get the slightest bit rattled if things went wrong.

Professional huntsmen, especially in Leicestershire, are the subject of much critical assessment over the dinner table by Hunt followers whose keenness on the Chase is not matched by real knowledge of hounds and hound work, nor do many have the opportunity to compare their huntsman with those elsewhere.

I noticed that when Masters mounted Jim well he went well; if the horse-flesh was not so good, he rode accordingly. He was a survivor; he hunted his hounds, and he got to the end of a hunt across challenging country. The big crowds of hard-riding thrusters, and would-be thrusters, on

Saturdays and Wednesdays never seemed to worry him. I greatly admired his professionalism at all levels. He was a total devotee to the English hound, and he knew how to keep them fit for their work on both sides of the country. His speech after a Quorn puppy show, was a masterpiece of humorous understatement. He referred to two sorts of hounds: 'the Belvoir hounds – and them other hounds', and he confessed with mock seriousness that it was somewhat difficult to judge 'them other hounds' because they were apt to be bred from such a variety of sources. He said with gravitas, and a twinkle in his eye, that he knew the Quorn country pretty well because 'when the wind is in the right quarter, the Belvoir hounds is apt to run in here quite a bit. . . '.

He was not exaggerating; some of the best runs I have had in the Quorn country, have been with the Belvoir hounds, and vice versa. To be fair, the very best 'away' hunt I had with the Belvoir occurred when the Quorn hounds were coughing and could not hunt, so the Belvoir was invited into the country to a meet at Hickling. They promptly found a fox and obligingly hunted it back into their own country, giving us a great ride across the Vale, swooping down on Hose Thorns across the green lane from south to north, having ridden parallel to Canal Lane from the Long Clawson end. In the afternoon, however, they excelled themselves, achieving a ten mile run from Curate's, right across the Quorn Monday country westwards, crossing the Fosse A 46 road, where lorry drivers were somewhat astonished to see the Prince of Wales holding up his hand asking them to slow down as hounds ran over the road. Hounds then swooped past Willoughby-on-the-Wolds, ran through Ella's covert and over the delectable grass and fences past Turnpost farm, going on down to Wysall in the dusk where they got among fresh foxes. I hacked back to Geoff Brooks's yard at Widmerpool that evening in the haze of a foxhunting heaven. This hunt occurred when Jim's successor, Robin Jackson, was hunting hounds. One of the best days I can recall with Jim as huntsman was his very last, when the Belvoir farmers demonstrated in practical terms that they thought the world of the retiring huntsman. He was a truly wonderful ambassador for the sport, and did so much himself to maintain excellent relationships with every farmer and landowner throughout the country.

Although it was a wet end of season the Vale farmers offered the Hunt an 'open day' – we could go anywhere – provided everyone, subscribers included, paid a special cap for the day, to be devoted to Jim's retirement testimonial fund. We had a grand hunt in the morning, and I cannot resist quoting part of my account of Jim's final hunt in the Vale – from Hose Thorns. I was mounted on my mare, Josephine, as second horse, and was among only a small mounted field for the last draw of the afternoon:

The black, tan and white bitches slip into the Thorns. We wait on the roadside: only thirty-four of us left in the mounted field, out of a contingent of one hundred and four.

Several of us hold up our hats as Charlie peeps out of the covert; he dodges back inside. An evening hunt? Is it too much to hope for?

Hats up again as the fox steals out covert, and we wait with bated breath while he runs south over Mr Jack Palmer's fabulous grass.

Jim's unmistakeable 'Gone Away' blows triumphantly, and the pack tumbles out of covert, almost gliding over the grass. Mr Henson, our thrusting Field Master, sets off and we rattle over the fly-fences. Josephine is pulling hard; she feels as if she had just started the day.

The other hunters apparently feel the same. We take a pull before the stiff in and out over the Green Lane, then on over Mr Richard Chandler's marvellous grassland, and hooray, hounds are swinging right over Mr Sneath's and across the Canal Lane. It is a thrilling jump on to the verge, across the lane, and straight over the next hedge, with hounds screaming on our left flank.

We gallop on over Mr John Wiles's land, and jump a formidable cut-and-laid with solid timber on top – specially prepared for a Melton Hunt Club ride – and on to Mr John Doubleday's farm. It is still all grass, and hounds are hurtling ahead.

We turn right to leap perhaps the biggest fence of the day, with a dyke rather than a ditch on the landing side. I spot a top hat lying on the brink, and there is a fearful crash as someone lands in the ditch.

Josephine flies it like a bird, and I vow never to make fun of her again. We gallop on over Mr Ken Egglestone's and Mr Brian Wiles's farms, crossing the Clawson-Hickling lane and going on to Sherbrooke's. Hounds hunt their fox into the dense covert; the fox is given best.

Time: just under thirty minutes. But how do you measure the pleasure in terms of minutes? 'Better one hour of glorious life, than half an age without a name . . .' says the poem.

Jim Webster has been flying ahead of us all day, close to his beloved hounds. Stuart Coley's whipping-in has been impeccable. Robert Henson asks Jim to blow for home, and then calls for three cheers from the small mounted field at Sherbrookes. Members of the field warmly thank the huntsman for today – and, of course, for all the days he has given to so many foxhunters.

Major General F. B. Wildbore-Smith joined John King in his Mastership for the final season, 1971–2, and remained in office in the subsequent Mastership with Mr Nicholas Turner, who farms an extensive estate at Ropsley, Lincolnshire, and Mrs Ann Reid-Scott.

Others who served as Masters during the 1970s and '80s (see Appendix for exact dates) were Mr John Hine, Mr Robert Henson, Mr John Blakeway, and Mr John Parry, all mainly concerned with the Leicestershire side of the country. In charge of days on the Lincolnshire side were Mr Philip Watts, Mr Charles Harrison, Mr James Knight, and Mrs Marjory Comerford.

John Hine was a successful, entrepreneureal Midlands businessman from the Derbyshire borders who learned to ride across country as an adult, but he was a natural athlete, having been a successful rugby player. He has a delightful personality, is an excellent organizer, and made sure that the Hunt servants were well mounted. During his two seasons at the helm, 1974–6, the Belvoir enjoyed some excellent sport. I shall never forget the marvellous day after the Melton Hunt Club ride from Scalford in 1975; hounds ran all day in great circles around the Wednesday country. I recall, with others, losing hounds at one point and retiring to an inn at Scalford for refreshment – it had an all day licence – only to hear hounds outside the village, and rejoining them for the last part of an exciting evening hunt.

The cross-country ride, and some of the hunting, were captured in a splendid documentary film *Wednesday Country*, made by former BBC television sports director Alan Mouncer, and for which I wrote the script and recorded the commentary. It was good enough to be shown on a national cinema circuit throughout Britain, and contained plenty of pro-hunting points which needed publicity at the widest possible level.

John Hine had some exciting business happenings at that time; he resigned from the Belvoir – much to the regret of many in the mounted field – and went to the High Peak as Master, proving that he could hunt hounds as well as performing as an excellent Field Master in Leicestershire.

Robert Henson's Mastership, from 1980–8 was a great boon to the Hunt; putting it simply, hunting with Henson was always sheer fun. He was brought up to hunting; his father, Gino Henson, was one of the great characters of Lincolnshire farming, and delighted in breeding and producing young hunters; he was a Master of the Blankney, but hunted a lot with the Belvoir and many other packs. His eldest son, Richard, still hunts with the Belvoir, and remains one of the best men across country, no matter what he is riding. His brother, Bill and his wife Val, hunted for many years with the Belvoir, although now mainly hunting in Yorkshire with the West of Yore. Bill has made a great success as Director of Burghley Horse Trials.

Robert Henson has a sunny personality, is a remarkably good horseman across country, and adores foxhunting. He put these qualities to the best possible use in making sure that hunting with the Belvoir was hugely enjoyable for all of us lucky enough to subscribe during the 1980s. We shall always owe him an enormous debt for a tremendous amount of fun. He gave the sort of lead over the Saturday and Wednesday countries which made you reflect afterwards: 'Did I really do that?' He was not so well mounted at first, but with the co-operation of his wife, Sarah – a former event rider of distinction – soon rectified this, and struck up an excellent relationship with Jim Webster, mounting him well, and helping to ensure that Jim's final seasons are remembered with special pleasure.

In 1983 Robert and his Joint Master, Charles Harrison, a shrewd Lincolnshire farmer who has done much for British eventing, made a splendid decision in appointing a young Scots huntsman, Robin Jackson, to replace Jim Webster on his retirement. Jackson was only twenty-seven but he had already won a good reputation as huntsman of the Lanarkshire and Renfrewshire, and the Grove and Rufford where Bill Henson was a Joint Master. When the Belvoir huntsman's post became vacant, Robin recalled: 'I thought I was a bit young, but as the job might not come up again for twenty-five years, I thought I would have a go.' He says his first opening meet at Long Clawson was 'the most frightening experience ever.' It did not show at the time; we had a splendid day, as I recorded in *Horse and Hound*. Robin went on to make a great success as huntsman of the Belvoir. The mounted fields were particularly hard riding on the Leicestershire side during the 1980s when we were fortunate to experience mostly open seasons, with comparatively few stoppages for bad weather. The drier seasons tended to produce poor scenting abilities, but Robin and the Belvoir bitch pack frequently produced good hunts when some other packs were finding the conditions extremely difficult. He was particularly pleased with the 1989–90 season when there were many good hunts with long points. Most remarkable was an eighteen mile run in December, 1989, when the Belvoir hounds had met at Plungar. They found below Langar village and ran to Bingham, Whatton, Granby Gap and back to Plungar where they caught their fox. This run included a seven mile point; it was a great hound hunt, but it was a testing ride for those members of the mounted field who endeavoured to stay with them, over huge acreages of arable land. I have to confess I was one of the large body of the field who did not partake, but waited unavailingly for hounds to return to the venue for a change to second horses at Langar airfield. When they did return it was nearly dark, and the second horses were never called upon!

In the 1991–2 season, Robin Jackson was equally pleased with hounds and with scenting conditions, but he had made a firm decision to give up his career as huntsman at the age of thirty-six, after nine seasons at Belvoir. It was a great disappointment to his many admirers in the country, but his change of lifestyle was his personal choice: 'If I don't make the change now, I think it will be too late in a few years' time,' he said. He and his wife

Dorothy and their children settled in the Belvoir country, and Robin became a salesman for a horse feed company.

Robert Henson had been joined in the Mastership in 1983 by Mr John Blakeway who retired at the end of the 1990–1 season, aged sixty-five. He was one of the most popular and successful of the Belvoir's recent Masters, forming a great team with Robert Henson. In his youth he was a successful amateur rider in National Hunt racing, winning the Kim Muir Memorial Chase at Cheltenham in 1946. His father was one of the founders of the Cotswold Vale Farmers' pack, and John was to serve as Joint Master of the Croome in his native West Midlands. He adores Leicestershire, and drove from his home in Gloucestershire to hunt with the Belvoir, combining his Mastership with such roles as Chairman of the British Show Jumping Association, and Honorary Director of the Horse of the Year Show.

A few in the Belvoir country wondered at first whether such a mature foxhunter was taking on the Field Mastership on Wednesdays and Saturdays at the right stage in his life. They were soon given the answer: John is a superb man across country, balancing his horses beautifully, taking on all obstacles with an iron nerve, and maintaining enough discipline without cramping the field's freedom unnecessarily. Like Robert Henson, he maintained a very happy atmosphere in the Belvoir hunting field, and we much regretted his resignation which also meant losing the regular attendance of his charming wife, Rosemary.

Another who the years treat extremely kindly is John Parry, of Allington, who rendered great services as the Hunt's Honorary Treasurer. He used to perform as Field Master earlier in the post-war years, and I recalled him, dressed in top hat, giving a great lead. John joined the Mastership for the seasons from 1987–9, and soon showed that he had lost none of his skills as Field Master.

'Steady' he would say, and people were steady. Then he would give a good lead over a fence, and we could be sure that we would be in the pound seats following him during a good hunt over any country. His wife, Jean, is one of only two ladies still riding side saddle regularly in the Belvoir mounted field. The other is Mrs Charlotte Rodriguez of Ashby Folville who goes particularly well on the Leicestershire side.

James Knight performed great services for the Belvoir on the Lincolnshire side, being a member of a keen sporting family in the Lincolnshire farming community. Marjorie Comerford, the former international three-day-event rider suffered a grievous riding accident during her Mastership but through sheer courage has made a great recovery, and it is good to see her still in the mounted field.

Everyone in the Belvoir country was delighted when Mr Joseph (Joey) Newton joined the Mastership in 1989, ensuring continuity from within the country. Few could be as well qualified: he is the son of the Honourable Mrs Ursula ('Urky') Newton, the redoubtable Honorary Secretary of the Melton Hunt Club (Chapter Eight) and the late Lance Newton who founded the Club and was a devoted foxhunter. Joey, a grandson of Lord Rank, farms extensively in the Wednesday country at Saltby. He was a top-class amateur rider in point-to-points and in 'chasing under Rules, and therefore knows how to mount himself effectively to take on a country where he has hunted all his life, and has the advantage of considerable backing and support from his wife, Emma.

After John Blakeway's resignation, Joey has taken on the Field Master's role single-handed on Wednesdays and Saturdays. His own farming experience is a great advantage in his relationships with farmers and landowners throughout the Belvoir country. The Lincolnshire side of the country is nowadays in the hands of Joint Masters Mrs Barry ('Tor') Owen and Mr John Martin who work hard to help ensure that the doghound pack continue to produce consistent sport.

Robin Jackson's successor as huntsman, Martin Thornton made an excellent start in the 1992–3 season, despite the period of exceptional rain up to Christmas which rendered so much of Britain's countryside waterlogged, followed by a severe frost. It was good to see his fourteen-year-old son, Bob, crossing the country behind his father with such enthusiasm and skill, accompanied by his mother, Sally, going equally well. Martin was previously huntsman of the Zetland, and the Bicester with Whaddon Chase; he hunts the fox with tremendous enthusiasm and persistence; hounds are encouraged to hunt their fox to the logical end, no matter what terrain they enter.

Watching the Belvoir hounds continues to give as much pleasure to the followers from roadsides and hilltops as they afford to those of us endeavouring to ride across the country.

As with its Masterships, the Belvoir had benefited from excellent Hunt Secretaries: Major Horton after the war and Brigadier Cooper from 1957–70; to be succeeded by Mr Tom Hudson, the popular horse shows public address commentator; then came the late Mr David Faulkner – who died in the hunting field – Major Peter Postlethwaite, and since 1988 Mr Tim Hall-Wilson. His appointment is another welcome sign of continuity, since his grandfather was the former Joint Master Major Charles Tonge, of Barrowby, referred to earlier, and his maternal grandfather, Colonel Swan was Field Master.

Nowadays, foxhunting with such a major pack in modern conditions, calls for up-to-date equipment, and Belvoir sportsmen of the past would no doubt be amazed to see the present Hunt Secretary making telephone calls from horseback on his radio 'phone during a day's hunting.

'It's invaluable in ensuring prompt fence mending, calling for medical aid in emergencies, and many other purposes – but not, of course, in any way to assist the huntsman in hunting the fox,' says Tim.

This present outline of Belvoir history must not end without the fullest tribute to Charles, 10th Duke of Rutland, who succeeded his father as long ago as 1940, and has remained staunch to the best interests of the Belvoir Hunt and the hounds, which are his property. He takes a special interest in the breeding and welfare of the pack, and ensures that Belvoir Castle's historic kennels are preserved as their true home. Built in 1802, the kennels are contained in a square building with a raised octagonal centre and four corner towers. There is a small room in the raised centre, where in sterner times the kennel boy would sleep; his task was to ring a bell to summon the huntsman if hounds began to fight in the kennel during the night. Hounds exercise in the Castle grounds, and the final meet of the season is always at the Castle. The puppy show at the kennels during the summer conveys the spirit of continuity which has ensured the flourishing history of the great Hunt.

These will surely always be the Duke of Rutland's hounds, and thanks to the guardianship of successive ducal owners, and the pack's central role in the life of the countryside all around Belvoir Castle, the future of foxhunting in this great Shires country must surely continue to offer so much pleasure to generations of sportsmen in the twenty-first century – especially those who relish the challenge of throwing their hearts over the fences of the Vale of Belvoir.

The present Duke of Rutland wrote:

I am immensely proud of my hounds, they are as much a part of Belvoir and Belvoir tradition as the Castle itself. That is why I am so anxious to ensure that the breeding policy should follow our distinctive traditional lines of colour and conformation. These undoubtedly have evolved over the two hundred years that the pack has been in existence. Soon after the first war, one of the Hunt Masters tried to introduce an element of white Welsh hound into the breeding. This caused great offence and was immediately changed.

My family have always taken pleasure in collecting works of art, including many sporting pictures. We are fortunate at Belvoir to have many pictures of the hounds, huntsmen and horses painted by famous artists such as Ferneley who, as a young man, used to paint the farm carts on the estate.

These pictures hang in the castle and are a frequent reminder of the Belvoir Hunt, and are part of our heritage. Also we have a remarkable collection of Hunt diaries covering a period of over one hundred years, up to the start of the last war.

These describe every day's hunting, written by the huntsmen at the end of each day. They show, only too clearly that the tradition and sport today is still very much the same, hunting the same country with many familiar names of meets and coverts. Foxhunting today is a popular sport giving great pleasure to people from all walks of life as well as farmers and those who live in the country.

I am pleased that my hounds have such a high reputation for speed and sport, that our Hunt staff and Masters have an equally high reputation. Field sports and foxhunting are part of our British way of life, and I truly believe they have had some influence on the formation of our character.

13

The Cottesmore in the Eighteenth and Nineteenth Centuries

If I were given my choice of a place to live
in, and a pack to hunt with, I would say, let
me live near Oakham and hunt with the
Cottesmore every day they are out

The origins of the Cottesmore Hunt are not crystal clear. No doubt there
were private packs in the area hunting deer for centuries, and fox would
have been hunted also, although, as mentioned previously, the latter sport
was considered much inferior until the great forests of England were
cleared.

It was claimed by the Lonsdale family, and has been generally accepted
since, that a pack of foxhounds was brought down by road from Lowther
Castle in Westmorland by Henry, Viscount Lowther to Fineshade Abbey,
Northamptonshire, in 1666, and were then sold to Mr Thomas Noel of the
Earls of Gainsborough family in 1695. They had family connections in the
East Midlands, wanted to run their hounds in the forests of Rockingham,
centred on the Castle which overlooks the Welland valley on the southern
borders of Leicestershire and Northamptonshire. There were other good
hunting areas to be encountered on the long trek south from Westmorland,
but their home in the Fells was, and is, the environment for hunting on

foot; it was necessary to travel elsewhere for the thrill of the Chase on horseback. They made a wonderful choice in deciding to hunt the country which became the Cottesmore, and the family was to prove instrumental in ensuring the Hunt's survival and development through much later stages of its history.

The pack which Henry Lowther first brought to the East Midlands would have contained Fell foxhound blood: a distinctive breed with a high domed skull, and open 'hare' feet, adapted to hunting on the steep sides of Fell slopes in the Lake District. These hounds are good scenting, but inclined to be independent. They have been used as outcrosses with foxhounds hunting elsewhere in the British Isles, even as far afield as the Exmoor under the Mastership of Captain Ronnie Wallace.

A curious joint Mastership arrangement has much to do with the foundation of the Cottesmore and its northern neighbour, the Belvoir. John, 3rd Duke of Rutland (1696–1779) arranged with the Earl of Cardigan, the Earl of Gainsborough, Lord Gower and Lord Howe, that each should pay £150 annually to defray the cost of hounds, horses and other costs for a pack of foxhounds. These hounds were to be kept from 15 October to 30 November at Croxton Park on the Duke of Rutland's estate; from 1 December to 31 January at Cottesmore; from 1 February to 31 March at Thawson; from 1 April to 14 October 'at such places as shall be determined by the parties.'

The Hunt establishment comprised one huntsman, six whippers-in, a steward, and two cooks; clearly the refreshment of the followers was an important consideration.

This joint aristocratic venture hunted a huge area up and down the East Midlands until the early eighteenth century. The costs greatly increased, and in 1732 the Earl of Gainsborough separated from the arrangement and took twenty-five couples of hounds which he began to hunt in the country now known as the Cottesmore. The Gainsborough seat is at Exton, east of Oakham, the county town of old Rutland.

At Belvoir there was recorded a surprisingly heavy correspondence between the Duke of Rutland and the Earl of Gainsborough as to the rightful ownership of a certain large caldron used for cooking the hounds' food! Clearly the noble gentlemen had an eye for detail, and the splitting of the joint Mastership probably indicated the difficulties of keeping everyone happy.

They had hunted a large territory, including great parts of Leicestershire, Northamptonshire, Rutlandshire and Nottinghamshire. The practice of moving hounds to kennels at different times of the season was common in many parts of Britain. The aristocracy would visit a country, enjoy a change of scene, and then move on to fresh hunting fields.

The Earl of Gainsborough died in 1751 and his eldest son was then only a boy of eleven. Meanwhile in 1756, the widowed Countess married Mr Thomas Noel and he and the 6th Earl retained the hounds. Tom Noel's huntsman was Arthur Abbey, according to Dick Christian, who was born at Cottesmore, and describes Abbey as, 'a big, heavy man with a rasping, strong voice'. Accounts kept by Tom Noel, and preserved by the Gainsborough family, indicate that Arthur Abbey shared the huntsman's role with a close relative, perhaps his brother, William Abbey, and that John Abbey also acted as a whipper-in. They were paid £35.12s.6d. per annum from 1771–84. In relative terms hounds were highly valued, since those that were sold fetched about five a couple. The accounts indicate that about fifteen Hunt horses were kept during the winter months, and about five during the summer when the rest were out at grass. Even better than the accounts, is the hunting diary of Tom Noel from 1766, continuing, with some blanks, for about thirteen seasons. They are the cryptic, workmanlike jottings of a down-to-earth foxhunter and contain no personal information, but they do indicate a great deal of excellent fox-hunting in the very areas hunted by the Cottesmore today.

Much of the hunting was in woodland, now far more open, which falls in the modern day Monday and Thursday countries. The tally of foxes killed per season is much smaller than the Cottesmore is achieving in the early 1990s: over seventy or eighty brace have been accounted for in each recent season. In 1767 twenty-nine and a half brace were killed: eleven brace in Leicestershire, seven in Lincolnshire and eleven and half in Rutland. In seven years the numbers (counted in brace) killed were: 1766, forty-one; 1769, forty-two and a half; 1772, forty-three and a half; 1767, twenty-nine and a half; 1768, fifty-six and a half; 1771, forty-four and a half.

It is impossible to deduce exactly how much smaller the fox population was in the late eighteenth century, but Hunt tallies are a good monitor, and it is clear that the fox population was certainly significantly smaller than today. After nearly two centuries of sporting conservation by the Hunts, including the preservation of coverts and protection of litters during the breeding season, it appears that the Leicestershire fox population is notably larger today.

So much for the arguments against foxhunting; in terms of conservation, the fox has benefited from organized foxhunting which has meant real investment in its habitat and a cull based on sporting requirements, rather than attempted pest extermination. Those anti-hunting groups who claim to be friends of the fox conveniently ignore evidence of this kind.

Christmas Eve, 1768, was recorded in typically laconic tone by Tom Noel's diary entry: 'Found at Burley Park, ran to Barnsdale, to ye Park, back to Barnsdale, to Armley, to Hambleton Wood, to Linding Goss, to Wing Goss, to Glaston, to Morcot, to South Luffenham, to North Luffenham Town, to Normington Park, ran to Ketton Stone Pitts, killed.' This was hardly likely to be a hunt after one fox, and at Normington park it refers to an 'untapige', an obscure term often used by Tom Noel. It may be derived from the French piege, a trap or snare, and could indicate that the run came to an untimely end through the fox being trapped. The countryside was probably full of traps at that time when rural larders depended heavily on trapped game or fish in the locality. Fox trapping became far less common once foxhunting developed as a premier sport in the countryside, since landlords learned to protect the fox from trapping or shooting so that they would not commit the social 'crime' of having blank coverts when they were drawn by the Hunts. Blank days are virtually unknown in modern foxhunting in the Cottesmore country, but in 1767, Tom Noel recorded on 10 December 'Tryed Pryers Coppey, Tampions Coppey, Launde Park Wood, the Great Wood, Lodington Redish, Tugby, Skevinton, Tilton, Ouston, Lady Wood, Orton Park Wood, Barleythorpe Bushes, and did not find.' One simply cannot imagine a blank day in this country where the same coverts exist today. Mr Noel began by hunting over a large, fairly undefined country which as time went on and foxes became more numerous, was gradually reduced to its present limits.

This was the period when Hugo Meynell was creating the Quorn Hunt to the west, and his influence clearly mattered greatly to his neighbours in the definition of Hunt boundaries. Although it was some years before his style of hunting hounds was emulated successfully by his neighbours.

In 1766 Tom Noel, acting on behalf of the Earl of Gainsborough, made an agreement with Mr Meynell regarding coverts and boundaries. Meynell achieved a good deal, since the following coverts – all nowadays in the Cottesmore country – were to be neutral, that is they could be drawn by both Quorn and Cottesmore packs: Owston, Launde Tilton, Skeffington, Loddington, Tugby, Allexton, Stockerston Woods, Easton Park, and the woods near Holt. Billesdon Coplow, now Quorn Friday country, was neutral, but the Cottesmore were not to draw Ashby Pastures, and no coverts on the Quorn side of Billesdon Coplow were to be drawn by Lord Gainsborough. Mr Meynell agreed in future not to draw Prior's Coppice, Brown's and Tampion Coppice, Lady Wood, Orton Park and Burton Gorse.

The agreement foreshadowed the shape of the hunting countries as we know them today, and which were to be finally defined and registered by the creation of the Masters of Foxhounds Association in 1881.

The 6th Earl of Gainsborough never married, and with Tom Noel having died, probably in 1788 – although this date is disputed – there was a problem of Mastership succession, but this was solved by the Lowther family. Sir William Lowther, known in the family as 'William the Good', who became the first Lord Lonsdale in 1807, bought the hounds about three years before he inherited the Lowther estates. He was immensely wealthy, with huge estates in Yorkshire, Westmorland and Cumberland. His miners brought his wealth to the surface by exploiting rich seams of coal under the Irish Sea; there was also iron ore to be mined from the Fells. But his heart was in Leicestershire. Foxhunting was his passion. He spent at least seven months a year hunting, and when he took over the pack he set about a scientific study of hound breeding.

At first he rented Stocken Hall, but later rented Cottesmore House, where he kennelled his hounds, and this is how the Hunt derived its name. The first Lord Lonsdale was the true founder of the Hunt. At the end of the hunting season he rode the two hundred miles back to Lowther with the pack; he could not bear to be parted from his hounds. The journey each way lasted nearly four weeks.

In 1802 Sir William became Viscount Lowther and the pressure of responsibilities in running his Westmorland estates caused him to sell his hounds to Sir Gilbert Heathcote of Normanton Park, ancestor of the Earls of Ancaster. He was a great sportsman, owning many racehorses, including Amarto who won the Derby. His studman was Dick Christian, made famous through the writings of *The Druid*. Dick was a garrulous fellow, but he knew plenty about hunting and his comments on the relative performances of the Cottesmore and Quorn hounds probably have much validity. Arthur Abbey and later Philip Payne hunted hounds for Sir William Lowther in his first Mastership, and for Sir Gilbert Heathcote, with Dick Christian whipping in. Dick described Payne as a, 'first rate little fellow'.

After four seasons William Lowther bought back the hounds, and was to remain Master for the best part of half a century, remaining in office until 1842.

With his enthusiasm, his wealth, and his devotion to orderly hound breeding, why did not the first Lord Lonsdale get far more credit for the development of foxhunting than his neighbour, Hugo Meynell? The answer was probably that Meynell was evolving a quickness and a dash in hunting the fox which much appealed to the Meltonian followers who were rapidly improving the quality of the horses they were bringing to the hunting field. When Lord Lonsdale bought back the hounds from Heathcote he employed a huntsman with an unfortunate name, Slacke. Unfortunately, the sport was still conducted by Slacke in the old style, whereby the fox was walked to death by large hounds, giving tongue melodiously, and studiously working out the line with immense patience but not much pace. Meanwhile, the Quorn hounds were perfecting the art of chasing the fox to death; the 'quick thing' was already happening, much to the delight of the well mounted followers.

Alas, the Master of the Cottesmore hounds and his huntsman were jibed at by the sporting parson, the Reverend John Empson, of Saxby, who wrote in 1816:

> My outset commenc'd with the Cottesmore Pack, Where the Master's dead slow and the Agent Slacke; So decidedly Slack, and so deadly slow, That the whole of the system appeared So-so.

John Empson was a hard rider in the hunting field, earning the nickname 'The Flying Parson' and it is likely that he had received the rough edge of Lord Lonsdale's tongue, and was paying him back. Modern hunting correspondents never indulge in such rudery; what a pity, but then Englishmen were far more accustomed to calling a spade a bloody shovel in the early nineteenth century.

Earl William and his Hunt staff used to wear hairy flat-topped hats, and it is believed that Surtees thereby obtained the idea of the 'Flat Hat Hunt', with Lord Scamperdale as Master, immortalized in *Soapy Sponge's Sporting Tour*. Surtees had travelled the length of Britain as a hunting correspondent before he wrote his novels.

We should not condemn the Cottesmore hounds at that time. They were undoubtedly a great pack, and highly effective. Dick Christian averred that they had the longest runs, and they were accomplished killers of foxes in their fine, wild country.

The new style of foxhunting was undoubtedly spreading, but it was to be later in the nineteenth century before the Meltonian set truly appreciated the full possibilities of the Cottesmore country. Its great coverts and its wildness meant that blank days were virtually unknown; it was always possible to find a fox somewhere. The country rode heavier than the Quorn or the Belvoir in a wet season, but there was grass throughout the Cottesmore, and improved drainage meant the riding possibilities opened up on the sea of old turf.

The first Lord Lonsdale's Mastership was not especially aimed at satisfying smart visitors from London. The Cottesmore has always had a much larger residential element than the Quorn, and it is clear the Earl's friends and neighbours were his primary consideration in providing sport on the purist lines he liked best. Picking up hounds and galloping them on to the line of another fox likely to provide a quick spin over the grass was definitely not his style. Having hunted the country for more than half a century, apart from a short break, he resigned his Mastership in

1842, only two years before he died, and the horses and hounds were sold.

Sir Richard Sutton was his successor, bringing his own existing establishment from the Burton country to the Cottesmore. A celebrated picture of 'Sir Richard Sutton and the Quorn hounds', painted by Sir Francis Grant, which hung in the Leicester County Club was really the Cottesmore; the church in the background was Langham. The confusion no doubt arose because Sir Richard gave up the Cottesmore after five seasons and took the Quorn (Chapter Four). The Hunt trundled along for several decades without sharing much in the lustre attaching to the Quorn and the Belvoir.

Sir Richard's successor was Mr Henley Greaves, who has been described as 'a heavy man and hot tempered'; he became well-known in Warwickshire hunting circles later. He was succeeded in 1852 by Mr Higginson Burrowes who gave up three years later. He hunted a pack 'drawn from various sources'.

Sir John Trollope was persuaded to take over the Mastership at a time when there were few contenders. Sir John, who was created Lord Kesteven in 1868, hunted the whole country which then extended from Bourne in Lincolnshire to Tilton in Leicestershire from east to west, and had an almost equal area from north to south. He is credited with breeding a much improved pack for the Cottesmore, but clearly the whole country was a huge commitment for him. He relied heavily on the Belvoir kennel for stallion hounds, and built up a pack with great hunting abilities in a country which was exceptionally demanding on hound and horse. On the Lincolnshire side there was much rough ground, and huge dykes; on the Rutland and Leicestershire sides, there was the constantly undulating landscape, with stiff timber to be jumped out of heavy going.

At the beginning of this century T.F. Dale, the excellent hunting historian wrote:

> If I were given my choice of a place to live in and a pack to hunt with, I would say, let me live near Oakham and hunt with the Cottesmore every day they are out. The country is wilder and, if I may say so, less artificial than some other parts of the grass countries, and in consequence the foxes are stouter and wilder, and for that reason possibly leave a better scent.
>
> Doubtless other packs can show bursts as brilliant for the satisfying daily bread of hunting, but for runs that are long but not tedious, for chases that are hunts but not slow, the Cottesmore, like its neighbour the Belvoir, is the country.
>
> For more than a quarter of a century now this Hunt has been

thoroughly worked and well hunted, and the tide of fashion has flowed towards it. It is still a Hunt to settle in and take pride in.

Dale averred however that 'with the exception of part of the Tuesday and Saturday countries, I may say plainly that the Cottesmore is not as a riding ground equal to the Quorn or Mr Fernie's. There are parts, too, of the Tuesday, or Leicestershire country that are very rough; and Tilton, Loddington, Tugby, Skeffington and Launde are places where none should venture unless he has a stout horse.'

It will be seen that the Lowther family again had much to do with the strengthening of the Hunt's fortunes during the latter part of the nineteenth century, to which Dale refers.

However, it is clear that Mr Tailby of Skeffington who helped form the Fernie country (Chapter Ten) achieved much in exploiting the potential of the Cottesmore country from Skeffington up to Whissendine.

In 1857 Sir John Trollope entered into an arrangement with Tailby whereby the latter took the area described above on loan, as fully recounted in my account of the Fernie history. Sir John took his hounds to Little Bytham and hunted from Casewick until 1870.

Colonel Henry Lowther was pressed to become Master, with a subscription of £400 a year. He employed a huntsman, Lambert, who was quick and intelligent; he raised the pace of hunting in the Cottesmore country, employing the more modern techniques evolved by Meynell, and the Meltonians began to visit the Cottesmore country more frequently and in greater numbers. The Colonel wisely bought fifteen couple of hounds for £1,300 from Tailby who had showed such good sport, and these undoubtedly helped Lambert enormously. He became 3rd Earl of Lonsdale in 1872 and continued to hunt the hounds until his great weight and ill health forced him to resign in 1876, when he loaned his pack to Lord Carrington for four years on condition that he might resume the Mastership at the end of that period if he wished. Most important, Henry Lowther from the start of his Mastership took back the country lent to Tailby, and thus restored to the Cottesmore its full territory. He was the second son of William, the 2nd Earl Lonsdale. After service in the Lifeguards, Henry became MP for West Cumberland, but lived at Asfordby near Melton Mowbray, which was rented by his father. Henry's father bought Barleythorpe on the Melton road, outside Oakham, as a hunting box for his son. When he succeeded to the Earldom Henry built kennels and stables on a lavish scale at Barleythorpe, laying the foundation stone on 1 March 1872; hounds used them for the first time in November 1872. Alas, his passion for foxhunting was equalled by his passion for food: he had hunted five days a week for many years, but on retiring from the Army he put on so much weight that no horse could carry him. When he died aged fifty-eight, he weighed twenty-two stone, and it took eight men to lift his coffin into the family mausoleum. He left four sons and two daughters; the second son, Hugh, was to become one of the most famous personalities in British social and sporting life, and certainly one of the most prominent of foxhunters in Leicestershire. Hugh was only nineteen when his father died suddenly; the eldest brother, St George, was aged twenty, and he suffered from ill health which was to end his life only six years later. He was, however, an excellent horseman and inherited Barleythorpe and the Cottesmore hounds from his father. He inherited a fortune which produced an income greater in one week than Hugh and the younger brothers received for one year. St George had many other interests, including a passion for sailing the oceans in his steam yacht. He was technically Master of the Cottesmore for two seasons, but Lord Carrington continued in office until 1880 when the agricultural depression forced him to resign.

The Hunt Committee accepted an offer made by Mr William Gosling to purchase the hounds from Lord Lonsdale in 1880 and present them to the country. The valuers, Mr Drake of Shardloes and Mr Lane Fox of Bramham, fixed the price at £900; less than a third of the price which the Duke of Portland and the Behrens brothers gave for the Quorn hounds when they bought them and presented them to that country. Arrangements to make packs of hounds belong to the country rather than a family were being taken in a great many hunting countries. It enabled continuity to be achieved despite changes of Mastership made necessary by human frailty, or business failure. Such aristocratic family packs as the Duke of Rutland's and the Duke of Beaufort's remained impervious to such new social pressures, but on the whole, ownership of the hounds by the country proved a beneficial move in most subscription Hunts. Constant selling of hounds when Masterships changed otherwise resulted in destruction of kennel breeding lines carefully built over many years.

The old foxhound sales at Rugby ceased between the world wars, and the modern Masters of Foxhounds Association ruled that registered foxhounds shall not be sold, but may be drafted from one registered pack to another by arrangement between Masters and/or Committees.

In 1888 St George, Earl of Lonsdale died, leaving Hugh Lonsdale the inheritor, at the age of twenty-five, as the 5th Earl of Lonsdale, Viscount Lowther and Baron Lowther of Whitehaven; an immensely rich and powerful nobleman. A life of extravagance, high society entertaining, and sporting endeavour was well and truly launched; the effects were to be considerable in Leicestershire (Chapter Five).

The immediate impact on the Cottesmore country was that Hugh

Lonsdale wished to take the Mastership on his terms. He offered to let Barleythorpe and the kennels to Mr William Baird on condition that Baird would give up the kennels to him at the end of two years. By now, the Cottesmore had a Hunt Committee, a significant creation, fitting in with the purchase of the hounds for the country to hold permanently, and therefore officially owned on behalf of the country by the Committee. The Chairman from 1880 was Lord Aveland, who was created Earl of Ancaster in 1892; the other members were Mr J.H. Finch of Burley-on-the-Hill, and Mr William Gosling, with Mr W. Wing as secretary. They were not amused by the terms of Hugh Lonsdale's letter to Mr Baird. At the time Hugh was Master of the Woodland Pytchley and was hunting hounds himself with great success. As a second son and not expecting to inherit the Earldom, he had led an adventurous, sporting life; schooling horses, riding races, boxing, and indulging in the raffish delights that London could offer an aristocratic young bachelor. He was already displaying the impulsiveness, physical courage and need for the limelight which was to come into full flower when he inherited the family millions.

Within three weeks of becoming the Earl he purchased a team of chestnut carriage horses for £1,000 and thereafter collected horses assiduously. His horses had to be not less than sixteen hands, six feet round the girth and each leg had to have not less than eight and three-quarter inches of bone.

'Master', the 10th Duke of Beaufort, who was Hugh's godson, told me that Lonsdale certainly had a remarkable ability to handle horses, as a rider and trainer. 'Master' could recall his godfather putting on a show in the stables by entering the boxes of manifestly fierce stallions and calming them very quickly by handling them fearlessly.

Doubtless, the old squires of the Cottesmore country had heard more than a few details of young Hugh's early exploits and they were not prepared to hand over the fortunes of the Hunt to his immaturity at this stage. There were also memories of the 1850s when the Hunt's fortunes had been at a low ebb, and Hugh's grandfather, William Lonsdale had declined to help.

Despite the six year-long Mastership of Hugh's father, Henry, it was felt in the country that the Lowther's hereditary claim on the Cottesmore Mastership had been broken. The Committee decided to sever its dependence on the Lonsdale kennels and stables at Barleythorpe. Not for the last time, Hugh repaired his relationships in the Cottesmore swiftly, and behaved with characteristic generosity. He agreed to continue letting Barleythorpe to William Baird, the new Master, until the new kennels were completed. He had further offered to sell the Hunt land adjoining Barleythorpe to build new cottages and stables, and to lend the existing kennels in forming a new Hunt establishment. He would give any stone required from his own stone pit. This offer was declined, as the feeling against him at that time was too strong. The Committee decided to pay £100 an acre to Lord Willoughby de Eresby for the land on which the Cottesmore kennels still stand, at Ashwell, on the Wymondham road from Oakham.

It was a decision which in 1992 is hard not to regret. The Committee built huge Victorian barrack like buildings; fine for a time when labour was plentiful and cheap, but desperately unworkable in the late twentieth century. Worse, the construction of a sewerage farm nearby, and Ashwell prison opposite, ensured that the kennels was less than attractive for housing or business development at a time when the Hunt badly wished to move because busy road traffic outside had made hound exercise very dangerous. The Barleythorpe site has rear access to a lane ascending to some of the best and still unspoilt country in the Cottesmore, ideal for hound exercise at all times of the year. However, at the time it was no doubt a very good decision. Landowners who backed the decision to build new kennels were: Edward Frewen of Cold Overton, Mr Hamlyn of Langham, R. Heathcote of Manton, Edward Monckton of Fineshade, William Pochin of Edmondthorpe, Edward Dawson of Launde Abbey and Colonel Palmer of Withcote.

The new kennels were completed by the builder, Mr Hollis of Cottesmore, in 1889; the price of £6,777 was £1,200 less than the estimate! The design was based on that of Lord Middleton's kennels at Birdsall in Yorkshire, and the building was intended to accommodate one hundred couple of hounds, fifty horses, and houses for the Hunt staff. Hounds were put into the building on 5 November 1890, and killed a fox after a good hunt the next day.

For the Cottesmore, the best part of the weighty decision making in 1880 was the appointment of Mr William Baird as Master. He was a capital success, staying in office for twenty-one seasons of excellent sport. 'Willie' Baird was a true hunting man, and could hunt hounds himself if occasion demanded. He employed two excellent huntsman in William Neal and George Gillson, father of the George Gillson who was to hunt the Cottesmore later, and grandfather of the Gillson who was to hunt the Warwickshire with such success in the next century. George Gillson senior had been hunting the Belvoir hounds until Mr Baird took him to Cottesmore. Mr Baird drafted new blood into the Cottesmore kennels at first, using the Belvoir, Fitzwilliam, and Holderness Kennels.

Chatty old Otho Paget described Baird as:

A very excellent Master. . . . He was very quiet with his field, and for that reason when he did speak his order was immediately obeyed.

If he saw a gateway to which the over eager and impetuous crowd was surging with the pack evidently about to throw up in the field beyond, he would block the exit with his horse and remain there Sphinx-like until the situation was clear again.

I hardly think he cared much about competing with the hard riding crew in a fast burst, but he was a fine horseman and ready to jump a big fence when necessary.

Perhaps what he enjoyed most was to act as his own second whip, and by riding forward get a view of a beaten fox.

Baird lived in Oakham at Deanscroft, a large house now occupied by the headmaster of Oakham school next to Steven's House residential premises. Later the family moved to Cold Overton.

This was clearly a successful Mastership, with the Master paying a sizeable part of the expenses himself. However, subscriptions were being taken, and in 1891 they were extended to include ladies. Hitherto, those ladies who hunted were not asked to pay. As I have described earlier, the presence of ladies in the hunting field was controversial in varying degrees up to the late nineteenth century.

The paying of caps for a day's visit by a stranger was introduced in 1893, on a suggestion from the Quorn which had the heaviest influx of visitors. There was a joint agreement by the Leicestershire Hunts to charge a cap of £2 on non-subscribers.

When Willie Baird resigned in 1900 the Cottesmore was immediately plunged into trouble over the Mastership. Hugh Lonsdale had given up the Quorn two years earlier (Chapter Four) and was still hankering to take up his 'inheritance' at the Cottesmore. The Committee was split on the issue. Some had approached Mr Fernie, but he declined and remained in his own Harborough country. There was a proposal that Hugh Lonsdale be offered the Mastership, but it was strongly opposed by others. The Yellow Earl's rigorous regime at the Quorn was fresh in the memory of Leicestershire foxhunters. Whilst his generosity and expenditure had been outstanding, his tendency to rule with a rod of iron, and his explosive temper in the field was inevitably a drawback for many who simply went hunting for fun – an example of the tension between a Master and his field which is not unknown in the late twentieth century in certain Hunts. Lonsdale was to be disappointed again. Lord Ancaster and Sir Arthur Fludyer proposed that Mr Evan Hanbury should be offered the hounds, and he won on a vote of four to two. They referred the matter to the general Hunt meeting where Lonsdale, although proposed by Lord Kesteven and supported by Lord Exeter and Mr Wiliam Pochin, was defeated by a large majority.

Hugh Lonsdale showed that he was a big man who could rise above such disappointments. He promptly stood up and seconded Evan Hanbury for the Mastership, who was elected unanimously.

14

The Cottesmore in the Twentieth Century

Master, Master, faster, faster!

The Cottesmore took off at the start of the twentieth century in a blaze of popularity among the Meltonians who looked for an outstanding ride, and this was largely because Hanbury brought from Essex as huntsman, Arthur Thatcher, and mounted him exceedingly well. Thatcher, as referred to in the Fernie history, was a huntsman who understood fully that in the Shires it was worthwhile taking trouble to be an entertainer. He caught plenty of foxes as well, too many according to some. Thatcher was especially effective in catching foxes in the large Cottesmore woodland coverts; woodland hunting is an art some huntsmen never really acquire. The Meltonians liked him, however, because of his prowess in providing the 'quick thing'; he would lift his hounds adeptly and with great opportunism to ensure a fast hunt in the open, either catching the fox above ground at the end of a tremendous gallop of about twenty-five or thirty minutes; or the fox just escaping to ground at the conclusion of such a burst. Thatcher would then pick up hounds quickly and cast them on to find another fox with extraordinary swiftness.

Lord Lonsdale, however, did not admire Thatcher; he disliked most of Thatcher's technique, and in 1904 wrote a 3,000 word critique of Thatcher's hunting errors which is a classic dissertation on the sport. It was never meant to be disclosed, but it became public many years later. Although intended to be couched in kindly terms, it is devastating stuff; quite extraordinary, since it was written to another man's servant. He accused Thatcher of being 'the headless huntsman' – of constantly changing foxes, or going to a holloa. The Earl quoted some examples of this and sternly told the huntsman that his technique 'is not foxhunting'.

Hugh went further: 'Your hounds are probably one of the greatest disgraces in England at the present time. They hunt like draghounds, not like foxhounds. You have no idea when you once start with a fox of identifying your line, whereas you ought to be able to see whether your hounds take up a fresh scent or not, and you ought to have stopped your hounds three times on 12 December and gone back and identified your line, when you could have killed your fox. But your hounds cannot identify a fox for you, and that I realize.'

During this imperial telling off, the Earl assured Thatcher that it was written 'entirely and solely in your own interests, and there is nobody in the world except my confidential secretary, Clarke, who is aware that I have written or said a word to you.'

Even more crushing, Hugh Lonsdale offered to take the huntsman down to Badminton to speak to the Duke of Badminton, and to see his hounds catch foxes in what the Yellow Earl considered to be the right manner.

It was all the more amazing because Thatcher was being hailed as a great success by the majority in Leicestershire, and other accounts state that he certainly caught foxes in addition to providing supremely entertaining hunts. He was often compared to Tom Firr; some claimed hunting with Thatcher was more fun than the Quorn's greatest genius.

Evan Hanbury, who lived at the Manor House in Braunston, is the great grandfather of Joss Hanbury, currently the Squire of Oakham and owner of the family house and estate, Burley-on-the-Hill. Evan had an equable temperament, was a bold rider, and a good administrator. He was unlikely to have allowed trumpetings from the Yellow Earl to have disturbed him, but it would be fascinating to know if he was aware of the Yellow Earl's letter to Thatcher.

Mr Hanbury as a Master clearly had an excellent relationship with his huntsman. There is a story that one day Thatcher dismounted to open a gate. Hanbury was riding his great horse, 'Jumping Josh', and he told his huntsman: 'You should have jumped the gate, Arthur. We would have pounded the field.' On the following Tuesday, Thatcher was riding his best horse, but Evan Hanbury was not so mounted. On the Melton to

Oakham road a gate was locked, and Arthur Thatcher popped over it and went on to kill his fox at Stapleford. The Master and field were delayed, wrestling with the gate. When Hanbury at last came up to Thatcher he said: 'You shouldn't have jumped that gate on to the middle of the road.' 'You should have, sir,' said Thatcher with a straight face but a twinkle in the eye which always disarmed.

Thatcher was noted as a 'poacher' of foxes from adjoining countries. If he lost a fox near the Hunt boundary he would dart over the border to a covert where he knew there were foxes, sometimes employing an accomplice to stand by the neighbouring covert, lifting his hat as if to indicate that a fox already being hunted by the Cottesmore hounds had gone there, and could thus be hunted on without complaint. He was also accused of being adept at the art of chopping a fox in covert; slipping it into a capacious Hunt coat pocket, and then dropping it in a ditch as having been killed at the end of another hunt where in fact his hounds had lost their fox.

Whatever he was, or was not, guilty of, Thatcher had tremendous hound control, was a superb horseman, and a highly intelligent observer of foxes and their ways. It would not be possible to have lifted foxhunting to something of an entertainment art form if he had not possessed these qualities. There is no doubt that the Thatcher period at the start of the century was a time of radical change; a judgement history was to make about Thatcherism on a national scale much later in the century.

When Mr Hanbury resigned in 1907 Thatcher was snapped up by Mr Fernie, as related in the Fernie Hunt history. Lonsdale had joined the Hunt Committee two years earlier, and he applied for the Mastership when it became vacant. There were serious reservations about the Yellow Earl in the Cottesmore country still, but Hunts have seldom allowed such reservations to be the deciding factor if the applicant appears to have the means to pay for their sport on a munificent scale. Committees may live to regret such decisions, but they usually fall into the category of 'it seemed a good idea at the time'. The Cottesmore Committee unanimously elected Hugh Lonsdale as Master, with a subscription guaranteed of £2,000 a year; the one condition was that he should employ a professional huntsman to hunt the hounds. So much for the Cottesmore's 'tradition' of amateurs; it is a much more recent practice than many have imagined. It is highly likely that the Committee feared that the wayward Earl just might care to hunt hounds himself again, as he had done in his youth with the Woodland Pytchley.

Times may change, but adults seldom alter radically, and Lord Lonsdale soon set about spending money lavishly on the Hunt, but at the same time demanding levels of obedience, not to say servility, from one and all who were part of an autocracy many found far too rigid.

The Quorn's mounted field, comprising many winter visitors, was far different to that of the Cottesmore where there was such a large percentage of permanent residents. They were not prepared to be dressed down by the lordly Field Master on their own land, nor that of their neighbours.

Predictably it took just one season for all the old animosities against the Yellow Earl to be burning fiercely again. They did not like his habit of having long discussions at the covert side, holding up the sport, and they hated his bombastic tickings off. Their suspicions about his intentions were confirmed when he formed a pack of doghounds, presented them to the country, and asked permission to hunt them himself for an extra two days a week. The Committee gave grudging permission, but was then horrified to find that Hugh felt he could hunt them any two days of the week he chose, which meant that sometimes his pack would appear in the cream of the country. His own professional huntsman was Sam Gillson, and there is in existence another remarkable letter from the Earl to Gillson, reminding him of his duties. Like the Thatcher letter, it was meant to be confidential and to 'assist' the huntsman to produce better sport. The letter indicates clearly that Hugh Lonsdale certainly knew a very great deal about foxhunting, and about the art of riding across country. This in no way made his advice easier to take. However, if modern foxhunters were to read Lonsdale's letters to his huntsmen carefully they would learn a great deal about their sport which would be of considerable help even in today's conditions. He warned Gillson never to 'play tricks' as huntsman; never to gallop from fox to fox, changing every ten minutes. Clearly, there was to be no retention in the Cottesmore of the faults he thought he saw in Thatcher. Hugh praised Gillson for his care of the hounds, and his management of the kennels, but was highly critical of the huntsman's riding. The Yellow Earl's dissertation on riding to hounds across Leicestershire in this letter is masterly. He emphasized three rules: 'First, convey to your horse what you mean and require him to do it. Second, judge the speed that will carry you over. Third, never try to jump a fence you don't think your horse can jump, for you will lose his confidence and he will fail you in an emergency. Watch the last two strides, that is the crucial moment for speed or walk.'

He advised his huntsman: 'Remember this: the art of riding over fences in Leicestershire is timing; steadying going to them, and it is the last two strides well timed and a stride well placed that crosses the country to the credit of horse and man, and with ease to the horse. To trot and walk a fence is childish and ignorant. You must convey to your horse what you want to do, and further than that you must realize that the horse understands before you try, whatever it is.'

He then launches into a detailed exposition on hunting the fox; throughout, his tone is sympathetic and helpful to his huntsman. A huntsman's job is a lonely one, and only a fool would despise a Master who took such an intense interest and bothered to give of his own very considerable skill and experience.

His remarks about the mounted field are splendid: 'I know people crab. What are they? Who are they? Remember those who know don't ever crab; those that know nothing always crab, and no one pays any attention. No man is perfect, and no man can make scent any more than he can control the weather. You have done what was possible – your best – and no man can do more.'

It is to be hoped that this letter gives an insight into the character of the Yellow Earl, revealing far more depth than his more public utterances and more impulsive acts may indicate.

Alas, his first Mastership of the Cottesmore was to end acrimoniously. The Committee protested about him hunting the doghound pack in March 1910, at the same time warning that owing to falling subscriptions, they could not guarantee £2,000 for another year. Lonsdale wrote back within a week stating that he would resign unless he was guaranteed the £2,000 for the 1911–12 season, and given a free hand to hunt the season as seemed best to him. The Committee, chaired by Sir Arthur Fludyer, accepted his resignation. The other members of the Committee were Lord Willoughby and Lord Gainsborough, and Messrs H. Gosling, John Gretton, H. Noel, W. Baird, A. Duncan, G.H. Finch, C. Fitzwilliam and H. Finch, Honorary Secretary.

Hugh Lonsdale clearly had not expected this, and refused to accept the decision. He withdrew his resignation, and called for a vote of confidence from a general meeting of the Hunt. Here, the vital factor in Hugh Lonsdale's favour came to the fore: he was a true countryman who understood thoroughly the ordinary farmer and the middling to small landowner. He could always command their support; many adored him. They did not mind him publicly putting the mounted gentry in their place; they had time for Lordy. His giant cigars, his four-in-hand carriages which gave way to a yellow Rolls-Royce, the style and panache of his public life, did not offend country folk, because he always had time for them. He took the trouble to know their names, their family history, and he spoke to them as if they mattered greatly to his life – as they did, since he hunted over their land. If the average Englishman in late Victorian and Edwardian times 'loved a Lord', he certainly loved Lord Lonsdale in particular.

There was a packed meeting, with the farmers and landowners hastening to the rescue. Lord Cowley, who lived at Cold Overton, proposed that the resignation be officially withdrawn – and Hugh Lonsdale was elected for the ensuing season.

There were some unpleasant repercussions, as well as a good deal of publicity which did the Hunt no good. First, Henry Finch resigned as secretary; he was known as 'Uncle Mop' and was highly popular with the subscribers. Although their view had been overturned by the farmers, the subscribers of course mattered enormously in terms of ensuring that the Hunt existed at all.

Meanwhile, in May 1910 Hugh Lonsdale received a severe financial blow: a disaster at the Wellington Pit, one of the coalmines he owned at Whitehaven. In an explosion some one hundred and thirty-four men lost their lives; the pit was out of action, and the Earl's income was cut substantially. One result was that he could no longer hunt hounds on the scale he had been accustomed to at the Quorn and the Cottesmore. In January 1911 he resigned from the Cottesmore Mastership, informing the press at the same time. The 1910–11 season had not been a happy one for the Cottesmore; a tendency to take hounds home early had grown up, earning the Hunt the nickname 'the Early Closers' among the Meltonians. Perhaps because of his financial position the Earl found it difficult to keep the Hunt staff and himself quite as well horsed as in the past.

Otho Paget notes, however, that the season 'was extraordinarily open and all three packs had good sport'. The Cottesmore had a new huntsman that season: Tom Isaac, son of Charles Isaac, who had whipped-in to the Pytchley and then hunted the Fernie hounds with so much success. Tom had served first in Ireland with Lord Milton's hounds in County Wicklow, then with the Fitzwilliam, the West Norfolk and the Blankney. Alas, he was to die tragically young in 1913 from pneumonia contracted from a chill; a fate which befell more than a few who worked out of doors before modern care and drugs were developed to render pneumonia a non-life threatening disease.

As a huntsman, Tom showed immense early ability, and seemed to have a great future, producing excellent sport for the Cottesmore for two seasons before his death. The Cottesmore's Mastership solution on the resignation of the Yellow Earl proved a happy one: the appointment of General John Brocklehurst, later Lord Ranksborough; he was sixty at the time, not especially wealthy, but a great and gallant foxhunter, and exceedingly popular with everyone involved in the Hunt. He appointed as Field Master John Maunsell 'Cat' Richardson, one of the great horsemen of the Shires, who won the Grand National twice: on Disturbance in

1873, and the following year on Reugny. Alas, he did not survive long to enjoy leading the Cottesmore field; he died the following year.

Meanwhile sport was excellent; things were not perfect, but the Cottesmore field was enjoying itself as usual. Most were innocently unaware that the political rumblings in Europe were about to change, or claim, the lives of so many. One who believed war was coming was General Brocklehurst, and in 1913 he advised the Cottesmore Committee that the Hunt subscriptions should be insured against the outbreak of war. The Committee did not think the risk was great; Brocklehurst resigned, and was succeeded for two seasons by an American sportsman, Mr R.E. Strawbridge. He was generous, well intentioned, but inevitably somewhat handicapped through lack of lifelong background in British foxhunting.

When the Great War came Strawbridge intimated that he could not continue the Mastership. By 1915 the war was already taking its toll on the younger men; the Cottesmore's future seemed doubtful. William Baird, Evan Hanbury and Herbert Gosling, all veterans, agreed to hunt the country until someone else could be found, but the prospects seemed bleak. It was then Hugh Lonsdale showed his true strength of character, his ability not to harbour grudges, but to work for what he regarded as the real priorities. He was up to his eyes in war work, but he stepped in and took the Cottesmore hounds for the next six years, ensuring its continuity during the war, and its revival in the immediate post-war years. For that alone, he deserves a special place in the history of hunting in Leicestershire. In answer to criticisms that the maintenance of hunting was not essential to the war effort, he used to reply: 'What on earth are officers home from the front going to do with their time, if there is no hunting for them?' One of his favourite remarks was 'lovely fun'; he ensured that foxhunting in the Cottesmore country survived the First World War, and remained fun in the final pastoral hey day of Leicestershire; the between-the-wars years.

After the war Hugh Lonsdale was over sixty, but he continued to hunt the country with George Leaf as huntsman, having transferred in 1915 from the Quorn where he had the onerous responsibilities of succeeding Tom Firr. Lonsdale had always ridden hard; in his youth he once jumped in and out of the east and west junction railway near Bishops Ichinton. In the Quorn country at Great Dalby he cleared a double oxer, afterwards measured at thirty-three feet four inches from take off to landing; a jump commemorated in a painting by Basil Nightingale which hung in the Hogarth Room at Lowther Castle. He was of the rank of horseman who would not enjoy his hunting unless he could still cross the country well. He continued as Master for two more seasons of excellent sport, and retired at the age of sixty-three in 1921, never hunting again, but remaining on the Cottesmore Committee for some years as a much mellowed counsellor. He spent his final years during the Second World War at the Stud House at Barleythorpe, having relinquished his Lowther residence and Carlton House Terrace in London, for financial reasons in the mid-1930s. He died at Barleythorpe in 1944, aged eighty-seven. In one of the last letters he ever wrote, he said: 'Life has been such lovely fun. There is nothing much I can do now, but they can never take my memories away from me. . . .'

He died childless and was succeeded in the Earldom by his younger brother, Lancelot, who lived at Ashwell, and was exceedingly popular in the Cottesmore and earlier in the Quorn country, acting as Hugh's right-hand man, and deputizing for him often in the Earl's absence – times when the field much appreciated the lull from Hugh's iron discipline.

Hugh Lonsdale was succeeded in the Cottesmore Mastership in 1921 by James Baird, son of the former Master Willie Baird. He engaged James Welch as his huntsman, having transferred from the Warwickshire where he had hunted hounds since 1915, having previously been first whipper-in. He had started with the Blackmore Vale as a second horseman in 1900, then travelling to Ireland as second whipper-in to the County Waterford, and moving to the VWH and first whipper-in with the Blackmore Vale again, and the Middleton. Altogether, it was a thorough and strenuous career; Welch was well fitted to take on the great hunting country which the Cottesmore represented. He was a true professional in every sense, capable of riding a big country with neat horsemanship, and hunting a high-class pack of hounds.

He certainly passed on his talent as a horseman: his son, Fred Welch, became one of the most successful showjumping riders in post-war Britain, and still runs a yard in Berkshire where he brings on potential jumpers. Earlier in his career he ran a yard at Burley-on-the-Hill.

When James Welch left the Cottesmore in 1931 he hunted the Blankney for six years and then moved to the Woodland Pytchley.

Guy Paget in his *Bad 'uns to Beat* says that James Baird was an excellent Master, but hot tempered at times . . . 'he carried on the hard swearing tradition of the Cottesmore. It's funny that nearly all our Masters have been hard swearers, while the Pytchley have never had to desert the firm courtesy established by the Lords of Althorp.'

Paget claimed that some in the Cottesmore field did not always show the 'loyalty and obedience they should have to their CO and so brought more retribution on their heads.'

Baird's Joint Master from 1928–30 was Colonel Sydney Green, described by Paget as a 'very cheerful fellow, Grinning Green, we called him. . . . It was a great shock to us when he shot himself in the August of 1931, but to show what a good fellow he was, he had made all the arrangements, so as not to let down his partner for the coming season.'

The Cottesmore Committee knew just where to look for a new Master. The reputation already earned by the Master and amateur huntsman of the North Cotswold was making itself well-known throughout the hunting world. Chetwode 'Chetty', or 'Chatty', Hilton-Green was born in 1895 and brought up in Alderley on the Beaufort–Berkeley borders. He saw Will Dale hunt the Beaufort, and Will Rawle the Berkeley; both remarkable role models. Chetty was brought up to hunt, and at Eton took the familiar route for future MFHs, being Master and huntsman of the Eton College Beagles. His fag was the Marquess of Worcester, who was to be one of the greatest Masters of the twentieth century as the 10th Duke of Beaufort. Chetty served throughout the 1914–18 War with the Royals, surviving its horrors, but suffering severe wounds which threatened his life.

He went to Christchurch College, Oxford, as a late graduate and took the Christchurch Beagles. In 1921 he became Joint Master and huntsman of the Mendip pack, which were harriers at that time, hunting their excellent upland country of grass and walls in Somerset and Wiltshire. From the start he showed great talent as a huntsman, producing marvellous sport in a fine, wild country. In 1924 he took the North Cotswold hounds and his skills developed still further, making the most of that country's hills and the excellent Pebworth Vale, then all down to grass and fences.

In 1929 he went to that great grass country, the Meynell, probably one of the most difficult to hunt well. It has a varied terrain of grass vale, with fly fences guarded by scoops, and a walled upland above Ashbourne. Foxes can be difficult to find, and even harder to catch, since this a wild country where earth stopping can be a major problem.

Hilton-Green continued to prove his worth for two seasons in the Meynell country, and accepted an invitation to hunt the Cottesmore as Master in 1931. He certainly proved to be the right man in the right place at the right time. The Cottesmore country was perhaps at its best: virtually all down to grass, but with the benefit of much improved drainage; the coverts were matured and well stocked with foxes; there was a keen, hard riding field, mounted largely on the sort of blood horses which nowadays find their way all too often into such sports as eventing instead of the hunting field.

Lady (Nairne) Tate, wife of Sir Henry Tate, one of the Cottesmore's greatest Masters, summed up Hilton-Green in the 1930s thus: 'The wonereful pack he bred, the sport he showed and his genius in the handling of hounds will remain forever in the memory of those who had the good fortune to enjoy those seasons between the wars when he made foxhunting history.'

Captain Ronnie Wallace, one of the greatest huntsmen of this century, saw Hilton-Green at his best, and Wallace's judgement is: 'Major Hilton-Green was such a wonderful huntsman because he hunted the fox with his hounds, and at the same time he could keep several hundred very well mounted horsemen at bay.'

Sir Henry Tate, President of the Cottesmore, still with a marvellous memory at the age of ninety, told me in 1992:

> Chetty was certainly one of the two best huntsmen I saw with the Cottesmore; the other was Simon Clarke much later.
>
> Chetty was capable of pleasing the purist who wanted to see a fox found, hunted and caught by hounds at the end of a hunt in which the pack hunted accurately and persistently. At the same time he was capable of entertaining a large mounted field.
>
> I would not describe him as the greatest horseman; he certainly crossed the country adequately, but he was highly strung, almost nervous at times. I think he suffered quite a lot of stress at times, but of course he loved hunting the Cottesmore country.

Hilton-Green had a remarkable memory and was keenly interested in history. He had a prodigious interest in hound pedigrees, which served him well in breeding a superb pack. He is recalled as a great raconteur, a man of wit and charm, a connoisseur of wine, and inclined to indulge this passion all too enthusiastically in later life.

The Hunt reports in *Horse and Hound* during Hilton-Green's Mastership make mouth-watering reading for any foxhunter who knows the country today. At that time vast tracts of the country now down to plough were all grass, and hounds hunted by Chetty Hilton-Green swooped over miles of country which are virtually unrideable in the same way today. It would nowadays be necessary to stay on tracks, or keep in single file along hedgerows in skirting huge acreages of winter wheat and other crops such as oilseed rape, strangers to the country before the war.

Even when down to grass, the Cottesmore was considered a special challenge for a heavyweight rider, since it is full of inclines, and the ground rides deeper in wet conditions than most of the neighbouring Quorn, Belvoir and Fernie countries. This may be one reason, however, why the Cottesmore country invariably carries a good scent, even in a comparatively dry season.

One Hilton-Green hunt which Sir Henry Tate recalls especially, was a run from Oakham pastures westwards across the Cottesmore country, going over the Quorn boundary and concluding in the Friday country at Ashby pastures. This involves a point of about ten miles, with some marvellous country to cross; swooping down off Burrough Hill into the Quorn country's delectable old turf and fences. Lord Sefton was a great success as Field Master, ensuring that the field had a great lead in following what was undoubtedly a great pack of hounds.

Oliver Moss was employed as Hilton-Green's kennel huntsman and first whip, Moss having served previously with the Portman and the Blackmore Vale in Dorset. Moss stayed with the Cottesmore until 1934 when he left to become huntsman of the Old Berks.

The great mainstay of the Cottesmore kennels for many years was Herbert Norman, formerly a whipper-in to Capell at the Belvoir, and later to Welch at the Cottesmore. He stood down to second whipper-in when Moss arrived, but resumed as first whipper-in and kennel huntsman, with his son John as whipper-in. He is remembered as a particularly attractive horseman to watch in the hunting field: neat, balanced, apparently unhurried, and making his fences look easy whether he was riding an experienced horse or a green one. He had spent part of his early life as a nagsman.

Hilton-Green lived at Ketton and later at Burrough-on-the-Hill, but moved into a flat at the Hunt Kennels during the cubhunting season. His first wife, Lady Dorothy, a member of the Grosvenor family, was a great help in managing the equestrian side of his hunting establishment, making his horses and organizing his equestrian needs. Some who hunted with Chetty say that he was not a particularly stylish horseman, not having good hands and sitting back at his fences in the old style, but like a great many other amateur huntsmen who are good hound men, somehow he always managed to stay near enough to his hounds. He favoured large, powerful horses, with less Thoroughbred blood than most Leicestershire hunters at that time, but they performed well for him in tackling the stiff gradients often to be found in the Cottesmore country.

His second wife, Lady Helena Fitzwilliam, daughter of Earl Fitzwilliam, known to all in the hunting world as 'Boodley' was a gifted horsewoman and one of the most popular personalities in Leicestershire. She was able to help her husband considerably with his horses. During the Second World War she played a great part in keeping the Cottesmore country going for her husband who was away on active service although still holding the Mastership until 1946. Herbert Norman, continued to hold the fort at the kennels during the war. His son, John, who whipped in, served in the war.

Chetty's second marriage broke up after the war, and Boodley went to Ireland with Lord (Toby) Daresbury who moved from the Belvoir Mastership to take the County Limerick country as Master and huntsman. Boodley adored this country of grass, huge banks and stone walls. She married Toby Daresbury in 1966, but alas she died in a fall on the flat while hunting with the Limerick only four years later. Chetty was forty-five when the Second World War broke out, but despite his age succeeded in bluffing his way into his old regiment, the Royals. His ship was torpedoed while he was travelling to serve in North Africa. A destroyer came to the rescue, and as Chetty was being pulled up on to the deck, a sailor who was helping him said: 'I thought it was about time you had your second horse, sir.' The man was one of Chetty's Hunt staff before the war.

By the end of the war he was one of the oldest Majors in the front line, serving in Europe after the North Africa campaign. The war had taken its toll, but his love of hunting was undimmed. He had one last season with the Cottesmore, but was a shadow of his former brilliance. He still had the skill, but he had formerly been equipped with quickness of action to effect his technique; time and the stress of war had taken their toll.

He then became Joint Master and huntsman of the Berkeley in his native Gloucestershire in 1946, but after one season went to Ireland to hunt the Ballymacad for a season. Six seasons with the Old Berks then followed, and despite ill health and pain, he went on to hunt the Craven for three seasons; finally hunting the Tivyside in Wales for three seasons until 1962 when he retired, and spent his last years in Badminton village.

In his obituary, published in *Horse and Hound* on 11 January 1964, Nairne Tate averred: 'History will, no doubt, pass the verdict, but it is easy to visualize him standing in that great gallery with Frank Freeman, Arthur Thatcher and Tom Firr.'

Nairne Tate and her husband Henry, the 4th baronet, came to hunt in Rutland and Leicestershire in 1927 soon after their marriage. Sir Henry had been educated in Rutland at Uppingham School, and recalls seeing the Yellow Earl mount his horse before a meet in the town. His own early hunting was with the Flint and Denbigh, the delightful Welsh border country where his family had estates. They both adored hunting, and country life; Nairne was an accomplished landscape painter, and wrote well. For many years she contributed model Hunt reports on the Cottesmore's sport under the initials NT. There was an occasion in the post-war years when someone mischievously wrote a parody of her report, with many sly digs at the Mastership and some of the hunting folk who were landowners. Unfortunately, *Horse and Hound* published the report, which caused much amusement among many, but fury among a few in the Cottesmore country. There was a thorough inquest, with subscribers being asked to show examples of the script produced by their typewriters, but the culprit was never found, although the hoaxer's identity was deeply suspected.

At first in the 1920s Henry and Nairne rented a suite at the Crown Hotel in Oakham. He recalls being awakened by scores of hunters at exercise from stables in the town.

'The hunting country was a paradise; it was nearly all grass,' he recalls. 'It was not the guaranteed ride that the Quorn could offer in those days, but the Cottesmore offered quite a challenge, especially in a wet season.

'The coverts were, and still are, marvellous; plenty of large, well-grown coverts where foxes can always be found. Most of them were beautifully sited.

'Everyone made a fuss about Ranksborough Gorse because it features in Bromley-Davenport's poem (*The Dream of an old Meltonian.*)

'Actually I would not say it produced quite the cream of the sport, and jumping the Whissendine brook on the other side of the Melton road was something of a puzzle. There are a number of tributaries and sometimes it was difficult to say whether one had jumped the Whissendine brook, or something else.'

The Burton Flats, the valley lying north of the Cottesmore below Burton Lazaars was all grass and fences with ditches. Sir Henry recalls many good hunts in that area, with hounds frequently running further north into the Belvoir country at Garthorpe where the three Melton Hunts now hold their point-to-points.

Sir Henry's cousin was the late R.W. 'Micky' Gossage, of Sauvey Castle Farm, Withcote, who served as Hunt secretary from 1939 to 1970 when he died after fracturing the base of his skull in a hunting fall. He was buried at Knossington, and in the first hunt in the area after the funeral the Cottesmore hounds hunted a fox over his grave; this phenomenon has occurred elsewhere after the deaths of hunting people.

Henry and Nairne Tate rented Launde Abbey in the 1930s and made many friends. As a serving officer in the Grenadier Guards, Sir Henry's war started early, and he had virtually no hunting during those years, but it was fortunate for the Cottesmore that he made firm friends with the late Cyril Heber-Percy who had hunted the Cotswold for ten years before the war and had also been brought up on the Welsh borders where country lore was deeply instilled in him.

He recalled his happy childhood in *Us Four*, one of a number of books he wrote which earned high praise as evocations of rural life. Others were *Hym*, the story of a fox, and *While Others Sleep*, a poacher's story.

Heber-Percy recalled that 'the Cotswold hunted five days a week and

I never missed one day in the ten years. By the season's end I rather longed to get my boots off and go ferreting.'

He had a tough war, being injured at Falaise, taking command soon after the Normany landing when both his commanding officer and second-in-command were wounded. He was awarded DSO and MC.

The Cottesmore was indeed fortunate when these two military gentlemen took the hounds in 1946. Henry knew the country and the people intimately; he built a new house, Preston Lodge, and bought the adjoining Owston Wood, the unfailing draw for the Cottesmore hounds. His estates included that other great covert, Prior Coppice. Meanwhile Launde Abbey was sold to the Church of England commissioners, and is still used as a religious retreat.

Sir Henry hunted the doghounds in the Monday and Thursday country, much of it to the east of the A 1, and Cyril hunted the bitch pack in the Tuesday and Saturday country in Rutland and Leicestershire to the west. Together, they put the Cottesmore on a firm footing in the post-war years. There was still a great deal of grass; and hunting folk coming home after the war found the country and the company congenial. The Cottesmore was confirmed still further as the residential pack in Leicestershire. Yet visitors were certainly made to feel at home.

Herbert Norman was second whipper-in during the '30s to Chetty Hilton-Green, becoming first whipper-in and kennel huntsman in 1938 and continuing in service throughout the war, providing invaluable continuity. Herbert whipped in after the war to Cyril Heber-Percy and Sir Henry Tate. Herbert was a great favourite with the Cottesmore farmers, like many a professional contributing much as an ambassador for the sport.

His son, John Norman started in Hunt service as a second horseman with the Cottesmore in 1932, became second whipper-in 1937, returning to the Hunt after war service, and became first whipper-in and kennel huntman in 1953, after the tragic death of his father who took his own life after suffering from depression when the Cottesmore pack was hit by a devastating attack of hard pad.

Sir Henry Tate put an enormous amount into the Cottesmore country in every sense: he had served on the Committee before the war, and after the war was at one time Hunt Chairman, as well as being Joint Master and huntsman. He is modest about his own hunting prowess, but undoubtedly produced a great deal of sport with the doghounds. He especially recalls an extraordinary hunt, achieving an eleven mile point, starting at Greetham Wood and finishing at Forty Foot Dyke. Sir Henry is one of the most urbane and affable of personalities; invaluable qualities in a Master of Foxhounds. It is still recalled with some awe that on one occasion a cantankerous farmer shot a fox in covert just after Sir Henry's doghounds had found it, and were about to start a hunt. 'Thank you very much,' said Sir Henry imperturbably, 'you have saved me a great deal of trouble.'

'Of course, there is glamour in hunting a pack of hounds in Leicestershire,' Cyril Heber-Percy once recalled. 'But you had to be more professional; not bringing out a cigarette in the hunting field, not dining out any evening during the season except Saturdays, only going out for Sunday lunch.'

During the summer they sent out the cubhunting ponies overnight to the far corners of the country, and the hounds would follow in their van. They would exercise hounds and at the same time meet as many farmers as possible over whose land they would be hunting later. Henry Tate recalls that he used these excursions as much as possible to visit historic churches.

In 1951 Mr Malcolm McAlpine, of Burton Lazaars, joined the Mastership, and remained in office for eighteen years. He was a generous and devoted supporter of the Hunt. He was not a thrusting rider, but thoroughly enjoyed all aspects of the Chase. Legend has it that his groom, who accompanied him in the hunting field, was inclined to encourage him to keep in touch with events by shouting: 'Master, Master, faster, faster!'

From 1953–8 Mr Marcus Kimball, now Lord Kimball, was Joint Master and amateur huntsman. He had previous experience as Joint Master and amateur huntsman of the neighbouring Fitzwilliam. Already, however, he had to fit in his sporting life with political ambitions. 'The Hunt Chairman was not at all amused when I told him I had to give up hunting hounds for a while during the season in order to fight a bye-election,' Marcus recalls. He won the bye-election for Gainsborough, Lincolnshire, in 1956, and held the seat until 1983, being knighted for political services in 1981 and created a Life Peer four years later. He was brought up in a political tradition; his father, Major Lawrence Kimball was MP for Loughborough, but Marcus was also brought up to know and enjoy country sports, hunting with the Cottesmore since childhood, and maintaining fishing and shooting at its best on his Scottish estate.

Foxhunters throughout Britain owe Lord Kimball an immense debt for his work in preserving the sport during his chairmanship of the British Field Sports Society from 1964–81. This was a crucial period during which Marcus Kimball proved his mastery of House of Commons procedure in ensuring that anti-hunting legislation never reached anywhere near the statute book, even during Socialist legislations. He was still hunting with the Cottesmore and the Quorn in the 1992–3 season and as a most experienced politician in the House of Lords his counsel and help continued to be invaluable to the cause of country sports. His contribution to the survival of hunting and other country sports should never be underestimated. All too few members of the BFSS realized just how much their sport depended on the skills and devotion of their Chairman. He would have made a fine Master of Foxhounds for many more years, but political duties forced him to resign in 1958. He was to serve as Field Master during the Mastership of Captain Simon Clarke. Marcus used his talent for public speaking to good effect in controlling the field. I recall one Cottesmore visitor, who had clearly not read Surtees, asking with bafflement why the Field Master had called him a 'a hairdresser' when he holloaed away a hare.

The resignation of the Mastership in 1958 was a major turning point in the Hunt's history. Henry Tate and Cyril Heber-Percy, with support from Mr McAlpine had provided great stability and an emphasis on the precept that hunting with the Cottesmore was not just a jolly across superb riding country; there was much emphasis on the true values of venery.

'We were keen to keep the amateur tradition in the Mastership and I was lucky indeed to get Bob Hoare to come here from the West Norfolk country,' Sir Henry recalls. 'Bob was a remarkable man in so many ways; he had a tremendous personality. He was not a great huntsman, but he intended everyone to enjoy themselves in the hunting field, and they certainly did throughout his Mastership.'

Major Robert Hoare was fifty-five when he took the Cottesmore; not an age when most men would undertake a four-day-a-week Leicestershire pack after twenty-one years as a Master and amateur huntsman in Norfolk. He never lacked confidence; had a bubbling cheerfulness, enormous energy and drive, and an ability to get his own way. He had the trim, spry figure of the true horseman, and took care to mount himself well.

Good humour and confidence on the part of the huntsman quickly spreads throughout the hunting field, not least to the hounds. It was just as well, since from Bob Hoare's Mastership the Cottesmore was to see an acceleration of the change from superb old turf to huge blocks of arable farming, all too often involving the uprooting of hedgerows. The wheat and barley barons were in the driving seats of the post-war agricultural journey to greater prosperity, thanks to new markets opening for corn, and British farming subsidies.

The Cottesmore lost more grassland than its Leicestershire neighbours, although all were to see a major change in the nature of their terrain. The major prize remained: the farming community still welcomed the Hunts, and hunting folk took great care to ensure that relationships remained firm with the new arable farmers. There were more than a few cases of newly wealthy arable farmers taking up hunting on a grand scale in Leicestershire for the first time; paying large subscriptions to hunt on the grass that remained. That grass was increasingly to be found on the smaller farms, often tenant, which continued to raise sheep or cattle.

'In the last three years the problem of ploughed land has become appalling,' Bob Hoare told me in 1966. 'I think my hounds are going marvellously over the plough. It is the riding after hounds which is spoilt. Hounds had a terrific hunt recently, but we got completely left behind because the pack started the hunt across a sea of wheat which was unrideable.'

Nevertheless, the Cottesmore retained some superb stretches of grassland; best of all the area between Oakham and Knossington. Here, the land was kept down to grass and fences largely because the owners and farmers were keen hunting folk. The Honourable Mrs Ursula ('Urky') Newton, Mr Edmund Vestey, Mr and Mrs Richard Watson – Tessa Watson being a daughter of Bob Hoare – Mr and Mrs John Hawksworth, and latterly Mr and Mrs David Samworth, and Mrs Betty Cross, were among those who kept much of the land intact as a superb example of Rutland pastoral upland country at its best; neat hedges criss-crossing the meadows of old turf, undulating and offering different vistas from every field.

Bob and Betty Hoare made the Cottesmore country their home, living at Hambleton Hall, the manor house which is now on the peninsular within Rutland Water, and Bob's energies and enthusiasms also included owner-ship of the Crown Hotel in Oakham.

The legendary story about Bob Hoare's Mastership, which was told yet again at the superb address by Dennis Fleming at his memorial service in St Martin in the Fields church, summed up his determination that the mounted field should enjoy their hunting. A senior foxhunting pundit was visiting the Cottesmore. He was more than a little appalled by what he considered the 'larking' of the mounted field when hounds were not actually running, plus a tendency to press hounds too much when they were hunting. Before hounds were to draw another covert, he said to the Master: 'Come on, Bob. Now's your chance. Get the field together and tear them off a strip.' 'My dear chap,' said Bob with his wide smile. 'We only hunt up here for fun, you know.'

On relinquishing the Cottesmore Mastership in 1969, Bob Hoare demonstrated his resilience and drive by taking on the South Notts pack from 1970–3, and he quickly made many new friends and admirers. Leicestershire foxhunters made a point of going to the South Notts at the end of the season to enjoy some romps over the grass and walls on the Derbyshire side of that country.

There was one occasion when Bob, leaving a farmhouse where a huge field had much enjoyed a major Hunt breakfast, had an unfortunate fall in leaping a wall, and broke his false teeth, making it impossible for him to blow the horn. He had a great gift for treating triumph or disaster as a friend, and he continued hunting hounds, someone having been despatched to find some new dentures to improve the horn blowing during the day when delivered to him in the hunting field.

He shone as a dinner host and after dinner speaker. I recall attending one rather dull dinner followed by equally uninspired speeches, but the whole occasion took off when Bob spoke, snapping everyone to attention with some racy stories and delivering some serious points as well.

He was an inspired choice as campaign manager of the British Field Sports Society's giant effort to raise a Fighting Fund worth £250,000 in the early 1970s. The money was vitally needed to help combat an increasing political and public relations threat to the sport. Bob journeyed many miles, and hosted innumerable social fund raising functions, to ensure the Fighting Fund's success. It was a great achievement for the sport he loved, an example to some others who simply sit back when they have ceased to occupy centre stage in the foxhunting theatre.

Alas, the hard work and strain probably contributed to a heart attack which Bob suffered, causing his sudden collapse and untimely death in London in 1976 much to the grief of many throughout the sporting world. The Fighting Fund achieved its target, and was instrumental in enabling the BFSS to continue its fight successfully through the 1970s and '80s.

Two exceptional amateur huntsmen were to carry the Cottesmore forward into the 1990s: Captains Simon Clarke and Brian Fanshawe. Both have strong Gloucestershire connections, and have family traditions of foxhunting at its best, shaping their own achievements in hound breeding and handling hounds in the hunting field.

Simon's stepfather was the late Major Gerald Gundry, Joint Master with the 10th Duke of Beaufort. Gerald was not only a great foxhunter in every sense, but a remarkable personality, a great humorist and a benevolent dictator on behalf of the Duke throughout that important hunting country based on the Badminton estate where the Hunt kennels is still regarded as one of the most influential sources of top-class hound breeding.

Simon imbibed foxhunting at its best during his boyhood, hunting with his stepfather, who carried the horn most effectively with the Duke of Beaufort's doghounds, and with the 10th Duke; 'Master' to everyone in the hunting world and beyond, who hunted his own hounds for forty-seven years with immense prowess. At one time the family had four serving Masters and three amateur huntsmen in office simultaneously: Gerald, Simon and his sister Susan and her husband Willy Poole who has deservedly earned much acclaim as a humorous sporting writer. Gerald's son Robin Gundry is nowadays earning much praise as Joint Master and huntsman in the delectable Welsh Borders country of Sir Watkin Williams-Wynn.

As one who was lucky enough to hunt occasionally with Simon Clarke in the South Dorset country, I can testify that he won a reputation as an exceptional huntsman from his earliest days in Mastership. The South Dorset has a wet, deep vale as well as much upland. It is a well foxed country, but a testing one for the huntsman. Nevertheless, it has produced some excellent huntsmen, and none better than Simon Clarke when he was offered the Cottesmore Mastership. As Sir Henry Tate has averred, Simon recalled the great days of Chetty Hilton-Green by achieving the exceedingly difficult feat of entertaining those who came to Leicestershire to ride whilst more than satisfying the purists who want to see hounds hunt their fox, a subject on which we have already noted the Yellow Earl's views! It was essential that such tactics were employed to the full. The country simply did not have enough grass to ensure that a huntsman could keep a large mounted field happy by lifting hounds off a hunted fox if it ran off the pasture on to plough; or constantly putting hounds on the line of fresh foxes holloaed away in areas likely to provide galloping and jumping on the grass.

Simon produced excellent hunts, scoring notable points, and thereby ensuring that the mounted field tasted a diversity of country. He generally made it possible that his hunts had a beginning, a middle and an end. There was to be no hunting resulting in what Gerald Gundry used to describe as 'mystery tours' when discussing the tactics of a professional huntsman he was wont to criticize.

The distinguished racing writer Ivor Herbert revisited his native Leicestershire to report a Melton Hunt Club ride in the Cottesmore country. He reported: 'Afterwards, the Cottesmore hounds, under their highly praised Master, Simon Clarke – "easily the best up here this season" several people murmured – met and moved off.'

Alas, it proved to be a comparatively short Mastership; Simon departed after seven years, in 1976, to take the Duke of Buccleuch's in Scotland, and later moved south again to the South and West Wilts country where he has made his home. He is now hunting the New Forest hounds with much success. During the 1991–2 season he performed great services for the Campaign for Hunting.

The Cottesmore Committee had not sufficient time to find another amateur huntsman to continue the tradition, and in any case there was a strong local team ready to take over. Their huntsman was to be Simon Clarke's excellent first whipper-in, Peter Wright, born to Hunt service. His grandfather was Joe Wright, huntsman of the Cheshire; his father, also Joe, was huntsman of the Woodland Pytchley. Peter was first whipper-in at the

Grafton, and was exceedingly experienced in all branches of the huntsman's craft.

The Masters were Mrs Di Hellyer, Mrs Joan Gibson and Mr David Samworth. Mrs Hellyer's husband, Major Tim Hellyer, had been Field Master with much success, and Joan Gibson's husband, George, was one of the most popular equine veterinary surgeons in the Midlands, heading the family practice in Oakham where her son Michael is still a partner. Her elder son, David Gibson, runs the Barleythorpe stud, breeding valuable flat horses, and is currently Chairman of the Thoroughbred Breeders' Association. David Samworth is a highly successful businessman, and a devoted foxhunter living just over the Quorn border near Twyford.

The Mastership lasted five years, a valuable contribution to foxhunting in Leicestershire. Mrs Hellyer took a special interest in the hound breeding and bred Cottesmore Baffle, winner of the Peterborough bitch championship in 1979. Mrs Gibson, a much sought after judge in the equestrian world, was an exceptional 'Master of the Horse' and ensured that the Hunt horses were top-class, and Mr Samworth was an enthusiastic and able Field Master.

When this Mastership ended in 1981 there was some controversy in the country – let us be frank, and say there was a Hunt row – over whether the professional huntsman should continue under the next Mastership. However, huntsmen are employed by Masters, not Committees, unless the Masters are merely acting for the Committee. The new Mastership was to include another distinguished amateur; there was a strong body of opinion that it was time to make a change in that direction again, even though some supporters went so far as to demonstrate with placards at a meet in favour of retaining Peter Wright. The row was even reported in the national press.

It was not the happiest of atmospheres for a new amateur huntsman to enter Leicestershire, but the incumbent was a remarkable man of considerable resolve: Captain Brian Fanshawe. If anyone can claim to have hunted the Cottesmore according to the popular song 'I did it my way' it is 'the Captain' as he was invariably known. The tall figure, with distinctive nose, dominated the Cottesmore for the next eleven seasons, and those of us lucky enough to have hunted with him will not forget the experience.

I wrote when he retired in 1992, after a total of twenty-six years as an amateur huntsman: 'He is just about the last of the really formidable amateur huntsmen. . . .'

' "What did he say?" is the most frequent appeal from someone who has earned a thunderous rebuke.'

' "Better not to ask old boy" is the most helpful response. . . .'

'Fortunately, the huntsman's decibel level is not matched by clarity, and once you get used to it, you accept that everything he says and does from the moment hounds move off from the meet is totally dedicated to ensuring that his beloved hounds will catch foxes. His own verve, determination and remarkable vigour is imparted to the way his pack hunts.'

Brian is a rare manifestation of top-class horseman and hound man; a combination which so seldom seems to exist. His parents, Major and Mrs Dick Fanshawe, both hunted the South Oxfordshire hounds. Ruth Fanshawe, now Lady Dulverton, hunted them solely towards the end of the war. Her late brother was the famed huntsman and hound breeder, Sir Peter Farquhar of the Portman.

Brian was a keen amateur rider, and won the National Hunt Chase in 1967 on Master Tammy. He joined the Warwickshire Mastership in 1963 and was Field Master before hunting the hounds. There followed glorious fun as Master and huntsman of the Galway Blazers. He and his wife Libby adored the grass country and the myriad limestone walls. After returning to England, Brian took the North Cotswold in 1975 before coming up to Leicestershire in 1981.

David Samworth and Joan Gibson continued in office, and Joss Hanbury completed a quartette. Joss, as Squire of Oakham, and a major landowner in the country, could not have been more appropriate as a Cottesmore Master. His laid back style as Field Master pleased subscribers immensely; he gave a great lead across country with no fuss, nor recrimination against any of his followers. He was always in a good humour, offsetting the occasional thunderstorms of temperament coming from the huntsman.

Brian Fanshawe was especially popular with the farmers, and his meticulous management of the country was highly successful in keeping it open to the Hunt. He worked exceedingly well with Cyril Smith, the Cottesmore's excellent terrierman, in management of the coverts and earth stopping. Bolting and digging are carried out by Cyril with professional expertise, strictly according to the Masters of Foxhounds Association's new rules.

Very soon after his arrival Brian undertook the onerous task of Chairman of the Leicestershire action committee which organized the Hunts' response to the first attempt by the Labour group to ban hunting on Council owned land (Chapter Eight). His powers of leadership and his energy were great assets, and he employed them again in the same role in 1992 when a repeat attempt by Labour councillors was once again foiled.

Fanshawe and his hounds demonstrated that the very best foxhunting can only be achieved when the huntsman and pack are united in the belief that their primary purpose is to end a hunt by catching the fox.

Long points were achieved, and there were notable excursions over the borders of the Fernie, Quorn, and Belvoir.

The Cottesmore retained its position as the pack which the purist hound lover especially enjoyed following and observing. Brian was also well aware of the priorities of his mounted field, and ensured as much fun as could possibly be gained from the grass country remaining. He was careful of the interests of the one-horse owner, drawing his best coverts in the Tuesday country during the morning so that everyone had a chance to enjoy the grass and fences, instead of waiting for the smaller late afternoon field with second horses. He was not always deliriously popular with those of us endeavouring to change to our second horses, since he was inclined sometimes to have his own second horse delivered to him in the hunting field and carry on hunting while we would struggle back to our horse boxes and then endeavour to find hounds, fearful we would miss the afternoon hunt.

But what sport we all enjoyed! His last season, 1991–2, was one of his best, despite it being one of the worst scenting anyone could remember: a drought produced bone-hard going, and many blue hazy days.

The Christmas Eve hunting from Somerby saw a nine mile hunt in the morning and a fifteen mile hunt, with a five mile point, in the afternoon, concluding far into the Quorn Friday country.

A vintage hunt in the Tilton hills, much of it on plough, was a seventy-two minute run, hounds covering about ten miles, and catching their fox in the open.

I hope I shall not forget the pleasure of the last good Tuesday evening hunt with Brian hunting hounds. They went away at last from the depths of Little Owston wood, after much patient woodland hunting. There were only a few of us, led by Rosemary Samworth as Field Master, and a red, sinking sun was drawing long shadows. With a great cry the Cottesmore bitches ran to Ladywood, sometimes checking and working it out themselves, only to surge on again; there was not a great scent. They crossed the Gwash and ran up past Brian's house into the Ladywood covert, then hunted their fox up to Orton Park covert which has figured in Cottesmore hunting throughout the Hunt's history. The Master blew for home, and we hacked down to Ladywood to say our goodnights. There were a few more days before his retirement, but this was the one I prefer to remember. The ills of the late twentieth century were rammed home when scores of Hunt saboteurs turned up at Brian's very last fixture, east of the A1 at Toft, Lincolnshire, home of Leslie Dungworth who joined the Mastership in 1984 and continued in office until Brian retired. Leslie performed great services in organizing the Monday country, and the Hunt has also benefited enormously from the fund raising efforts of his wife, Jeanne, as Chairman of the Hunt Supporters' Club. It was another stroke of good fortune when Leslie was succeeded in the Mastership by his son, Roger.

Joss Hanbury performed the extraordinary feat of simultaneous Joint Mastership of the Quorn and Cottesmore until 1990 when he gave up the latter, much to the regret of his many friends in the country. They were even more upset when his Quorn Mastership ended so grievously after the fox digging video film coup by the anti-hunting lobby (Chapter Seven).

He was succeeded in 1990 in the Cottesmore Mastership by David Samworth's wife, Rosemary, a lifelong devoted foxhunter who was fulfilling a long held ambition in taking a Mastership, having brought up a family of four. Before her marriage, as Rosemary Cadell, she won the Melton Hunt Club's annual cross-country ride for four successive years, mounted on Major Bob Hoare's great horse, Double Vision. As Field Master of the Cottesmore, Rosemary has showed that she can still give a tremendous lead across Leicestershire. I have thoroughly enjoyed trying to keep somewhere near her during some excellent hunts over the grass and fences between Knossington and Oakham. Lady Field Masters have been rare in Leicestershire (Ulrica Murray Smith with the Quorn, 'Boodley' Hilton-Green during the war years with the Cottesmore); Rosemary Samworth shows that this is one more role which should never be considered a male preserve in future. Interestingly, I have noted that it is lady members of the field who tend to dislike 'taking orders' from a female Field Master, whereas the gentlemen of the field generally find this no problem especially those who have been married for some years.

Tony Ruddle of the famous Rutland family brewers' firm bearing that name, joined the Mastership in 1988, and has backed the Hunt most generously in every way. After Brian Fanshawe's departure, Rosemary Samworth, Tony Ruddle and Roger Dungworth formed a strong, locally based Mastership, with Brian's former kennel huntsman Neil Coleman hunting hounds. The amateur tradition was broken again, but in the harsh economics of the 1990s the Hunt was indeed fortunate to have such a team, and Neil quickly proved a top-class huntsman, handling the Cottesmore pack with the skills he had learned from the Captain during a long apprenticeship which started back in the North Cotswold country.

Brian Fanshawe retired at the age of fifty-five electing to give up hunting hounds while still at the top; we shall remember him hunting hounds with all his powers as a hound man and a great horseman until the day he handed over the horn. In 1992 he became Director of the National Hunting Club and Campaign for Hunting to defend the future of the sport to which he has contributed so much. He was also running a racing syndicate, with horses trained by his son, James, who has achieved so much in his first seasons as a Newmarket trainer.

The 1992–3 season started as one of the wettest on record, with sport being suddenly halted at Christmas by a desperately hard frost. Although hounds ran very well in the wet, it was an exceedingly difficult season in which to organize sport on water-logged farmland, and the toll on horses is always heavy in such conditions. The new Mastership and huntsman rose to the challenge: the Cottesmore continued to provide some of the best sport achieved in Leicestershire, especially on the Tuesdays.

My Hunt histories, as I warned, have had to focus mainly on Masterships and huntsmen, but of course no Hunt runs successfully without effective Hunt Chairmen and Committees. Sir Henry Tate, after his great Chairmanship, was created Hunt President and was still filling the role splendidly in his ninety-first year. Colonel Billy Smith, Colonel Stephen Eve, Major 'Tat' Hubbard, David Samworth and now Robin Sturgess, have all helped steer the Hunt as Chairmen through the turbulent post-war years of change.

The Cottesmore has been exceedingly lucky in long terms of office by its Hunt secretaries. Henry Finch, as I reported retired in 1907 after twenty-two years as Hunt Secretary. Major Tom Cavenagh of Withcote was a great Honorary Secretary between the wars; succeeded in 1939 by R.W. 'Mickey' Gossage who performed great services, until tragically dying in office in 1971, when he was succeeded by Miss Joanna Spencer of Braunston, one of the pillars of Rutland; totally devoted to its traditions and the best interests of its residents.

Since 1981 the Hunt has been fortunate in having Mr Michael Stokes of Owston as its unflappable, totally dedicated Honorary Secretary, coping with the multitude of problems besetting modern Hunt establishments and keeping the subscribers happy.

It is true that the Yellow Earl would not recognize, and would not wish to recognize, the changed nature of the vast acreages of Cottesmore country nowadays under the plough.

Yet, as a true hound man, he would certainly recognize the brilliance of the modern Cottesmore pack which can hunt the fox accurately over huge arable fields as well as skimming over the remaining grass. Their cry, their accuracy, their persistence would bear favourable comparison with any pack which has hunted this great country.

We who endeavour to follow them should be grateful to the formidable foxhunters of the past whose enthusiasms and expertise have ensured that a great sporting tradition thrives within the Cottesmore boundaries today.

15

The Fun of it

Again our hearts lifted as hounds ran without check across the lane, and over the swell of another Rutland undulation

The immense amount of time and effort expended on hunting in Leicester-shire would hardly have survived into the late twentieth century if sport had deteriorated as much as some veterans will darkly aver.

As I write this chapter I am glowing from a marvellous day with the Cottesmore hounds this very week in November 1992. It helps me to emphasize as strongly as possible that this book is no mere record of a dry-as-dust archaic sporting pastime.

Foxhunting is vibrantly alive. Despite all the horrors perpetrated on our countryside in the name of 'progress'; in conservationist terms a euphemism for increased financial profit by ruthless farming methods, Leicestershire is still a marvellous setting for the sport which has made it famous.

Two days ago I tasted foxhunting at its best. The Cottesmore hounds met at Shorne Hill, Brooke, at the home of a redoubtable foxhunter, Miss June Curwen, in her sixty-fifth season as a member of the mounted field in this hunting country where she was bred. She was brought up at Withcote and hacked to her first school at Knossington on a pony. After Miss Curwen's meet, hounds were put into the famous Priors Coppice covert, overlooking the villages of Braunston and Brooke. The monks who lived at Brooke Priory constructed a series of fishponds from the narrow River Gwash, and its tributaries. They also ensured a supply of game from the Priors Coppice covert established to the west of the Priory. A Leicestershire conservation group now owns the coppice, but the sporting rights are retained by the former owner, Sir Henry Tate, one of Rutland's greatest foxhunters, of whom more later.

Hounds were soon speaking joyously on the line of a fox which ran eastwards over the grass and fences carefully preserved and enhanced by the owners, Colonel and Mrs Reggie Purbrick; Lizzie Purbrick is one of Britain's leading horse trials riders – show me a horseman's land, and you will see conservation which would delight the most ardent of 'Greens': proper hedgerows, old turf, and patches of covert where wildlife abounds.

The pack marks their fox below the Priory. They speak with a melodious, clear voice. They are now hunted by Brian Fanshawe's former kennel huntsman and first whipper-in, Neil Coleman, who imbibed the Captain's forceful style of hunting, and handles the pack with a combination of zest and tact.

Foxes are afoot everywhere by now, and the pack quickly catches one in a patch of covert on the land at Brooke of Mr and Mrs Richard Watson; he a veterinary surgeon, she the daughter of the late Bob Hoare, another former Cottesmore Master and huntsman of great fame.

Before the mounted field has time to think of relaxing, the quick Cottesmore bitches are giving tongue with chiming notes on the line of yet another fox, found on the Watson land by the Gwash.

And who are we, the mounted field? Privileged, feudal squires? The idle rich? Arrogant aristocrats about to ride roughshod over the peasantry? Such are the emotive terms which the Animal Rights Movement serves up in its dish of hatred against all who go foxhunting. The truth, in the late twentieth century, is perhaps even more remarkable. The Cottesmore field, like all others, is a remarkable cross-section of society, young, not-so young, and some at an age when many would prefer resting by the fireside to risking life and limb over fences on a pulling hunter in all weathers. Our Field Master is a lady: Rosemary Samworth, wife of a Leicestershire businessman, David Samworth, who has made a great success of his career in the food industry by his own acumen and sheer hard work; nothing elitest and hereditary about their well-deserved achievements. Yes, there is a Lord in the mounted field, a Life Peer: Lord Kimball, whose peerage is recognition of many years of public service as former MP for Gainsborough. He is still heavily involved in government; hunting is his favourite recreation.

Who else? Farmers, housewives, a roofing contractor, a pawnbroker from Essex, a jeweller, a large-scale motor trader, a solicitor, a lady doctor, a horse dealer, a journalist; all sorts of professions and jobs – all people bound together by a common love of the countryside and the sight of a good pack of hounds hunting over it, preferably seen between the ears of a good horse.

We are in for a marvellous tour today. Hounds scream away above the village of Braunston, swing left, and run hard southwards, parallel to the Wisp, the long straight road to Braunston from Withcote. We jump timber rails out of tufty old turf; we steady our horses as best we can, for this is a wet season, with deep going. There are calls from the Field Master to 'keep in'; we must be careful to mark the pastures as little as possible, so we ride close to the hedgerows. At the rear of the field are two riders in tweed coats; their job is to ensure that farm gates are all closed, but everyone in the field is mindful of this obligation. We have a Hunt fence mender out on the roads in a van; he will repair any rails broken by a jumping horse, or fill in any gaps in hedges.

Half way alongside a tributary of the Gwash, we find the only way ahead is to cross this brook; it is narrow, but the banks are steep, clad in brambles, and decidedly trappy. Rosemary Samworth's horse slides carefully down half-way, and leaps to the opposite steep bank. We follow one by one, some horses making a neater job than others. My grey mare, Lucy, is marvellous at such obstacles, a skill she learned in her youth in Ireland, and she deals with the brook with reassuring ease. We breast a swell of land to look down on the beautiful Withcote estate, owned by Captain and Mrs Michael Cavenagh. They are both experienced riders, and their estate is well fitted with jumps for horse trials and hunter trials. Hooray! Hounds are swooping down over the Withcote grass, still speaking; clearly we are hunting a travelling dog fox, making a far point.

We gallop downhill, pull our horses back to take on a timber fence not to be trifled with, and then hurtle down to jump a gate into a field short of the beautiful Withcote manor house.

Still hounds surge ahead, and we gallop across grass to Lover's Walk, the narrow path which runs alongside the narrow River Chater, and past the ruins of Sauvey Castle; an eerie spot this, where it is all too easy to conjure up scenes of bloody battles in pre-history, up to medieval times. This is an ancient settlement, and the old moat and wrecked ramparts are evidence of the need for defence against marauders in England's turbulent past.

No time for reflection now; hounds are running south alongside the stream; we jump a timber fence from all-too slippery mud, ride past the castle's mound, and into the lane from Whatborough crossroads to Launde.

Again our hearts are lifted as hounds run without check across the lane, and over the swell of another Rutland undulation. The field, now somewhat reduced to about forty riders, continues to follow hounds; sometimes leaping timber, sometimes stopping while an electric fence is by-passed, always with as much care as possible for the land we are so fortunate to be able to rider over, thanks to the co-operation of farmers and landowners. This is sheep and cattle country, and we are especially careful to keep well clear of grazing flocks.

We take to the lane to Oxey Farm now as hounds run above us, attended by Neil Coleman and his whipper-in. There is a check; hounds feather over the grass; now they have it again, and run ahead. They swing right, and they are skirting Robin a 'Tiptoe Hill. This owes its name to the felon who was hanged from a tree on top of the hill. They left him overnight swinging from the bough, but it bent and he was able to keep alive by standing on tip toe. Next morning he was found still alive, and was pardoned. Hounds check here. The huntsman casts them widely, but they are unable to pick up the scent. The fox is given best; most of the horses are showing signs of having performed a lot of work in heavy going.

Those of us with second horses, change them at Whatborough crossroads where the horse boxes are gathered. Hounds are taken to draw Owston Woods, the famous covert whose boggy environs have sucked shoes off horses for generations while hounds hunt whole families of foxes up and down the dense woodland. The wood is said to be 'paved with horseshoes and riders' curses'. It is a reminder of the great hunting forests which once dominated the East Midlands when the stag, not the fox, was the premier beast of the Chase.

The major problem for the huntsman is to eject a fox into the open, and to sustain the pressure so that it runs far from the wood instead of skirting back all too quickly. The problem for the mounted field is to be at the right part of the wood's circumference when hounds go away. It is all too easy to miss a run. On this occasion hounds hunt enthusiastically in Owston Big Wood for an hour, while the small mounted field wait patiently at various points around the wood in the hope of holloaing away a fox. We get one brief excursion, but the fox doubles back to the wood after three fields.

Then the huntsman goes to the Preston Lodge side of the Withcote lane which bisects the wood. This is Little Owston, a much more likely place for a run in the open. Hounds chime away with a great cry; we see a fox steal away from the covert to cross the Oakham to Tilton road, but not a hound follows. They are intent on the line of another inside covert. I ride round the covert, and hack slowly round its northern edge.

Hounds are speaking on my right. At the far end from the lane there is small knot of riders, David and Rosemary Samworth and two others. They motion me to keep quiet, and we watch a fox running up the hedgerow towards Cheseldyne. Then there is a crash of hound music, and the huntsman sounds the thrilling notes of 'Gone away!' It never fails to make the hairs stand up on the back of my neck.

The Cottesmore hounds surge out of covert on the line of the fox. They run to the left of the next covert, Cheseldyne, and head over the grass towards Ladywood, lying below the fold of hills overlooking Braunston. We jump several sets of rails, and canter across the grass towards Ladywood, the famous covert and the white faced house next to it where Brian and Libby Fanshawe live. Our horses splosh down through the muddy banks of the stream below Ladywood. We canter over the Knossington lane, and wait while hounds scream through the Ladywood covert to our left.

Yes, they are away, and we are in the heaven of grass and fences above Ladywood. My chestnut gelding, Hughie, is pulling like a train; he adores hounds, and knows full well that he is in for a good hunt.

Hounds run towards Braunston above the Knossington lane. We jump timber, and some of the delectable fly fences which criss-cross the old turf. The going is very wet, but Hughie makes nothing of it, springing in great arcs over the clipped hedges, and landing far out over the Cottesmore scoops which guard them. If a horse lands in one, or puts his feet into one on take off, it can put bring him down, especially when the going is heavy.

Hounds check by the Leicestershire lane; this is a narrow field lane which the mounted field cross by jumping hedges or timber in a somewhat tricky in and out. The huntsman goes back to a knot of hounds feathering in the open; suddenly they are running hard up the hill. We enjoy more grass and fences in pursuit.

Dusk is coming in fast against a band of scarlet and amber sunset. Ahead the shadows are lengthening away from Orton Park Wood covert. The pack runs into the covert, and we scamper round the edge. Hounds are running through the covert on our left. Has the fox gone on towards Cold Overton or Ranksborough?

When hounds emerge from the covert they falter and dwell, casting again on the grass. The fox may have run ahead, but it has gained much valuable time. Darkness is coming fast, and the Master decides it is time to blow for home.

There are now about six riders in the hunt. We say our goodnights and warmest thanks, and I hack back with Andrew and Jane Collie, down over the grass towards Withcote. It is dark when I walk Hughie towards the welcoming glow from the barn door where Mick Smith is giving the horses their evening feed.

The evening hunt lasted only thirty-five minutes; the point was no more than two and half miles, although we covered more than that, but the 'quick thing' remains one of Leicestershire's greatest delights – and to enjoy such a hunt in the late twentieth century in an area which has nurtured foxhunting at its best for over two hundred and fifty years is a remarkable testament to the loyalty which the sport has secured through good times and bad.

Our progress across country, traversing entirely privately owned land, was achieved by a marvellous mixture of old loyalties and friendships, careful liaison, and a country tradition that has miraculously survived all the social upheavels of the twentieth century.

Paradise is not lost.

Bibliography

A History of Leicestershire and Rutland, Roy Millward (Phillimore 1985).

Bad 'Uns to Beat, Guy Paget (Collins 1936).

British Hunting, Arthur Coaten (Sampson Low Marston 1909).

British Hunts and Huntsmen, Vols I, II and III, J.N.P. Watson (Batsford 1986).

British Sporting Art in the Twentieth Century, Stella Walker (The Sportsman's Press 1989).

English Foxhunting, Raymond Carr (Weidenfeld and Nicolson 1976).

English Sporting Prints, F.L. Wilder (Thames and Hudson 1974).

Famous Foxhunters, Daphne Moore (Spur Publications 1978).

Fields Elysian, Simon Blow (J.M. Dent 1983).

Foxhunting, A. Henry Higginson (Collins 1948).

Foxhunting, The 10th Duke of Beaufort (David and Charles 1980).

Foxhunting in the Shires, T.F. Dale (Grant Richards 1903).

Foxhunting in the Twentieth Century, William Scarth Dixon (Hurst and Blackett 1925).

Foxiana, Isaac Bell (Country Life).

Good Sport 1885–1910, Cuthbert Bradley (Routledge).

Hounds of the World, Sir John Buchanan-Jardine (Grayling Books 1937).

Hunting, The Duke of Beaufort and Mowbray Morris, Badminton Library (Longmans 1889).

Hunting Reminiscences of Frank Gillard, Cuthbert Bradley (Edward Arnold 1898).

Huntsmen of Our Time, Kenneth Ligertwood (Pelham Books 1968).

John Leech and the Victorian Scene, Simon Houfe (Antique Collectors Club 1984).

Jorrocks's England, Anthony Steel (Methuen 1932).

Leicestershire and its Hunts, Charles Simpson (Bodley Head 1926).

Leicestershire and the Quorn Hunt, Colin D.B. Ellis (Edgar Backus 1951).

Magic of the Quorn, Ulrica Murray Smith (J.A. Allen 1980).

Memories of the Shires, T. Otho Paget (Methuen 1920).

Nimrod's Hunting Reminiscences, 'Nimrod,' Charles James Apperley (Bodley Head 1926).

Observations on Foxhunting, Colonel Cook (Edward Arnold 1922).

Peculiar Privilege, David C. Itzkowitz (The Harvester Press 1977).

Scarlet and Corduroy, Lionel Edwards (Eyre and Spottiswoode 1941).

Silk and Scarlet, 'The Druid' (Vinton and Co. 1859).

Squire Osbaldeston, His Autobiography, ed. E.D. Cuming (Bodley Head 1922).

The Best Season on Record, 'Brooksby', Captain Pennell-Elmhirst (Routledge 1884).

The Book of the Foxhound, Daphne Moore (J.A. Allen 1964).

The Chase, The Road and The Turf, 'Nimrod', Charles James Apperley (Edward Arnold 1898).

The Cream of Leicestershire, 'Brooksby', Captain Pennell-Elmhirst (Routledge 1883).

The Foxhunters' Bedside Book, compiled by Lady Apsley (Eyre and Spottiswoode 1949).

The Harboro' Country, Charles Simpson (The Bodley Head 1927).

The History of the Belvoir Hunt, T.F. Dale (Archibald Constable 1899).

The History of Foxhunting, Roger Longrigg (Macmillan 1975).

The History of Hunting, Patrick Chalmers (Seely Service 1936).

The Politics of Hunting, Richard H. Thomas (Gower 1983).

The Quorn Hunt and its Masters, W.C.A. Blew (John C. Nimmo).

The Sporting Empress, John Welcome (Michael Joseph 1975).

The Yellow Earl, Douglas Sutherland (The Molendinar Press 1980).

Thoughts on Hunting, Peter Beckford (first published 1781, J.A. Allen 1981).

Tom Firr of the Quorn, Roy Heron (Nimrod Book Services 1984).

APPENDIX I

Leicestershire in Words and Pictures

References are made in the text to writers and artists who have recorded and celebrated the virtues of foxhunting in Leicestershire.

Nimrod 1777–1843

This was the pseudonym of Charles James Apperley. Although he was lampooned by some, including the great sporting novelist, R.S. Surtees, who called him 'Pomponious Ego', Apperley made a major contribution to sporting journalism, raising the role of the hunting correspondent to a much higher level than that of the local scribbler. His hunting tours first appeared in *Sporting Magazine* in 1822 and greatly increased its circulation. He was equipped with five hunters and a hack, and toured Britain, reportedly earning the huge sum of £20 per page of copy. He worshipped Leicestershire, and conveyed the hectic fun of riding with the Shires packs better than anyone else. He was an exceptional horseman, a fervent foxhunter, but he suffered from admiring the titled aristocracy to excess, and from a shortage of money to indulge his sport at the level he enjoyed most. His transparent snobbery earned him the enmity of Surtees, who may also have been guilty of some sour grapes, since Apperley was an incomparably better horseman. Surtees, himself a hunting correspondent early in his career, did not much care for Leicestershire, and referred to it tartly in his own collection of hunting tour reports.

Apperley was born in Denbighshire and was educated at Rugby, he served in the cavalry, and then became feted as the greatest hunting correspondent of the early nineteenth century. His fortunes waned alas, and he spent some years in Calais as a debtor, before returning as he said, 'like a hare doubling back to die in the country', expiring in London at the age of sixty-five. Thoroughly recommended are his *Hunting Tours, Hunting Reminiscences* and *The Chase, the Road and the Turf*.

Brooksby 1845–1916

The pen name of Captain Edward Pennell-Elmhirst who was the industrious hunting correspondent for *The Field* in the late nineteenth century. He adopted his pseudonym from the hunting lodge at Brooksby, in the Quorn Friday country, nowadays the county Agricultural College, where he used to stay when hunting in Leicestershire.

He was an excellent horseman, and another example of a scribe who had problems in paying top prices for his horses. He was described by Otho Paget as 'The best man I ever remember for getting a bad horse across Leicestershire, and he was always to be seen in the first flight.' Pennell-Elmhirst was a Master of the Woodland Pytchley for just one season (1880–1), and is best tasted in his *The Cream of Leicestershire*, published in 1883 and the *The Best Season on Record* which referred to 1883–4. His aim was to convey the excitement of the hunting field as vividly as possible, and his prose is full of references to 'a brilliant little burst', or 'a scent on which a pack of Pomeranians could have run, and in which the Cottesmore bitches simply revelled'.

His writings are full of fun, and if you peruse them carefully you will find much wisdom and wit, if tactfully expressed. For example, he was well ahead of his time in pointing out that the top hat was scarcely the most convenient, nor the safest, form of head protection.

George John Whyte-Melville 1821–78

Whyte-Melville was a poet and novelist who brought the Shires hunting field alive with perception, wit and humour. His novel *Market Harborough – Or How Mr Sawyer Went to the Shires*, first published in 1861, is a marvellous evocation of a visitor's first experiences of hunting in Leicestershire and Northamptonshire. Horse dealing and a touch of romance enliven the tale.

Whyte-Melville died in the hunting field in a fall whilst hunting with the VWH on 5 December 1878. His poem *The Good Grey Mare* provided the title for the magazine *Horse and Hound*, which still bears on its front page a quotation from that work, 'I freely admit that the best of my fun I owe it to horse and hound.'

Otho Paget

Paget wrote as 'Q' for *The Field* from 1882 until 1919. His *Memories of the Shires* published in 1920, is full of good things. His comments are somewhat acidic at times, but he is totally lacking in pomposity or self-importance. He confessed gloomily in 1919 when he returned from service in The Great War, that after being its hunting correspondent for nearly thirty years, *The Field* was only prepared to pay him a third of what he formerly received, and this was not enough to keep a horse. He remarks, 'In addition to this, I have taken unto myself a wife, and the necessary expenses attached thereto.' His nephew, the late Lord Reggie Paget, told me that Otho was always somewhat parsimonius and was apt to invite one to his house only between meals.

William Bromley–Davenport 1821–84

He was a Cheshire landowner and MP, hunted with the Quorn and wrote two poems with Leicestershire as the setting, *Dream of the Old Meltonian* and *Lowesby Hall*. The former has been described as one of the best depictions in verse of an imaginary run. The poem relates an MP falling asleep in the House to recall a fast burst across the Cottesmore country from Ranksborough Gorse. It was in this mode:

> Oh! gently, my young one; the fence we are nearing
> Is leaning towards us – 'tis hairy and black,
> The binders are strong, and necessitate clearing,
> Or the wide ditch beyond will find room for your back.

Bromley-Davenport used the poem to promote the hunting field as a place where all sections of society met:

> Select is the circle in which I am moving,
> Yet open and free the admission to all,
> Still, still more select is that company proving,
> Weeded out by the funker and thinned by the fall!

Yet here all are equal – no class legislation,
No privilege hinders, no family pride –
In the 'image of war' show the pluck of the nation,
Ride, ancient patrician! democracy ride!

In Lowesby Hall, a parody in the accents of Tennyson, the hunting MP put into verse a memorable forecast of Britain without foxhunting:

For I looked into its pages, and I read the book of fate,
And saw foxhunting abolished by an order of the State;

Saw the heavens filled with guano, and the clouds of men's command,
Raining down unsavoury liquids for the benefit of land;

Saw the airy navies earthwards bear the planetry swell,
And the long projected railroad made from Halifax to H-1;

Saw the lands yield their acres of centuries of wrongs,
Cotton lords turn country gentlemen in patriotic throngs;

Queen, religion, State abandoned, and the flags of party furled,
In the Government of Cobden, and the dotage of the world.

Guy Paget

Paget was father of Reggie Paget and was a gifted writer. His works should be read by Leicestershire foxhunters, notably in *Rum 'Uns to Follow, Bad 'Uns to Beat, Wit and Wisdom of the Shires, The Flying Parson and Dick Christian*, and his great history of the Pytchley Hunt. Also recommended are: the writings of T.F. Dale, whose works include the history of the Belvoir; Cuthbert Bradley, who wrote the biography of Frank Gillard; and Colin D.B. Ellis for his immensely readable, *Leicestershire and the Quorn Hunt*.

Foxhunting has been the inspiration of much that is best in Britain's unique tradition of sporting art. Here are some especially associated with Leicestershire:

Charles Simpson 1885–1971

Simpson was the writer and highly accomplished artist who left two marvellous tributes to Leicestershire: *The Harborough Country* and *Leicestershire and its Hunts*; beautifully illustrated with his own drawings, and colour reproductions of his oils and water-colours.

Henry Alken senior 1785–1851

Alken was a foxhunter, and a horseman who schooled young horses, explaining why his Leicestershire pictures, often water-colours with pencil, abound with equestrian endeavour and mishaps: horses fall into ditches, run away, and riders are frequently seen taking huge risks. Among his many notable works was a set of eight scenes of the Quorn Hunt, engraved by F.C. Lewis in 1835. Christmas cards, table mats, calendars and china have borne Alken's work for over a century. Henry Alken's father, Samuel Alken, was a successful engraver. Henry's brothers, Samuel junior, George and Seffrien all became artists, and their output was prodigious, but the reputation of Henry as a painter of the hunting field outshone the others.

John Ferneley senior 1782–1860

Ferneley was son of a wheelwright and carpenter at Thrussington, in the Quorn Friday country, and decorated the foreboards of wagons sent in for repair. His talent was observed and encouraged by the young 5th Earl of Rutland, and Ferneley was apprenticed to another Leicestershire-born artist, Ben Marshall (1768–1835) who was to base himself at Newmarket and become famous for his racehorse portraits. Ferneley settled in Melton Mowbray and painted the local sporting scene, and his studio at Elgin Lodge became a meeting place for the Melton elite to discuss sport and admire his pictures which he sold for remarkably modest prices. They have been much in demand ever since. They include marvellous scenes of Hunt scurries which convey the action, landscape and boundless horizons of Leicestershire.

Lionel Edwards 1878–1966

Long considered to be the outstanding sporting artist of the twentieth century, Edwards' gift for landscape makes his hunting works immediately recognizable to foxhunters. He roamed far and wide, but there is a considerable body of Leicestershire work among his drawings, water-colours and oils. His great understanding of the Chase shines through his work; it is always technically correct and a sheer delight. His *Leicestershire Sketch Book*, first published in 1935, was re-published in 1991. Edwards had hunted with over 80 packs, and he declared that Leicestershire, 'is the pick of our foxhunting countries'. However, he described it as 'delectable and distinctly expensive country' and thanked those Hunt Secretaries who had 'let me down lightly' in the payment of caps. In another book *Scarlet and Corduroy*, he described Leicestershire somewhat wryly as a paradise for the hunting man, but 'rather an overcrowded paradise, perhaps, and with a somewhat mixed company of angels!'.

Cover picture

The dust jacket illustration for this book is a scene of the Belvoir running from Clawson Thorns in 1963. It was specially commissioned from Lionel Edwards by Norma and John Bowles of California, USA. Mr Bowles, a distinguished US newspaper publisher and businessman with interests in Loughborough, and his wife are devoted foxhunters who hunted in Leicestershire regularly. They commissioned Lionel Edwards to paint five pictures depicting hounds hunting from their favourite coverts in Leicestershire. No commercial prints have ever been made of these fine works in oils. The Belvoir picture depicts the Joint Master, Lord King (then Mr John King), with the Honorable Lady King behind, followed by Mr and Mrs Bowles. We are grateful for their permission to reproduce this picture.

Snaffles (Charlie Johnson Payne) 1884–1967

The great caricaturist and painter of the hunting field based himself at Oakham before 1912, and became a warm friend of 'Doc' Gibson, the notable veterinary surgeon, father of George Gibson whose wife, Joan, was to become Joint Master of the Cottesmore. Snaffles adored hunting with the Cottesmore and described it as 'a glimpse of Paradise – anyway it was the sort of place I would have Paradise to be in those days: miles of glorious pasture, intersected by timber and stake and bound fences stretching away to the far horizon with never a thought of wire, wheat or slippery tarred roads, and every yard of it rideable.'

Cecil Aldin (1870–1935), G.D. Armour (1864–1949), G.D. Giles (1857–1941), Michael Lyne (1912–89), Peter Biegel (1913–86) John Kenney (1911–72) and Sir Alfred Munnings (1878–1959) are among those who have captured the glories of Shires hunting on canvas in the twentieth century.

Among contemporary hunting artists in Leicestershire born and bred, Neil Cawthorne, whose many attractive paintings in the Quorn country have included the Prince of Wales at the Prince of Wales Covert in Baggrave Park in 1979.

John King (born 1929)

The Lionel Edwards tradition lives on in John King's work. He was a close family friend and neighbour of Edwards. He is exceedingly talented and versatile in pencil, water-colour, and oils and has hunted in most parts of the British Isles, and his work has often graced the pages of *Horse and Hound*, sometimes illustrating Foxford's Hunting Diary. His work had been much in demand as retirement presentations for leading Masters of Foxhounds. A bold rider to hounds, he adores Leicestershire, and his paintings include the retirement presentation works for Mrs Ulrica Murray Smith in the Quorn country, and Mr Robert Henson in the Belvoir. We are grateful for his permission to reproduce some of his fine pencil works in this book.

APPENDIX II

Masters and Huntsmen of the Quorn

Seasons	Masters	Huntsmen
1696–97 to 1751–52	Thomas Boothby	Edward Chesterton (alias Parsons)
1753–54 to 1799–1800	Hugo Meynell	John Raven
1800–01 to 1803–04	Earl of Sefton	John Raven and S. Goodall
1804–05	Earl of Sefton and Lord Foley	?
1805–06	Lord Foley	J. Harrison
1806–07 to 1816–17	Thomas Assheton Smith	The Master
1817–18 to 1820–21	George Osbaldeston	The Master (Tom Sebright occasionally)
1821–22 to 1822–23	Sir Bellingham Graham	?
1823–24 to 1826–27	George Osbaldeston	The Master
1827–28 to 1830–31	Lord Southampton	Dick Burton, G. Mountford
1831–32 to 1832–33	Sir Harry Goodricke	G. Mountford
1833–34 to 1834–35	Francis Holyoake	G. Mountford
1835–36 to 1837–38	Rowland Errington	G. Mountford
1838–39	Lord Suffield	C. Treadwell
1839–40 to 1840–41	Thomas Hodgson	Webb, Tom Day
1841–42 to 1846–47	Henry Green	Tom Day
1847–48 to 1855	Sir Richard Sutton	Tom Day, Jack Morgan, R. Robinson
1856–57 to 1862–63	Earl of Stamford and Warrington	Ben Boothroyd, John Treadwell
1863–64 to 1865–66	S.W. Clowes	John Goddard
1866–67 to 1867–68	Marquis of Hastings	Charles Pike, Thos. Wilson
1868–69 to 1869–70	J.C. Musters	The Master and Frank Gillard
1870–71 to 1883–84	J. Coupland	F. Gillard, J. MacBride, Tom Firr
1884–85 to 1885–86	Lord Manners	Tom Firr
1886–87 to 1889–90	Capt. W.P. Warner	Tom Firr
1890–91 to 1892–93	Capt. W.P. Warner and W.B. Paget	Tom Firr
1893–94 to 1897–98	Earl of Lonsdale	Tom Firr (1872–99)
1898–99 to 1904–05	Capt. J. Burns Hartopp	Tom Firr, Walter Keyte, Tom Bishopp

1905–06 to 1917–18	Capt. F. Forester	Tom Bishopp, George Leaf, The Master (N. Capel assisting)
1918–19	Committee	Walter Wilson
1919–20 to 1927–28	W.E. Paget and Major A.E. Burnaby	Walter Wilson
1928–29 to 1929–30	Major A.E. Burnaby	Walter Wilson (1918–19), George Barker
1930–31 to 1931–32	Major Burnaby and Sir Harold Nutting	George Barker
1932–33 to 1939–40	Sir Harold Nutting	George Barker
1940–41 to 1946–47	Committee (Major W.P. Cantrell–Hubbersty, Acting)	George Barker
1947–48	Mrs Cantrell–Hubbersty and F. Mee	George Barker
1948–49 to 1950–51	Mrs Cantrell–Hubbersty, F. Mee and Major the Hon. R. Strutt	George Barker
1951–54	Major the Hon. R. Strutt	George Barker (1929–59)
1954–60	Lt. Col. G.A. Murray Smith	Jack Littleworth (1959–67)
1960–85	Mrs Ulrica Murray Smith	
1960–62	Lt. Col. T.C. Llewellyn–Palmer and Capt. E.O. Crosfield	
1962–65	Brig. R.G. Tilney	
1965–72	Capt. J.J.A. Keith	Michael Farrin (1967–)
1975–83	Mr A.J.M. Teacher	
1972–85	Capt. F.G. Barker	
1985–91	Mr J. Bealby	
1985–91	Mr E.R. Hanbury	
1985–91	Mr W.B. Hercock	
1991	Mrs D.E.H. Turner	
1991	Mr A.R. Macdonald–Buchanan	
1991–	Capt. F.G. Barker	
1992–	Mrs D.E.H. Turner	
1992–	Mr A.R. Macdonald–Buchanan	
1992–	Mr C.H. Geary	
1992–	Mr R.T. Thomas	

1991–2 Season Committee

Mr D.C. Samworth, Chairman
Mr K.J.M. Maddocks Wright, Vice-Chairman

Mr R.A. Barber	Mr D. Headly
Mr T.H. Barton	Mr F.A. Hewitt
Mr C.G. Brooks	Mr P. Mann
Dr T.B. Connors	Col. Sir Andrew Martin

Mr D. Cotton
Mr P. Copley
Mrs J.S. Crosfield
Mr G. De Lisle
Mr H. Eggleston
Mr M. Hardy

Mrs U. Murray Smith
Mr J.A. Partridge
Mr I.H. Phillipps
Mr R. Thomas
Mr D.W. Wilson
Mrs L.E. Weldon

Hon. Secretary, M.J. Hemphrey

Subscribers

Mr R.W. Abbott
Mr & Mrs Abel Smith
Mrs B.F. Abraham
Mr N.J.R. Alexander
Mr M.E.R. Allsopp
Mr M.J. Allured
Miss S. Ames
Mrs V. Anderson
Miss J. Anderson
Mr A.J. Arkwright
Mr M.C. Ashton
Mr J.S. Ashworth
Mr R.A. Aston
Mr & Mrs M.R.L. Astor
The Hon. Lady S.H.V. Astor

Miss S.L. Bailey
Mr R.A. Baillie
Miss S. Baillie
Mrs V.E. Barclay
Mr C.T. Barclay
Mrs L. Barker
Mrs P. Barker
Mr T. Barlow
Mrs S. Barnett
Mr T.H. Barton
Miss E. Barton
Miss H. Barton
Mrs H.G. Bates
Mr P.V. Bathurst
Miss C. Baxter
Mr A. Bealby
Mr C. Bealby
Mr & Mrs M.J. Bell
Mr R.S. Benson
Mr D. Biggins
Mr D.J. Birch
Mrs M. Black
Mr D. Bland

Mr & Mrs D.R. Bloor
Mr J. Bottomley
Mr R.C. Boucher
Mr R.G. Boyce
Mrs J. Bradwell
Mr R.D.F. Bream
Miss J.A. Bream
Mr M.F. Bream
Mr K.M. Brennan
Mr R.P. Brett
Mrs J.M. Brewer
Mr & Mrs M. Brewin
Mrs E.D.P. Brook-Lawson
Miss G. Brooke
Messrs C.G. & R.D. Brooks
Mr M.D. Brooshooft
Mrs J.L. Brown
Mr T. Brown
Mr N.W. Budgen
Mr & Mrs G.C.C. Bull
Capt. W.H. Bulwer-Long
Capt. T. Bulwer-Long
Mr O.A. Burge
Mrs E.A. Burrows
Mr C. Burton
Mr & Mrs J.H.R. Buxton
Miss E.L. Bywater

Mr P.G. Cairns
Mrs D.J. Camp Simpson
Mr A.H. Canvin
Lt. Col. N.H. Carding
Mr C.D.P. Cave
Mrs D. Chandler
Mr M.G. Chatterton
Mr A. Clarke
Mr M. Clayton
Miss T. Cleeve

Mr G. & The Lady Rose Clowes
Mr C.M. Coll
Mr & Mrs A.D. Collie
Dr T.B. Connors and Family
Mr A.D. Cooke
Mr G.A. Coombe
Mrs J. Coope
Mr & Mrs P. Cottrell
Mr & Mrs I.M. Crawford
Mrs J.S. Crosfield
Mr & Mrs D. Crossley Cooke
Mr J. Cunningham
Mr & Mrs M. Cursham
Dr R.S. Damazo
Mr R. Dashwood
Mr & Mrs E.H. Davey
Mr M.E.T. Davies
Mrs P.M. Day
The Squire De Lisle
Mr & Mrs E. De Lisle
Mr J.S. Dobson
Mr J.E. Dobson
Mrs K. Drage

Mr J.A.C. Edwards
Mr H. Eggleston
Mrs C. Elliott
Mr K. Ellwood
Mr B.V. Elson

Mr T. Fairburn
Mr C. Farnsworth
Mr D.G. Field
Mrs T.H. Fieldhouse
Mrs V. Fitchett
Mrs F.E. Fletcher
Mrs M. Flint

Mr T. Flint
Mrs C.R. Frank
Mr M. Freestone
Mr C.J. Fryer

Mr & Mrs G.B. Gamble
Mr & Mrs T.F. Garner
Mr C.H. Geary
Mr H.D. Gee
Mr J.B. George
Miss E.B. Godfrey
Mr M.W. Goode
Mr C. Gordon-Watson
Mr W.B. Green
The Hon. Mrs Edward
  Greenhall
Mrs E.M. Grey
Guards Saddle Club
Mr T. Gwyn-Jones

The Revd Haldane-
  Stevenson
Miss C. Hammonds
Mr C. Hardy
Mr M.J. & Miss J.S. Hardy
Mrs K.A.A. Harrington
Mr O. Harris
Mr R.C. Harrison
Miss C. Harrison
Mr P.W.E. Harvey
Sir Stephen Hastings
Mrs S. Hatton
Mr D. Headly
Mr & Mrs J.E. Heathcote
  Ball
Mrs A. Hellyer
Mr & Mrs R.G. Henson
Mr & Mrs B. Henton
Miss A.M. Hepplewhite
Miss D.B. Hepplewhite
Mrs J. Hibbert
Mrs B.P. Hill
Mrs G.N. Hodson
Mr N.J. Hollick
Mrs C. Holmes
Messrs R.C. & J.R. Holt
Household Cavalry
  Regiment
Mrs B.A. Housley
Mr & Mrs G.P.C.
  Howard
Mr P.C.V. Hudson
Mr & Mrs S.G. Hulse

Mr S. Humphrey
Mr R. Hunnisett
Mr W. Hutchinson

Mrs L. Irwin

Mrs A.M. James
Mrs M. James
Mrs G. Jewson
Mrs B.L. John
Mr & Mrs C. Jones
Mrs M.E. Jones
Mr R.G. Jones

Mrs A. Kelly
Mr R. Kernohan
Mr P.J. Kerry
The Lord Kimball
Kings Troop R.H.A.
Mr G.J. Kitchen
Miss A. Knott

Miss R.J.M. Leverton
Mrs C.E. Llewellyn
Miss H. Lodge
Mrs S. Lonsdale

Mr & Mrs K.J.M.
  Madocks Wright
Mrs S.A. Maine
Sir Rupert Mann
Col. Sir A. Martin
Mrs L.G. Mattews
Mrs J.M. Maxted
Mrs M.D. McAlpine
Mr L. McDonald
Miss F. McKim
Major & Mrs R. Mclaren
Mr P. McNicole
Mrs N.L. McRoberts
Miss S. Mee
Mr R.F.B. Mildmay-
  White
Lt. Col. Sir John Miller
Miss R. Minson
Mrs J.S. Morant
Mrs B. Morgan
Mr & Mrs R.S. Morley
Mr W. Morris
Mr & Mrs P.R. Morritt
Mr & Mrs H. Morton
Miss C. Mucklin
Mrs U. Murray Smith

Mr D. Naylor-Leyland

Mr & Mrs J. Newton
The Hon. Mrs R.L.
  Newton
Miss J. Nixon

Dr & Mrs N.W.
  Osborne
Mr D.P. Owen
Mr R.A. Oxford

Lady Laura Palmer
Mrs R.M. Parker
Cllr. R.A. Parkinson
Mr & Mrs T. Parr
Mr & Mrs J. Partridge
Mrs J.N. Paxton
Mr N. Pearson
Mr N.A. Pegge
Mr & Mrs I.H. Phillipps
Mr V. Phillipps
Miss G.L. Phillipson
Mr & Mrs R.F.S.
  Pickering
Mrs. M. Pitts
Mr G.M. Pope
Mr M.J. Portsmouth
Mr R. Price
Mr A. Puddy
Mrs E. Purbrick
Mrs M. Pyrah
Mrs P.C. Pytches

Mrs O. Radford
Mr & Mrs S. Rayns
Mrs M.E. Redding
Mrs B. Rich
Miss S. Rich
Mr & Mrs T.G.
  Richardson
Mr M.J. Roberts
Mr A. Robertson
Mrs C. Rodriguez
Mr & Mrs Ross Wilson
Mrs J.S. Rumph

Mr R.P.A. Sale
Mr & Mrs D.C.
  Samworth
Mr G.L. Sanders
Mr & Mrs G.C.
  Sanderson
Mr A.G. Schroeder
Mr C. Scotney
Mrs A. Scruby

Mr J. Gillies Shields &
Family
Mr B.J. Simspon
Sir Benjamin Slade
Mr & Mrs J.R. Smith
Mr J.L. Smith
Mr A.J. Sparrow
Mr P.J. Stanton
Mrs H. Stockdale-Wright
The Hon Mrs T.
Stopford Sackville
Mr C.T. Sullivan
Miss P. Swarbrick
Mrs B.L. Symington

Mrs L. Taylor
Mr & Mrs S. Taylor

Mr D.F. Thorpe
Mr J.M. Tinsley
Mr B. Townsend
Mrs J. Trosper
Miss P.K. Turner
Mrs S. Turner
Mr N. Turner

Major & Mrs G. Vallance
Mr G.M. Nicholl Vere
Mrs A.M. Vinton

Mr & Mrs A.J. Waldron
Sir Stephen Waley-Cohen
Mrs J. Watkins
Mr & Mrs R.J.
Watmough

Mrs S. Watts
Mrs L.E. Weldon
Mr M. Wells
Miss A. Welsh
Mr A.H. Westropp
Mrs E.A. Whall
Mr P. Whitechurch
Major D. White
Mr M.P. Whitehouse
Mr & Mrs D.H.C.
Williams
Mr E.F. Williams
Mr C.F. Woodhouse
Mrs M.B. Woodhouse
The Hon. Mrs C. Wynn

APPENDIX III

Masters and Huntsmen of the Fernie

Season	Masters	Huntsmen
1853–56	Richard Sutton	Richard Stutton (1853–56)
1856–57	W.W. Tailby	Tom Day (1856–57)
1857–63	W.W. Tailby	Jack Goddard (1857–63)
1863–72	W.W. Tailby	Frank Goodall (1863–72)
1872–76	W.W. Tailby	W.W. Tailby (1872–76)
1876–77	W.W. Tailby	Dick Christian (1876–77)
1877–78	W.W. Tailby	Richard Summers (1877–80)
1878–80	Sir Bache Cunard	
1880–88	Sir Bache Cunard	William Grant (1880–88)
1888–07	C.W.B. Fernie	Charles Isaac (1888–1907)
1907–19	C.W.B. Fernie	Arthur Thatcher
1919–21	Mrs. Fernie	Arthur Thatcher
1921–23	Mrs. Fernie & Mrs. Faber	Arthur Thatcher (1907–23)
1923–24	Lord Stalbridge	Lord Stalbridge
1924–28	Lord Stalbridge & Major H.A. Wernher	Lord Stalbridge (1923–28)
1928–32	Col. Sir H.A. Wernher & A.C. Edmonstone	Bert Peaker
1932–34	Col. Sir H.A. Wernher A.C. Edmonstone & Cmdr. F.J. Alexander	Bert Peaker
1934–35	Col. Sir H.A. Wernher & Cmdr. F.J. Alexander	Bert Peaker
1935–37	Lady Zia Wernher, Cmdr. F.J. Alexander & Capt. J.D. Hignett	Bert Peaker
1937–39	Sir Julian Cahn, Bart.	Bert Peaker
1939–40	R. Wright	Bert Peaker
1940–46	The Committee	Bert Peaker
1946–48	Col. J.D. Hignett & Col. P.H. Lloyd	Bert Peaker (1928–1948)
1948–56	Col. J.D. Hignett & Col. P.H. Lloyd	Walter Gupwell
1956–57	Col. P.H. Lloyd & Capt. B.F.G. Currie	Walter Gupwell
1957–58	Col. P.H. Lloyd, Capt. B.F.G. Currie & Capt. W.A. Gillilan	Walter Gupwell

1958–60	Col. P.H. Lloyd & Capt. W.A. Gillilan	Walter Gupwell
1960–62	Col. P.H. Lloyd, Capt. W.A. Gillilan & Col. G.A. Murray Smith	Walter Gupwell (1948–62)
1962–65	Col. G.A. Murray Smith & Major R.B. Collie	Col. G.A. Murray Smith
1965–66	Col. G.A. Murray Smith	Col. G.A. Murray Smith (1962–66)
1966–69	Col. G.A. Murray Smith, Capt. W.A. Gillilan & A.S. Clowes	Bruce Durno
1969–71	Col. G.A. Murray Smith & A.S. Clowes	Bruce Durno
1971–72	Col. G.A. Murray Smith & Capt. B.R. Bell	Capt. B.R. Bell and Bruce Durno (1971–72)
1972–83	Col. G.A. Murray Smith & J. Cowen	Bruce Durno
1983–	J. Cowen, A.C. Hinch, & J.R. Millington	Bruce Durno (1972–)

1991–2 Season Committee

MR D.C. Stewart, Chairman

R.M. Bernstein
Mrs. M.J. Brankin–Frisby
Mrs B.J.E. Briggs
E.F. Broughton
E. Brudenell, D.L.
J.G.P. Buxton (Hon. Treasurer)

W.V. Ellingworth
I.S. Gilbert
N.P.T. Hall
J.D. Hammond
Mrs E.L. Higgs
Lt. Col. J.D. Hignett, D.L.
J.M. Hignett

W.H.P. Johnson
Mrs C.B. Maeers
D.L. Parker
R.D. Parker
E.L. Symington
R.G. Watson

Hon. Secretary, F.B. Hill

Subscribers and donors

R.E. Adams
Mr & Mrs C. Aldous & family
T. Aldous & Miss G. Aldous
N. Anderson
R.A. Andrews
Mr & Mrs D. Attfield
D.J. Austin & Dr. M.J. Austin
Miss P. Austin
Mrs G.M. Barber

Miss A.E. Barlow
Mr & Mrs D.J. Beaty
Mrs M.R. Beesley
N.R.J. Bell
Mr & Mrs J.M. Bentley
Mrs A. Bergman
R.M. Bernstein
J. Bevin & Partner
Mr & Mrs R.J.W. Bird
P.A. Bland
S.A. Blyth & Miss H. Blyth

Mrs J. Bolton–Carter
J.G. Bowers
J. Bowie
Mrs B. Braint
Mrs M.J. Brankin–Frisby
Miss M.K. Branin–Frisby
Mr & The Hon. Mrs R.D.F. Bream
Mrs B.J.E. Briggs & family
S.J.M. Brisby
Mrs S.F. Brockman, Mrs

R.P. Cory & Miss N. Cory
Mrs A. Brooks
M. Broome
E.F. Broughton
M.W. Brown & Miss H.M. Mace
W.R. Brunton
Mrs E.A. Burton
Mr & Mrs J.G.P. Buxton
Miss R. Buxton
H. Buxton
Mrs C. Carnduff
Mrs L.M. Carrier
R.G. Chamberlain
A.J. Chapman
Miss A.K. Chapman
Mr & Mrs J.N. Cheatle
Mrs S. Clarke
Mr & Mrs R.C.G. Clowes
Mrs D.J. Cowen
G. Cowen
P.E. Cowen
I.P. Crane
Viscount Cranely
Mr & Mrs J.C. Crisp & family
T.M. Curtis
M. Curtis-Bennett
Mrs J. Darby & Mrs. L. Newton
R.F. Davey
Miss E.M. Davison
Debdale Horses
Miss S.M. Dixon-Smith
Miss S.J. Dodd
R.L. & S.D. Edgson
Mrs S. Edmunds
W.V. Ellingworth
D. Esden
Miss F.E. Everett
Mrs H. Forster & T. Forster
G.N. & S.J. Frankham
J.M. Franklin
J.E. Gardiner
Miss E. George
Miss C. Gibbins
I.S. Gilbert
W. Gilbertson-Hart & Miss L. Jones-Fenleigh
F.H. Gilman

W.G. Ginns
Miss A. Gray
J.S. Greenwood
Viscount Grimston
Mr & Mrs N.P.T. Hall & family
Mr & Mrs J.D. Hammond
D. Harding
Miss K. Harpham
J. Harrison
Miss J.D. Harrison
Mrs M. Hastings
Mr & Mrs J.P. Hawksfield
J.E. Heathcote-Ball
Mr & Mrs G. Henderson
Mr & Mrs R.W. Heyman
Mr & Mrs E.L. Higgs
A.D. Hignett
Lt. Col. J.D. Hignett
Mr & Mrs J.M. Hignett & Miss C. Hignett
F.B. Hill
Miss A. Hinch
Mrs P.D. Hinch
Miss T.A. Hockridge
Mr & Mrs R. Hodges
A. Holder
Mr & Mrs T.A. Holliday
J.A. Hoon
C.S. Hurst
Mr & Mrs P. Hutchinson & family
Miss C. Hutton
Miss H. Hutton
Mrs L. Hutton
J.J. Inglesant
W.H.P. Johnson
Miss N. Kay
R.C. Kelton
S.F. Knowles
R.D. Leach
Mrs L. Lillie
Mrs J.P.A.M.P. de Lisle
Miss C. de Lisle & J. de Lisle
Mr & Mrs J.N. Lloyd
Mrs L.N. Loake
Mr & Mrs J. Mackaness & family
Mr & Mrs C.B. Maeers & family

J.C.F. Magnay & family
Mr & Mrs A. Marchant
Mr & Mrs S. Marlow-Thomas
K.W. Martin
Mrs D. Mason
J.K. Matthews
Mrs C.M. Miller-Davis
C.R. Millington
P.J. Millington
C.M. Moore
Mrs J.L. Morris & family
S.G.B. Morrison
M. Munro-Kerr
G. Myerson
J. Neale & Mrs J.E. Cartwright
P.I. Neal
J.W. Nichols
K. Nourish
Mrs D.E. Oakley
The Earl of Onslow
Mrs J.W. Painter & family
C.I. Parker
D. Parker
Mr & Mrs R.D. Parker
G.W. Paul
Mrs P.G. Pawley
Miss E. Pawley
Mrs V. Peach
The Pegasus Club
F.R.S. Pentney
Mrs J.P. Polito & family
N. Pomfret
Miss Powells staff
Miss S. Randall
Mrs J.D. Readett-Bayley & family
D.R.F. Rhimes
Mrs R.D. Roberts
Mrs D.S. Robinson
Miss N. Rogers
Mrs V. Royds
Mr & Mrs C.J. Russell
Mrs M.C.C. Sandell
Mr & Mrs P.J. Sanders
Mrs M. Saunders-Watson & family
J.D.V. Seth-Smith
M. Skinner
D.W. Sleath & family

J.C. Smith
Mrs J.E. Spence & Miss
R. Spence
Miss D.B. Stanhope
A.J. Steward & family
A.N. Stewart
D.C. Stewart
B.S. Stokes R.J. Strong &
family
G. Stubbs
S.J. Sugden
Mrs K. Swarbrick
Mrs E.L. Symington
A. Tacy
Mrs D.H.S. Thompson
G. Thompson

Mr & Mrs H.D.
Thompson
M.C.B. Thompson & Mrs
A. Pyper
Mrs D.M. & N. Toms
H.W. Turcan
Mr & Mrs W.J. Turcan
& family
N. Turley
Mrs E.M.K. Turner
The Earl of Verulam
Mrs M. Vickers
Mr & Mrs A.M. Vinton
Mrs J.M. Walker
Mrs R.G. Watson
Mrs M.A. Watt

Mr & Mrs G.F. Welby
Miss A. Welch
P.R. Wells & family
D.A. West
Miss N.J. Wheeler
Mr & Mrs P.K. Wheeler
Miss K. Wilkinson
V. Winnington
Mrs J.W.T. Wood &
family
R.W. Wright

Honorary Life Members
Col. Sir Andrew Martin
Miss E.M. Powell
R.G. Watson

APPENDIX IV

Masters and Huntsmen of the Belvoir

Seasons	Masters	Huntsmen
1730–79	3rd Duke of Rutland	
1742–70	John Marquis of Granby	
1779–87	4th Duke of Rutland	John Smith
1784–91	(Lord George Cavendish Sir Carnaby Haggerston as managers)	
1791–99	Mr Perceval	Newman
1799–1830	5th Duke of Rutland	'Gentleman' Shaw (1804–16)
		Thomas Goosey (1816–42)
1830–58	Lord Forester	Will Goodall (1842–59)
1859–88	6th Duke of Rutland	James Cooper (1859–70)
1888–96	7th Duke of Rutland	Frank Gillard (1870–96)
1896–1912	Sir Gilbert Greenall	Ben Capell (1896–1912)
	(later 1st Lord Daresbury)	
1912–24	Major T. Bouch	Dick Woodward (1913–19)
		Major Bouch (1919–24)
1912–14	Lord Robert Manners	
1924–28	Capt. M.O. Roberts	Nimrod Capell (1924–28)
1928–31	Mr Charles Tonge	George Tongue (1928–56)
1928–30	Mr P.S. Akroyd	
1930–39	Col. F.G.D. Colman	
1934–47	2nd Lord Daresbury	
1939–47	10th Duke of Rutland	
1947–64	Lt. Col. James Hanbury	Jim Webster (1956–83)
1952–54	Lt. Col. F. Bowlby	
1954–55	Lt. Col. James Seely	
1955–66	Lord Belper	
1956–64	Lt. Col. H.L.V. Beddington	
1958–72	Mr John King (later Lord King)	
1971–73	Major General F.B. Wildbore-Smith	
1972–78	Mrs Ann Reid-Scott	
1972–74	Mr N.J. Turner	
1974–76	Mr J.S. Hine	
1976–78	Lord Belper	
1978–79	Mr R.P. Watts	
1978–88	Mr Robert Henson	
1980–83	Mr N.G.W. Playne and Mr N.J. Turner	

1983–88	Mr C.F. Harrison	Robin Jackson (1983–92)
1983–92	Mr John Blakeway	
1987–89	Mr J.M.C. Parry	
1983–90	Mr R.J. Knight	
1989–	Mr J.R. Newton	
1990–	Mrs D.B. Owen	
1991–	Mr J.R. Martin	Martin Thornton (1992–)

1991–2 Season Committee

Lord King of Wartnaby, Chairman
J.G. Richardson, Hon. Treasurer
T. Hall–Wilson, Hon. Secretary

A. Applewhite	B.R. Marriott
R.D. Chandler	R. Miller
R.H. Chatterton	Lady Sarah McCorquodale
M.S.B. Cross	B. Pitman
Dr. M. Fitzpatrick	M. Powles
C. Henson	Mrs. J.R. Stevenson
P.R. Jordan	Col. G.L. Wathen
I.E. Manchester	C.F. Harrison

Life members, K. Botterill, and J.E.P. Knight

Subscribers

R.W. Abbott
R.J. Aldous
A. Armstrong
E.F. Astley–Arlington
R.A. Aston
Miss A. Bailey
Miss R.J. Bailey
Mr. & Mrs. R.A.J.
  Beauchamp
C.E. Bee
Mr. & Mrs. M.J. Bell &
  family
Mrs. F. Bell–Irving
Miss A. Bellamy
Mr & Mrs. C. Benson
Mrs. P. Bertelsen
Mrs. Z. Black
K. Botterill
P. Bottosley
Mr. & Mrs. R.N.C.
  Boucher
J.C. Boyce
R.G. Boyce

Mr. & Mrs. H.
  Brockbank
J.A. Bradley
C. Brown
M.J. Brown
T. Brown
Miss M. Bruns
Mrs. J. Bullard
D.A. Burge
Miss F. Burridge
Miss R. Capriles
A.R.P. Carden
Mrs. B.E. Chandler
B. Chapman
Mr. & Mrs. R.H.
  Chatterton
Mrs. M. Comerford
J.R. Cornwall
His Honour Judge
  Coulson
Miss C.R. Cox
Cranwell Saddle Club
M.S.B. Cross

Miss C. Crossley
W. Cursham
Dr. R. Damazo
Miss J.T. Daniels
Dr. G. Daws
Miss J. Dawson
Mrs. P. Day
D. Donegan
J. Duffin
P.L. Durlacher
G.A.D. Emerson
Mrs. D.E. Etty
D.G. Field
Mrs. C. Fisher
Mrs. J.M. FitzHerbert
Dr. M. Fitzpatrick
D.R. Foster
Miss P. Foster
R.E. Gardiner
Miss H. Garner
Mrs. F. Gibson
Miss J. Gibson
C. Gordon–Watson

The Hon. Mrs. M.A.
Greenall
Mrs. M.A. Greetham
Mrs. C. Hale
W.R. Halliday
A.A. Hasbly
Mrs. B. Hardstaff
Mrs. S.A. Harington
Mr. & Mrs. J. Henderson
B.O. Heath
Mrs. J. Heerbeck
C.W. Henson
J.R. Henson
Officers of Household
Cavalry
Mrs. A.N. Hurst
Mrs. V. Hutchinson
S. Inguanta
L.W. Jackson
Mr. & Mrs. P.R. Jordan
The Lord King of
Wartnaby
Mrs. F.V. Le Measurier
Miss J. Lee
S.R. Lee
Miss T.A.R. Lee
Mrs. J. Loxton
Miss V. Loyd
Mrs. R. & Miss C.
Mallalieu
Mr. & Mrs. C.
Manchester
Mr. & Mrs. S.D.
Manchester
Miss C. Marshall
Mrs. L. Maxfield–Gullett
Melton Hunt Club
Lt. Col. Sir J.M. Miller
B. Mitchell
D. Mitchell
A.F. Money
Dr. E. Monteith

Mrs. M.A. Morris
Lady Sarah McCorquodale
Mrs. R.S. McCorquodale
The Hon. Mrs. R.L.
Newton
Mrs. J.M. Newton
Mrs. D.M. Nicholls
Mrs. E. Norman
F. & N. Page
Lady Laura Palmer
Mrs. S.E. Parr
Mr. & Mrs. J.M.C. Parry
R.E. Pattinson
Mrs. J. Paxton
Mrs. J.J.H. Payne
A.D. Pease
G. Pitman
N.G. Playne & family
Mrs. M. Poluszunska
Major C.P.R.
Postlethwaite
Mrs. M. Powles
J.A.J. Price
A.D. Puddy
Miss. M. Ray
Mrs. A. Reid Scott
J.G. Richardson
Mrs. E. Rigden
Mrs. S.A. Roberts
Miss K. Roberts
Mrs. O. Robinson
Miss S.M. Robinson
Mrs. C.A. Rodriguez
Mrs. P. Rothera
Lady de la Rue
D. Savage
D.S. Shanks
S.P. Sharkey
Mrs. M.J. Shields
Miss P. Sizer
J.J.B. Skinner
R. Slater

J.F.E. Smith
Mrs. V.J. Smith
E.J.H. Smith-Maxwell
A.J. Sparrow
Miss. S. Spence
Mrs. E. Spicer
H.A.B. Stroud
C.T. Sullivan
Mrs. J. Summers
Miss. J.R. Sutcliffe
N.D.E. Sykes
Mr. & Mrs. S. Taylor
Miss H. Thompson
J.M. Tinsley
P.C. Tinsley
Mrs. D.E.H. Turner
N.J. Turner
Mrs. S.J.E. Turner
Mr. & Mrs. R.P. Turner
C.J. Vale
Mrs. S. Van Cutsen
T.M.G. Vestey
Mr. & Mrs. A.M. Vinton
Mrs. C. Wainwright
Mrs. H. Wallace
Mrs. R.J. Walker
A.E. Walton
Mrs. V.C. Ward & family
C.A. Warde–Aldam
Col. & Mrs. G.L. Wathan
The Hon. M.R.M. Watson
Miss J. Webb
Brigadier E.J. Webb–
Carter
Mr. & Mrs. E. Wesley
C. Whitton
G.A. Widdowson
Mrs. J. Wildridge
Mrs. G. Willett
Mrs. M. Willson
T.F. Winterton
A.J. Woodward

APPENDIX V

Masters and Huntsmen of the Cottesmore

Seasons	Masters	Huntsmen
1732–88	Mr Thomas Noel	Arthur Abbey (exact dates unknown)
1788–1802	Sir William Lowther (created 1st Earl of Lonsdale)	Philip Payne
1802–06	Sir Gilbert Heathcote	
1806–42	1st Earl of Lonsdale	George Slacke (1806–?)
1842–47	Sir Richard Sutton	Ben Morgan (1842–47)
1847–52	Mr H. Greaves	John Treadwell (1847–52)
1852–55	Mr H. Burrowes	
1855–57	Sir John Trollope	
1857–70	Sir John Trollope and Mr Tailby	Frank Goodall (1861–64) Jack West (1867–76)
1870–76	Col. Henry Lowther (created 3rd Earl of Lonsdale)	Jack Barber
1876–78	4th Earl of Lonsdale	William Neil (1876–88)
1878–80	Lord Carrington	
1880–1900	Mr William Baird	George Gillson (1888–1900)
1900–07	Mr Evan Hanbury	Arthur Thatcher (1900–07)
1907–11	Hugh, 5th Earl of Lonsdale	Sam Gillson (1907–11)
1911–13	Maj. General Brocklehurst (created Lord Ranksborough)	Tom Isaac (1911–13)
1913–15	Mr R.E. Strawbridge	
1915–21	Hugh, 5th Earl of Lonsdale	George Leaf (1915–21)
1921–31	Mr W.J. Baird	James Welch (1921–31)
1928–1930	Col. S.J. Green	
1931–46	Major C.C. Hilton–Green	Major C.C. Hilton–Green (1931–46)
1946–58	Lt. Col. Sir Henry Tate	Lt. Col. Heber–Percy and Lt. Col. Sir Henry Tate (1946–58)
1946–58	Lt. Col. C. Herber Percy	
1953–69	Mr M.D. McAlpine	
1953–58	Mr Marcus Kimball (created Lord Kimball)	Mr Kimball (1953–58)
1958–69	Major Robert Hoare	Major Hoare (1958–69)
1969–76	Capt. Simon Clarke	Capt. Simon Clark (1969–76)
1976–81	Mrs Andrew Hellyer	
1976–85	Mr D.C. Samworth	

1976–89	Mrs Joan Gibson	Peter Wright (1976–81)
1981–89	Mr E.R. Hanbury	
1981–92	Capt. B.E. Fanshawe	Capt. B.E. Fanshawe (1981–92)
1984–92	Mr L. Dungworth	
1988–	Mr A. Ruddle	
1990–	Mrs D.C. Samworth	
1992–	Mr R. Dungworth	Neil Coleman (1992–)

1991–2 Season Committee

Lt. Col. Sir Henry Tate, President   Mr. P.R.G. Sturgess, Chairman

Mr M. Vergette	Lady M. Pridden
Mrs R. Watson	Prof. E. Lamming
Maj. J. Hawksworth	Mr R. Wright
Mrs E. Gilman	Mr N. Hubbard
Mr S. Campbell	Mr D. Hollis
Capt. R. Micklethwait	Mr R. Dungworth
Mr W. Cross	Mr M. Clayton

Secretary, Mr. N.A. Stokes   Hon. Treasurer, Mr N.J. Cheatle

Subscribers

Mr D. Aldridge
Mr M. Allsop
Mrs P. Anderson
Mr A. Austin

Mr M. Bolton
Mr J. Bee
Miss E. Byng
Mr J. Barson
Mrs S. Knight
Miss L. Bates
Mr R. Brett & Family
Mrs C. Blackwell
Mr S. Bergman
Mr & Mrs C. Bradstock
Miss D. Barker
Mrs L. Bevan
Mrs A. Burnaby-Atkins

Mr S. Campbell
Miss H. Campbell
Mr N. Cheatle
Mrs B. Chorlton
Mr & Mrs T. Clarke
Mr M. Clayton
Mr G. Cohen
Mr A. Collie

Mr A.D. Cooke
Mr A. Cooke
Mr & Mrs P. Cooke
Mrs B. Coulson
Mr G. Cowan
Mr B. Cross
Mrs W. Cross
Mr J. Culshaw
Miss J. Curwen
Mrs A. Cuthbert

Mrs J. Dale
Mr & Mrs S. Dale
Miss R. David
Mr P. Davies
Mr E. De Lisle
Mr D. Dixon
Mrs P. Dixon-Smith
Mr P. Durlacher

Mr G. Edmondson
Mr P. Escombe
Mrs A. Edmonds
Mrs B. Eve
Mrs J. Ervin
Mr C. Ellis

Mrs R. Ferrand
Mr T. Fowler
Miss L. Ferguson
Mrs P. Ferguson
Mr G. Fuller

Mr K.E. Gaymer
Mrs E. Gilman
Mr T. Garner
Mrs T. Gordon-Cooper
Mrs A. Grundy
Mr D. Gee
Mrs P. Gee
Ms. J. Giese
The Hon. Mrs D. Gibbs
Mrs V. Guess
Mrs J. Gibson
Mrs F. Grey-Cheape
Mrs E. Garnier
Miss A. Griffiths
Miss E. Godfrey

Lady C. Hales
Sir Stephen Hastings
Mr S. Hammond
Mr R. Haddow
Mr E.R. Hanbury

Maj. J. Hawksworth
Mr J. Hawksfield
Mrs A. Hellyer
Mr & Mrs D.
  Hill-Brooks
Miss S. Horne
Mrs C. Humphries
Mr R. Hunnisett
Mrs C. Hunter-
  Coddington
Capt. J. Haywood
Mrs R. Hoare
Household Cavalry

Miss E. Inman
Mrs G. Iveson

Mr M. Johnson
Mr D. Jones
Mrs S. Jones
Mrs E. Jones Fenleigh
Mr P. Judd

Mrs A. Kanter
The Lord Kimball
The Hon. V. Kitson
Kings Troop R.H.A.

Prof. E. Lamming
Mr N. Ley
Mrs H. Llewellyn
Mrs C. Lowes

Mrs D. McAlpine
Mrs A. McRoberts
Mr P. McNicols
Mrs J. Mills
Mrs E. Mellows
Mrs P. Mayo

Mrs L. Matthews
Miss R. Matthews
Mrs D. Maxwell
Capt R. Micklethwaite

Mrs E. Nelson-Parker
Hon. Mrs R.L. Newton
Mrs J. Nicholson
Mr A. Nicholson

Mrs S. Parker
Mr J. Partridge
Mrs J. Partridge
Mrs J. Paxton
Mr R. Payton
Miss L. Pearce
Mr N. Pegge
Mrs J. Pick
Mrs F. Plummer
Mr M. Pocock
Lady M. Pridden
Mr J. Pridmore
Miss J. Pritchard
Mrs G. Price
Mrs R. Ralli
Mrs H. Reynolds
Mr M. Roberts
Mr A. Robertson
Miss J. Ross
Lady N. Ruddle
Mrs B. Rich
Mrs D. Rollo

Mr D. Samworth &
  Family
Miss J. Spencer
Mr S. Shelsher

Miss P. Seckington
Mrs P. Sillars
Mrs C. Skinner
Mrs J. Smeeton
Mrs M. Smith
Mr K. Smith-Bingham
Mrs B. Senior
Mr R. Sturgess
Miss K. Scott
Mrs J. Sturrock
Mr B. Stokes
Miss J. Stevens

Mr T. Tarratt
Miss C. Tarratt
Mr S. Taylor
Mr J. Thwaite
Mrs R. Todd
Mr M. Trollope-Bellew
Mr R. Turner

Mr M. Vergette
Mr E. Vestey

Mr R. Walker
Miss S. Waddilove
Mrs D. Watson
Mrs R. Watson
Miss R. Willis
Mr A. Waldron
Mrs A. Warrington
Mr P. Warrington
The Hon. M. Watson
Mr E. Welford
Miss V. White
Maj. A. Warre
Mr G. Williams

Mr & Mrs J. Young

Index

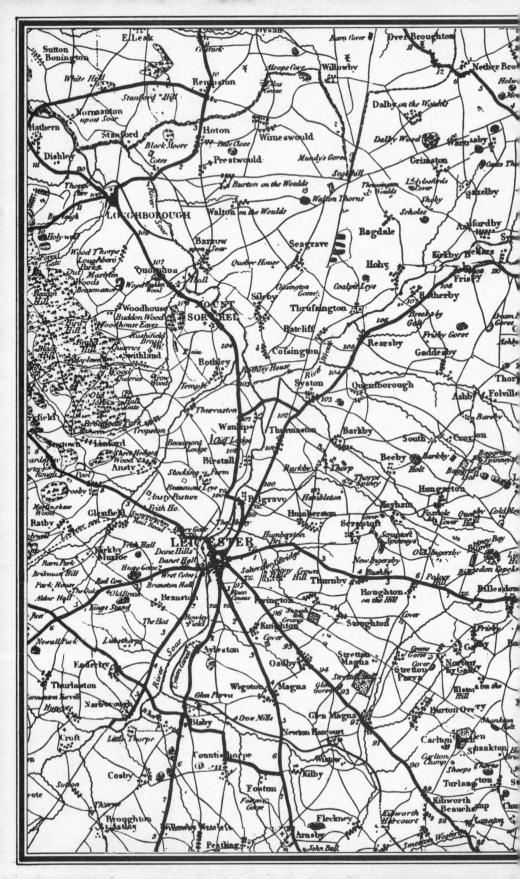